Photograph by John Amburg.

Writing about Vietnam

A Bibliography of the Literature of the Vietnam Conflict

*A
Reference
Publication
in
Literature*

Writing about Vietnam

A Bibliography of the Literature of the Vietnam Conflict

SANDRA M. WITTMAN

G.K.HALL &CO.

70 LINCOLN STREET, BOSTON, MASS.

Library of Congress Cataloging-in Publication Data

Wittman, Sandra M.
      Writing about Vietnam: a bibliography of the
literature of the Vietnam conflict/ Sandra M. Wittman
        p. cm. – (A Reference publication in literature)
        ISBN 0-8161-9083-6
        1. Vietnamese Conflict, 1961-1975 – Bibliography.
      2. Vietnamese Conflict, 1961-1975 – Literature and the
war – Bibliography. I. Title. II. Series.
      Z3226.W58   1989
      [DS557.7]
      016.959704'3 – dc20   89-15553
                             CIP

This publication is printed on permanent/durable acid-free paper
MANUFACTURED IN THE UNITED STATES OF AMERICA

This work is dedicated to all those whose lives

were touched by Vietnam

Contents

Preface

The purpose of this bibliography is to gather together the most complete and current list of materials written about the Vietnam Conflict in the following areas:

Novels

Adventure novels

Personal narratives/biographies

Anthologies

Poetry

Dramas

Short stories

Literary criticism/secondary sources

Bibliographies

Dissertations/theses

Teaching materials

Periodicals with a Vietnam emphasis

Histories, documents, and political science treatises are not included. The included materials cover the period from 1954 to the end of 1988. One exception is the inclusion of Andre Malraux's *The Royal Way,* published in 1935, which is generally considered to describe events that foreshadowed American involvement in Vietnam much as Graham Greene's *The Quiet*

American (1955) does. Works written by those who had firsthand experience in Vietnam as well as those who did not are cited.

Because the Vietnam War was not an isolated event, I felt it was also important to include materials in the genres that reflect the French period just prior to American involvement, the antiwar activities in the United States during the war, Vietnam after the fall of Saigon, the plight of refugees, and the readjustment of American soldiers returning home as well as materials that deal with American involvement in the actual fighting. Works describing events in Cambodia and Laos are included if those events occurred during the fighting in Vietnam.

It is hoped that this compilation will be a useful reference tool for researchers, teachers, students, and the general reader.

RESEARCH METHODS

The items listed in this bibliography were located using basic library tools such as reference books, indexes, and abstracts. *Books in Print, Short Story Index, Play Index, Fiction Catalog, MLA Bibliography, Book Review Digest, Book Review Index, Resources in Education, Newsbank, Masters Abstracts, Dissertation Abstracts, Bibliographic Index, Current Journals in Education, Humanities Index, Essay and General Literature Index, Access, Education Index, Reader's Guide to Periodic Literature,* and *Library Literature* were used. Volumes for the years covered by the bibliography were checked. The resources of the BRS and Dialogue databases were searched, particularly the Arts and Humanities Citation Index, ERIC, Dissertation Abstracts, MLA, Books in Print, Magazine Index, and Popular Magazine Review Online. Infotrac was also used.

The OCLC library database system was used to verify bibliographic data and availability of items. Other major bibliographies in the field, particularly those by John Newman, Merritt Clifton, F. C. Brown, and Catherine Calloway, were helpful in locating titles. Individual items in each of these bibliographies were checked and verified, and were obtained for examination whenever possible. Many works included in this bibliography also have their own bibliographies; each item in these bibliographies was checked and verified. Every effort was made to examine and annotate each item included in this bibliography to give the reader a description of the work and its purpose, scope, or plot. If an item's existence could be verified but the item could not be obtained for examination, it was listed unannotated. If an item's existence could not be verified, it was not included. In the citations, American first editions are preferred. ERIC document (ED) and journal (EJ) numbers are included in citations for those items that are available form the ERIC clearinghouses.

NOVELS

Hundreds of novels use Vietnam in their plots. The novels chosen for inclusion in this bibliography fit the criteria outlined in this preface and utilize Vietnam as an integral plot element or an important aspect of character development. Juvenile literature is included. Annotations in this section are plot summaries. Those novels considered the most important in Vietnam literature are identified as such in the annotation. If a novel was not available for review, plot summaries were constructed from all available book reviews.

ADVENTURE NOVELS

The section on adventures novels is included because this subgenre of Vietnam War novels is a growing phenomenon. Included in this section are only those novels that are part of a series of adventure novels, such as those by Nick Carter, Don Pendleton, Jonathan Cain, Jack Buchanan, and others. These novels emphasize the adventures that form the plot rather than Vietnam, the Vietnam War, or their attendant issues. They could be set in any hot spot on the globe, as are many of the authors' other series titles. Vietnam serves only as a convenient, topical backdrop. For this reason, and because of the similarities of plot, these novels are unannotated in this bibliography.

PERSONAL NARRATIVES/BIOGRAPHIES

Firsthand accounts of the subjects outlined in the opening of the preface are listed in the Personal Narratives/Biographies section. Included are accounts by soldiers on both sides, journalists, and civilians. Collections of letters are also cited. Some titles that appear to be histories are listed if they contain a significant amount of eyewitness testimony and reflection. Although many personal accounts were published in periodicals, these are not included in this bibliography.

ANTHOLOGIES

A work is listed in the Anthologies section if it contains selections from more than two genres. In other sections of this bibliography, cross-references alert the reader that the full annotation of the work is included in Anthologies.

POETRY

The poetry collections included contain only poems that deal with the Vietnam War. General Vietnamese poetry is not included. No attempt has been made to locate or list individual poems.

DRAMA

Only those plays that a reader may obtain in printed form are included in this bibliography.

SHORT STORIES

The short stories are arranged in two sections: collections and individual short stories. In short-story collections in which the works of only one author are represented, the contents are listed in the annotation. This is also true in collections of short stories by Vietnamese authors in which the short stories have not been printed elsewhere. Individual short stories are listed by author, accompanied by citations to collections and periodicals where they may be located.

LITERARY CRITICISM/SECONDARY SOURCES

The indexes, abstracts, and databases listed earlier in this preface were utilized to locate literary criticism of Vietnam War literature. In some cases a book review is included if the review presents general information pertinent to the study of this genre of literature. No attempt was made to compile a list of the existing books reviews.

BIBLIOGRAPHIES

Only those bibliographies with listings that include the genres detailed at the outset of this preface are included. Purely historical bibliographies were excluded. If a work cited in other areas of this bibliography contains a bibliography, it is mentioned in the annotation.

DISSERTATIONS/THESES

Only those institutions of higher education that list their doctoral dissertations and master's theses in *Dissertation Abstracts International* or *Master's Abstracts* are included, unless a dissertation or thesis was cited in another source and could be verified.

TEACHING MATERIALS

Teaching materials included describe techniques for teaching the Vietnam War in social science and literature classes from elementary school through higher education. Articles evaluating history textbooks on the Vietnam War were excluded.

PERIODICALS

Only those periodicals whose major emphasis is, or was, the Vietnam War are included in this bibliography.

Acknowledgments

No book such as this is written alone, and I would like to acknowledge the assistance of those who made it possible. I would like to thank the board of trustees, the administration, and the faculty of Oakton Community College, Des Plaines and Skokie, Illinois, for their faith in my work, shown by granting a sabbatical leave that enabled me to complete this project, begun two years before. I am also grateful to all members of the library staffs of both of Oakton's libraries and to my friends and colleagues. I am very fortunate to live in an area with an abundance of fine libraries and library services. Their resources were invaluable to me, particularly those of the Central Serials Service, Northwestern University, Rosary College, and the Des Plaines, Skokie, and Arlington Heights public libraries. Most of my appreciation, however, is reserved for Esther Marks, for her tireless scouring of the country on her OCLC terminal, locating hundreds of items for me, and for Norman Kopp, for his computer expertise, but most of all for his continual encouragement, patience, and devotion.

Introduction

The war in Vietnam left a wound on my generation that hasn't healed. It has closed with the infection still raging inside. The longer we ignore it, the worse the infection grows."

-Mark Baker
Nam (1981)

Unlike World War II veterans, American veterans of the Vietnam War did not come home together at the end. Instead, after their tour of duty, they returned separately throughout the war. They were not met with bands, parades, or any show of enthusiasm by the American people, whose ambivalence toward the war extended to its reception of the war's participants. Those veterans who returned from Vietnam with their terrible physical, spiritual, and psychic wounds, needed to talk about their experiences, but people simply didn't want to hear. The feelings were too potent, the war too painful even for those who didn't go to Vietnam. For the veteran, there was no one to talk to and nothing to read to help clarify his experiences.

Although outside the scope of this bibliography, Peter Aichinger's *The American Soldier in Fiction, 1880-1963* (1975) provides excellent background material on the literature of other wars.[1] Little creative literature described the Vietnam War while it was in progress, however, and the early literature was like the literature of other wars, with overtones of heroism and patriotism. Robin Moore's *The Green Berets* (1965), and John Wayne's role in the subsequent movie, fostered the idea that this was an "ordinary" war where both winning and being a hero were possible; it led many young men to volunteer for service in Vietnam. Veterans knew better. The early literature of the war was usually not written by those who had been in Vietnam.

Some of the early novels, such as Eric Ambler's *State of Seige* (1965) or James Bassett's *The Sky Suspended* (1968), do not even refer to Vietnam directly; their stories are set in fictional countries. Others, like *The Gooney Bird* (1968) by William C. Anderson, present Vietnam as another Korea – the Korea Americans knew from the popular TV series "M.A.S.H." Much of the early drama, such as *Hair* and *Xa*, was experimental and strongly antiwar. Poets took an active role in protesting the war, their view represented by writers such as Denise Levertov, John Balaban, Daniel Berrigan, Robert Bly, and Allen Ginsberg.

It became apparent very early that Vietnam could not be written about in the same manner, using the same literary styles, that had been appropriate for other wars in America's history. This war was not like any other. It was fought in a country whose history, culture, religion, and values are quite different from ours, a country that had not threatened us personally. The actual battle tactics differed; what worked in the world wars did not work in the jungle warfare of Vietnam. There was never clear indication that America would do whatever was necessary to win. Land was taken and given up and retaken-again and again. Problems within the military were rampant, from financial corruption to racism, low morale, drug addiction, theft, murder, and suicide. Soldiers knew that moral support from the American people was lacking. Literature had to compete with the evening news to try to tell Americans a story they thought they already knew. As Valentine Cunningham wrote, "If literature is to be news, Vietnam fictions are about events that were news before literature got near them. And it is quite a task to make what is so familiar seem new enough to strike."[2]

Eventually the veterans began to write of their experiences, compelled by their need to tell others what it had really been like over there and perhaps by an even more urgent need to come to terms with the experience personally – to make some sense of it. These writers expressed themselves most often in poetry and short stories. Publishers were cautious about publishing Vietnam material, wondering if there was an audience for it. Movie makers felt the same. In response, some veterans established their own publishing house, the 1st Casualty Press, for the work of veterans and their friends. The 1st Casualty Press, which took its name from Aeschylus's phrase, "In war, truth is the first casualty," was formed in the early 1970s by members of Vietnam Veterans Against the War, including Larry Rottman, Jan Barry, and Basil Paquet. The group borrowed money to publish an anthology of veterans' poetry, *Winning Hearts and Minds,* after the manuscript had been rejected by forty-two publishers. The press also published *Free Fire Zone,* a short-story collection. Both books were later published by McGraw-Hill. (The history of the 1st Casualty Press is fully discussed in Carolyn Slocock's article "Winning Hearts and Minds: The 1st Casualty Press.")[3]

In the late 1970s, the desire of the veterans to tell began to match the desire of the American public to hear and, only very recently, of teachers to teach. Philip Caputo's 1977 *A Rumor of War* was a landmark personal narrative that ushered in a whole new literary style that combines the best elements of nonfiction and the novel. Thus the new journalism was born, also exemplified in Michael Herr's *Dispatches* (1977).

Vietnam War novelists owe a debt to Joseph Conrad's *Heart of Darkness* and Joseph Heller's *Catch-22,* echoes of which are found in many of the novels. Science fiction and mystery are often the genres of choice, and the use of the supernatural is common. This is not surprising given a war where euphemisms such as body counts and kill ratios were coined, where villages were destroyed to save them, where napalm hideously burned villagers and Agent Orange threatens the unborn children of veterans, where Americans committed atrocities against civilians and a child could be as dangerous as a fully armed Vietcong. Michael Hastings' mystery *The Unknown Soldier,* Steven Hardesty's supernatural *Ghost Soldiers*, and Jean and Jack Dann's Vietnam War science fiction short-story anthology *In the Field of Fire* are examples.

With the passage of time, some of the emotions surrounding the Vietnam War have started to cool and the process of reflection has begun. The dedication of the Vietnam Veterans Memorial, the Wall, in Washington, D.C., on 13 November 1982 seemed to give the nation permission to finally deal with the war. The trickle of literature about the war has become a flood of poems, plays, short stories, novels, and personal narratives. Many novels of the early 1980s, such as Charles Coleman's *Sergeant Back Again,* John Del Vecchio's *The 13th Valley,* and Jack Fuller's *Fragments,* were critically well received.

By this time, scholars were aware that Vietnam War literature was rapidly becoming a subgenre of twentieth-century American literature, and they responded with histories and studies, tracing the major styles and themes and comparing them with those of other wars. These studies no longer comprise only single articles in literary journals but also book-length critiques. Some fine examples are Timothy Lomperis's *Reading the Wind,* William Searle's *Search and Clear,* and James Wilson's *Vietnam in Prose and Film.* Journals such as *Critique* and *Modern Fiction Studies,* among others, have devoted whole issues to the study of Vietnam War literature.

Thus far the experiences of two minorities – the African-American soldier and the nurse – have not been fully explored. Attempts to depict the African-American soldier and the racial problems prevalent throughout the war appear in a few novels, such as John William's *Captain Blackman* (1972), and more recently in Wallace Terry's nonfiction book *Bloods* (1984). Until Lynda Van Devanter's 1983 nonfiction narrative *Home before Morning,* the nurse in Vietnam was to be found only in superficial romantic novels, such as those by Ellen Elliot, Della Field, Evelyn Hawkins, and Suzanne Roberts – all called *Vietnam Nurse.* The story of the Australian soldier is also told in only a small number of novels, such as David Alexander's *When the Buffalo Fight* (1980).

An increasing number of adventure novels is published each year in which valiant Americans rescue POWs and MIAs and perform other heroic deeds. On the screen Rambo wants us to think we won the war in Vietnam. This is cause for concern at a time when we have just begun to examine our national guilt over the war, and it is potentially dangerous if it fosters a climate that encourages further "adventures" in other people's countries. Americans are apparently still ambivalent about the Vietnam War, and these novels are a symptom of the difficulty involved in coming to grips with the first U.S. military defeat. Intellectually, Americans are examining the war; emotionally, this is not yet fully possible.

Even though Larry Heinemann won the National Book Award in 1987 for *Paco's Story,* critics have welcomed relatively few Vietnam novels wholeheartedly. The great Vietnam War novel may yet have to be written, even though some feel that Tim O'Brien has done just that with *Going After Cacciato.* As is evident from the materials listed in this bibliography, most of the novels about the Vietnam War have not come to grips with its meaning; their authors simply want to tell a good rousing adventure story. The personal narratives come much closer to telling it like it was – sometimes taking a personal toll on the author. Neil Sheehan's Pulitzer-Prize winning *A Bright Shining Lie* (1988) took twenty years to complete. In the 1980s, fewer Vietnam War poems have been written, and many of the dramas have centered on the plight of the war veteran, the standard for such plays being set by David Rabe's *Sticks and Bones.*

Vietnam War literature in English includes very few accounts of the war from the Vietnames perspective. Two novels, Anh-Duc's *Hon Dat* (1969) and Phou Loung's *The Men of Company 97* (1971) present the North Vietnamese view and are, of course, decidedly anti-American, as are the short-story collections *The Ivory Comb* and *The Mountain Trail.* The South Vietnamese view is presented in Tran Van Dinh's novels *No Passenger on the River* and *Blue Dragon, White Tiger.* Several Vietnamese leaders, including the South's Nguyen Cao Ky and the North's Vo Nguyen Giap, have given their personal accounts of and explanations for the fall of South Vietnam. The personal cost of the war for ordinary Vietnamese citizens is poignantly described in works such as Huynh Quang Nhuong's autobiographical *The Land I Lost* and the poet Tich Nhat Hanh's *The Cry of Vietnam.* Although the war has been over for some time, the number of Vietnamese accounts in English does not seem to be increasing. This is unfortunate, as Americans need to see both sides of the conflict to come to any true understanding of it.

What is perhaps most heartening in the recent flood of information on the Vietnam War is that scholars are studying it and elementary, secondary, and college and university educators are beginning to find ways to teach their students about it. A number of juvenile novels, like Rachel Anderson's *The War Orphan* and Ann Nolan Clark's *To Stand Against the Wind,* tell the story of the Vietnam War refugees, the boat people, to native-born American students whose classmates often include Vietnamese refugees. Students in school now were either children or unborn when Saigon fell. Growing up in the last decade, they had little chance to hear much about it. Educators are now making an effort to teach the history and the literature of the war, to determine what lessons from our experience there should be imparted to those who will someday be our leaders.

Today, visitors are able to enter the one-time concentration camp at Dachau, outside Munich, Germany. On the path the visitor walks when leaving the camp, a marker has been erected that states "Never Again" in several languages. It would be comforting to think that after Vietnam we could say "Never Again" and mean it. As so many of the writers listed in this bibliography feel, however, history teaches us that the basic nature of human beings has not been changed by thousands of years of experience on this planet. Unfortunately, "adventures" like Vietnam will recur. Knowing this, writers continue to write, to exhort, to warn, and teachers continue to teach. The human animal is nothing if not hopeful. The desire of the writers whose work is represented in this bibliography is in one sense the same as my purpose in compiling it–to fuel the hope that we can be better and to offer a memorial to those whose lives were destroyed.

NOTES

1. Peter Aichinger, *The American Soldier in Fiction, 1880-1963* (Ames, Iowa: Iowa State University Press, 1975.)

2. Valentine Cunningham, "The Weight of War," review of Robert Roth's *Sand in the Wind* in *Times Literary Supplement,* 14 March 1975, 269.

3. See entry 1539 in this volume for further information on Slocock's article.

Novels

1   Aaron, Chester. *Hello to Bodega*. New York: Atheneum, 1976.
     The main character, Gil Stuart, is a Vietnam veteran haunted
by a war-time incident, trying to make a go of a ranch-commune, where
he forbids the use of guns and drugs. Serious vandalism occurs on his
ranch, and he must find the culprits and come to terms with his past.
This was the author's master's thesis from San Francisco State
University. Appropriate for grades 8-10.

2   Abel, Robert. *The Progress of a Fire*. New York: Simon & Schuster,
     1985.
     A Vietnam veteran who had been a photojournalist in Vietnam
suffers from delayed stress years after the end of the war. He and
another veteran protect an Asian artist being terrorized by a motorcycle
gang.

3   Abrahams, Peter. *Hard Rain*. New York: Dutton, 1988.
     In this mystery-thriller, a bargain arranged at the Woodstock
rock festival results in a poor man going to Vietnam instead of a rich
one. Jessie Shapiro, ex-wife of the man who profited from the bargain
twenty years before and has disappeared with their daughter, must
embark on a cross-country search for them.

4   Alexander, David. *When the Buffalo Fight*. Richmond, Australia: Hutchinson, 1980.

This Australian novel describes the life of ordinary soldiers in Vietnam, based on the author's experiences in 1965-66, and contains detailed descriptions of life on the base and in combat. The author expresses the opinion that Australian troops were the best in Vietnam, particularly at ambushes, and compares their activities to those of the Americans.

5   Ambler, Eric. *State of Siege*. New York: Knopf, 1965.

Although the small Southeast Asian country in this novel is called Sunda, the story mirrors events in Vietnam as the capital is attacked by rebel insurgents and defended by government forces. The story is told by a British engineer. Published in England as *The Nightcomers*.

6   Amos, James. *The Memorial*. New York: Crown, 1988.

Jake Adams recalls his experiences in Vietnam while standing in front of the Wall. In an extended flashback, he relives the battle of the Ashau Valley and describes its affect on him.

7   Amos, W. J. *M. I. A. Saigon*. Los Angeles: Holloway House, 1986.

8   Anderson, Jack, and Bill Pronzini. *The Cambodia File*. Garden City, N.Y.: Doubleday, 1981.

This is a fact-based novel about the tragic events in Cambodia: the corrupt regime of Lon Nol, the take-over by the Khmer Rouge and the infamous Pol Pot, and the ensuing bloodbath in the country. The characters are both American and Cambodians. Mystery novelist Pronzini and Washington columnist Anderson severely criticize American foreign policy.

9   Anderson, Kent. *Sympathy for the Devil*. Garden City, N.Y.: Doubleday, 1987.

An effective novel in which the main character, Hanson, comes to Vietnam as a naive, liberal, college-educated young man. A series of atrocities and deaths, the horror of battle, and the despair of this particular war, make him into a hardened soldier.

10   Anderson, Rachel. *The War Orphan*. Oxford: Oxford University Press, 1984.

       Simon's parents adopt Ha, a Vietnamese orphan boy. This is the story of how Simon comes to understand Ha, what he has been through, what war means, and perhaps even something about himself. The author is the mother of an adopted Vietnamese boy.

11   Anderson, Robert A. *Cooks and Bakers: A Novel of the Vietnam War*. New York: Avon, 1982.

       The main character is a young soldier, naively hoping for a victory, but, as he matures, he comes to realize that this is not possible. His attitudes, particularly toward patriotism and heroism, change as he experiences real combat and sees real death.

12   _____. *Service for the Dead*. New York: Arbor House, 1986.

       The main character, Mike, relives his war adventures throughout this novel. In fact, they often are more real to him than the things around him in the present – particularly his home and parents. He and his war buddies create a surreal, movie-like world of the war that never really existed, but one in which he feels more comfortable than he does at home.

13   Anderson, William C. *The Gooney Bird*. New York: Crown, 1968.

       A humorous story about an odd-lot assortment of characters who pilot a C-47, the World War II gooney bird, into Vietnam to kill Vietcong and end the war. One of the few novels to use a humorous approach.

14   Anh-Duc. *Hon Dat*. Hanoi: Foreign Languages Publishing, 1969.

15   Archibald, Joe. *Special Forces Trooper*. New York: McKay, 1967.

       Stan Rusat joins the army and volunteers for the Special Forces when he is expelled from West Point. He learns to handle discipline and the anxieties and stress that he will face in combat.

16   Arnold, William. *China Gate*. New York: Villard, 1983.

       A gang of teenaged Americans living in Taiwan are led by Bryan White who is determined to amass the wealth his father lost to the Chinese. The reader follows White and the others as they grow up and become more and more ruthless and corrupt. The Vietnam War is the backdrop against which most of the action is set as the characters carry on business in Vietnam. The corruption of capitalism and the failure of American Asian policy are major themes.

17   Atkinson, Hugh. *The Most Savage Animal*. New York: Simon & Schuster, 1973.
      This Australian novel centers around the activities of the International Committee of the Red Cross in its efforts to help the wounded in Vietnam at Quong Lo field hospital where plague has broken out. Action is centered on Pierre Salem, the organization's president, and Dr. Adam Thompson, the overworked field doctor.

18   Avery, Everett. *Vietcong Terror Compound*. New York: Star Distributors, 1979.

19   Baber, Asa. *The Land of a Million Elephants*. New York: Morrow, 1970.
      The land of Chanda resists the efforts of outsiders to bring a neighboring war to its land. Told in the manner of an ancient folk tale, this antiwar story effectively contrasts the horrors of Vietnam and Laos with echoes of a better place and time, now only a fantasy.

20   Baier, L. S. *Vietnam, "The Filthy Liars" and You: A Nautical and Political Saga You Will Never See*. Portland, Oreg.: Self-published, 1970.
      Navy Captain, Jim Daniels, veteran of three wars, is asked to take the *S. S. Morningstar*, a supply ship, to Saigon. The Vietcong don't want the ship to dock. This is the story of the adventures of the captain and crew in which the author has a chance to give his opinion on foreign affairs.

21   Baker, Kenneth Wayman. *Alone in the Valley*. Pompano Beach, Fla.: Exposition Press of Florida, 1987.
      The story of Daniel Perdue's tour of duty in the Central Highlands of Vietnam in 1965 is told.

22 Baker, Richard E. *Feast of Epiphany*. Tacoma, Wash.: Rapier Press, 1981.

An infantry platoon engages in combat near Pleiku just as the war is heating up.

23 Baker, W. Howard. *The Judas Diary*. New York: Lancer, 1969.

24 Balaban, John. *Coming Down Again*. San Diego: Harcourt Brace Jovanovich, 1985.

Balaban, a volunteer in Vietnam during the war, tells the story of John Lacey and his attempt to rescue two friends being held in a Thai prison for drug smuggling. The story is set against the background of the war and depicts the drug culture of that time and the psychology of those who fought in Vietnam.

25 Ballinger, Bill S. *The Spy in the Jungle*. New York: New American Library, 1965.

Joaquin Hawks, the hero of several novels by the author, secretly enters North Vietnam in search of top secret missile installations in this adventure novel – one of the earliest novels to be set in Vietnam.

26 Barfield, H. Eugene. *Treachery on the Double*. Hicksville, N.Y.: Exposition Press, 1979.

A spy thriller in which four enlisted men, CIA operatives based at Bang Phya Airfield in Thailand, are charged with locating a mysterious agent involved with the Chinese and Albanians in a drug smuggling operation in Vietnam during the war.

27 Barrus, Tim. *Anywhere, Anywhere*. Stamford, Conn.: Knights Press, 1987.

The story of gay Vietnam veterans who return home to find rejection for being gay and a gay world that doesn't understand them or their experiences.

28 Bassett, James. *The Sky Suspended*. New York: Holt, Rinehart & Winston, 1968.

An action adventure tale in which an ex-WWII hero and adventurer, Frederick Cragg, agrees to help the people of Theitvanne, a thinly veiled Vietnam, stop supplies to the communists after the Americans withdraw.

29   Bausch, Robert. *On the Way Home*. New York: St. Martin's, 1982.
        Michael Sumner, an escaped POW who everyone believed to be dead, suddenly returns home. The author details the stress Sumner and his family experience as they adjust to his presence.

30   Bax, Martin. *The Hospital Ship*. New York: New Directions, 1976.
        The hospital ship *Hopeful* sails the oceans as a world holocaust occurs. On the ship are two mental cases being treated, one a prostitute from Saigon, who symbolizes the events in Vietnam and Indochina in general that led to the collapse of civilization.

31   Beatty, David L. *Don't Tread on My Tire Rubber Sandals: A Tale of Vietnam*. Boonville, N.Y.: Willard Press, 1969.
        Beatty's novel follows the journey of Captain Fervent from Ft. Bragg to Saigon where he is assigned to a headquarters job. He has a plan for using French nationals to ferret out the Vietcong – a plan in which no one seems to have much interest. No combat is described.

32   Bennett, Jack. *The Voyage of the Lucky Dragon*. Englewood Cliffs, N.J.: Prentice-Hall, 1981.
        After the fall of Saigon, a Vietnamese family flees the Communist re-education camps in a fishing boat bound for Australia. Written for grades 7-9.

33   Biderman, Bob. *Letters to Nanette*. San Francisco: Early Stages, 1982.
        A college student enlists to get a better chance at a good position in the army just as the Vietnam War is beginning to heat up. His story is told in the form of letters to his girlfriend.

34   Biersach, Frank J., Jr. *So Cruel World*. Taiwan?: n.p., 1968.
        The author says that this is a novel about war, greed and morality, based on actual events that happened in Vietnam. A Vietnam

family befriends an American officer, Riley, in Saigon, while the family's sons take opposite sides in the war.

35   Blacker, Irwin K. *Search and Destroy*. New York: Random House, 1966.
An adventure story in which a group of Special Forces commandos led by Colonel Barney Fannin secretly infiltrate North Vietnam to destroy an enemy base near Hanoi. Published in England as *The Valley of Hanoi*.

36   Blair, Cynthia. *Battle Scars*. New York: Ballantine, 1983.
The long shadow of the war touches the main characters as the hero, a Vietnam veteran, falls in love with a woman whose brother died in the war.

37   Boatman, Alan. *Comrades-in-Arms*. New York: Harper & Row, 1974.
Marine Robert Harding is shot in the back by another Marine in Vietnam. Although the motive for this is unknown, the man is later murdered for it. As Harding is recuperating, he reminisces with other Marines about the war, giving the reader a view of the camaraderie among men in war as well as the emotional and spiritual damage done by war.

38   Bodey, Donald. *F. N. G.* New York: Viking Press, 1985.
F.N.G. stands for "fucking new guy," Gabe Sauers, the main character of this novel, who presents his memoir of his tour as an infantry private in Vietnam. The author depicts the sights and sounds of the war, the drive to simply survive, and the typical conflicts with career officers.

39   Bograd, Larry. *Travelers*. New York: Lippincott, 1986.
A boy is haunted by the image of the father he never knew who died in Vietnam. He sets out to find out more about him. Written for high school students.

40   Bosse, Malcolm J. *The Incident at Naha*. New York: Simon & Schuster, 1972.

A mystery in which a woman and her lover, Virgil, a black Vietnam veteran haunted by memories of a massacre in Vietnam, attempt to solve the murder of a member of Virgil's former Vietnam unit.

41 _____. *The Journey of Tao Kim Nam*. Garden City, N.Y.: Doubleday, 1959.

Tao Kim Nam was once a landowner in North Vietnam. The Communist presence forces him to flee and become a refugee in Vietnam prior to American involvement. On the run, he learns how to survive.

42 _____. *The Man Who Loved Zoos*. New York: Putnam, 1974.

A mystery in which a Vietnam veteran, who now only feels comfortable with animals, is murdered after discovering secret FBI activities. His aunt, a librarian, attempts to reveal his murderer.

43 Boulle, Pierre. *The Ears of the Jungle*. New York: Vanguard Press, 1972.

This French novel deals with the attempts of Madame Ngha, chief intelligence officer of North Vietnam, to foil the efforts of the Americans who have dropped devices throughout the jungle that pick up the sounds of truck convoys.

44 Boyd, Candy Dawson. *Charlie Pippin*. New York: Macmillan, 1987.

Eleven year old Charlie tries to understand her father by studying about the Vietnam War in which he fought. He returned home a bitter, rigid man. Her research reveals that her father is a decorated war hero. Written for grades 5-7.

45 Boyne, Walter J., and Steven L. Thompson. *The Wild Blue*. New York: Crown, 1986.

This novel describes the history of the Air Force from 1947 through Vietnam, where part of the novel is set. Their activities in Vietnam, including the torture of Air Force pilots by the North Vietnamese is chronicled. The novel is filled with details about the planes these men fly.

46   Briley, John. *The Traitors*. New York: Putnam, 1969.
       Five Americans on a patrol in Vietnam are ambushed, captured, and forced to walk along the Ho Chi Minh trail to prison. They are repeatedly lectured with propaganda by Evans, an American defector, who wants them to participate in a mission against the U.S. to free one of their leaders imprisoned in the South.

47   Britton, Christopher. *Paybacks*. New York: Popular Library, 1985.
       The author, a Marine Vietnam veteran, describes the grueling life of basic training through his character Mike Taggart, a Marine defense counsel who must defend a sergeant accused of beating a new recruit to death. The sergeants activities in Vietnam play a role in the story. Mystery.

48   Brooke, Dinah. *Games of Love and War*. London: Jonathan Cape, 1976.
       Also published by Harcourt, Brace in 1976 under the title *Death Games*, this novel deals with a neurotic European woman, Elspeth, her father, and his mistress in Vietnam after American troops have withdrawn.

49   Brooke, Joshua. *Just a Little Inconvenience*. New York: Dell, 1978.
       Kenny Briggs and Frank Logan were boyhood friends who fought together in Vietnam where Briggs lost an arm and leg. Briggs feels Logan's cowardice under fire resulted in his injuries. Their confrontation and Briggs' readjustment at home are shown.

50   Brossard, Chandler. *Raging Joys, Sublime Violations*. Wheaton, Md.: Cherry Valley, 1981.
       An acidly bitter and irreverant satire of the war in Vietnam and the characters who ran the show from Nixon to Bundy, Kennedy to Kissinger. Even Pat Nixon and Martha Mitchell aren't ignored.

51   ____. *Wake Up, We're Almost There*. New York: Richard W. Baron, 1971.
       In this eccentric novel, the sexual fantasies of a Greenwich Village grocer are told. He imagines himself as a multitude of characters, two of which are a black infantryman in the Central

Highlands of Vietnam and an American soldier of Indian descent who defects to the Vietcong.

52   Brown, Wesley. *Tragic Magic*. New York: Random House, 1978.
       Melvin Ellington, a black conscientious objector serves five years in prison, returns home and confronts a friend who went to Vietnam and lost a hand.

53   Bunch, Chris. *A Reckoning for Kings: A Novel of the Tet Offensive*. New York: Atheneum, 1987.
       The story of the war is told from the point of view of Major Dennis Shannon, an army intelligence officer, and North Vietnamese general Vo Le Duan. The novel moves from the American characters to the Vietnamese as the war progresses and events lead up to Tet.

54   Bunting, Josiah. *The Lionheads*. New York: George Braziller, 1972.
       The author of this well-received first novel is a Vietnam veteran and West Point instructor. He tells the story of George Lemming, self-seeking commanding general of the 12th Division, called "The Lionheads," and their involvement in actions just around the time of Tet. The novel emphasizes the details of military action.

55   Buonanno, C. *Beyond the Flag*. New York: Tower, 1981.
       A combat novel describing action by Marines serving with Australian soldiers in Quang Tri province in 1969.

56   Burke, Martyn. *The Laughing War*. Garden City, N.Y.: Doubleday, 1980.
       Barney, a comedian who is a favorite of the Vietnam GIs, incurs the wrath of a colonel who subsequently arranges for him to be involved in an operation that leaves him trapped in a city under fire. The author was a journalist in Vietnam.

57   Butler, James. *Song Yam Sat – River of Death*. Reseda, Calif.: Mojave Books, 1979.

Dick Brown is the commander of a river patrol guarding the Mekong Delta area from the enemy. Told episodically, this is one of the few pictures of action along the rivers.

58   Butler, Robert Olen. *The Alleys of Eden*. New York: Horizon Press, 1981.

Cliff Wilkes is drafted after marrying his college sweetheart and is sent to Vietnam where he serves well until his marriage comes to an end and he is involved in a Vietcong prisoner's death. He deserts and lives with a Vietnamese bar girl, eventually returning home to Illinois after the fall of Saigon where neither of them are able to fit in, and he is still a fugitive. The author of this novel served as an intelligence officer in Vietnam.

59   ____. *Sun Dogs*. New York: Horizon Press, 1982.

In Butler's second novel, the main character, Wilson Hand, is a private investigator involved in a case dealing with leaked information about American oil reserves. He is bothered by continual flashbacks to the time he was a POW with the Vietcong.

60   ____. *On Distant Ground*. New York: Knopf, 1985.

Butler describes the journey of a soldier who relives his experiences in Vietnam during his court-martial trial for releasing a Vietcong prisoner. During the retelling of events in Vietnam, he realizes that he may have fathered a child by his Vietnamese girlfriend. He returns to Vietnam, just prior to the fall of Saigon, to confirm his suspicions and find the child.

61   Butterworth, William E. *Air Evac*. New York: Norton, 1967.

Ken Maddox, a college graduate who had dreamed of medical school, joins the army and becomes a pilot of a medical helicopter in Vietnam in the hope that he will not have to kill.

62   ____. *Helicopter Pilot*. New York: Norton, 1967.

Tony Fletcher, a young, very successful advertising executive, is drafted and becomes a helicopter pilot. The story emphasizes the training and experiences of the pilot during the Vietnam years, although Vietnam is not mentioned and Fletcher does not see combat in the novel. Written for grades 7-9.

63 _____. *Orders to Vietnam: A Novel of Helicopter Warfare*. Boston: Little, Brown, 1968.

This is the story of Bill Byrnes, a young West Point drop-out and army draftee from a military family, who trains to be a helicopter pilot. He is decorated for bravery in Vietnam, thus proving himself in the eyes of his army general father. Written for grades 7-9.

64 _____. *Stop and Search: A Novel of Small Boat Warfare off Vietnam*. Boston: Little, Brown, 1969.

Eddie Czernik joins the Naval Reserve Officer's Training Program in order to get training to become a marine biologist and instead ends up in Vietnam serving on the stop and search missions of Vietnamese boats that may be supplying the Vietcong. Written for grades 6-9.

65 Calin, Harold. *Search and Kill*. New York: Belmont Books, 1982.

66 Cameron, Lou. *The Dragon's Spine*. New York: Avon, 1968.

An action adventure story in which the remains of an ambushed Green Beret team become involved with a Montagnard tribe in the mountains of the Central Highlands of Vietnam.

67 Campbell, Ewing. *The Rincon Triptych*. Fort Worth, Tex.: Latitudes, 1984.

Hunt Crofford, recovering from a wound received in Vietnam, returns home to Texas and tries to find work. He seems unnaturally tranquil – or overly restrained. Flashbacks of memories of his early years with his mother intrude on his life.

68 Camper, Frank. *The Mission*. New York: Manor Books, 1979.

An action adventure story about a secret military operation in Laos. One team member jeopardizes the others.

69   Caputo, Philip. *Delcorso's Gallery*. New York: Holt, Rinehart & Winston, 1983.

One of the major Vietnam novelists tells the story of Nick DelCorso, a Vietnam veteran photojournalist who returns to Vietnam to record the fall of Saigon and later goes to Beirut to record events there. An interesting presentation of the role of the news media in events.

70   _____. *Indian Country*. New York: Bantam, 1987.

Chris Starkmann had enlisted in Vietnam to oppose his pacifist father and to be with his Indian friend, but the death of his friend in the war and his experiences there haunt his return home and push him toward madness.

71   Carabatsos, James. *Heroes*. New York: Berkley, 1977.

This book is based on the author's screen play. Jack Dunne is a Vietnam vet, a former combat paratrooper. In the early scenes, he ends up back in the veterans' hospital after causing a brawl in a recruiting office. When he is released, he decides on his dream – to run a worm farm. Photographs from the film.

72   Carn, John. *Shaw's Nam*. Indianapolis: Benjamin Books, 1984.

Jimmy Shaw, a black soldier, is serving with the army in Vietnam in 1968 as a member of a searchlight army unit attached to Marine infantry. A searchlight unit drove searchlight mounted jeeps. The author gives an account of the cooperation between the two services and the racial tension between the black and white soldiers, an experience with which the author, a black Vietnam vet, is familiar. The main character temporarily loses his hearing in an explosion and is in a coma for over a week before being sent home.

73   Carroll, James. *Fault Lines*. Boston: Little, Brown, 1980.

One of the four characters in this novel is a Vietnam War draft dodger whose brother died in the war. He leaves Sweden to return to the States after a ten year exile in order to start his life over.

74   _____. *Prince of Peace*. Boston: Little, Brown, 1984.

Frank Durkin, a college professor, tells the story of Father Michael Maguire, a former Korean war vet and POW, becomes actively involved in the antiwar movement after visiting Vietnam during the war and is eventually excommunicated. Carroll delineates the upheaval going on in the Catholic Church at the same time as the country was in turmoil over Vietnam.

75 Carroll, John. *Token Soldiers*. Boronia, Australia: Wildgrass Books, 1983.

The token soldiers of the title are Australian troops fighting in Vietnam with less support, and, if possible, less understanding of their role, than their American counterparts. This novel describes some of the actions seen by these men.

76 Carver, James. *The Shadows of Go-Yeu*. New York: Walker, 1971.

Lieutenant Marron asks to be assigned to work with a Vietnamese village following his tour of duty. He is assigned to Go-Yeu with Captain Early who has no understanding of the Vietnamese people or his own team members. Marron deals with the smuggling going on in the village and the mysterious death of his predecessor.

77 Cassidy, John. *A Station in the Delta*. New York: Scribners, 1979.

The main character in *A Station in the Delta* is Toby Busch, a CIA agent living in the provinces in the Mekong Delta area and gathering information about the impending Tet Offensive, information that is ignored by his superiors. An interesting look at the role of the CIA.

78 Certo, Dominic N. *The Valor of Francesco D'Amini*. New York: Manor Books, 1979.

Jason Davenport tells the story of a Marine platoon and its actions in a small village around the time of Tet, action that eventually causes tragedy within the platoon.

79 Chalker, Jack L. *A Jungle of Stars*. New York: Ballantine, 1976.

In this science fiction novel, Paul Savage is murdered while on jungle duty in Vietnam. After his death, his spirit is contacted by an extraterrestrial being who enlists him to help his people in a intergalactic battle.

80   Chandler, David. *Captain Hollister*. New York: Macmillan, 1973.
        Captain Hollister re-enlists in the army and returns to Vietnam where he works on the graves registration detail. His job is to write letters of condolence to the families of dead soldiers. The decision of whether or not to tell the truth about how each man died weights on him. He eventually becomes involved in a drug smuggling operation in this novel.

81   Chapel, Ernie. *Dateline: An Loi*. New York: Paper Jacks, 1988.
        Reporter Ernie Chapel describes combat against the Vietcong around An Loi, a small security base with one infantry battalion. Some of the action is described from the point of view of Phat, a Vietcong soldier. Chapel is haunted by the image of the Vietcong prisoner wearing a Mickey Mouse t-shirt.

82   ____. *Dateline: Phu Loi*. Toronto/New York: Paper Jacks, 1987.
        The author, who may be using a pen name, shares the same name with the main character, a reporter in Vietnam. There is an attempt to make the book look like a true story as Chapel is going to tell the "real" story of the war that he saw in 1968; the story that couldn't be printed then. This is the story of his adventures with his helicopter pilot friend, Mike Carmack. This is the first in what may be the beginning of a series featuring Ernie Chapel.

83   Chaplin, Gordon. *Joyride*. New York: Coward, McCann and Geoghegan, 1982.
        Two teenage boys living in the American community in Bangkok steal a motorcycle and ride into Vietnam to see the war up close. Their adventures are presented.

84   Charles, Robert. *Sea Vengeance*. New York: Pinnacle, 1974.
        The North Vietnamese hijack a British merchant ship.

85   Charyn, Jerome. *War Cries over Avenue C*. New York: Donald I. Fine, 1985.

Howard Biedersbill goes to Vietnam as a demolitions expert and returns a twisted shadow of the man he was. He and his equally twisted girlfriend become involved in the underground world of crime in this novel.

86   Clark, Alan. *The Lion Heart: A Tale of the War in Vietnam*. New York: Morrow, 1969.

Jack Lane, a 35-year-old Special Forces trooper, has left his home and family to serve in Vietnam as an advisor. Disappointed in the South Vietnamese, he is transferred to work with an American unit peopled by assorted psychotics and misfits. He is killed in a disastrous military operation. Glossary of terms included.

87   Clark, Ann Nolan. *To Stand against the Wind*. New York: Viking Press, 1978.

A young Vietnamese refugee living in the United States remembers his life in a small village in Vietnam before and during the war. Grades 4-7.

88   Clark, Johnnie. *Semper Fidelis*. New York: Ballantine, 1988.

Shawn McClellan was a Marine in Vietnam. His action-filled experiences and those of his closely-knit platoon are depicted. The senselessness of the battles, but also their life/death exhilaration, are shown. At the end, McClellan is wounded and returns home to the inevitable readjustment and lack of understanding of those at home. Glossary of terms. Clark also wrote the personal narrative *Guns Up!*

89   Cleary, Jon. *Spearfield's Daughter*. New York: Morrow, 1983.

Cleo Spearfield, daughter of a famous Australian politician, goes to Vietnam as a war correspondent. She writes of a massacre which is suppressed by her editors, after which she resigns and goes to London. A woman battling in a man's world is the theme.

90   Coleman, Charles. *Sergeant Back Again*. New York: Harper & Row, 1980.

An interesting novel in which the main character, Andrew Collins, is sent to a mental hospital in Texas after his shattering experiences as a medic in Vietnam. Reminiscent of *One Flew Over the Cuckoo's Nest*, the inhabitants of the ward relive their experiences. For them, Vietnam is still every bit as real as the ward in which they find themselves.

91   Collingwood, Charles. *The Defector*. New York: Harper & Row, 1970.
      The author was the chief foreign correspondent for CBS. His novel is a suspense thriller about a television commentator who goes on a secret mission to Hanoi to bring a defector safely to the West.

92   Connolly, Edward. *Deer Run*. New York: Scribners, 1971.
      Two Vietnam veterans sent up a commune on a farm in Vermont and gain the friendship of the old farmer, Ritter, who gave them the use of the place. They live quietly until violent acts are directed against them by the enraged townspeople. The main character, Josh, becomes violent himself, which eventually results in tragedy and the end of the commune.

93   Cook, Kenneth. *The Wine of God's Anger*. Melbourne, Australia: Lansdowne Press, 1968.
      Cook's main character is a young Australian who deserts while on leave from the Vietnam War. Like American soldiers, he too wanted to save a country from communism but becomes disillusioned about that and his other ideals as well. He continually struggles with the beliefs of his Catholic upbringing. Numerous battle scenes throughout the novel.

94   Coonts, Stephen. *Flight of the Intruder*. Annapolis, Md.: Naval Institute Press, 1986.
      The author, an ex-Navy flier, describes air raids over North Vietnam from the deck of an aircraft carrier. The main character, Jake Grafton, is worried about the deaths he causes but does not see from his plane. However, when his best friend is killed, he sets out to bomb the Communist Party headquarters in Hanoi.

95   Coppel, Alfred. *A Land of Mirrors*. San Diego: Harcourt Brace
        Jovanovich, 1988.
               A suspense novel in which the main character, Megan Wells,
        receives a call from her husband in the middle of the night. However,
        he supposedly had died seventeen years before in Vietnam. He warns
        her that their daughter is in danger, and she sets out on a quest to save
        her.

96   Corder, E. M. *The Deerhunter*. New York: Jove/Exeter Books, 1978.
               Corder has novelized Deric Washburn's screenplay of the film
        The Deerhunter. Several families from a poor Allegheny Mountain town
        are shown before some of the young men go to Vietnam. Some are
        killed in action, and others find their lives shattered beyond repair.

97   Cortesi, Lawrence. *The Magnificent Bastards of Vietnam*. New York:
        Tower Publications, 1968.
               The novel describes the actions of a group of infantrymen
        fighting the Vietcong.

98   Costello, Michael. *A Long Time from Home*. New York:
        Kensington/Zebra, 1984.
               An action adventure tale in which Army sergeant Harry Pitts
        searches for a helicopter pilot who caused the death of several men on
        a previous mission. Although from a family of soldiers, Pitts is shocked
        by what he sees in Vietnam and fights out of a sense of duty to his lost
        friends and a need for revenge.

99   Couper, J. M. *Lottery in Lives*. Boston: Houghton Mifflin, 1970.
               An Australian youth faces a dilemma after registering for the
        National Service, knowing he will probably be sent to Vietnam.

100   Coutant, Helen. *First Snow*. New York: Knopf, 1974.
               Lien, a Vietnamese refugee adjusting to life in the U.S., spends
        her first winter in New England with her dying grandmother who
        schools her in Vietnamese values and customs. Drawings by Vo-Dinh
        Mai. Written for grades 3-5.

101   Coyne, John. *Brothers and Sisters*. New York: Dutton, 1986.
        A family saga of the Irish-American DeLacy family. One of the sons, Emmett, returned from Vietnam broken and troubled by nightmares.

102   Cragg, Dan. *The Soldier's Prize*. New York: Ballantine, 1986.
        In this fiction based on fact story, the men of the 18th U.S. Infantry see action during the 1968 Tet Offensive. Career army soldiers are portrayed.

103   Crawford, William. *Gunship Commander*. New York: Pinnacle, 1973.
        The main character is a colonel in charge of a helicopter unit. He is an angry, violent man and ulitmately an ineffective leader. The author provides a great deal of information in the descriptions of the land, the machines, and the warfare itself.

104   _____. *The Marine*. New York: Pinnacle, 1972.
        Frank Garrison, Marine pilot and former POW, stands trial for killing another POW who collaborated with the enemy while imprisoned by the North Vietnamese. Prison conditions are graphically described.

105   Crosby, Alexander. *One Day for Peace*. Boston: Little, Brown, 1971.
        Junior high school student Jane Simon is very upset over the death of her friend, the milkman, in Vietnam. She writes to the President, asking him to explain why the U.S. is fighting and organizes a committee in her town to plan a peace parade. Appropriate for grades 6-10.

106   Crowther, John. *Firebase*. New York: St. Martin's, 1976.
        A murder and series of racial incidents form the basis for the plot which involves Alpha company of the 11th Infantry Brigade in Vietnam. The other enemies of the soldier are shown – boredom, apathy, liquor and drugs, and racial tension, among others.

107   Crumley, James. *One to Count Cadence*. New York: Random House, 1969.

Crumley describes army life before Vietnam through his character Slag Krummel who was based in the Philippines with an intelligence monitoring unit prior to being wounded in Vietnam. He reminisces on his experiences in the Philippines where life was boring. Then his unit was ordered to establish a monitoring station in the jungles of Vietnam. Krummel comes into conflict with another soldier, Joe Morning, and in battle emerges as a real leader.

108 Cunningham, Ben. *Green Eyes*. New York: Ballantine, 1976.

Green Eyes was adapted from the Lorimar television production; the story conceived by Eugene Logan and David Seltzer. Seltzer wrote the original teleplay. The main character, Lloyd Dubeck, a black Vietnam veteran, returns to Asia to search for his girlfriend, Em Thuy, and their child, who he has never seen.

109 Currey, Richard. *Fatal Light*. New York: Dutton/Seymour Lawrence, 1988.

Richard Currey was a Marine medic. He tells the story of a combat medic in Vietnam, an everyman figure who is never named. This is a rite of passage book in which the young medic comes of age as he sees sickness, poverty, and the terrible deaths of soldiers and civilians. Juxtaposed against this ugliness are the fond memories he shares with the reader of his family, his home and his girlfriend, Mary. This is a beautifully written book.

110 D'Alpuget, Blanche. *Turtle Beach*. New York: Simon & Schuster, 1983.

D'Alpuget, an Australian novelist, tells the story of Judith Wilkes, a journalist, who travels to Malaysia to report on the plight of the boat people – the Vietnamese refugees. She learns of the political and moral questions the presence of these people has raised.

111 Daniels, Norman. *Operation VC*. New York: Pyramid, 1967.

112 Davis, George. *Coming Home*. New York: Random House, 1971.

The author is an Air Force Vietnam veteran. Eleven narrators alternate in telling parts of the story of combat flying in Vietnam. Racial tensions are explored through the characters of Ben and Stacey, roommates from two races. Neither of the two main characters comes home.

113 Davis, Patti, and Maureen Strange Foster. *Home Front*. New York: Crown, 1986.

A popular novel by the daughter of President Reagan concerns the life of Beth Canfield (a character similar to the author) who opposes the Vietnam war but loves a high school classmate who is in Vietnam on the front lines. She rebels against parental manipulation. Thinly disguised portraits of the President and Nancy Reagan.

114 Dean, Nell M. *Nurse in Vietnam*. New York: Julian Messner, 1969.

Called a "Career Romance for Young Moderns" on the title page, *Nurse in Vietnam* tells the story of nurse Lisa Blake and her experiences in a hospital in Manila and later in Saigon during the war. The love story is a large part of this novel which appears to have been written for teenaged girls.

115 DeBorchgrave, Arnaud, and Robert Moss. *The Spike*. New York: Crown, 1980.

Robert Hockney, a journalist, visits a Vietcong encampment and a Marine infantry company in battle during the Tet Offensive. Later he uncovers Soviet infiltration in the U.S. government and media. A spy thriller.

116 Del Vecchio, John M. *The 13th Valley*. New York: Bantam, 1982.

One of the best of the Vietnam War novels, *The 13th Valley*, tells the story of three men involved in a major combat mission in the Khe Ta Laou Valley in 1970. Realistic portrayals of the men, their fears before and in battle, the companionship they find in each other, and their actions in the final jungle battle. Maps, glossary, chronology of Vietnamese history.

117 DeMille, Nelson. *Word of Honor*. New York: Warner, 1985.

Ben Tyson, a decorated Vietnam veteran, is an electronics executive in New York. One morning he learns that a book has been published that names him as one of those involved in a military massacre in which nuns, children, and other civilians were killed in a raid on a French hospital in Hue. The army recalls him to active duty in order to try him for murder. This is a well-written, exciting story.

118 Dennis, Charles. *Stoned Cold Soldier*. London: Bachman & Turner, 1973.

This is the story of a twenty-four year old GI who shot his entire platoon in Vietnam while stoned on dope. His superiors try to cover-up the incident, a reporter tries to discover the truth, and a lawyer tries to prevent the soldier from being convicted and court-martialed.

119 Derho, John. *The Rocky Road*. San Luis Obispo, Calif.: Man to Man Press, 1979.

The main character, a conscientious objector, is sent to Vietnam toward the end of his military obligation. He keeps a low profile and tries to stay out of trouble and alive, all the while, commenting on the action around him.

120 Dewlen, Al. *Next of Kin*. New York: Doubleday, 1977.

A father whose son has died in Vietnam receives an ugly anonymous letter demeaning his son's death in the war and goes looking for the letter-writer. An examination of the affect of the boy's death on his family.

121 Dibner, Martin. *The Trouble with Heroes*. Garden City, N.Y.: Doubleday, 1971.

Captain Paul Damion is in charge of a nuclear submarine. He refuses to follow orders to bombard a Vietnamese village believed to be hiding enemy troops because of the innocent inhabitants that would be killed. He turns his command over to another officer. As a result, a court of inquiry is called to investigate the incident. Well-written and readable.

122 Dickason, Christie. *Indochine*. New York: Villard Books, 1987.

Nina, Eurasian daughter of a man who dealt in opium in order to obtain weapons to repel the French from his country, finds her life thrown into chaos when her home is bombed and her mother killed. She is forced into the underworld of Vietnamese society where she becomes powerful. Vietnam is seen from the the 1920s through the Vietnam War. Published in England as *The Dragon Riders*.

123 Didion, Joan. *Democracy*. New York: Simon & Schuster, 1984.
 The noted essayist and novelist describes the wife of an American politician involved with a CIA operative. At the height of the war, she travels to Saigon just before the fall in 1975. She is able to leave on one of the last planes.

124 Diehl, William. *Hooligans*. New York: Villard, 1984.
 A sensational novel that describes the activities of Jake Kilmer, federal agent and Vietnam veteran. His war on crime is interrupted with his "Nam Diary" where the horrors of Vietnam are compared to the horrors of the urban jungle.

125 ____. *Thai Horse*. New York: Villard Books, 1987.
 An adventure novel in which a secret agent returns to Southeast Asia to locate his friend who had disappeared fifteen years before. The Thai horse of the title refers to an organization involved in drug trafficking.

126 Dodge, Ed. *Dau: A Novel of Vietnam*. New York: Macmillan, 1984.
 Morgan Preston goes to Vietnam in 1965 and is assigned to a unit than transports supplies, the wounded, and the dead by helicopter. He tells his story and that of the men he knows. After his discharge, physically and mentally wounded himself, he returns home and spends time in a mental institution, trying to come to terms with his experiences. A well-written, powerful novel.

127 Doliner, Roy. *The Thin Line*. New York: Crown, 1980.
 An action adventure novel in which the main character, Jack Sullivan, an ex-CIA agent, becomes involved in a CIA sponsored drug smuggling operation in Vietnam in 1963.

128 Doolittle, Jerome. *The Bombing Officer*. New York: Dutton, 1982.
 The author was a U.S. information officer in Laos. His main character, Fred Upson, attached to the U.S. embassy in Laos, is in charge of approving or dismissing requests to bomb various areas. The author decries the total disregard for human life in American policy with regard to the "rules of engagement," a euphemism for target practice. Upson becomes disillusioned with these practices.

129 Downs, Hunton. *The Compassionate Tiger*. New York: Popular Library, 1960.

The author was a U.S. foreign service officer and cultural editor of the Voice of America at the time the novel was written. He traveled by jeep through Vietnamese and Cambodian jungles, interviewing hundreds of people – French, Chinese, and American. The main character is Daniel King, an American soldier of fortune serving with the French during the IndoChina war involved with a plantation owner, his mistress, and a Vietnamese mandarin. The story is full of betrayal and double dealing.

130 ____. *The Opium Strategem*. New York: Bantam, 1973.

A suspense novel based on fact about opium trafficking in southeast Asia involving the CIA, the military, and the international Mafia. The hero is Lee Kopit, a former Special Forces captain who works for a secret military group. He returns to Vietnam and becomes involved in an internicene battle among the drug traffickers.

131 Dunn, Marylois. *The Man in the Box: A Story from Vietnam*. New York: McGraw-Hill, 1968.

The center of the story is a Montagnard village that is victimized by both the Americans and the Vietcong. A young boy, Chau Li, rescues a Green Beret who is being tortured in the same way as the Vietcong tortured and killed his father. He helps the American to safety and becomes a refugee in the process. A thoughtful, effective story.

132 Durand, Loup. *The Angkor Massacre*. New York: Morrow, 1983.

This novel charts the events in Cambodia between 1970-75, during the regime of the infamous Khmer Rouge. A sub-plot involves an American deserter in Vietnam who is smuggled to Sweden.

133 Durden, Charles. *No Bugles, No Drums*. New York: Viking Press, 1976.

Jamie Hawkins is a southern soldier who feels he has stumbled into a surreal movie in Vietnam. He fights against the army and everything around him, trying to hold on to his sanity. He tells his story in the first person, relating the death of his best friend and the traitorous activities of another soldier whom he later kills. Considered to be one of the major novels of Vietnam War literature.

134   Durham, Harold. *Strawman*. New York: Kensington/Zebra, 1987.
        The adventures of jet pilot Michael Kelly includes combat, romance, and conflict with a superior officer.

135   Dye, Dale A. *Platoon*. New York: Berkley, 1986.
        The author is a Vietnam veteran who served as an advisor to the film *Platoon*. This is the story of Chris Taylor and the men of his platoon in Vietnam. Taylor becomes an everyman of the war.

136   _____. *Run between the Rain Drops*. New York: Ballantine, 1985.
        Dye, himself a journalist during the war, tells the story of two war correspondents involved in the battle for Hue.

137   Eastlake, William. *The Bamboo Bed*. New York: Simon & Schuster, 1969.
        One of the major books of Vietnam War literature, *The Bamboo Bed* is considered by many to be the *Catch 22* of this war. The main characters are Captain Knightbridge and his aid Lieutenant Janine Bliss, who involve themselves in nonmilitary matters in the helicopter, The Bamboo Bed, above the battles, and Captain Clancy, an old-fashioned kind of soldier. The book is surreal, blackly humorous, and heavily symbolic.

138   Ebert, Alan, and Janice Rotchstein. *The Long Way Home*. New York: Crown, 1984.
        The story of the Tiernam family, seen in a previous novel, *Traditions,* as they cope with the affect of the Vietnam War on their lives. In this popular fiction, one of the main character's children is a war hero and former POW, another deserted and fled to Canada, and the daughter is an antiwar activist.

139   Edell, Ed. *A Special Breed of Men*. Guilderland, N.Y.: Ranger Associates, 1984.
        Young and inexperienced Sergeant Raymond Heller commands a patrol in Vietnam. His combat experiences are described. He is wounded, falls in love with his nurse, and eventually returns home.

140   Edgar, Ken. *As If*. Englewood Cliffs, N.J.: Prentice-Hall, 1973.
        A popular novel in which Tom Welland, a Korean War veteran, and his pilot Kramer are in love with the same woman. They work together in Vietnam, eventually being captured and held in a POW camp, where several escapes occur. Later Tom returns to the U.S. and must decide between his ex-wife and Holly, the girl both men love.

141   Edgerton, Clyde. *The Floatplane Notebooks*. Chapel Hill, N.C.: Algonquin Books, 1988.
        A family saga of the Copelands of Listre, North Carolina, who gather every year in May to clean the family gravestones and swap family history and stories. All the family eccentrics show up including the patriarch, Albert, who has been building an amphibious plane for a decade. Two fun-loving, mischievous cousins, Mark and Meredith, are sent to Vietnam where Meredith is maimed. The author was an Air Force pilot.

142   Edwards, Ellis. *Operation Golden Buddha*. Boulder, Colo.: Paladin Press, 1986.
        Three ex-Green Berets concoct a scheme to steal a golden Buddha from a temple in Cambodia. The action takes place in Vietnam and Cambodia at the time of the fall of Saigon.

143   Ehrlich, Jack. *Close Combat*. New York: Pocket Books, 1969.

144   Eickhoff, Randy Lee. *A Hand to Execute*. New York: Walker, 1987.
        A mystery thriller set during the time of the Tet Offensive in which a reporter based in Saigon, Con Edwards, sets out to find the killer of his assistant, a man he did not like, but whose killer must be found.

145   Elegant, Robert A. *A Kind of Treason*. New York: Holt, Rinehart & Winston, 1966.
        Gerald Mallory, a writer, is given an assignment to go to Vietnam to write about the Vietnamese reaction to the war and the effect it is having on them. He learns that this job has another side to it: he will also be working for the CIA, trying to determine the source of

an information leak that is aiding the Vietcong. An effective mystery thriller.

146 Elliott, Ellen. *Vietnam Nurse*. New York: Arcadia House, 1968.
     Australian nursing sister Joanna Shelton's father is a missionary doctor, missing in Vietcong territory. She is brought to Vietnam to lead the search for him through the jungle.

147 Ellison, James Whitfield. *The Summer after the War*. New York: Dodd, Mead, 1972.
     John Packard is a Vietnam veteran recently returned home and trying to adjust. He has decided that he would like to be a writer and attends a writer's conference. His ideas of writing, and those of the author are presented. A love affair between the main character and an older woman is also a major part of the plot.

148 Ely, Scott. *Starlight*. New York: Weidenfeld & Nicolson, 1987.
     The starlight of the title refers to a device used by sniper Tom Light to aid in shooting at night. Light appears to have mystical powers to the men in his unit. The horror of war is shown through the battle scenes that abound in this surreal novel that was the author's master's thesis at the University of Arkansas.

149 England, Barry. *Figures in a Landscape*. New York: Holt, Rinehart & Winston, 1968.
     Two POWs escape their prison camp and must struggle to survive. One is an experienced soldier while the other is young and untested. This short novel is set in an unnamed country and in an unnamed war, but the setting resembles Vietnam.

150 Everett, Percival. *Walk Me to the Distance*. New York: Ticknor & Fields, 1985.
     Recently returned Vietnam veteran, David Larson, is driving across Wyoming. When he arrives at the town of Slut's Hole, he meets an odd assortment of characters and becomes involved in a kidnapping case involving a Vietnamese girl that eventually results in a lynching.

151 Faherty, Pat. *The Fastest Truck in Vietnam*. San Francisco: Pull/Push Press, 1983.

"Crash" Piper is a Marine truck driver who spends his time at a base near Da Nang where he never sees action or the enemy, spending his time alleviating his boredom through drinking, whoring, smoking dope, and racing his truck.

152 Fairbairn, Douglas. *Shoot*. Garden City, N.Y.: Doubleday, 1973.

Rex, the narrator, is a WWII vet who goes on a hunting trip with four other friends. While there, they see several men on a ridge. The men see them and suddenly shoot at them, grazing Rex's friend Pete on the head. They shoot back, hitting one of the men on the ridge in the face. They assume he is dead, but no notice appears in the paper. Knowing they will return next weekend, Rex enlists the help of Ogilvie, a burned-out Vietnam vet and several of his friends. Together they return to the sight of the shooting for a real Vietnam-style firefight.

153 Ferrandino, Joseph. *Firefight*. New York: Soho, 1987.

The main character is an infantryman trying to survive the Vietcong, the enemies the jungle throws against the men, the deaths of friends, and open conflict with a superior officer. Another grim look at the Vietnam War from an author who served as an infantryman himself in this war.

154 Fick, Carl. *The Danziger Transcript*. New York: Putnam, 1971.

Newspaper reporter Peter Danziger had an opportunity to interview Vietcong in depth during his assignment in Vietnam. Upon returning home, he provides information on what he has learned to Major Pike, an intelligence officer, who interrogates him mercilessly.

155 Field, Della. *Vietnam Nurse*. New York: Avon, 1965.

156 Fleming, Stephen. *The Exile of Sergeant Nen*. Chapel Hill, N.C.: Algonquin Books, 1986.

Sergeant Nen had been a Vietnamese soldier for most of his life. Now living in the U.S. and working in his family's restaurant in Alexandria, Virginia, following the end of the war in which he heroically helped others escape, he tries to adjust to life in the United

States and in the refugee community in particular, while remembering his adventures as a paratrooper during the war.

157　Fleming, Thomas. *Officer's Wives*. Garden City, N.Y.: Doubleday, 1981.
　　　A story of four West Point graduates and their wives. The couples are followed from 1950-1975. We see the women's joys, fears, and frustrations as the men's careers advance as well as the change in attitude toward the military that occurred during these years. Some of the novel is set in Saigon during the officers' tours while the Diem government was being overthrown.

158　Flowers, A. R. *Demojo Blues*. New York: Dutton, 1985.
　　　Tucept Highjohn and two other black veterans try to adjust to civilian life after the Vietnam war, remembering the racial discrimination they experienced in Vietnam. Feeling rejected, he becomes a student of the local hoodooman, a master of the occult.

159　Ford, Daniel. *Incident at Muc Wa*. Garden City, N.Y.: Doubleday, 1967.
　　　This well-written novel, one of the major novels of the genre, features Corporal Stephen Courcey, a demolitions expert working in the highlands with a group of commanding officers that are nothing less than fools. The camp at Muc Wa is held through several attacks but finally lost and the main character is killed. This book was reissued in 1979 by Jove under the title *Go Tell the Spartans*, the same title as the film based on the book which is available in videotape.

160　Ford, Richard. *The Ultimate Good Luck*. Boston: Houghton Mifflin, 1981.
　　　Quinn, a Vietnam veteran who still has flashbacks to the war and is trying to adjust to civilian life, becomes involved in drug smuggling in Mexico.

161　Franklin, Mark. *The Mother-of-Pearl Men*. London: John Murray, 1985.
　　　Michael Bishop, a civilian employee in Saigon during the late 1960's, becomes involved in a plot to help a defector escape from the Vietcong. Americans are not major characters in the book, but the war is ever present.

162 Frazer, Michael. *Nasho*. West Melbourne, Australia: Aries Imprint, 1984.

An Australian novel of the Vietnam war in which atrocities against civilians are shown through the murder of the narrator's fourteen year old mistress.

163 Freeling, Nicholas. *Tsing-Boom*. New York: Harper & Row, 1969.

A murder mystery set in Vietnam in 1954 against the backdrop of the French in Indochina that is solved by Dutch police inspector Van der Valk.

164 Freemantle, Brian. *The Vietnam Legacy*. New York: Tor, 1984.

Efforts are made to rescue three American MIA's believed to still be held in Vietnam.

165 French, Robert. *Vietnam: Both Sides*. New York: Manor Books, 1979.

Carl Reddin is the hero of this unbelieveable adventure novel in which an ex-football star goes to Vietnam, is captured by the Vietcong, and held prisoner.

166 Fuller, Jack. *Fragments*. New York: Morrow, 1984.

One of the major Vietnam novels, *Fragments* tells the story of two soldiers destined for Vietnam. Morgan, a draftee who narrates the story, and Neumann. They join the Blue Team that carries out special missions. The two soldiers represent different points of view about how to survive. Neumann, an exponent of free will and an instinctive fighter, feels he must take charge, while Morgan, a more cautious person, believes in fate and in letting others decide what is best. In the course of the narrative, both are wounded, and Neumann kills a Vietnamese family.

167 Garfield, Brian. *The Last Bridge*. New York: McKay, 1966.

A group of commandos try to free an American captain from a Vietcong prison and in the process blow up a vital railroad bridge.

168 _____. *Relentless*. New York: World, 1972.

A group of fugitives, led by an ex-Green Beret expelled from the army for the murder of Vietnamese civilians, has stolen one million dollars in cash. They flee from the FBI into the Arizona mountains where they are caught by a blizzard and tracked by a local Navajo policeman – also a Vietnam vet.

169 Gangemi, Kenneth. *The Interceptor Pilot*. London: Marion Boyars, 1980.

James Wilson was a Korean War fighter pilot who has agonized over his role in that war. Now he hears disturbing reports about a new war. He gives up his university teaching post, leaves his family, and joins the North Vietnamese to intercept American planes. He eventually becomes dangerous to both the Americans and the Russians. The novel reads like a movie script with directions for the cameramen with lines like "Cut to a shot of Wilson in his cockpit."

170 Gentry, Claude. *Love and War in Vietnam*. Baldwin, Miss.: Magnolia, 1970.

An adventure novel of an American soldier's journey through the jungles of Vietnam, fighting the enemy along the way. A Vietnamese girl is his partner in these adventures.

171 Gilkerson, Seth. *The Bastard War*. Great Neck, N.Y.: Todd & Honeywell, 1986.

A Vietnam veteran's story is told in flashbacks. He remembers particularly a woman resistance fighter who fought with real heroism and saved American lives.

172 Gillis, Gerald, L. *Bent, but not Broken*. Orangeburg, S.C.: Sandlapper, 1986.

Mike Billingsley, a successful soldier, survives three wounds in Vietnam and returns home. The reader follows him through his basic training and tour of duty.

173 Gilson, Jamie. *Hello, My Name Is Scrambled Eggs*. New York: Lothrop, 1985.

Tuan Nguyen arrives in the U.S., a Vietnamese refugee, to live with the Trumble family in a small town in Illinois. Their son, Harvey, a seventh grader, tries to mold him into an "American Kid." Written for grades 4-7.

174 Giovannitti, Len. *The Man Who Won the Medal of Honor*. New York: Random House, 1973.

David Glass, a draftee sent to Vietnam, kills some Americans after he witnesses them murdering prisoners. He seems to get away with this act without being caught. In fact, he is awarded the Congressional Medal of Honor. During the award presentation ceremony, he commits an unbelievable act of violence. The novel is written as if the main character was describing events in his diary.

175 Glasser, Ronald. *Another War, Another Peace*. New York: Summit, 1985.

In this well-written novel by the author of *365 Days*, the growing friendship of two men, David, a young doctor sent to Vietnam, and his driver, Tom, is told. Interesting character development.

176 Glick, Allen. *Winter's Coming Winter's Gone*. Austin, Tex.: Eakin, 1984.

Subtitled "There Were Other Tragedies Besides Dying in Vietnam: An American Struggle," this novel tells the story of nineteen year old David Schrader, his tour in Vietnam, and the difficulty of his readjustment. At home with fellow survivor Mingo Calderone, he confronts the violence of the war, the things he did, and how it affected his life. This novel was reissued by Bantam in 1987 under the title *The Winter Marines*.

177 Godey, John. *The Talisman*. New York: Putnam, 1976.

A gang of Vietnam Veterans, led by a World War II vet, conspire to steal the body of the Unknown Soldier from Arlington National Cemetery to secure an activist's release from prison.

178 Gold, Jerome. *The Negligence of Death*. Seattle: Black Heron Press, 1984.

Ray Dickinson is a sergeant in the Special Forces. This novel tells of his experiences and the men he knew prior to his being wounded. He returns home briefly and returns to Vietnam. The book's emphasis is on death and the valuelessness of human life in such a war.

179 Graham, Gail. *Cross-Fire: A Vietnam Novel.* New York: Pantheon, 1972.

      The author lived in Vietnam and was captured by the Vietcong from whom she escaped. *Cross-fire* tells of an American soldier who becomes separated from his platoon. He meets four Vietnamese children, the only survivors of a raid on their village. Although there is mutual hate and suspicion on both sides, they band together for safety and try to get to civilization, but all five are killed by Americans. Written for grades 7-12.

180 Grant, Bruce. *Cherry Bloom.* Sydney, Australia: Aurora Press, 1980.

      Although this novel is set in Singapore after the war, the Vietnam War plays a role. The title character is the wife of the head of British intelligence in Singapore. The characters criticize American involvement in Vietnam and analyze it's tactical mistakes.

181 Graves, Richard L. *Rolling Thunder.* New York: Pocket Books, 1977.

182 Greene, Graham. *The Quiet American.* New York: Viking Press, 1955.

      One of the most influential and prophetic novels of Vietnam War literature, *The Quiet American* describes American involvement in Vietnam before fiction became fact. The story involves a British journalist interacting with an American sent from Washington on a mysterious mission.

183 Grey, Anthony. *Saigon.* Boston: Little, Brown, 1982.

      A long book that traces the history of Vietnam from 1925 through the war and the fortunes of the Joseph Sherman family. An attempt to tell the whole story of Vietnam that has generally been considered successful by the critics.

184 Griffin, W. E. B. *Brotherhood of War.* Book V: *The Berets.* New York: Jove, 1985.

      The story of the Green Berets during the early days of the Vietnam War. Part of a series, three volumes of which are about Vietnam.

185 ___. *Brotherhood of War*. Book VI: *The Generals*. New York: Jove, 1986.

    The Generals continues the story started in *The Berets* with many of the same characters and tells the story of raids on POW camps in North Vietnam.

186 ___. *Brotherhood of War*. Book VIII: *The Aviators*. New York: Putnam, 1988.

    The main character is a helicopter pilot involved in the Army's Air Assault Division charged with fighting guerilla warfare in Vietnam.

187 Groen, Jay, and David Groen. *Huey*. New York: Ballantine, 1984.

    The authors are brothers who served in Vietnam. David Groen was a helicopter pilot as is the main character, John Vanvorden. The story is similar to many in this genre with descriptions of the horrors of combat and the deaths of friends. Action scenes with helicopters, the ubiquitous symbol of the Vietnam War, are utilized throughout.

188 Groom, Winston. *Better Times than These*. New York: Summit Books, 1978.

    One of the major novels, *Better Times than These* tells the story of Bravo Company in Vietnam in 1966. The men of the company endure a long sea voyage and then a long jungle trek before engaging in a battle that kills many of them. The interactions of the men and their relationships with people back home, the dangers of the jungle, the loss of friends are all reported by the author who experienced them himself in Vietnam.

189 ___. *Forrest Gump*. Garden City, N.Y.: Doubleday, 1986.

    Forrest Gump is considerably less than bright as is obvious as he tells the story of his life in misspelled first-person narration. His zany adventures include his becoming a hero during the Tet Offensive and earning the Congressional Medal of Honor.

190 ___. *Gone the Sun*. New York: Doubleday, 1988.

    Vietnam veteran and small town newspaper editor Beau Gunn becomes involved in murder and fraud in this thriller.

191 Grosback, Robert. *Easy and Hard Ways Out*. New York: Harper's Magazine Press, 1975.

Written with black humor and a cast of weird characters, this novel tells the story of the test of new Navy plane that has a flaw in its missile avoidance system. A fact that is being covered up as it is tested over North Vietnam with tragic results. Published by Carroll and Graf in 1984 as *Best Defense*.

192 Hadley, J. B. *The Point Team*. New York: Warner, 1984.

A Green Beret veteran, "Mad Mike" Campbell, takes on a mission to save the Amerasian son of Lt. Frank Vanderhoven, USAF, shot down over Vietnam. Eric was left behind after the fall of Saigon. His wealthy grandfather pays Campbell one million dollars to take five mercenaries into Vietnam to get him out.

193 Halberstam, David. *One Very Hot Day*. Boston: Houghton Mifflin, 1967.

One of the major novels, *One Very Hot Day* describes what should have been an easy assault on a Vietcong rest camp across the Ap Thanh Thoi canal, but something goes terribly wrong and the Americans fall into a trap. The story is told from the point of view of two Americans who led the raid and of the Vietnamese lieutenant who countered it. The action takes place on one day.

194 Haldeman, Joe W. *The Forever War*. New York: St. Martin's, 1975.

The Forever War is a science fiction novel that follows the career of William Mandella from private to major in an intergalactic war that has been fought for 1,000 years. The author draws on his Vietnam War experiences, and the parallels are obvious.

195 ____. *War Year*. New York: Holt, Rinehart & Winston, 1972.

War Year tells the story of the one year tour of duty in Vietnam of nineteen-year-old John Farmer, away from home for the first time. The experiences are typical of many of the real soldiers in this war.

196 Hardesty, Steven. *Ghost Soldiers*. New York: Walker, 1986.

This is an interesting story of Vietnam and the supernatural. When an American helicopter crashes at night in the Central Highlands, Captain Oliver Foley and his men of Bravo Company are sent out to find the crew. As they begin to search, each of the men enters into his own fantasy, an alternate reality. They are all killed in an ambush. Then they rise from the dead and fight the battle the way it should have been fought.

197 Hardy, Rene. *Sword of God*. Garden City, N.Y.: Doubleday, 1954.

Jeane Kernez is trying to find his brother Dom Angelico, the abbot of a monastery in a remote area of Vietnam. Angelico has been taken prisoner by the Viet-Minh. Kernez tries to save him with tragic results.

198 Hardy, Ronald. *Place of Jackals*. Garden City, N.Y.: Doubleday, 1955.

Captain Roget is a French army chaplain in Vietnam and Laos during the French involvement in Indochina. Roget feels a great inner turmoil over his wavering faith and is tested by temptations put in his path and the horrible conditions he experiences. A compassionate act allows him to save his soul and his vocation.

199 Harper, Stephen. *Live till Tomorrow*. London: Collins, 1977.

The protagonist, Barber, is an American who stayed on in Saigon after his tour of duty to open a business. Now Saigon is about to fall and Barber tries to help a Vietnamese friend and his family leave Saigon. He describes the chaos of the last days and hours as people beseige the American embassy, a scene that the author witnessed as a British reporter in Vietnam.

200 Harris, Thomas. *Black Sunday*. New York: Putnam, 1975.

Michael Lander is a former Navy pilot and Vietnam War POW whose experiences have made him bitter and dangerous. Arab terrorists contact him to blow up the Super Bowl in retaliation for American aid to Israel. Landers is the perfect choice for assassin as he will be piloting the blimp above the game.

201 Harrison, Jim. *A Good Day to Die*. New York: Simon & Schuster, 1973.
An alienated intellectual worried about ecology teams up with a Vietnam veteran knowledgeable in guerilla tactics in the Florida Keys, and they destroy dams as they try to save spawning game fish.

202 Harvester, Simon. *Battle Road*. New York: Walker, 1967.
Michael Hunter has vanished in Saigon, and his Australian colleague, Dorian Silk sets out to find him, finally locating him in a Vietcong prison camp from which he must be rescued in this story of suspense and intrigue.

203 Hasford, Gustav. *The Short-Timers*. New York: Harper & Row, 1979.
Marine William "Joker" Doolittle is sent to Vietnam as a combat reporter. Toward the end of his tour, his attitude earns him a place in a military action in Hue during the time of the Tet Offensive. He becomes a leader. The surreal quality so evident in many Vietnam novels appears in *The Short-Timers*, a major work. The film *Full Metal Jacket* was based on this novel.

204 Hastings, Michael. *The Unknown Soldier*. New York: Macmillan, 1986.
The unknown soldier from the Vietnam War is about to be buried in Arlington National Cemetery, and former CIA agent Walt Meredith must learn the identity of the body. This is a fascinating mystery thriller.

205 Hathaway, Bo. *A World of Hurt*. New York: Taplinger, 1981.
Jeff Madsen is excited to be going to Vietnam and comes to worship an older sergeant who fills in for the father he lost as a child. When the sergeant is killed, the reality of war becomes apparent. He is sent home after an insubordinate act. The author also follows the experiences of Sloane, a soldier Madsen met in basic training.

206 Hawkins, Evelyn. *Vietnam Nurse*. New York: Zebra, 1984.
Sybil Watkins is a nurse in the 555th Field hospital near Long Binh, Vietnam. The novel describes her life and work and presents the usual love affair with a handsome Green Beret.

207 Healy, Jeremiah. *The Staked Goat*. New York: Harper & Row, 1986.
John Francis Cuddy is a private investigator from Boston in a series of mysteries by Healy. When an army buddy from Vietnam is murdered, Cuddy sets out to find the killer and instead finds a crime that has its origin in Vietnam.

208 Heckler, Jonellen. *Safekeeping*. New York: Putnam, 1983.
Judy Greer is the wife of a POW held by the North Vietnamese. She has never received a letter from him since his capture several years before. Her antiwar activities have alienated her from others on the army base where she lives and from her twelve year old son, Kevin. Kevin's football coach, Major Joseph Campbell comes into their lives, bringing what each needs, but causing a difficult choice to be made.

209 Heffernan, William. *The Corsican*. New York: Simon & Schuster, 1983.
Peter Bently is an American intelligence officer in Vietnam in 1966 whose grandfather is a Corsican drug king. An organized crime thriller set in Southeast Asia that explores the drug trade.

210 Heinemann, Larry. *Close Quarters*. New York: Farrar, Straus & Giroux, 1974.
A classic novel of the war, *Close Quarters* follows the coming of age of Philip Dosier and his fellow soldiers in Vietnam where they learn that war is not like a John Wayne movie. Dosier comes home stunned by his experiences and deadened to emotions.

211 ____. *Paco's Story*. New York: Farrar, Straus & Giroux, 1986.
The National Book Award winner for 1988, *Paco's Story* relates the final Vietnam War battle of Paco Sullivan that nearly is the end of him. He recovers from his wounds and returns home to the intolerance of civilians and a job as a restaurant dishwasher, where he tries to come to terms with his experiences.

212 Hempstone, Smith. *A Tract of Time*. Boston: Houghton Mifflin, 1966.
Harry Coltart is an American agent working with Vietnamese tribesmen early in the war, where the politics of Saigon undermine American activities under the Diem regime. The author was a

correspondent in Vietnam and his character sees some of the things the author himself experienced including the self-immolation of a Buddhist monk.

213 Hennesey, Hal. *The Midnight War*. New York: Pyramid, 1967.
     An action adventure tale about Paul Partridge whose new invention, an improved tank, is tried out in Vietnam. The book is filled with all the elements guaranteed to sell – sex, betrayal, adventure.

214 Hentoff, Nat. *I'm Really Dragged but Nothing Gets Me Down*. New York: Simon & Schuster, 1968.
     Sam and Jeremy Wolf, father and son, are opposites in the debate over the issues of the sixties from the Vietnam War to drugs. Jeremy wants to resist the draft. His father is concerned that nothing disrupt his peaceful, materialistic life. In the course of the story, they come to a better understanding of each other and a workable solution to their disagreements. Written for junior high school and above.

215 Hershman, Morris. *Glory in Hell*. New York: Lancer, 1967.
     The story of a young man's coming of age during his tour in Vietnam as an infantryman.

216 ____. *Mission to Hell*. New York: Pyramid, 1968.
     An Air Force crew of five go on a mission to drop supplies and pick up wounded at Phu Kyu where Americans are surrounded by Vietcong. Their plane crashes in the jungle and they are captured. Eventually they escape and are rescued.

217 Heywood, Joe T. *Taxi Dancer*. New York: Berkley, 1986.
     Taxi Dancer tells the story of a corps of jet pilots flying bombing missions over North Vietnam. While on a mission, the main character is captured and spends six years as a prisoner of war.

218 Higgins, Jack. *Toll for the Brave*. New York: Fawcett, 1971.
     Toll for the Brave, written under Higgins's pseudonym Harry Patterson and also published in England (Long, 1971), relates the story of Ellis Jackson, an escapee from a Vietnamese prison camp who has

turned up at his seacoast home in England. The suspense builds, and bodies multiply, as it becomes apparent that someone, a Vietcong perhaps, is after him. Jackson begins to doubt his sanity.

219   Hiler, Craig. *Monkey Mountain*. New York: Belmont Tower, 1979.

A Vietnam veteran tells the story of his experience in Vietnam in which he was part of a group manning a radar unit on Monkey Mountain, near Da Nang. He describes the psychological effects the duty caused as well as the conflicts between ordinary soldiers and the career soldiers. An effective novel.

220   Holland, William E. *Let a Soldier Die*. New York: Delacorte, 1984.

The author was a helicopter pilot in Vietnam, and he utilizes his experiences in chopper warfare in describing the book's action. An accident occurs in which "friendly fire" kills several American soldiers, precipitating a psychological crisis for the story's hero.

221   Honig, Louis. *For Your Eyes Only: Read and Destroy*. Los Angeles: Charles, 1972.

An action adventure story about Lane Peters, journalist, given a secret mission that could bring an end to the war. He is thwarted by various enemies, the Vietcong, Bangkok's KPA, and the CIA itself.

222   Hoover, Paul. *Saigon, Illinois*. New York: Vintage, 1988.

Jim Holder is a twenty-two year old native of Indiana who is granted conscientious objector status and comes to Chicago to do his alternative service in a hospital. The deaths he witnesses at the hospital and the ones in Vietnam that he sees on the television each night keep the war very close to him. His relationships with his fellow hospital workers play an important role in this well-written novel by a prize-winning Illinois poet.

223   Horan, James David. *The New Vigilantes*. New York: Avon, 1975.

A group of ex-Marine POWs, who were nicknamed the Hounds of Tong Le Mai while in Vietnam, organize themselves into a vigilante group to fight urban crime in this action novel.

224 Huggett, William Turner. *Body Count*. New York: Putnam, 1973.
     In this well-received novel, Lieutenant Chris Hawkins commands a Marine platoon. The reader follows him through combat at Khe Sanh, R & R in Tokyo, and back to Vietnam for a terrible battle in which a hill is taken and then given up the very next day. A well-written novel with effective action scenes.

225 Hughes, Frank. *Everyday Heroes*. Norwalk, Conn.: Tower Books, 1982.
     Jim Howard flies bombing raids of North Vietnam from the deck of the carrier *Shangri-La* in 1966-67. The lives of the men and their families back in the States are depicted as well as the actions in which they are involved.

226 Hunt, Greg. *Mission to Darkness*. New York: Dell/Banbury, 1983.
     Reporter Lily Stratton is an eyewitness to the major historical events in Vietnam and Southeast Asia during the sixties, particularly the fall of the Diem government and the Tet Offensive. She accompanies combat missions and has a few adventures of her own.

227 Hunter, Evan. *Sons*. Garden City, N.Y.: Doubleday, 1969.
     Hunter has written a family saga of the Tylers, three generations that have fought in America's wars from World War I to Vietnam. The last Tyler, Wat, enters the Vietnam War reluctantly and is killed.

228 Hunter, R. Lanny, and Victor L. Hunter. *Living Dogs and Dead Lions*. New York: Viking Press, 1986.
     Tom Bishop still feels guilty about the death of his friend Joshua Scott in Vietnam over a decade earlier, experiencing flashbacks to the battles they fought. He travels to Joshua's wife's farm in Kansas and becomes involved in her life and in a dangerous situation with a psychotic killer. Action and suspense.

229 Hyman, Tom. *Riches and Honor*. New York: Viking Press, 1985.
     An interesting thriller that begins during World War II when an SS officer assumes the identity of a dying Jewish prisoner and travels to the United States. Years later, he is Ambassador to Israel and his

son is missing in Vietnam. His younger son sets out on a mission to rescue him, and he decides to accompany him.

230 Hynd, Noel. *Revenge*. New York: Dial Press, 1976.
   A former Vietnam War POW searches for the interrogator and torturer from the camp where he was held who is known as Imp. His search takes him from Vietnam to Europe in this action adventure thriller.

231 Ives, John. *Fear in a Handful of Dust*. New York: Dutton, 1978.
   An American Indian, Calvin Duggai, has been incarcerated in a mental hospital after psychological problems stemming from Vietnam War combat action that resulted in the deaths of five people. He plots to escape and kill the doctors that put him in the hospital.

232 Jackson, Blyden. *Operation Burning Candle*. New York: Third Press, 1973.
   A mystery thriller. Aaron Rogers, a black medical student who volunteers for Vietnam in the middle of his studies, is reported dead in battle. He resurfaces as the leader of a black fighting group from Harlem, an all veteran group who carry out robbery, murder, and mayhem in New York. Their eventual plan is to assassinate anti-black southern senators at the Democratic National Convention.

233 Jacob, John. *Long Ride Back*. New York: Thunder's Mouth Press, 1988.
   The author is not a Vietnam veteran, yet he effectively describes the tour of duty of Trent Jones in all its ghastliness. Jones lives in Chicago, and his narration jumps from past to present like the flashbacks to the war that the character experiences. Attention is given to the reception returning veterans received.

234 James, Allston. *Attic Light*. Santa Barbara, Calif.: Capra, 1979.
   Chase, the main character of *Attic Light*, is wounded in Vietnam and returns home. He receives a hostile reception from those at home reacting to the war, causing his alienation. He worries about a friend, still in Vietnam fighting the war. Later the friend is reported killed.

235 Jessup, Richard. *Foxway*. Boston: Little, Brown, 1971.

Terry Foxway returns home from Vietnam. His relationship with his girlfriend, Nina, is an important part of the novel. Terry is haunted by Vietnam memories, and the violence that was permitted in war, however, is not so easily turned off in peace.

236 Johnson, Annabel, and Edgar Johnson. *The Last Knife*. New York: Simon & Schuster, 1971.

This is an episodic novel in which five people, including an American Indian, a Chicano, a black, a white lawyer, and a motorcycle gang member, tell tales of protest against war and men's efforts to remain free to Rick, a young boy who hopes to go into the Marines. Ironically, his brother has just served time in prison for refusing to serve in the military.

237 Johnstone, William W. *The Last of the Dog Team*. New York: Kensington/Zebra, 1980.

Terry Kovacs belongs to a secret army organization, the Dog Team, where is happily employed for most of his life. He is involved in activities in Vietnam in the mid-1960s.

238 Jolly, Andrew. *A Time of Soldiers*. New York: Dutton, 1976.

Jolly's novel traces three generations of a military family in which the last member serves in Vietnam. The narrator is a priest who points out that men who fight for noble causes most often end up bringing unhappiness to everyone involved.

239 Joss, John. *Sierra, Sierra*. Los Altos, Calif.: Soaring Press, 1977.

Mark Lewis is a Vietnam veteran. Now at home, he dreams of breaking two world records in his sailplane. As he flies, monitored by the sister of his dead Marine buddy, Mark relives the air battles that he fought in Vietnam.

240 Just, Ward. *The American Blues*. New York: Viking Press, 1984.

Just uses the devise of a writer trying to find an end for his latest book about the Vietnam War. Writers block causes him to take his family off for a break in a secluded area where he spends time with a mystery writer and a young woman and is eventually able to return to the novel with insight into his memories that he seemed to lack before.

241 _____. *In the City of Fear*. New York: Viking Press, 1982.

Washington at the height of the Vietnam War is the setting for this novel of a congressman, Piatt Warden, his wife Marina, and Sam Joyce, a career soldier. Sam is summoned by the President to hear of schemes to win the war in Vietnam.

242 _____. *Stringer*. Boston: Little, Brown, 1974.

Stringer is an unsuccessful newspaperman who has avoided committed involvement. Now he is in Vietnam as a civilian with an army officer involved in planting electronic sensors in enemy territory. After the officer is killed, he must get out on his own.

243 Kaiko, Takeshi. *Into a Black Sun*. New York: Kodansha International, 1980.

The author of *Into a Black Sun*, first printed in Japan in 1968, is a Japanese reporter who observed events in Vietnam during 1964-65. His main character is semi-autobiographical and describes both the life in Saigon and the abject terror of being involved in combat and ultimately fleeing from the Vietcong. The author foreshadows how the war would ultimately end. The sequel is *Darkness in Summer*, in which one of the unnamed main characters is an ex-reporter obsessed with Vietnam. The story takes place in Europe after the Vietnam War.

244 Kalb, Bernard, and Marvin Kalb. *The Last Ambassador*. Boston: Little, Brown, 1981.

The authors, brothers and well-known television journalists, write about Hadden Walker, the last American ambassador to Vietnam who, even in the midst of shelling near the embassy and the fall of Saigon begins, believes that the U.S. can still avoid defeat.

245 Kalish, Robert. *Bloodrun*. New York: Avon, 1984.

A mystery in which the main character, a Vietnam veteran, journeys back to Asia to discover his brother's murderer.

246 Kaplan, Andrew. *Dragonfire*. New York: Warner Books, 1987.
North Vietnamese troops prepare to pursue Cambodian rebels illegally into Thailand. Michael Parker is sent by the CIA to prevent this in this action adventure novel.

247 Karl, S. W. *The Last Shall Be First*. New York: Manor Books, 1978.
This is the story of the career of a soldier who re-enlists in order to join the Greet Berets. His training and various missions are described. He is eventually dishonorably discharged for his part in a failed mission.

248 Karl, Terry. *Children of the Dragon*. San Francisco: People's Press, 1974.
Children of the Dragon is a children's book that describes the effect of American bombing in Vietnam on two children living in the country.

249 Karlin, Wayne. *Lost Armies*. New York: Henry Holt, 1988.
A well-written novel whose protagonist is Emmett Wheeler, a Vietnam veteran, who is a free-lance writer and teacher of Vietnamese refugees. Deer are being mutilated in the area, and one of the suspects is another veteran, a friend of Wheeler's. He is hired by a local paper to investigate the mutilations. Throughout, Wheeler remembers the war and evaluates its meaning.

250 Katzenbach, John. *In the Heat of the Summer*. New York: Atheneum, 1982.
Malcolm Anderson, a Miami newspaper reporter, gets a call from a psychotic serial killer and becomes involved in the hunt to find and stop him. The killer is a Vietnam veteran who relives his experiences in Vietnam through flashbacks.

251 Kauffmann, Joel. *The Weight*. Scottsdale, Pa.: Herald Press, 1983.
Jan, the son of a Mennonite preacher, must decide whether or not he will register for the draft or seek conscientious objector status. There is considerable peer pressure to register for the draft.

252   Keith, Jeff. *A Child's Crusade*. New York: Vantage, 1971.
      Jason Bates sees combat in Thailand, but his return home
finds him unable to adjust to home or family. He re-enlists and returns
to Asia, this time to Vietnam, where his sociopathic tendencies gain
ascendancy, and he murders a Thai girl.

253   Kempley, Walter. *The Invaders*. New York: Saturday Review Press,
      1976.
      North Vietnamese Colonel Linh and black American deserter
Eddie Palmer form a terrorist partnership in Saigon in 1968 which calls
for eventual explosions in New York City. Lieutenant Skilling discovers
the plot and tries to prevent it.

254   Keneally, Thomas. *Passenger*. New York: Harcourt Brace Jovanovich,
      1979.
      The antihero of *Passenger* is journalist Brian Fitzgerald who
was taught as a child that "All Asia was turning monolithic and Marxist
and was lusting with ideological ardour for Australia." Fitzgerald gets
involved in Vietnam and faces disillusionment of his long-held ideals
after his first killing. He comes to question Australia's involvement in
Vietnam and its other Asian adventures, feeling that Australians will
enthusiastically embrace the next Asian conflict.

255   Kim, Samuel. *The American POW's*. Boston: Branden Press, 1979.
      The author was a POW and so is his main character, Sammy
Kim, who is captured by the Vietcong and held under deplorable
conditions before he escapes. Sammy Kim falls in love with a Eurasian
doctor, Risabelle Kim, who is killed.

256   King, Annette. *The Magic Tortoise Ranch*. New York: Crown, 1972.
      One of the characters in this story of the establishment of a
commune and its problems with its neighbors is a Vietnam veteran
haunted by the war.

257   Kingery, Philip. *The Monk and the Marines*. New York: Bantam Books,
      1974.
      The main character is in the Navy but serves with a Marine
infantry unit. He had been a monk in a monastic order, thus the title.

Simply staying alive is no easy task amid the missions and attacks. The subject of fragging is explored as is the soldiers' feelings for the Vietnamese.

258 Kirkwood, James. *Some Kind of Hero*. New York: Crowell, 1975.

Eddie Keller returns home after spending four years as a POW in North Vietnam. Life presents a series of unhappy events at home including the end of his marriage and the serious disability of his mother. Eddie steals some negotiable securities, becoming involved in a movie-like chase. *Some Kind of Hero* is the basis for the film of the same name, available in videotape.

259 Klose, Kevin, and Philip A. McCombs. *The Typhoon Shipments*. New York: Norton, 1974.

An adventure mystery in which Dan Gilmore and Ralph Sidder, customs agents, work on cracking an international heroin ring operating in the U.S. Their investigations take them into Vietnam during the height of the war. Heroin, typically, is being shipped to the U.S. in the bodies of dead servicemen.

260 Kolpacoff, Victor. *The Prisoners of Quai Dong*. New York: New American Library, 1967.

Krueger, an army lieutenant is in a military prison at Quai Dong. When a young Vietnamese boy, suspected of being a Vietcong, is brought in for questioning, Krueger is ordered to help in the interrogation as he knows some Vietnamese. The major part of the story describes the brutal questioning of the boy that eventually results in his death by suicide. Krueger is reinstated for the information he supposedly gained from the boy, but which he actually invented.

261 Kopp, Frederick. *Something Like This Happens Every War*. Glendale, Calif.: Great Western, 1982.

The author shows the difficulty of Vietnam veterans' readjustment to civilian life caused by the hostile and bitter attitudes of those who did not go to war and have little understanding of what soldiers experienced there.

262 Kovic, Ron. *Around the World in Eight Days*. San Francisco: City Lights, 1984.

   The main character is a Vietnam War veteran who hitchhikes west from his hometown in Long Island. This is the story of his adventures, the people he meets, and his coming to terms with his war memories.

263 Kozak, Yitka R. *The Conscientious Objector*. Jericho, N.Y.: Exposition, 1973.

   This novel is divided into two parts: "Who Is a Conscientious Objector," and "Witnesses' Testimonies." Dave Zimmerman, on trial for draft evasion and international flight, fled to Canada upon receiving his draft notice. Later he returned and was arrested. His lawyer wants to plead that he is a conscientious objector, but Dave is uncooperative and apathetic. A courtroom drama ensues that explores the issues of conscientious objection, amnesty, the draft, and guilt and responsibility.

264 Kreuger, Carl. *Wings of the Tiger*. New York: Fell, 1966.

   Wings of the Tiger is the story of the life and loves of a group of Air Force pilots whose job is to destroy North Vietnamese airfields.

265 Kumar, P. J. *Roll Call of Death*. New York: Manyland, 1971.

   Role Call of Death describes the activities of an Indian journalist who is enlisted by the CIA to gain access to Americans held prisoner in North Vietnamese under terrible conditions. The hero manages this, but is killed just before the prison is liberated by an American raid.

266 Kurtzman, Joel. *Sweet Bobby*. New York: McGraw-Hill, 1974.

   Sweet Bobby is the story of a violent sociopath whose desertion by his father, abuse by his prostitute mother, and horrifying combat experiences in Vietnam make him seek control in acts of violence, usually directed against women. Description of his combat experiences with his friend Harvy are brief.

267 LaFountaine, George. *The Long Walk*. New York: Putnam, 1986.

   Stanley Baker, a doctor, tries to help Frank Turco, who has been a POW for over ten years and has lost his identity. He comes home to a hero's welcome and ends up in psychiatric care where Baker again attempts to save him.

268 Larson, Charles. *The Chinese Game*. Philadelphia: Lippincott, 1969.
　　　Captain Belgard is an army advisor in Vietnam early in the war. After being injured by a grenade, he develops the ability to foretell the future through a Chinese game of sticks with words on them. He eventually sees his own death.

269 Larteguy, Jean. *The Centurions*. New York: Dutton, 1962.
　　　Larteguy is a well-known French journalist who was based in Southeast Asia during both French and American involvements. This early novel is the story of French paratroopers in Indochina after the fall of Dien Bien Phu, and the effect of the war on the soldiers. The paratroopers' experiences in re-education Prison Camp One are depicted. *The Centurions* was later issued under the title *The Lost Command*. Its sequel is *The Praetorians*, in which these French soldiers go on to battle the Algerians using techniques learned in Vietnam.

270 ＿＿＿. *Presumed Dead*. Boston: Little, Brown, 1976.
　　　Swiss banker Hans Brucker travels to Vietnam to search for a man who is presumed dead. If his death can be confirmed, his wife stands to inherit the family fortune. Larteguy incorporates the atmosphere of the time, 1970, and the military operations he observed.

271 ＿＿＿. *Yellow Fever*. New York: Dutton, 1966.
　　　The story of two French journalists in Saigon and Hanoi following the fall of Dien Bien Phu in the mid-1950s. Interesting background to the American involvement.

272 le Carré, John. *The Honourable Schoolboy*. New York: Knopf, 1977.
　　　Another in the series of novels about George Smiley of the British Secret Service. Attempting to reorganize his network destroyed in *Tinker Tailor Soldier Spy*, Smiley tries to locate Karla, his Russian counterpart. The action takes place in Asia including Vietnam near the end of the war and in Cambodia.

273 LeBaron, Charles. *Fragments of Light*. New York: St. Martin's/Marek, 1984.

    The main character, Frito, is a doctor who grew up in Berkeley during the political activism of the 1960s This story takes him to a children's hospital in Cambodia while the Cambodians and Vietnamese are fighting.

274 Lederer, William J., and Eugene Burdick. *Sarkhan*. New York: McGraw-Hill, 1965.

    An American businessman and a professor in Sarkhan, an imaginary country recognized by readers as Vietnam, see the inevitability of a Communist take over although the American ambassador seems oblivious to it. Intrigue, action, and adventure. Also published as *The Deceptive American*.

275 ____. *The Ugly American*. New York: Norton, 1958.

    An important early novel about an imaginary country, Sarkhan, that shows an American ambassador who never bothers to learn the language or the culture. The novel is an indictment of American foreign policy mistakes abroad, particularly in Asia. *The Ugly American* is actually a series of twenty-one stories of Americans and Sarkhanese and their interactions. The authors' factual epilogue is included in hope that it will stimulate discussion and change. Prophetic and tragic from the vantage point of the 1980s.

276 Lee, Larry. *American Eagle: The Story of a Navajo Vietnam Veteran*. Madrid, N.Mex.: Packrat Press, 1977.

    Two-Luke Dancer, a Navajo Vietnam veteran, is haunted by his war experiences, the brutality of the war, and its affect on his own nature. *American Eagle* presents a series of Lee's adventures, in a picaresque style, as he tries to exorcise the demons.

277 Linn, Bill. *Missing in Action*. New York: Avon, 1981.

    Missing in Action is the story of an American POW's escape from a prison camp and his 350 mile journey through the jungle toward Saigon.

278 Linn, Edward, and Jack Pearl. *Masque of Honor*. New York: Norton, 1969.

Captain David Walsh is a black officer in Vietnam glowingly portrayed in a journalist's overblown article. Actually, Walsh is somewhat less than honorable. When he is awarded the Congressional Medal of Honor on the strength of the article, all of those involved with him are affected. He does have the courage, and honor, to decline the award.

279 Littell, Robert. *Sweet Reason*. Boston: Houghton Mifflin, 1974.

A series of zany adventures by the crew of an outmoded naval vessel patrolling the Vietnamese coasts during the war are the focal point of this novel. Sweet Reason is a mysterious pamphleteer who urges the men to disobey orders and resist the military whenever possible.

280 Little, Loyd. *The Parthian Shot*. New York: Viking Press, 1973.

Several members of a Green Beret team become missing persons on official records through a bureaucratic snafu. They decide to stay in the Mekong Delta area where they have been based and begin a business venture that involves both the South Vietnamese and the Vietcong.

281 Lockridge, Ernest. *Prince Elmo's Fire*. New York: Stein & Day, 1974.

Prince Elmo Hatcher is a backwoods boy from Indiana. When events disrupt his primitive family life, Prince Elmo's artistic talent provides a way for him to survive. Eventually, he is drafted and sent to Vietnam where he is wounded, captured, and returned to the U.S. The last part of the book is set in Vietnam.

282 Louang, Phou. *The Men of Company 97*. Hanoi: Neo Lao Haksat, 1971.

A propaganda piece about North Vietnamese soldiers effectively fighting against the United States.

283 McCarry, Charles. *The Tears of Autumn*. New York: Saturday Review Press, 1974.

A well-written thriller in which Paul Christopher, an intelligence officer, tries to link the assassination of President Kennedy to the assassination of Ngo Dinh Diem, President of Vietnam. Christopher feels that Kennedy's death was a revenge killing for the Diem assassination which may have been engineered by the Kennedy Administration.

284 McColl, Alex. *Valley of Peril*. New York: Tom Doherty Associates, 1987.

The main character is an advisor to the South Vietnamese in 1967-68. The Tet Offensive is part of the action.

285 McMahon, Thomas P. *Jink*. New York: Simon & Schuster, 1971.

A mystery novel in which a Vietnam veteran pilot, Major McKendrick, returns home to find that his family has been kidnapped.

286 McMath, Phillip H. *Native Ground*. Little Rock, Ark.: August House, 1984.

Christopher Shaw from Arkansas is involved in tank and infantry patrol in Vietnam.

287 McQuay, Mike. *The MIA Ranso*m. New York: Bantam, 1986.

After the fall of Saigon, Vietnam radios the U.S. that it has 2,045 POWs who will be returned to the U.S. for one million U.S. dollars in gold–or else they will be tried and executed. Nancy Henderson sees the picture of her husband, thought to be dead, on TV and bands together with other MIA wives to raise the ransom after the U.S. President states he will not give in to extortion.

288 McQuinn, Donald E. *Targets*. New York: Macmillan, 1980.

Major Charles Taylor, on his second tour in Vietnam, is involved in a undercover operation with the South Vietnamese to rout drug smugglers, black marketeers, and other criminals in the ugly underside of the war.

289 Maggio, Joe. *Company Man*. New York: Putnam, 1972.

An action adventure novel in which the main character is a CIA mercenary whose activities in Vietnam form part of the story. He performs actions designed to precipitate the Gulf of Tonkin Resolution and trains villagers to fight along the Vietnam-Laos border.

290   Magliocco, Peter. *Among a Godly Few*. Northridge, Calif.: Limited Editions, 1982.
     A self-published first novel about a young Hispanic military policeman coming of age in the 1960s with the Vietnam War as a backdrop.

291   Magnuson, Teodore. *A Small Gust of Wind*. New York: Bobbs-Merrill, 1980.
     An action adventure novel set in Saigon at the height of the war. A newsman is involved in a gold and drug smuggling operating with two other American civilians with bloody results.

292   Mahoney, Tim. *Hollaran's World War*. New York: Delacorte, 1985.
     Tom Hollaran is a Vietnam veteran who cannot adjust to civilian life and his two psychiatrists don't seem to be able to help him stop hearing the sound of helicopter blades. His life falls apart and he gets involved in a fellow veteran's crazy plot.

293   ____. *We're Not Here*. New York: Delta Books, 1988.
     Sergeant Bill Lemmen is drawing toward the end of his second tour of duty and is not anxious to leave as he has come to love the country as well as a Vietnamese woman.

294   Mailer, Norman. *Why Are We in Vietnam?* New York: Putnam, 1967.
     A major novel in Vietnam War literature by a major American writer, *Why Ae We in Vietnam?* is a story told by an eighteen year old boy on an Alaskan hunting trip prior to leaving for Vietnam. Vietnam is only mentioned twice in this novel, which has been alternately praised and ridiculed.

295   Maitland, Derek. *The Only War We've Got*. New York: Morrow, 1970.
     The author, a British war correspondent, points out, in a series of vignettes rather than in a well-developed plot, that many people made a lot of money out of the Vietnam War, namely businesses,

generals, ambassadors, journalists, and pimps and bar girls, to name a few. He ridicules major figures and institutions of the time. Settings range across Vietnam and include the events of the Tet Offensive. Satirical and blackly humorous.

296 Malraux, Andre. *The Royal Way*. New York: Harrison Smith & Robert Haas, 1935.

A very early novel that many feel is as prophetic as *The Quiet American*. Jerome Klinkowitz notes that Malraux "saw that the Indochina experience could be a metaphor for man's anguished alienation from an absurd society within a meaningless universe." The story is set in the 1920s and presents a dialogue between Claude, a French archaeologist plundering Siam for its ancient art work, and Perken, a Danish adventurer. The power of the jungle is an important image in the novel.

297 Mano, D. Keith. *War Is Heaven*. Garden City, N.Y.: Doubleday, 1970.

Mano has written a parable of the Vietnam War in his description of the imaginary Camaguay where a war is being fought by fanatics.

298 Martin, Ian Kennedy. *Rekill*. New York: Ballantine, 1978.

An adventure thriller in which a Vietcong officer tracks those involved in a massacre in a small village. Some of the action takes place in Albania.

299 Martin, Ron. *To Be Free!: Escape from a North Vietnam Prison*. New York: Vanguard Press, 1986.

The story of a POW in North Vietnam who endures the torture, humiliation, constant interrogation, deplorable food and sanitary conditions with only one thought – escape. Most of all, he fears that they will break him. He finally does escape on foot through the jungle to the sea in this effective novel.

300 Mason, Bobbie Ann. *In Country*. South Yarmouth, Mass.: Curley, 1985.
An effective and powerful novel, *In Country*, tells the story of Samantha Hughes, a recent high school graduate who wants some answers about the Vietnam War. Her father died in the war. Her mother can't really tell her anything about her father as they were only married a month before his death. Her uncle, with whom she lives, seems to be suffering ill effects from Agent Orange exposure in Vietnam, and she is attracted to another Vietnam vet who is emotionally scarred by the war.

301 Mathis, Edward. *From a High Place*. New York: Scribners, 1985.
Mathis writes a mystery series featuring Dan Roman, a private investigator, ex-cop, and Vietnam veteran from Butler Wells, Texas. Other titles in the series are *Dark Streaks and Empty Places*, *Natural Prey*, and *Another Path, Another Dragon*.

302 Meier, John. *The American Imperialist*. New York: Vantage, 1983.
The story of an Air America civilian pilot flying dangerous missions for the military in Vietnam early in the war.

303 Meiring, Desmond. *The Brinkman*. Boston: Houghton Mifflin , 1965.
A journalist, veteran of French fighting, a female Vietnamese communist, and an American CIA agent become involved with each other in Vietnam and Laos in 1959-60 with tragic results.

304 Melaro, HJM. *The Vietnam Story*. Willingboro, N.J.: Alexia Press, 1968.
A story based on fact with names and places changed, *The Vietnam Story* traces the history of Vietnam and the rise of the Vietcong movement. The story is basically about an American civilian interaction with U. S. soldiers, Asians and Eurasians during the war. Told in short-storylike vignettes.

305 Merkin, Robert. *Zombie Jamboree*. New York: Morrow, 1986.
Richard Heiser and David Becker are friends who find themselves unwillingly in Vietnam. Heiser sees the war as very serious

business, but Becker enjoys the surreal quality of the army and the war itself. Heiser is involved in a fragging incident.

306 Meyer, Nicholas. *Target Practice*. New York: Pinnacle, 1974.
     An effective mystery in which a former POW, accused by a childhood friend of having collaborated with the enemy while a prisoner, is found shot dead. It looks like suicide, but as the story proceeds, it comes to look more like murder.

307 Meyer, Ted. *Body Count*. New York: Expositon Press, 1982.
     Body Count is the story of three soldiers: Master Sergeant Carl Nevins, Korean War hero who is shocked by the atrocities he sees in Vietnam, Gary Butcher, an All- American football player who lost both legs in the war, and Eugene Weiss, a scholar. All three soldiers felt that they had been mistreated by the military, the government and their own countrymen. They band together and decide to go for a really big body count – in a New Jersey veterans' hospital.

308 Miceli, Frank. *The Seventh Month*. New York: Fell, 1969.
     An Italian-American soldier from the Bronx, recently returned from Vietnam and having difficulty adjusting, becomes involved in a series of misadventures.

309 Michaeles, M. M. *Suicide Command*. New York: Prestige Books, 1967.
     An action adventure novel in which the main character is involved in conflicts with an old friend, now his commanding officer, and dangerous missions that result in being captured by the Vietcong.

310 Michaels, Rand. *Women of the Green Berets*. New York: Lancer, 1967.

311 Miller, Kenn. *Tiger, the Lurp Dog*. Boston: Little, Brown, 1983.
     American paratroopers of a Long Range Reconnaissance Patrol (LRRP) in Vietnam feel great pride in their unit. They are a cohesive group whose mascot is a fleabitten dog called Tiger. On a mission, part of the team disappears. Against the better judgment of the platoon sergeant, a mission is planned to find the missing team members. A well-written, exciting story.

312 Millman, Lawrence. *Hero Jessie*. New York: St. Martin's, 1982.
Jessie Boone is slightly retarded and more than a little violent. He becomes obsessed with the Vietnam War as a result of his brother's experiences there and the endless television coverage. As a result he commits several violent acts against other people.

313 Molloy, Tom. *The Green Line*. Charlestown, Mass.: Charles River, 1982.
Returning Vietnam veteran Liam Fergus sinks in despair as he is unable to adjust to several tragedies and his own cynicism upon his return home.

314 Moore, Elizabeth Sims. *Bend with the Wind*. Port Washington, N.Y.: Ashley Books, 1980.
The story of a nurse in Vietnam early in the war.

315 Moore, Gene D. *The Killing at Ngo Tho*. New York: Norton, 1967.
One of the better Vietnam War novels, *The Killing at Ngo Tho* tells the story of Colonel Scott Leonard, an advisor to a South Vietnamese general with whom he has developed a friendship. The Vietcong infiltrate Ngo Tho and the two leaders work to find the traitor.

316 Moore, Robin. *The Country Team*. New York: Crown, 1967.
There is a Communist take over in Mituyan (Vietnam). Mike Forrester, owner of a plantation, becomes involved in all the attendant political intrigue.

317 _____. *Search and Destroy*. New York: Condor, 1978.
A military unit called Wildfire stages a disastrous mission into Cambodia during the Vietnam War. Later, the remaining members of the group team up to stage a robbery in Houston's Astrodome.

318 Moore, Robin, and Henry Rothblatt. *Court-Martial*. Garden City, N.Y.: Doubleday, 1971.
Based on a real incident, *Court-Martial* describes a military trial in which several Green Berets are accused off murdering a

Vietnamese double agent. Co-author Rothblatt was a Green Beret defense lawyer.

319 Moore, Robin, and June Collins. *The Khaki Mafia*. New York: Crown, 1971.

The story of corruption in army support services, such as the PX, in Vietnam during the war, based on a actual events. Australian co-author Collins entertained troops in Vietnam and testified about the corruption before a Senate sub-committee.

320 Morgan, Thomas B. *Snyder's Walk*. Garden City, N.Y.: Doubleday , 1987.

Jack Snyder, a journalist, covers a 1966 protest walk from Chicago to Washington, D.C., that ends in tragedy. The novel's action takes the reader to the battlefields of Vietnam.

321 Morris, Edita. *Love to Vietnam*. New York: Monthly Review Press, 1968.

The story of a correspondence between a Japanese man disfigured by the atom bomb in Nagasaki and a Vietnamese girl disfigured by napalm that ends tragically after the two correspondents meet and fall in love. An antiwar statement.

322 Morris, Jim. *Strawberry Soldier*. New York: Ace Books, 1972.

The author, a former Green Beret, tells the story of another Green Beret who fought with the mountain tribe, the Montagnards, and faces problems in readjusting when a wound sends him home.

323 Morrison, C. T. *The Flame in the Icebox: An Episode of the Vietnam War*. New York: Exposition, 1968.

Written during the height of the war and dedicated to those opposed to the war, this short novel is the story of an American infantry squadron ambushed and decimated by Vietcong. Those who survive are taken prisoner but eventually die when a rescue group fails in their mission. Vietnam is described as the flame in the "global icebox called the cold war." The novel seems propagandistic in its intent.

324 Morrison, James. *Treehouse*. New York: Dial, 1972.
       A story of a family that has adopted two unrelated children. Their own child is in Vietnam where he is eventually killed. The dynamics of the family and the relationship between the two adopted children, now adults, are shown as well as the affect of the war on all of them.

325 Mossman, James. *Lifelines*. Boston: Little, Brown, 1971.
       Dan Fenwick is a British journalist who has to resort to drunken binges to forget the things he saw in Vietnam which are described in some effective scenes.

326 Muller, Marcia. *There's Nothing to Be Afraid Of*. New York: St. Martin's, 1985.
       A mystery novel, one of a series featuring Sharon McCone, *There's Nothing to Be Afraid Of* finds McCone trying to discover who is behind the acts of terrorism directed against a group of Vietnamese refugees in San Francisco.

327 Mullin, Chris. *The Last Man out of Saigon*. London: Victor Gollancz, 1986.
       The fall of Saigon is described by the author, who covered the event as a British journalist. The main character is CIA agent McShane who is sent to Saigon to keep Vietnam in turmoil after the Americans leave.

328 Myers, Walter Dean. *Fallen Angels*. New York: Scholastic Books, 1988.
       A very powerful Vietnam War novel written for teenagers, *Fallen Angels* describes a story all too common. Richie Perry, 17, enlists to fight in Vietnam as a way out of a dead-end life in Harlem. He experiences all of the horrors of war as well as the racial conflict that existed among American troops, and he questions his religious faith and his moral values.

329 Myrer, Anton. *Once an Eagle*. New York: Holt, Rinehart & Winston, 1968.

A long novel that traces the personal history of Sam Damon, a career military man who fights from 1916 Mexico to Vietnam (which the author calls Khotiane).

330   Nagel, William. *The Odd Angry Shot*. Sydney: Angus & Robertson , 1979.
      Nagel portrays the life of Australian soldiers in the Vietnam war. The experiences aren't so different from those of American soldiers – the boredom, the terror of battle, the death of friends, but the perspective is interesting. The main character, Harry, fears that the Communists will take over Vietnam anyway, and that Australia won't welcome them home.

331   Nahum, Lucien. *Shadow 81*. Garden City, N.Y.: Doubleday, 1975.
      Shadow 81 is the story of a hijacked airliner and a clever blackmail scheme. Part of the story takes place in Vietnam toward the end of the war where an Air Force general and a fighter pilot conspire.

332   Naparsteck, M. J. *Hero's Welcome*. New York: Norden Publications, 1981.
      Unlucky Culver Orbanski is a would-be novelist who flunks out of college, is drafted, loses his right hand and right eye in enemy action in Vietnam, and adjusts to his return home through an alcoholic haze before finally becoming the novelist he wanted to be.

333   ____. *War Song*. New York: Leisure Books, 1980.
      War Song chronicles the adventures and adversities of Michael Cull, a young soldier in Vietnam. He lives in relative comfort and safety in Saigon but is slightly wounded in an enemy attack. Aided by a bureaucratic snafu, he deserts and goes to Canada.

334   Nash, Norman Harold. *The Last Mission*. New York: Vantage, 1978.
      The main character in *The Last Mission* bails out of his plane over enemy territory and is captured by North Vietnamese. He isn't held prisoner for long before he escapes.

335   Nazarian, Barry. *Final Reckoning*. New York: Seaview/Putnam, 1983.

Final Reckoning deals with Sam Clement, an ex-World War II black marketeer, and his family. His son is a wounded and disgruntled Vietnam veteran.

336 Nelson, Charles. *The Boy Who Picked the Bullets Up*. New York: Morrow, 1981.
Nelson's novel features a gay naval hospital medic in Vietnam in 1966-67, Kurt Strom, whose story is told through the letters he writes to his family and friends at home. He changes his personality and his adventures to suit the person to whom each letter is written. A different perspective on the war.

337 Newhafer, Richard. *The Golden Jungle*. New York: New American Library, 1968.
Matt Keane is a former "air ace" from Korea and Vietnam. Now he is fighting Communism in Cuba. Keane refers to his Vietnam war experience throughout the novel.

338 ____. *No More Bugles in the Sky*. New York: New American Library, 1966.
A "hawkish" novel of air combat in the Vietnam War, this is an adventure story of a group of ex-pilots from previous wars that, on a directive from the CIA, try to force the North Vietnamese into an action that will allow Washington to escalate the war. Published in 1966 by Signet as *The Violators*.

339 Nichols, John. *American Blood*. New York: Henry Holt, 1987.
The author of *The Milagro Beanfield War* has written a violent novel about a Vietnam veteran who returns home filled with terrible images of the death and destruction that he saw in the war. He cannot let go of the destructive impulses that were acceptable in Vietnam and is involved in a series of violent acts, particularly against women.

340 O'Brien, Tim. *Going After Cacciato*. New York: Delacorte, 1978.
Going After Cacciato, 1979 National Book Award winner for fiction, is probably *the* book of Vietnam War literature. Paul Berlin, shocked by the horror and hopelessness of the Vietnam War, walks

away from his unit into the jungle, hoping to make his way to Paris. He is pursued by a group of soldiers.

341 ____. *Northern Lights*. New York: Delacorte, 1975.

Harvey, a Vietnam veteran, and his brother Paul decide to ski home from a skiing weekend in Northern Minnesota and become lost in a blizzard where they are saved by the brother who was not the war hero. Although this book is not about the Vietnam War, critics, and the author himself, have noted that Vietnam is a "presence" in the novel.

342 Olemy, P. T. *The Transgressors*. New York: Caravelle Books, 1967.

One of the only novels that deals with the troops of entertainers that visited Vietnam during the war.

343 Olshaker, Mark. *Unnatural Causes*. New York: Morrow, 1986.

A medical mystery in which two doctors try to find out why small capsules are being found in the bodies of Vietnam veterans who are dying from what appears to be random and unrelated accidents. They uncover a germ warfare plot.

344 O'Rourke, William. *The Meekness of Isaac*. New York: Crowell, 1974.

Brian Kilpatrick has come from Kansas to school at Columbia only to find that he is drafted. He tries everything he can think of to avoid this, from applying for conscientious objector status to pretending to be a homosexual.

345 Page, Thomas. *The Spirit*. New York: Rawson, 1977.

American Indian John Moon is an ex-Green Beret so disturbed by his experiences in Vietnam that he seeks peace in the comfort of ancient religions and customs. When an image appears to him of Yeti, the mythical Bigfoot, he follows the image across Canada.

346 Parker, Gilbert L. *Falcons Three*. New York: Vantage Press, 1978.

Parker presents three main characters, Sergeants Thompson and Ryker and Warrant Officer Van Thanh and their beliefs, fears, and the war they fight against the Vietcong in a Ranger company in 1969.

The author spent over two years in Vietnam with a long range reconnaissance patrol unit.

347 Parker, T. Jefferson. *Little Saigon*. New York: St. Martin's, 1988.
A well-written mystery novel set in a Vietnamese refugee community in Orange Country, California, called Little Saigon. Chuck Frye searches for his older brother's kidnapped wife, Li, a well-known and loved Vietnamese singer. Parker describes the many underground organizations in existence still fighting the war.

348 Parque, Richard. *Firefight*. New York: Kensington/Zebra, 1986.
Another novel on the rescue theme, *Firefight* tells the story of a Vietnam veteran who left Vietnam seven years earlier but returns just before the fall of Saigon to rescue his wife and friends still being held prisoner.

349 _____. *Flight of the Phantom*. New York: Kensington/Zebra, 1987.
The main character, Vince Battaglia, is a jet fighter pilot who is unsure of the wisdom of American involvement in Vietnam. The author shows Vince's interaction with Vietnamese civilians and his imprisonment and rescue from a POW camp.

350 _____. *Hellbound*. New York: Kensington/Zebra, 1985.
Steve Randall, an American pilot in love with a Vietnamese woman, is shot down and held prisoner in Cambodia where he is rescued by the woman.

351 _____. *Sweet Vietnam*. New York: Kensington/Zebra, 1984.
Vic Benedetti is a pilot in Vietnam whose ambition is to shoot down his counterpart, the famous North Vietnamese pilot Colonel Tan, "Dragonman." A love story with a native woman plays an important role in the novel.

352 Paterson, Katherine. *Park's Quest*. New York: Dutton, 1988.
The author shows the affect of the war on the children of those who served. The main character, Park, comes to his grandfather's farm in Virginia to learn more about his father who died in Vietnam and his

father's family. He meets a Vietnamese-American girl named Thanh who may be his half-sister. Written for young readers.

353 Patterson, James. *Black Market*. New York: Simon & Schuster, 1986.
A thriller in which a group of ex-Vietnam veterans called the Green Band use their combat experience to commit acts of terrorism in New York.

354 Pelfrey, William. *The Big V*. New York: Liveright, 1972.
A first-person account of a young radio operator's tour of duty in Vietnam.

355 ____. *Hamburger Hill*. New York: Avon, 1987.
Based on a screenplay by James Carabatsos, *Hamburger Hill* describes an attack on a fortified enemy position. Many battle scenes.

356 Peters, Stephen. *The Park Is Mine*. Garden City, N.Y.: Doubleday , 1981.
An action-filled novel in which a deranged Vietnam veteran booby-traps Central Park. A group of ex-Vietnam guerrillas try to end his siege.

357 Petrakis, Harry Mark. *In the Land of Morning*. New York: McKay, 1973.
A Vietnam veteran returning home falls in love with a Vietnamese woman, only one of the characters and stories in this family saga.

358 Pfarrer, Donald. *Neverlight*. New York: Seaview, 1982.
Richard Vail, wounded in Vietnam, has a chance to come home, but he rejects this and returns to the battlefield where he is eventually killed. Vail's combat action is seen as well as the life of his wife in New Hampshire as she waits for him, not understanding his motives in remaining in the war.

359 Philburn, Dennis K. *Freedom Bird*. New York: Tor, 1987.

The story of Ryan James's tour of duty is a coming of age novel where the horrors of the war affect James's maturation process.

360 Phillips, Jayne Anne. *Machine Dreams*. New York: Dutton, 1984.
The saga of an American family that begins in the depression and ends with the Vietnam war and its affect on the family.

361 Pollard, Rhys. *The Cream Machine*. Sydney: Angus & Robinson, 1972.
A tale of Australian infantrymen in Vietnam filled with the conventional elements of Vietnam War novels. The soldiers views on the war, their alternating commitment to personal survival and then to the group, those at home that are protesting, but not fighting, the career officers, the jungle, the deaths in combat – all are part of the story. The title refers to the fact the soldiers think of themselves as the "cream" of the Australian forces.

362 Pollock, J. C. *Centrifuge*. New York: Crown, 1984.
Ex-Green Beret Mike Slater finds that members of his old unit from Vietnam are being murdered. Staying one step ahead of the killers, he discovers that something he saw in Vietnam gives him dangerous knowledge – knowledge that is a threat to someone. Exciting thriller.

363 ____. *Mission MIA*. New York: Crown, 1982.
Betty Detimore, MIA wife, pleads with Jack Callahan, former Green Beret, to save her husband and other men she has proof are still alive in Vietnam. Callahan organizes five ex-members of his old unit, and they plan a rescue mission.

364 Pollock, Lawrence. *Xin Loi (Sorry about That) Doc!*. New York: Vantage, 1971.
The author was a Marine medic in the 55th Evacuation Hospital. He provides a fictional, anecdotal account of a year in an army hospital in Vietnam that is based on his own experiences. The conditions under which they worked, what they saw, the bureaucracy, the battles are all depicted in detail, particularly the medical sequences.

365 Porter, John B. *If I Made My Bed in Hell.* Waco, Tex.: World Books, 1969.
     Captain Brakowski commands a unit in Vietnam whose members become more and more disillusioned with the war. Chaplain Grayson, the main character, comes to know these men and wants to help them, but the war is making him have doubts too – about his faith. The title comes from the Bible, "If I make my bed in hell, behold thou art there."

366 Powell, Hollis C. *The River Rat.* Smithtown, N.Y.: Exposition Press, 1982.
     Herb Poole is a commander of a landing craft (LCU) delivering supplies on the rivers, a "river rat," in Vietnam at the height of the war.

367 Powers, Charles. *A Matter of Honor.* New York: First East Coast Theater, 1982.
     The story of a young infantryman's year in Vietnam at the beginning of the build up. He survives the tour and returns home.

368 Pratt, John Clark. *The Laotian Fragments.* New York: Viking Press, 1974.
     Pratt, author of *Vietnam Voices* tells the story of Major William Blake, a pilot working with the Laotians on a secret operation who has disappeared and is listed as a MIA. The "fragments" of the title are his letters, notes, reports, jottings of his observations, etc., that are collected by an old professor and through which the story is told.

369 Proffitt, Nicholas. *The Embassy House.* New York: Bantam, 1986.
     In this interesting and powerful novel, Operation Phoenix, which finds and eliminates Vietcong from local villages, is described. Led by Captain Jack Gulliver, the Operation gains unwanted public exposure when an innocent man is killed and a cover-up of its activities is ordered. Those closest to Gulliver are exposed, and he must confront the conflict between his military assignment and his own values.

370 ____. *Gardens of Stone.* New York: Carroll & Graf, 1983.

An excellent novel of the friendship of two men who are assigned to the Honor Guard at Arlington National Cemetery in 1966. Also involved in their story is a young soldier who will be sent to Vietnam and killed. A story of friendship, love, duty, and the waste of war.

371 Proud, Franklin M., and Alfred F. Eberhardt. *Tiger in the Mountains.* New York: St. Martin's, 1976.

The main character attempts to free American pilots held in a North Vietnam prison by hijacking an Air France plane, diverting it to Hanoi, and offering the North Vietnamese a trade.

372 Pruitt, James N. *Striker One Down.* New York: Tom Doherty Associates, 1987.

A story of the mythic Salt and Pepper, a traitorous bi-racial duo, and their adventures in North Vietnam. Action adventure.

373 Raines, Jeff. *The Big Island.* New York: Beech Tree Books, 1987.

Jim Yamasaki, a Vietnam veteran, is a Hawaiian police chief who is involved in a war between Japanese gangsters, opium dealers, and a group of Mormons out to avenge the deaths of four missionaries. The book relies heavily on flashbacks to the Vietnam War as a key in understanding the main character.

374 Randle, Kevin, and Robert Cornett. *Remember the Alamo!* New York: Charter Books, 1980.

Through a top-secret process, a group of thirty-three Vietnam veterans are transported back to 1836 – with 1970s military equipment – to refight the battle of the Alamo. If the U.S. wins this time, a rich oil field will belong to the United States instead of to Mexico.

375 Reed, J. D. *Free Fall.* New York: Delacorte, 1980.

A former Green Beret hijacks an airplane and is tracked by his former commanding officer from the war.

376 Reeves, James R. *Mekong!* New York: Ballantine, 1984.

A novel based on the experiences of the author's friend, James C. Taylor, a Navy SEAL (Navy Special Forces), in Vietnam. Scenes of battles around the Mekong Delta and depictions of the flashbacks veterans experience are effectively done.

377　Reisner, Jack. *The Last Hope*. Honolulu: Cellar Mead, 1982.
　　　　A novel about the Joint Personnel Recovery Center in Saigon, whose job it was to free captured Americans, based on the authors' own experiences.

378　Rich, Curt. *The Advisors*. New York: Kensington/Zebra, 1985.
　　　　The story of Jerry Harris, an advisor to a South Vietnamese army unit which was significantly less than prepared to fight. The problems of dealing with his unit, especially the language problems, are told in diary and letter form. Harris's experiences in the field and his fears in and of battle are depicted.

379　Richards, Tony. *The Harvest Bride*. London: Headline, 1987.
　　　　Tom Auden, a journalist adversely affected by his experiences in Vietnam, must face these experiences when three former colleagues die mysteriously in London and he finds himself tracking down the killers.

380　Riggan, Rob. *Free Fire Zone*. New York: Norton, 1984.
　　　　The author was a medic in Vietnam as is his main character, Jon O'Neill, who remembers and relates his tour of duty in flashback. Internal conflicts between the men and the affect of the war on their spirit is described in this effective novel.

381　Rinaldi, Nicholas. *Bridge Fall Down*. New York: St. Martin's, 1985.
　　　　The story of a strange assortment of misfits trekking through a jungle to blow up a bridge, led by a crazy general. The country and the war are never mentioned but the parallels are striking enough to be Vietnam.

382　Rivers, Caryl. *Intimate Enemies*. New York: Dutton, 1987.

A romance in which Jessie McGrath, Kinsolving College provost and former antiwar protester, falls in love with Major Mark Claymore, head of the College's ROTC program and former Vietnam veteran who lost a leg in the war. Their previous activities relating to the war interfere with their relationship. Descriptions of the Major's war flashbacks are effective.

383   Rivers, Gayle, and James Hudson. *The Five Fingers*. Garden City, N.Y.: Doubleday, 1978.

A suspense thriller in which a special group named "The Five Fingers" is sent into China to assassinate Chinese and North Vietnamese leaders, including General Giap. Supposedly based on fact.

384   Roberts, Suzanne. *Vietnam Nurse*. New York: Ace, 1966.

385   Robertson, Dorothy. *Fairy Tales from Vietnam*. New York: Dodd, Mead, 1968.

Nine stories told in letters from Nguyen Dinh Thuan, a Vietnamese War refugee living Saigon, to his foster mother in the United States. The boy came from Haiphong with his mother, two brothers, and grandmother when the country was divided. The stories he tells describe the centuries long struggle of the Vietnamese for independence viewed through its folklore. Written for grades 4-6

386   Rohan, Donald. *The Browning Touch*. New York: Dial, 1979.

America's hasty retreat from Vietnam in 1975 left billions of dollars worth of military equipment behind. William Browning is given millions of dollars to give to the North Vietnamese to prevent them from selling the weaponry to America's other adversaries – China or Russia.

387   Rollins, Kelly. *Fighter Pilots*. Boston: Little, Brown, 1981.

The author was a fighter pilot in Vietnam and so is his main character, whose experiences from World War II to Vietnam are described.

388   Rooney, Frank. *Shadow of God*. New York: Harcourt, Brace & World, 1967.

The story of a U.S. Army company in retreat in an unnamed country in Asia while fighting in an undeclared war. The company is escorting five Catholic nuns who had been prisoners of war and forced into prostitution. All are pregnant in this sensational and incredibly unbelievable novel.

389 Rosen, Gerald. *Blues for a Dying Nation*. New York: Dial, 1972.
     This satirical novel, which exposes the American military establishment in all of its corruption and inefficiency, is meant to parallel events in Vietnam.

390 Ross, William. *Bamboo Terror*. Rutland, Vt.: Tuttle, 1969.
     An espionage tale set in North Vietnam very early in American involvement in which an ex-intelligence officer, Michael Hazzard, a detective from Tokyo, accepts a job from a Chinese named Chang to find a spy within his secret army.

391 Roth, Robert. *Sand in the Wind*. Boston: Little, Brown, 1973.
     One of the major Vietnam novels, *Sand in the Wind*, is characterized by well-developed characters and effective battle scenes and is the story of two soldiers, an officer and an enlisted man, in Vietnam around the time of Tet. The brutality of basic training is shown and seems almost more terrible than the graphic battle scenes depicted later, which also emphasize the atrocities committed by both American and South Vietnamese soldiers. A powerful novel.

392 Rothberg, Abraham. *The Other Man's Shoes*. New York: Simon & Schuster, 1968.
     Journalist Elliott Sanders is haunted by his Vietnam experiences including the memory of a soldier who died for him in Saigon and the stress of trying to live up to a famous father, also a journalist. His return to the States finds him involved in the antiwar demonstrations.

393 Rowe, John. *Count Your Dead*. Sydney: Angus & Robertson, 1968.
     Rowe, an Australian, was a professional soldier in Borneo, Malaya, and Vietnam. Although *Count Your Dead* was one of the first Australian novels to deal with the war, the main character Bill Morgan,

is an American. Morgan is in constant conflict with his commanding officer, who endangers his men and fakes body counts.

394   Roy, Gabrielle. *Windflower*. Toronto: McClelland & Stewart, 1970.
        Elsa, an Eskimo girl, has a brief encounter with an American GI stationed at a base near her home which results in the birth of a child, Jimmy. She raises the child alone, but eventually the blond boy longs for a life in the United States, and he runs away. After hearing on the radio that GI's have been sent to Vietnam, Elsa becomes convinced that her son is one of them, and she lives for reports about the war. A simple and rather sad story.

395   Rubin, Jonathan. *The Barking Deer*. New York: George Braziller, 1974.
        Based on a Vietnamese fable in which a tiger and an eagle fight to protect the very fragile barking deer, who is destroyed as a result, *The Barking Deer* depicts the relationship between Special Forces and Montagnard tribesman in Vietnam early in American involvement. Americans' inability to understand the Vietnamese is a major theme in this important novel in Vietnam War literature.

396   Runyon, Charles. *Bloody Jugle*. New York: Ace, 1966.

397   Rylant, Cynthia. *A Blue-Eyed Daisy*. New York: Bradbury, 1985.
        In one chapter of this novel for young readers, the main character, eleven year old Ellie Farley's Uncle Joe goes off to war. It is to be presumed it is the Vietnam War although it is not directly named. She is confused about wars and men killing one another and even more confused by her Uncle's silence upon his return. Joe doesn't talk of the war or of his experiences there.

398   Sadler, Barry. *The Moi*. Nashville: Aurora Publishers, 1977.
        Adventurer Mike Reider, Special Forces trooper imprisoned by the Vietcong, battles with Major Lim, American-trained Cong commander, in a duel of wills for survival. Both men learn about themselves in the conflict as they try to discover who is really the *moi* – a word meaning animal. Later republished as *Cry Havoc*.

399   _____. *Phu Nham*. New York: Tor, 1984.

Phu Nham is the story of top American sniper, Jim Rossen. His activities and an eventual duel with his Vietnamese counterpart form the basis of this novel.

400 Sanders, Pamela. *Miranda*. Boston: Little, Brown, 1978.
Miranda was a correspondent in Vietnam during the war and the description of her experiences there, told in flashback, are part of this novel.

401 Sanford, Barent. *The Chinese Spur*. New York: New American Library, 1983.
An adventure story of Tobias Godwin Porter, a wealthy American with a genius IQ and a black belt in karate, and his attempts to rescue his friend Matt Eberhart, a former U.S. ace fighter pilot, who is missing in the jungles of Southeast Asia.

402 Scarborough, Elizabeth. *The Healer's War*. New York: Doubleday, 1988.
Lt. Kitty McCully is a nurse in Vietnam who befriends two Vietnamese patients and becomes involved in a dangerous mission.

403 Scott, Leonard B. *Charlie Mike*. New York: Ballantine, 1985.
The author was an Army Ranger in Vietnam. *Charlie Mike* is the story of a specially-trained reconnaissance team whose motto is "Charlie Mike," which means continue the mission. The reader follows the group through several combat missions.

404 _____. *The Last Run*. New York: Ballantine, 1987.
Scott follows another group of Rangers as they infiltrate a valley held by the Vietcong in a gruesome battle.

405 Sellers, Con. New York: *Where Have All the Soldiers Gone?* Pyramid Books, 1969.
In this interesting story, the main character, Lee Boyd, is a conscientious objector who volunteers to be a medic rather than go to jail. He becomes involved with a Vietnamese prostitute and a professional killer and ends up fighting.

406 Seran, Val. *Vietnam Mission to Hell*. New York: Bee-line, 1966.

407 Shaplen, Robert. *A Forest of Tigers*. London: Andre Deutsch, 1958.
This very early novel is interesting in its depiction of the various factions jockeying for position in Vietnam: the French, the Americans, Emperor Bao Dai, and the Vietminh. The novel is set in Saigon between 1945-1955.

408 Sidney, George. *For the Love of Dying*. New York: Morrow, 1969.
An action adventure novel centering on the activities of a Marine unit in Vietnam.

409 Silliphant, Stirling. *Silver Star*. New York: Ballantine, 1986.
John Locke left Saigon in 1975, after the fall. He feels drawn back by his experiences there and more importantly, to find his son, born after the fall to his Vietnamese girlfriend. He returns with his ship *Steel Tiger* to Communist Vietnam.

410 Silver, Joan, and Linda Gottlieb. *Limbo*. New York: Viking Press, 1972.
Limbo focuses on the lives of the wives and families who wait for news of their men who are POWs in Vietnam. The author presents the very real problems of these families including raising children without a father, the loneliness, and the attempt to keep the memory of the prisoner alive in the family.

411 Simon, Pierre-Henri. *An End to Glory*. New York: Harper & Row, 1961.
An End to Glory is the story of Jean de Larson and his disillusionment with war and military service. Coming from a French military family, de Larson serves in Indochina and Algeria. He eventually leaves the army in disgust over what he sees. An interesting view of the French experience in Vietnam prior to U.S. involvement that mirrors the American experience.

412 Simpson, Howard R. *To a Silent Valley*. New York: Knopf, 1961.
General Betrand Cogolin of the French paratroopers in Vietnam before American involvement battles the Vietminh in the Lao Bang Valley. An authentic account of the siege.

413 Sinor, Paul. *Operation Bright Eyes*. Canton, Ohio: Daring Books, 1987.

Phong Quong is a Vietnamese artist and a refugee, one of the boat people, who has a photograph showing an American soldier, Captain Eddie Wilson, still being held in An Bac prison in Vietnam. His evidence sets a dangerous rescue mission in motion that involves Phong in its operations and makes his return to Vietnam necessary. His memories of life in Saigon after the fall display just how dangerous his part in the rescue is for him.

414 Sisco, Sam, and Bert Sisco. *The Littlest Enemy*. San Diego: Greenleaf, 1970.

A Special Forces captain attempts to aid in the evacuation of a Montagnard village prior to the village's destruction. The children, who are as effective as soldiers, thwart him at every turn with terrorist activities. An interesting view of children in the war.

415 Sloan, James Park. *War Games*. Boston: Houghton Mifflin, 1971.

In this effective and well-written novel, the narrator is a young soldier who wants to write the great novel of the Vietnam War – to be the Hemingway or Remarque of his generation. He gets transferred to Vietnam, but what he finds is a world full of corruption and petty bureaucracy as well as death and dying he sees on the combat mission he accompanies. An indictment of not only the Vietnam War, but of all wars.

416 Smalley, Peter. *A Warm Gun*. London: Andre Deutsch, 1972.

A satire intended to represent the Vietnam War, *A Warm Gun* is a black comedy of a war in which everyone from the president down is crazy.

417 Smith, Steven Phillip. *American Boys*. New York: Putnam, 1975.

Four soldiers assigned to Germany volunteer for the Vietnam War. The reader follows the tour of each of the volunteers through boredom, fear, and death to their return home, where they now find everything to be as meaningless as Vietnam. Effective.

418 Sparrow, Gerald. *Java Weed*. London: Triton Books, 1968.

The main character is a British journalist captured with two other reporters by the Vietcong. They escape and find protection by hiding in the java weeds in the Mekong River. Through a series of adventures, they reach safety and successfully file their stories.

419 Spetz, Steven. *Rat Pack Six*. Greenwich, Conn.: Fawcett, 1969.

The story of a major battle in which the narrator allows the reader to see the men and the strategies being planned by both sides before the confrontation.

420 Stead, C. K. *Smith's Dream*. Auckland, New Zealand: Longman Paul, 1971.

Christian Karlson Stead is an English professor and literary critic in New Zealand. The dream of the title is really a nightmare in which New Zealand is led by a dictator named Volkner who is supported by the United States. American "advisors" come in, carry out "search and destroy" missions and blow up towns to "save" them.

421 Stoll, Jack. *A Father Is Dying*. New York: New Earth, 1978.

A young soldier fighting in Vietnam is furloughed home to be with his father who is dying. He begins to reevaluate his life and his values and to question what it was that made him, and others like him, become a soldier.

422 Stone, Robert. *Dog Soldiers*. Boston: Houghton Mifflin, 1974.

Winner of a National Book Award, *Dog Soldiers* is one of the major novels of Vietnam War literature. The hero is John Converse, a newspaperman who collapsed in terror during a bombing in Cambodia. He subsequently acquires heroin, becomes involved in drug smuggling, and he and his wife become addicted as well. The heroin is symbolically used as an image of corruption and of the war itself. *Dog Soldiers* has been criticized as being a conventional chase thriller as well as being called the "best novelistic treatment of the American Involvement in Vietnam." Particularly effective is the novel's treatment of the effect of war on noncombatants both in Vietnam and at home.

423 Stone, Scott C. S. *The Coasts of War*. New York: Pyramid, 1966.

An early novel of the war that takes place in Kien Hoa province in the Mekong Delta area and concerns the actions of Navy men advising a Vietnamese force of 500 Chinese-style junks that patrol the coasts, stopping and searching thousands of fishing boats in search of Vietcong insurgents. Two Navy men are main characters as well as the commander of the Vietnamese junk force. Their mission is to prevent coastal reinforcement by the local Vietcong and protect the villagers.

424 ____. *Song of the Wolf*. New York: Arbor House, 1985.
The hero, John Dane, is half-Indian, named Snow-Wolf by his grandfather. He serves in the Korean War and later becomes a mercenary in Vietnam. His adventures are recounted, one of which involves saving American medics from the Vietcong.

425 ____. *Spies*. New York: St. Martin's, 1980.
A tale of international espionage in which Americans compete with the Russians for a precious object in the jungles of Laos and along the Mekong River during the war. A parody of spy fiction.

426 Stone, Tom. *Armstrong*. New York: Warner Paperback Library, 1973.
Set in a country that resembles Vietnam, *Armstrong* tells the story of Walker Armstrong, a young soldier involved in secret activities that result in the death of a double agent and eventually of his commanding officer. He becomes unhinged by events.

427 Straub, Peter. *Koko*. New York: Dutton, 1988.
A thriller from one of the masters of supernatural suspense, *Koko* is about four Vietnam veterans who meet at the Wall in Washington. During their reunion, they begin to discuss the possibility that one member of their old unit, a man missing for fifteen years, is responsible for a series of grisly killings across the country. They decide to find out.

428 Surat, Michelle Maria. *Angel Child, Dragon Child*. Milwaukee: Raintree, 1983.

A children's picture book that tells the story of a Vietnamese refugee child adjusting to an American school. Pictures by Vo-Dinh Mai. Grades K-3.

429 Tate, Donald. *Bravo Burning*. New York: Scribners, 1986.

The author, a war correspondent, follows Bravo Company, a company comprised of all types from a former drugged hippie to a superpatriot, led by crazy Lieutenant Colonel Frederick Gutmann who commands from a helicopter.

430 Tauber, Peter. *The Last Best Hope*. New York: Harcourt Brace Jovanovich, 1977.

A novel of the 1960s in which one of the characters is a soldier in Vietnam. Several battles in which he is involved are described.

431 Taylor, Laura. *Honorbound: A Novel of Love and Courage of America and Vietnam*. New York: Franklin Watts, 1988.

The author is the wife of a former Marine F-4 Phantom aviator and Top Gun. She tells the story of Eden and Matthew Benedict who marry before the Vietnam war. Matthew goes to Vietnam as a career Marine pilot where he is captured and held prisoner. Taylor describes the suffering of Matthew in the prison camp and of Eden waiting for word at home.

432 Taylor, Thomas. *A-18*. New York: Crown, 1967.

A-18 is a Special Forces team charged with capturing two Chinese generals who have deposed Ho Chi Minh and taken over North Vietnam in this action adventure war novel. The author is the son of General Maxwell Taylor.

433 _____. *A Piece of This Country*. New York: Norton, 1970.

Roscoe Jackson, black army advisor, is a respected leader in Vietnam late in 1965, but racial prejudice back home does not allow him to succeed in the way he has in the army. His responsibilities and experiences in Vietnam, juxtaposed with the life of his family back home as seen through his letters, and his conflict over whether or not to stay in the army, comprise the plot.

434 Thacker, Jada. *Finally, the Pawn*. New York: Avon, 1986.

The story of two soldiers in Vietnam, one of whom is killed during the course of the story while the other deserts after returning home, becoming involved with antiwar protestors.

435 Theroux, Joseph. *Black Coconuts, Brown Magic*. Garden City, N.Y.: Doubleday, 1983.

A young doctor who served as a medic in Vietnam escapes to American Samoa where he comes to terms with himself, his past, and his memories.

436 Thorpe, Stephen J. *Walking Wounded*. Garden City, N.Y.: Doubleday, 1980.

The story of Sherwood, a Vietnam veteran with a series of problems as a result of the war, who cares for his orphaned nephew and a army friend, a double amputee. The main character becomes involved with several other wounded people.

437 Tiede, Tom. *Coward*. New York: Trident, 1968.

The author was a war correspondent in Vietnam. He tells the story of Nathan Long, a conscientious objector in the army who goes on a hunger strike to protest the war. As a result he is sent to Vietnam. When a close friend is killed by a sniper, Long volunteers to go on the next mission in pursuit of the sniper with tragic results. The horrors of torture by the Vietcong are described in detail.

438 Toni, A. M. *The Buffalo Doctor*. Philadelphia: Dorrance, 1969.

The main character is a physician who works in Vietnam for a decade before the build-up of American involvement. His adventures include capture by the Vietcong.

439 Topol, B. H. *A Fistful of Ego*. Great Neck, N.Y.: Todd & Honeywell, 1985.

A futuristic novel in which an American president faces the threat of nuclear war at the end of the century. His experiences in Vietnam are described and play a role in his performance as president.

440 Tran Khan Tuyet. *The Little Weaver of Thai-Yen Village*. San Francisco: Children's Book Press, 1977.

Written in English and Vietnamese, this book is the story of Hien, a Vietnamese girl who is brought to the U.S. for medical treatment after the loss of her family. She relates her wartime experiences which are intended to aid in American children in understanding the experiences of refugee children. Translated by N. H. Jenkins with illustrations by Nancy Hom, this book, which was revised in 1986, was written for children in grades 3-6.

441 Tran Van Dinh. *No Passenger on the River*. New York: Vantage, 1965.

American trained South Vietnamese Colonel Minh returns to his homeland where he is disillusioned by the corruption he sees in the military. He becomes involved in a coup attempt in which he is killed.

442 _____. *Blue Dragon, White Tiger: A Tet Story*. Philadelphia: TriAm Press, 1983.

Tran Van Minh, a diplomat, resigns his position in Diem's government in protest over Diem's anti-Buddhist policies and remains in the United States working in the antiwar movement. He returns to Vietnam in 1967 to visit his dying father and becomes caught up in the war, joining the Communists at the time of the Tet Offensive. The blue dragon and white tiger of the title are the two powers the Vietnamese believe compete to rule mankind.

443 Trowbridge, James. *Easy Victories*. Boston: Houghton Mifflin, 1973.

Knox is a career intelligence officer in Saigon. He is lacking in any of the qualities that would make him a hero, and his work makes him a cynic who eventually becomes involved in illegal activities and the corruption rampant in Saigon during the war. The author served in Vietnam.

444 Tully, Andrew. *The Time of the Hawk*. New York: Morrow, 1967.

U.S. Senator Baldwin and his Vietnamese mistress are charged with preventing the withdrawal of American troops from Vietnam after a cease-fire. The author was a reporter in Vietnam and gives an interesting description of Vietnam.

445 Van Greenaway, Peter. *Take the War to Washington*. New York: St. Martin's, 1975.

A heavy-handed black comedy in which 500 Vietnam veterans hijack an aircraft carrier. The depiction of the President and the Congress is particularly acid.

446 Van Heller, Marcus. *Jungle Fever*. New York: Ophelia Press, 1971.

A British reporter and a Canadian journalist travel into Cambodia to interview prisoners held by the rebels.

447 Vaughn, Robert. *The Quick and the Dead*. New York: Dell, 1984.

The main character is a major general who serves in Vietnam and whose son is killed in the war.

448 ____. *The Valkyrie Mandate*. New York: Simon & Schuster, 1974.

An action adventure novel set in Vietnam under the rule of Diem. Madame Nhu is a character. The author is a Vietnam veteran.

449 Vaughn, Robert, and Monroe Lynch. *Brandywine's War*. New York: Bartholomew House, 1971.

The authors were chief warrant officers who served in Germany, Korea, and Vietnam. Written during their second tour in Vietnam, the novel is a comic view of both soldiers and civilians often described as Vietnam's *M*A*S*H* or *Catch 22*. The main character is Chief Warrant Officer W. W. Brandywine, a maintenance and aircraft recovery officer and flier of helicopters. His funny adventures and the characters he meets provide the plot.

450 Wager, Walter. *Swap*. New York: Macmillan, 1972.

Captain D. O. Garrison, a decorated and wounded Vietnam veteran, was saved in Vietnam by the skill of his surgeon Major Brodsky. He feels a debt to this man and subsequently undertakes a mission on the request of Brodsky's dying tycoon father to rescue a young Jewish relative, an orphan girl, who has been refused permission to emigrate from Russia. Vietnam scenes occur only at the beginning of the novel.

451 Walsh, Patricia L. *Forever Sad the Hearts*. New York: Avon, 1982.

Heroine Kate Shea is a nurse in a civilian hospital in Da Nang. She loses a man she loves in the war and faces the daily cases of napalm burns, dismemberment, children's agony and death, and the difficulty of working with limited supplies, which are often diverted by black market operations. No longer able to cope, she returns home. The author was a nurse in Vietnam.

452 Wandke, Richard D. *Vietnam Remembered*. New York: Vantage, 1985.

The author of *Vietnam Remembered* was a lieutenant colonel with the U.S. Army who served three tours in Vietnam. He describes the experiences of Dick West, a married man with children who goes to Vietnam, experiences the horrors of combat, falls in love with a Vietnamese woman, and returns home to readjust to normal life. The main character is a composite of people the author knew in Vietnam and is based on personal experience.

453 Wartski, Maureen Crane. *A Boat to Nowhere*. Philadelphia: Westminster, 1980.

Villagers protest Thay Van Chi's protection of a wandering orphan, and they seem to be right when he appears to side with the Vietcong when they arrive. However, the boy is acting so that he will have an opportunity to save them. The villagers become boat people, facing the terrible hardships and dangers these refugees endured. Illustrated by Dick Teicher. For elementary through junior high school students.

454 Webb, James H. *A Country Such as This*. Garden City, N.Y.: Doubleday, 1983.

Three 1951 graduates of West Point vow to stick together. The novel follows them, their careers, and their families from Korea to Vietnam, where the last part of the book is set. One of the characters becomes a POW. The events of the 1960s play an important role on the novel.

455 ____. *Fields of Fire*. Englewood Cliffs, N.J.: Prentice-Hall, 1978.

A Marine unit fights the Vietcong, unbelievable living conditions, the dangers of the jungle, and faces death and injury in this major novel of the Vietnam War. The reasons each man became a soldier is explained as the reader follows them through combat.

456 Weinberg, Larry. *War Zone*. New York: Bantam, 1985.
     Woody Glover and Del Griggs are boyhood, family enemies in Tennessee. When Woody's brother is murdered, evidence points to Del who enlists for Vietnam. With thoughts of avenging his brother, Woody follows him.

457 Werder, Albert. *A Spartan Education*. New York: Beekman, 1978.
     Wynn Jamison is a medic in Vietnam. He is sent home after being wounded in Cambodia, feeling that he was saved at the brink of death.

458 Wessler, David. *Half a World Away*. New York: Vantage, 1980.
     The author states that this book should be read as historical fiction although it is a thinly disguised personal narrative. "The primary purpose I had in writing this book was to give the American people my side, a soldier's side, to the Viet Nam War." He concludes, "In the years since the war, I only have two unfaltering thoughts about it: one, we were correct to have been in Viet Nam, and two, we did not fight the war correctly." The narrator of the story tells of his tour from arrival to Jungle Devil School at Phuoc Vinh as well as his combat experiences during the Tet Offensive in which he is wounded. Glossary.

459 West, Morris. *The Ambassador*. New York: Morrow, 1965.
     Maxwell Amberley is appointed ambassador to Vietnam during the crucial period. He becomes involved in an operation that results in the death of not only the Vietnamese President but also a man who he viewed as a son.

460 West, Paul. *The Place in Flowers Where Pollen Rests*. Garden City, N.Y.: Doubleday, 1988.
     The title of this novel is also the name of the main character, a Hopi Indian, and his son Oswald, an ex-Vietnam sharpshooter. Oswald's motivation for volunteering for Vietnam is explored as is his combat experiences. West uses the Vietnam War as a symbol of terror and chaos.

461 Weston, John. *Hail Hero*. New York: McKay, 1968.
An interesting viewpoint is presented in this story in which Karl Dixon leaves Yale University, enlists to fight in Vietnam, and then tries to explain to his parents why he enlisted.

462 White, Kent, Jr. *Prairie Fire*. Canton, Ohio: Daring Books, 1983.
The main characters are Sergeants Harper and McShane who lead teams of Asian mercenaries into Laos, code named Prairie Fire. Much of the action is set during the Tet Offensive.

463 White, Teri. *Tight Rope*. New York: Mysterious Press, 1986.
A mystery novel in which two Los Angeles detectives trace a series of murders to a former Green Beret who is planning to steal diamonds from local Vietnamese and the Mafia.

464 Whiteley, L. S. *Deadly Green*. New York: New American Library, 1987.
Five men, an explosive mixture of types, desert after a bloody battle in Vietnam. After wandering through dense jungle, they find a small village where they are welcomed. Their eventual discovery jeopardizes the lives of the villagers.

465 Williams, Alan. *The Tale of the Lazy Dog*. London: Anthony Bland, 1970.
A group plans to steal over a billion dollars in American currency from an airfield in South Vietnam.

466 Williams, Bill. *The Wasters*. New York: Macfadden-Bartell, 1971.
Neal Gilbert is an unstable soldier who becomes involved in the massacre of civilians in a small Vietnamese village. Part of the story is a court-martial trial much like that of the Calley case.

467 Williams, John A. *Captain Blackman*. Garden City, N.Y.: Doubleday, 1972.
The title character is a black soldier who is badly wounded while performing an act of heroism in Vietnam. Through his thoughts, the reader is taken on a tour of the experiences of the black soldier in

America's wars and the racial discrimination often faced, particularly in Vietnam.

468 Williams, Michael. *Door Gunner*. New York: Tor, 1987.
     Carl "Willy" Willstrom is a nineteen year old door gunner on a Huey. He is haunted by the deaths of fellow Americans he has seen and determines to seek revenge for their deaths on the Vietcong. Door gunners had one of the most dangerous jobs in Vietnam. This one dies at the end of the novel.

469 Williams, T. Jeff. *The Glory Hole*. London: Corgi, 1977.
     Jacob Sturm is an army medic. The gruesome sights take their toll, and he becomes a heroin addict and then a killer.

470 Willson, David. *REMF Diary*. Seattle: Black Heron Press, 1988.
     The main character never sees the enemy in Vietnam. He is a army office clerk in Saigon. What he does see is the bureaucracy, corruption, and endless paper-pushing of the war that is as much a part of it as the fighting.

471 Wilson, William. *The LBJ Brigade*. Los Angeles: Apocalypse, 1965.
     The narrator is an infantryman in Vietnam whose stream-of-consciousness narration describes the men who fight with him and alternately tell him that the war is unwinnable and not to think. Many of his friends are killed, and he is captured and later killed by American bombs.

472 Windisch, Charles. *Footsteps of a Hero*. New York: Dorrance, 1984.
     The story of a nineteen-year-old Marine fighting at the height of the war, but understanding neither the war nor his own motivations. The racial tension between black and white soldiers is presented.

473 Winn, David. *Gangland*. New York: Knopf, 1982.
     Dunkle is a Vietnam veteran who has great difficulty in readjusting after his return home. He enters into the counterculture of the late 1960s in his home state of California. The lifestyles and values

of this time are satirized. This novel was the author's master's thesis from the University of Colorado, Boulder.

474 Wise, Leonard. *Doc's Legacy*. New York: Richardson & Steirman, 1986.

"Doc" Ella returns to his farm in Iowa after spending ten years as a POW in Vietnam. He struggles to come to terms with his memories, especially the revenge he took on those who held him captive. He also must fight developers to save his land. Doc is a world-class poker player and images of the game abound.

475 Wizard, Brian. *Permission to Kill: Viet Nam '69-'69*. Port Douglas, Australia: Starquill, 1981.

Subtitled "A Warm and Open Look into a Cold and Closed-Off Situation," this is the story of helicopter warfare written by an author who was a doorgunner in Vietnam. He describes the relationships between the men and the actions undertaken.

476 Wolfe, Michael. *The Chinese Fire Drill*. New York: Harper & Row, 1976.

Mike Keefe is an army intelligence officer who is charged with ransoming two MIAs, one of whom is a Senator's son, after the war is over. The ransom to be paid is a million rounds of rifle ammunition. A glossary of GI English is included.

477 _____. *Man on a String*. New York: Harper & Row, 1973.

A suspense adventure story in which the author's character Mike Keefe reappears. He is a now a roving reporter-cameraman in Vietnam at the end of the war and becomes involved in finding a missing army payroll.

478 _____. *The Two-Star Pigeon*. New York: Harper & Row, 1975.

Wolfe's hero Michale Keefe tries to uncover and stop a conspiracy by an American general to overthrow the Vietnamese government and restore the monarchy.

479 Wolff, Tobias. *The Barracks Thief*. New York: Echo, 1984.

The main characters are three young men undergoing paratrooper training at Fort Benning before being sent to Vietnam. The emphasis of the novel is more on the motivations and relationship of the three men than it is on the training experience.

480 _____. *Ugly Rumors*. London: Allen & Unwin, 1975.
The author follows two friends from basic training to a relatively safe village in Vietnam, and traces the development of the characters and their ideals to the point that they no longer have anything in common to sustain a friendship when they return home.

481 Wolitzer, Meg. *Caribou*. New York: Bantam, 1986.
Becca Silverman, a twelve year old, is disturbed by the Vietnam War, in fact, by the idea of war in general. Her brother escapes to Canada to avoid the draft. She decides to paint a vivid antiwar picture as her entry in the school's art contest whose theme is patriotism. Written for grades 4-7.

482 Wolkoff, Judie. *Where the Elf King Sings*. Scarsdale, N.Y.: Bradbury, 1980.
Twelve-year old Marcie struggles to deal with her alcoholic father, a Vietnam veteran who is not able to cope with his return home. His traumatic experiences in the war have been a shadow over the whole family for the six years he has been home. A powerful addition to the juvenile literature on the Vietnam War. Written for grades 6-9.

483 Wood, Ted. *Live Bait*. New York: Scribners, 1985.
Canadian author Wood has created a mystery series that features a main character who is a Marine Vietnam veteran who uses his background and skills learned in the war to solve crimes. Other titles in the series are *Fool's Gold, Dead Center, The Killing Cold, Dead in the Water, Murder on Ice,* and *When the Killing Starts.*

484 Woodruff, Paul. *The Personal Success of First Lieutenant Peter Rosillo*. Austin, Tex.: Pawn Review, 1983.
An award-winning book by a Texas writer based on his experiences as an army advisor in the Mekong Delta in 1969-70. The

narrator, Don Howard, tells Rosillo's story. Rosillo has been secretly helping Cambodian mercenaries.

485 Wright, Glover. *The Hound of Heaven*. New York: Arbor House, 1984.
      A thriller in which the first part of the book takes place in Vietnam. Father Pierre Labesse was crucified by the Vietcong in their rampage against Catholics. Although brain dead, he lived for ten years. The Pope gave an order that he was to be canonized after his death, but when life supports were removed, he died and nine hours later he rose, walked to the window and proclaimed "Heaven is here." He later meets the soldier who saved him, who is now a priest himself.

486 Wright, Stephen. *Meditations in Green*. New York: Scribners, 1983.
      James Griffin, who will later refer to his time in Vietnam as "the lost years," was never an optimistic soldier in the war, but his experiences turned him into a drug addict and made his readjustment after his return home painful. A well-written novel.

487 Zeybel, Henry. *The First Ace*. New York: Pocket Books, 1986.
      A story of jet combat by an author whose own experiences parallel those of his hero, Cy Young, a Korean War veteran who fears that his adventures are over until he becomes a pilot in Vietnam.

488 _____. *Gunship: Spectre of Death*. New York: Pocket Books, 1987.
      The hero is a navigator of a AC-130, flying bombing missions along the Ho Chi Minh Trail into Vietnam, destroying enemy trucks on the ground.

489 Zimpel, Lloyd. *Meeting the Bear: Journal of the Black Wars*. New York: Macmillan, 1971.
      A futuristic novel in which the events of the 1960s are projected into the 1980s and 1990s. The Vietnam War is still being fought and black soldiers are being sent there by the thousands. At home a second Civil War is in progress with oppressed blacks waging guerilla warfare on city after city.

490　Zlotnik, Donald E. *Eagles Cry Blood*. New York: Kensington/Zebra, 1986.

　　　　The adventures of a Green Beret hero who risks his life in dangerous missions is told in this action novel.

Adventure Novels

491 Aarons, Edward S. *Assignment Cong Hai Kill*. New York: Fawcett, 1966. Assignment series.

492 Buchanan, Jack. *Blood Storm*. New York: Jove/Berkley, 1986. M.I.A. Hunter, no. 6.

493 ____. *Cambodian Hellhole*. New York: Jove/Berkley, 1985. M.I.A. Hunter, no. 2.

494 ____. *Exodus from Hell*. New York: Jove/Berkley, 1986. M.I.A. Hunter, no. 5.

495 ____. *Hanoi Deathtrap*. New York: Jove/Berkley, 1985. M.I.A. Hunter, no. 3.

496 ____. *M.I.A. Hunter*. New York: Jove/Berkley, 1985. M.I.A. Hunter, no. 1.

497 ____. *Mountain Massacre*. New York: Jove/Berkley, 1985. M.I.A. Hunter, no. 4.

498 ____. *Stone: M.I.A. Hunter*. New York: Jove/Berkley, 1987.

499 Cain, Jonathan. *Boonie Rat Body Burning*. New York: Kensington/Zebra, 1984. Saigon Commandos, no. 5.

500 ____. *Cherry-Boy*. New York: Kensington/Zebra, 1984. Saigon Commandos, no. 4.

501 ____. *Code Zero: Shots Fired!* New York: Kensington/Zebra, 1983. Saigon Commandos, no. 2.

502 ____. *Di Di Mau or Die*. New York: Kensington/Zebra, 1984. Saigon Commandos, no. 6.

503 ____. *Dinky-Dau Death*. New York: Kensington/Zebra, 1984. Saigon Commandos, no. 3.

504 ____. *Hollowpoint*. New York: Kensington/Zebra, 1986. Saigon Commandos, no. 11.

505 ____. *Mad Minute*. New York: Kensington/Zebra, 1985. Saigon Commandos, no. 9.

506 ____. *Sac Mau, Victor Charlie*. New York: Kensington/Zebra, 1985. Saigon Commandos, no. 7.

507 ____. *Saigon Commandos*. New York: Kensington/Zebra, 1983. Saigon Commandos, no. 1.

508 ____. *Suicide Squad*. New York: Kensington/Zebra, 1986. Saigon Commandos, no. 12.

509 ____. *Tortures of Tet*. New York: Kensington/Zebra, 1986. Saigon Commandos, no. 10.

510 ____. *You Die, Du Ma!* New York: Kensington/Zebra, 1985. Saigon Commandos, no. 8.

511 Carter, Nick. *Appointment in Haiphong*. New York: Charter, 1982.

512 ____. *Cambodia*. New York: Award Books, 1970.

513 ____. *Hanoi*. New York: Award Books, 1966.

514 ____. *Saigon*. New York: Award Books, 1964.

515 Derrick, Lionel. *Penetrator–Jungle Blitz*. New York: Pinnacle, 1982. Penetrator series.

516 Derrig, Peter. *Battlefield*. New York: Paperback Library, 1967.

517 _____. *The Glory of the Green Berets*. New York: Paperback Library, 1967.

518 _____. *The Pride of the Green Berets*. New York: Paperback Library, 1966.

519 Hawkins, Jack. *Blood Trails*. New York: Ivy/Ballantine, 1987. Chopper 1, no. 1.

520 _____. *Jungle Sweep*. New York: Ivy/Ballantine, 1987. Chopper 1, no. 3.

521 _____. *Kill Zone*. New York: Ivy/Ballantine, 1988. Chopper 1, no. 7.

522 _____. *Monsoon Massacre*. New York: Ivy/Ballantine, 1988. Chopper 1, no. 10.

523 _____. *Payback*. New York: Ivy/Ballantine, 1988. Chopper 1, no. 9.

524 _____. *Red River*. New York: Ivy/Ballantine, 1987. Chopper 1, no. 4.

525 _____. *Renegade MIAs*. New York: Ivy/Ballantine, 1987. Chopper 1, no. 5.

526 _____. *Suicide Mission*. New York: Ivy/Ballantine, 1987. Chopper 1, no. 6.

527 _____. *Tunnel Warriors*. New York: Ivy/Ballantine, 1987. Chopper 1, no. 2.

528 Helm, Eric. *Body Count*. New York: Pinnacle, 1984. Scorpion Squad, no. 1.

529 _____. *Chopper Command*. New York: Pinnacle, 1985. Scorpion Squad, no. 3.

530 _____. *The Fall of Camp A555*. Toronto: Worldwide Library, 1987. Vietnam: Ground Zero.

531 _____. *Guidelines*. Toronto: Worldwide Library, 1987. Vietnam: Ground Zero.

532 ____. *The Hobo Woods*. Toronto: Worldwide Library, 1987. Vietnam: Ground Zero.

533 ____. *Incident at Plei Soi*. Toronto: Worldwide Library, 1987. Vietnam: Ground Zero.

534 ____. *The Kit Carson Squad*. Toronto: Worldwide Library, 1987. Vietnam: Ground Zero.

535 ____. *The Nhu Ky Sting*. New York: Pinnacle, 1984. Scorpion Squad, no. 2.

536 ____. *P.O.W.* Toronto: Worldwide Library, 1986. Vietnam: Ground Zero.

537 ____. *The Raid*. Toronto: Worldwide Library, 1988. Vietnam: Ground Zero.

538 ____. *River Raid*. New York: Pinnacle, 1985. Scorpion Squad, no. 4.

539 ____. *Soldier's Medal*. Toronto: Worldwide Library, 1987. Vietnam: Ground Zero.

540 ____. *Tet*. Don Mills, Ontario: Worldwide Library, 1988. Vietnam: Ground Zero.

541 ____. *Unconfirmed Kill*. Toronto: Worldwide Library, 1986. Vietnam: Ground Zero.

542 ____. *Vietnam: Ground Zero*. Toronto: Worldwide Library, 1986. Vietnam: Ground Zero.

543 ____. *The Ville*. Toronto: Worldwide Library, 1987. Vietnam: Ground Zero.

544 Lansing, John. *AK-47 Firefight*. New York: Kensington/Zebra, 1985. The Black Eagles, no. 6.

545 ____. *Bad Scene at Bong Son*. New York: Kensington/Zebra, 1986. The Black Eagles, no. 9.

546 ____. *Beyond the DMZ*. New York: Kensington/Zebra, 1985. The Black Eagles, no. 7.

547 _____. *Boo Coo Death*. New York: Kensington/Zebra, 1985. The Black Eagles, no. 8.

548 _____. *Cambodia Kill-Zone*. New York: Kensington/Zebra, 1986. The Black Eagles, no. 10.

549 _____. *Duel on the Song Cai*. New York: Kensington/Zebra, 1987. The Black Eagles, no. 11.

550 _____. *Encore at Dien Bien Phu*. New York: Kensington/Zebra, 1987. The Black Eagles, no. 13.

551 _____. *Firestorm at Dong Nam*. New York: Kensington/Zebra, 1988. The Black Eagles, no. 14.

552 _____. *Hanoi Hellground*. New York: Kensington/Zebra, 1984. The Black Eagles, no. 1.

553 _____. *Lord of Laos*. New York: Kensington/Zebra, 1987. The Black Eagles, no. 12.

554 _____. *Mekong Massacre*. New York: Kensington/Zebra, 1984. The Black Eagles, no. 2.

555 _____. *Nightmare in Laos*. New York: Kensington/Zebra, 1984. The Black Eagles, no. 3.

556 _____. *Punji Patrol*. New York: Kensington/Zebra, 1984. The Black Eagles, no. 4.

557 _____. *Saigon Slaughter*. New York: Kensington/Zebra, 1984. The Black Eagles, no. 5.

558 Mackenzie, Steve. New York: *Ambush!* New York: Avon, 1987. SEALS, no. 1.

559 _____. New York: *Breakout!* New York: Avon, 1988. SEALS, no. 5.

560 _____. New York: *Target!* New York: Avon, 1987. SEALS, no. 4.

561 Morrell, David. *First Blood*. New York: Evans, 1972. Rambo.

562 _____. *First Blood, Part II*. New York: Jove, 1985. Rambo.

Based on a screenplay by Sylvester Stallone and James Cameron.

563 _____. *Rambo III*. New York: Jove, 1988.
Based on a screenplay by Sylvester Stallone and Sheldon Lettich.

564 Nik-Uhernik. *M-16 Jury*. New York: Kensington/Zebra, 1985. War Dogs, no. 2.

565 Pendleton, Don. *Dirty War*. Don Mills, Ontario: Worldwide Library, 1985. Mack Bolan.

566 _____. *Return to Vietnam*. Toronto: Worldwide Library, 1982. Mack Bolan.

567 _____. *Skysweeper*. Toronto: Worldwide Library, 1984. Mack Bolan.

568 Sadler, Barry. *Casca: The Eternal Mercenary*. New York: Charter Books, 1979.

569 _____. *Casca: The Legionnaire*. New York: Charter Books, 1984.

570 _____. *Casca: The Phoenix*. New York: Charter Books, 1985.

571 Scofield, Jonathan. *Junglefire*. New York: Dell, 1982. Freedom Fighters, no. 15.

572 Sherman, David. *Knives in the Night*. New York: Ivy, 1987. Night Fighters.

573 _____. *Main Force Assault*. New York: Ivy, 1987. Night Fighters, no. 2.

574 _____. *A Nghu Night Falls*. New York: Ivy, 1988. Night Fighters, no. 5.

575 _____. *Out of the Fire*. New York: Ivy, 1987. Night Fighters, no. 3.

576 _____. *A Rock and a Hard Place*. New York: Ivy, 1988. Night Fighters, no. 4.

577 Teed, Jack Hamilton. *Cobra Kill*. New York: Kensington/Zebra, 1984. Gunships, no. 3.

578 ____. *Fire Force*. New York: Kensington/Zebra, 1982. Gunships, no. 2.

579 ____. *The Killing Zone*. New York: Kensington/Zebra, 1981. Gunships, no. 1.

580 ____. *Sky Fire*. New York: Kensington/Zebra, 1986. Gunships, no. 4.

581 Whittington, Harry. *Burden's Mission*. New York: Avon, 1968.

582 ____. *Doomesday Mission*. New York: Banner, 1967.

Personal Narratives/Biographies

583 Adler, Bill, ed. *Letters from Vietnam*. New York: Dutton, 1967.
     This is the first collection of letters home compiled prior to the end of the war. The only criterion for inclusion was that the writers were involved in the war and had something to say. Writers were soldiers, nurses, parents, volunteers working with Vietnamese peasants, Red Cross workers, U.S. civilian personnel, and Vietnamese citizens. The letters are reproduced just as they were written. Particularly poignant is the letter from a U.S. soldier to his seven-year-old son in which he tries to explain the responsibilities of being a soldier and a father.

584 Albright, John, John A. Cash, and Allan W. Sandstrum. *Seven Firefights in Vietnam*. Washington, D.C.: U.S. Government Printing Office, 1970.
     The accounts of seven confrontations in Vietnam told by men involved in the actions. Glossary, maps, index.

585 Allen, George. *Ri*. Englewood Cliffs, N.J.: Prentice-Hall, 1978.
     Ri is the story of American medic Ken Anderson and his attempts to adopt Ri, an eight year old Cambodian boy who had lost a leg and his whole family. This is one of the few stories from the war which focuses on the plight of the child victims and also one of the few to show the good of which American enlisted men were capable.

586 Anderson, Charles R. *The Grunts*. San Rafael, Calif.: Presidio Press, 1976.

    The Grunts is the story of one, 106-man Marine company during a fifty-eight day combat operation. The author emphasizes the role of "the grunt," the ordinary infantryman, and how the war affected him as well as the type of reception he received upon returning home.

587 ____. *Vietnam: The Other War*. San Rafael, Calif.: Presidio Press, 1982.

    Anderson was assigned to "service and support" in "the rear" near Da Nang in 1968 during the first half of his tour of duty. He describes life here and all of the diversions from standard operating procedure needed to make things work. An entertaining look at the Vietnam soldier's life away from the battlefield.

588 Anderson, William C. *Bat-21*. Englewood Cliffs, N.J.: Prentice-Hall, 1980.

    Based on the story of Lieutenant Col. Iceal E. Hambleton, USAF, code named Bat-21, who was shot down over enemy jungle in 1972. He was valuable to both the U.S. and the Vietnamese because of the highly secret military information he possessed. The story describes the twelve days both sides tried to find him. Our side mounted the largest one-man rescue operation in Air Force history. The author notes that changes made in the story were necessary to protect classified information.

589 Bain, David Howard. *Aftershocks: A Tale of Two Victims*. New York: Methuen, 1980.

    Former Marine combat veteran Louis Dorian Kahan, suffering from psychological problems, encountered a teenage girl – My Hanh, a Vietnamese refugee – in Queens. He interrogated, raped, and killed her. This is the story of both of the victims, made more significant by the increase of crimes by veterans suffering from post- traumatic stress syndrome. Bibliography.

590 Baker, Mark. *Nam: The Vietnam War in the Words of the Men and Women Who Fought There*. New York: Morrow, 1981.

    This is a very powerful, honest, and touchingly written book, and one of the classics of Vietnam literature. Baker interviewed both men and women, officers, enlisted men of all kinds, pro and antiwar veterans, asking them "What was Vietnam *really* like?" Baker, who was a college student during the war, said "I just wanted to record what they could remember about the intersection of their lives with the Vietnam War and the consequences of that experience. They seemed to feel obligated to relate their stories clearly and accurately for the sake of dead friends, dying ideals, and a personal sense of worth and honesty." Effective introduction.

591 Barnes, Scott, with Melva Libb. *Bohica.* Canton, Ohio: Bohica Corporation, 1987.

In 1981, the author was asked to participate in a mission to investigate reports of live American prisoners in Laos – Operation Grand Eagle. The title refers to the secret telex code. The author maintains – and provides proof – that there are MIAs in Laos and that the government wants the evidence suppressed. A huge book filled with supporting documentation.

592 Basel, G. I. *Pak Six: A Story of the War in the Skies of North Vietnam.* New York: Jove, 1987.

Basel was a Lieutenant Colonel in the USAF. In *Pak Six,* he describes his experiences and adventures as a fighter pilot over Vietnam in 1967, until he was wounded in a plane crash eight months later. Photographs. This is one in a series of paperbacks by Jove. Other titles include *Infantry in Vietnam, A Distant Challenge,* and *West to Cambodia.*

593 Baskir, Lawrence M., and William A. Strauss. *Chance and Circumstance: The Draft, the War, and the Vietnam Generation.* New York: Knopf, 1978.

A study of the Vietnam generation and how the war affected the fifty-three million Americans who came of draft age between 1964 and 1973. Discussed are "avoiders," evaders, deserters, and exiles. Personal accounts of experience are found throughout the book. Charts of the statistics are impressive as is the breakdown of just what segment of the population actually fought. Extensive bibliography and notes.

594 Baxter, Gordon. *13/13 Vietnam: Search and Destroy.* New York: World, 1967.

The author, a Texan, was a photographer in Vietnam. He tells the story of the Marine battalion India Company and the battle to secure the village of Tha Binh in which thirteen U.S. soldiers died. In this photographic essay, the streets and people of Saigon and the village of Loc Tan are shown and described. Color and black and white photos. Introduction by Chet Huntley.

595 Beesley, Stanley W. *Vietnam: The Heartland Remembers*. Norman: University of Oklahoma Press, 1987.

An excellent, poignant oral history of thirty-three Oklahomans who speak "for heartland America." All were involved in the war, either as soldiers or as family members who waited – mostly ordinary people forced into extraordinary circumstances. The author was a Ranger team leader in Vietnam who was twice awarded the Bronze Star.

596 Benavidez, Roy P., and Oscar Griffin. *The Three Wars of Roy Benavidez*. San Antonio, Tex.: Corona, 1986.

Benavidez was a Mexican-American who grew up in poverty in El Campo, South Texas. He served in Vietnam and won the Distinguished Service Cross for rescuing several men in a fire fight. He kept going back into the battle until all of the fallen were safe. He had to spend twelve years searching for evidence and witnesses until he was finally awarded the Congressional Medal of Honor in 1981. He has since campaigned for veterans rights.

597 Bernard, Edward. *Going Home*. Philadelphia: Dorrance, 1973.

Bernard was an Army major who served three tours in Vietnam in Special Forces and Airborne as a paratrooper. He says that this is "the story of every man who has fought in this or any other war." He describes his training at Aberdeen and Ft. Bragg and his battle experiences in Vietnam including being wounded. He feared he would be unable to fit in back home.

598 Berrigan, Daniel. *Night Flight to Hanoi: War Diary with 11 Poems*. New York: Macmillan, 1968.

Berrigan, the well-known radical priest, poet, and peace activist during the Vietnam War, tells of his trip to Hanoi and Laos with a coalition of various peace groups to try to secure the release of American POWs. He speaks not only of what he saw, but expresses his commitment to peace. He says "When, at what point, will you say no to this war? We have chosen to say, with the gift of our liberty, if necessary our lives, the violence stops here, the death stops here, the suppression of the truth stops here, the war stops here." Eleven poems by the author are woven throughout the narrative.

599 Berry, John Stevens. *Those Gallant Men: On Trial in Vietnam*. Novato, Calif.: Presidio Press, 1984.

The author was chief defense counsel for the Second Field Force in Vietnam in 1968-69. He describes his experiences in defending soldiers on a variety of charges from "fragging" to theft. Considerable attention is given to his most famous case in which he defended Green Beret Leland Brumley accused of the murder of a double agent. He also aided Vietnamese. A fascinating and different view of the war.

600 Bisignano, Flavio. *Vietnam – Why?: An American Citizen Looks at the War*. Torrance, Calif.: Frank Publications, 1968.

The author, an educator and ex World War II Navy man, made two trips to Vietnam during the war – as a merchant seaman and later as a journalist. He describes his experiences with combat troops. His purpose was to come to some understanding of our involvement.

601 Blakey, Scott. *Prisoner at War: The Survival of Commander Richard A. Stratton*. New York: Anchor Press/Doubleday, 1978.

Richard Stratton was a Navy pilot taken prisoner when his plane crashed on a combat mission over North Vietnam. He was held for six years. The book is based on interviews with Stratton in which he described his experiences. Blakey also describes the ordeal of Stratton's family. Bibliography of books, films, documents, and articles relating to POWs.

602 Bleier, Rocky, with Terry O'Neil. *Fighting Back*. New York: Warner, 1975.

Bleier, a Pittsburgh Steelers halfback, relates his experiences of being drafted, fighting in Vietnam, being gravely wounded, and recovering.

603 Block, Mickey, and William Kimball. *Before the Dawn*. Canton, Ohio: Daring Books, 1988.

Block was a Navy commando who lost a leg in Vietnam. He tells of his return to the United States, his stay in several VA hospitals which resulted in alcohol and drug addiction. He becomes a dedicated Christian which turns his life around.

604 Boettcher, Thomas D. *Vietnam: The Valor and the Sorrow*. Boston: Little, Brown, 1985.

The author was an Air Force liaison to the press in Vietnam, 1968-69. He has written a popular history of the war based in his experiences. The book is subtitled "From the Home Front to the Front Lines in Words and Pictures." Over 500 pictures.

605 Borton, Lady. *Sensing the Enemy: An American Woman among the Boat People of Vietnam*. Garden City, N.Y.: Dial, 1984.

Borton volunteered to work with the Quakers in a hospital in Quang Ngai, Vietnam, in 1969 and served two years. In 1980, she returned to a Malaysian island, Pulau Bidong, to work with the boat people, the Vietnamese refugees.

606 Bowers, Curt, as told to Glen Van Dyne. *Forward Edge of Battle: A Chaplain's Story*. Kansas City, Mo.: Beacon Hill Press of Kansas City, 1987.

Chaplain Bowers worked with men in the front lines during the war. He was a pastor of the Church of the Nazarene. He tells of how he came to Vietnam, the moral questions raised throughout his experience there, what he saw, and the people for whom he provided spiritual care. The book is religious in content with Bible passages cited throughout to emphasize points.

607 Boyle, Richard. *Flower of the Dragon: The Breakdown of the U.S. Army in Vietnam*. San Francisco: Ramparts Press, 1972.

Boyle was a correspondent in Vietnam. He describes the ugly events within the U.S. military including racial problems, drug addiction, fragging, and mutiny. An eyewitness account.

608 Bozek, David A. *Artillery Medic in Vietnam*. New York: Vantage, 1971.

A diary-like account of a tour of duty in Vietnam in 1969. The author was an artillery medic.

609   Brace, Ernest C. *A Code to Keep: The True Story of America's Longest-Held Civilian Prisoner of War*. New York: St. Martin's, 1988.

Ernest Brace, America's longest-held captive POW in Vietnam, tells his story. Brace was Korean War Marine, a decorated pilot who had lost his rank and was dishonorably discharged in 1961 for deserting the scene of an aircraft accident. He later flew secret missions for the CIA, was captured, imprisoned in North Vietnam in one of the infamous bamboo cages, and ended up in the Hanoi Hilton. He describes escape attempts and an imprisonment of over seven years. He was granted a full pardon by President Ford and decorated for courage while imprisoned. A well-told story. Photographs, maps, forward by Sen. John McCain, another POW.

610   Brandon, Heather. *Casualties: Death in Vietnam, Anguish and Survival in America*. New York: St. Martin's, 1984.

A different approach is taken here in that those who suffered at home are profiled – thirty-seven survivors tell of their hope, fear, mourning (public and private), their changing feelings toward the war, and their efforts at healing. These are the stories of the mothers, father, sisters, brothers, children, lovers, wives, friends, and grandparents of soldiers who died in Vietnam. All classes and ethnic groups are represented. The author is a Vietnam veteran counselor. This book breaks your heart.

611   Branfman, Fred. *Voices from the Plain of Jars: Life under an Air War*. New York: Harper & Row, 1972.

Branfman notes that most of the civilian Vietnamese were peasants rather than urban populations. This book tells the story, in their own words, of the peasants of the Plain of Jars in Northeast Laos during five years of American bombing, 1964-69. There were over 25,000 attack sorties, 75,000 tons of bombs dropped and their 700 year old society destroyed. These essays were written from refugee camps. This is one of the few books that deal with the story of the peasant victims. Maps.

612   Brant, Toby L. *Journal of a Combat Tanker, Vietnam, 1969*. New York: Vantage, 1988.

Brant states that his book is "a journal of impressions, anecdotes, and memories that made an imprint upon my mind in the brief time I served in Vietnam." He strives to convey to readers how it felt to be in the war and gives the reader the sights and smells of the place. From Charleston, Illinois, he enlisted in the army at eighteen. Brant fought in the M-48-A3 tank as a gunner and commander near Cu Chi in 1969. He lost both legs in a booby trap.

613   Brennan, Matthew. *Brennan's War: Vietnam, 1965-1969*. Novato, Calif.: Presidio Press, 1985.

Brennan was a member of the Flashing Saber Blues of the 9th Cavalry and served thirty-nine months in Vietnam, making over 400 helicopter assaults with "The Headhunters," the 1st Air Cavalry Division reconnaissance squad. He describes his eagerness as a teenage volunteer to be involved in the war, and the brutality that he observed. Photographs.

614   ____, ed. *Headhunters: Stories from the 1st Squadron, 9th Cavalry, Vietnam, 1965-1971*. Novato, Calif.: Presidio Press, 1987.

Brennen further describes the activities of the Headhunters, one of the most effective squads in Vietnam during the war. The author collected stories from the others members of the group.

615   Briand, Rena. *No Tears to Flow: Women at War*. Melbourne, Australia: Heinemann, 1969.

Briand was a woman journalist free-lancing in Vietnam for three years. She gives a short history and describes the experiences she had, life in Saigon, and her observations of the Vietnamese people, including the tribesmen, the American and Australian soldiers and leaders as well as those fighting with the Vietnamese.

616   Bridwell, E. R. *Manchu Delta: A Vietnam War Story*. Helena, Mont.?: E. R. Bridwell, 1986.

617   Briscoe, Edward G. *Diary of a Short-Timer in Vietnam*. New York: Vantage, 1970.

Briscoe was a surgeon in Vietnam, serving near China Beach and Danang. His introduction discusses the meaning and psychological ramifications of the term "short-timer." The diary begins on the day he was first called a short-timer and tells of his experiences which are filled with graphic medical details. Black and white photographs, glossary.

618 Broughton, Jack. *Going Downtown: The War against Hanoi and Washington*. New York: Orion, 1988.

Broughton, an air force fighter pilot, presents the story of the bombing campaign waged against North Vietnam. The book includes an introduction by Tom Wolfe and photographs.

619 ____. *Thud Ridge*. Philadelphia: Lippincott, 1969.

Col. Broughton (USAF) gives his account of aerial operations against Hanoi across Thud Ridge–the line of hills the F-105 Thunderchiefs (the "Thud") followed into Hanoi. The author carried a miniature tape recorder on missions and actual cockpit dialogue is recorded.

620 Brown, Gerald Austin. *No Sad Songs*. Fort Worth, Tex.: Branch-Smith, 1973.

A collection of letters by Captain Gerald Austin Brown to his mother, Grace Spaulding, and others. Captain Brown was killed in Vietnam in 1967.

621 Browne, Corinne. *Body Shop: Recuperating from Vietnam*. New York: Stein & Day, 1973.

A collection of personal narratives from amputee veterans who recovered in Letterman General Hospital in San Francisco in 1970-71. The soldiers reminisce about their lives before the war, give accounts of the day they were wounded, and describe their adjustment to life afterward. Glossary.

622 Browne, Malcolm W. *The New Face of War*. Indianapolis: Bobbs-Merrill, 1965.

Browne was a Pulitzer Prize-winning Associated Press journalist in Vietnam. He describes the things he saw including a vivid description of the famous self-immolation of Buddhist monk Quang Duc in 1963 in Saigon. The author gives his opinions on the progress of the war. The title of the book indicates the fact that Vietnam was different from any other war. Preface by Henry Cabot Lodge.

623   Broyles, William. *Brothers in Arms: A Journey from War to Peace*. New York: Knopf, 1986.
   The author of this interesting account served as a Marine lieutenant in Vietnam, leading a platoon near Da Nang in 1969. Later, he became editor in chief of *Newsweek*, a job he left in 1984 to return to Vietnam to discover the meaning of the war. He traveled to both the north and south and spoke to members of the Vietcong against whom he had fought.

624   Bryan, C. D. B. *Friendly Fire*. New York: Putnam, 1976.
   This is the story of Sergeant Michael Mullen of Black Hawk County, Iowa. Sgt. Mullen's death in 1970 was attributed to "nonbattle" causes. His parents attempted to discover how he really died and ended up being investigated by the FBI. *Friendly Fire* illustrates one family's disillusionment with the government over the issue of Vietnam. This is one of the early Vietnam classics. A made-for-television version of the story is available on videotape.

625   Butler, David. *The Fall of Saigon: Scenes from the Sudden End of a Long War*. New York: Simon & Schuster, 1985.
   Butler was a reporter in Vietnam and made three trips there during the war. His book describes the events leading up to the fall of Saigon, which he witnessed, and a minute by minute description of the fall itself. Butler emphasizes the people involved in the story–both American and Vietnamese.

626   Byerly, Wesley Grimes. *Nam Doc*. New York: Vantage, 1981.
   Byerly volunteered to serve with USAID's Project Vietnam in 1967 for a minimum sixty-day tour as a doctor. The book is written in diary form and tells of his experiences, the people he met, the Tet Offensive, which occurred during his tour, and the conditions under which he worked in a hospital in Rach Gia near the Gulf of Siam. An interesting view of the Vietnamese attitude toward medicine is presented. This is a very "up" book. Glossary.

627 Byrd, Barthy. *Home Front: Women and Vietnam.* Berkeley, Calif.: Shameless Hussy Press, 1986.

   Home Front is the story of nine women and how the Vietnam War affected them through the loss or mental or physical crippling of someone they loved. Some of these men returned but were essentially destroyed by the war. Included are stories of MIA wives and women who bore children deformed as a result of their husband's contact with Agent Orange.

628 Calley, William Laws, with John Sack. *Lieutenant Calley: His Own Story.* New York: Viking Press, 1971.

   Calley spent 100 days in conversation with John Sack, author of *M*, in which he explained his account of what happened at My Lai and after his return to the United States. A military jury found him guilty of premeditated murder in 1969. Half of this book first appeared in *Esquire* magazine. The British edition is called *Body Count: Lieutenant Calley's Story.*

629 Caputo, Philip. *A Rumor of War.* New York: Holt, Rinehart & Winston, 1977.

   This is one of the major books of Vietnam War literature. Caputo, a young Marine infantry officer for sixteen months in Vietnam, beginning in 1965, presents a grim, honest picture of the war. The soldiers' enemies were boredom and climate as much as the Vietcong. Caputo gives the reader a feeling for what fighting in a war is like. A film version of *A Rumor of War* is available on videotape.

630 Carhart, Tom. *The Offering: A Generation Offered Their Lives to America in Vietnam – One Soldier's Story.* New York: Morrow, 1987.

   Carhart, a 1966 West Point graduate, describes his experiences on his tour of duty. Throughout, the author questions the West Point code of conduct and the nature of men, war, and politics. He commanded a long-range reconnaissance platoon and was twice wounded.

631 Chanda, Nayan. *Brother Enemy: The War after the War – A History of Indochina since the Fall of Saigon.* San Diego: Harcourt Brace Jovanovich, 1986.

The author was the Indochina correspondent for the *Far Eastern Economic Review*. He describes conditions and events in Indochina since the fall of Saigon based on interviews with major figures in all of the countries with an interest in this area, plus his own observations and experiences. Notes, chronology.

632 Chanoff, David, and Doan Van Toai. *Portrait of the Enemy*. New York: Random House, 1986.

The authors show us the lives of the enemy through first-person accounts of North Vietnamese terrorists, militant monks, propaganda chiefs, factory workers, artists, former Vietcong and southern opposition leaders. It is interesting to see their fears, hopes and dreams told for once – to see that the other side has a human face. The authors conducted interviews with Vietnamese exiles in the United States, Europe, and in Southeast Asian refugee camps. Coauthor Daon Van Taoi was an antiwar student leader at Saigon University during Thieu's regime.

633 Chesley, Larry. *Seven Years in Hanoi: A POW Tells His Story*. Salt Lake City: Bookcraft, 1973.

Chesley was shot down on a night mission in 1966, flying to bomb a cave area in North Vietnam where he was captured. He was held prisoner for seven years in the infamous Hanoi Hilton. He describes life as a POW, the inhuman conditions at the prison, and the comfort he found in his religious faith.

634 Chinnock, Frank W. *Kim: A Gift from Vietnam*. New York: World, 1969.

Chinnock went to Vietnam to adopt a war orphan. This is the story of how he finally was able to bring her to the United States and the difficulty of her adjustment to her new life.

635 Clark, Johnnie M. *Guns Up!* New York: Ballantine, 1984.

A Marine machine gunner in Vietnam, Clark describes his tour and his friends, Chan and Red, and the battles they fought together. He joined the Marines at 17 and served during the 1968 Tet Offensive. He was wounded three times.

636 Cleland, Max. *Strong at the Broken Places*. Waco, Tex.: Chosen Books, 1980.

After graduating from college, where he had been in ROTC, the author volunteered for active duty in the First Air Cavalry Division in 1966. He was sent to Vietnam in 1968 and was wounded when a grenade exploded. He lost his right hand, right leg and knee, and severely injured his left leg and his windpipe. He describes the survival from wounds and the painful healing process. His faith in God helped him to adjust to his disability. Later, Cleland served as head of the Veterans Administration under President Carter.

637 Clodfelter, Michael. *Mad Minutes and Vietnam Months: A Soldier's Memoir*. Jefferson, N.C.: McFarland, 1988.

Clodfelter describes his enlistment at seventeen and the seventeen months he spent in country in Vietnam, being wounded twice. He received decorations for bravery in battle. Maps.

638 Coe, Charles. *Young Man in Vietnam*. New York: Four Winds Press, 1968.

Told in a series of vignettes, this is a war memoir of a twice-wounded Marine lieutenant's year in Vietnam. He describes his arrival, the field camp, his friends, and his first contact with the enemy. *Young Man in Vietnam* is a very personal story of one man's war with no attempt to pronounce on war's larger meaning.

639 Coe, John J. *Desperate Praise: Australians in Vietnam*. Perth, Australia: Artlook Books, 1982.

Desperate Praise is "a collection of stories, memories, and diaries of Australian soldiers, both regulars and national servicemen, who served in Vietnam." The collection includes the first person accounts of fourteen contributors including one by the editor who spent eighteen months in Vietnam in 1968-69. The book is dedicated to the 496 Austrlians who died in Vietnam. Glossary, historical appendix, and a note on Australian involvement included.

640 Colvin, Rod. *First Heroes: The POW's Left Behind in Vietnam*. New York: Irvington, 1987.

Colvin explores the question of whether or not there are still POWs in Vietnam. Included are thirteen personal narratives by members of MIA families.

641 Cook, John. *The Advisor*. Philadelphia: Dorrance, 1973.
The author was an American advisor in Vietnam for two years as part of the Phoenix program, a counterterrorist group working to stop Vietcong atrocities perpetrated on local farmers who would not cooperate. He tells of his work in the Di An district, and how it was affected by the war.

642 Corson, William R. *The Betrayal*. New York: Norton, 1968.
Corson, an ex-Marine who was in charge of a group of "pacification" teams charged with winning hearts and minds, describes his experiences and explains what must be done to win the war and what is being done wrong. The content is more heavily opinion than personal narrative, but is interesting from an 1980s viewpoint.

643 Daly, James A., and Lee Bergman. *A Hero's Welcome: The Conscience of Sergeant James Daly versus the United States Army*. Indianapolis: Bobbs-Merrill, 1975.
James Daly, a young black from Bedford-Stuyvesant, enlisted in the army, applying for conscientious objector status, which he never received. He ended up a POW in Hanoi before he even had a chance to fire his rifle. He spoke out against the war. After his return to the U.S., he and a group of his friends were faced with treason charges that were eventually dropped.

644 Dedera, Don. *Anybody Here from Arizona? A Look at the Vietnam War*. Phoenix: Arizona Republic, 1966.
The *Arizona Republic* sent two correspondents to Vietnam, Don Dedera and Paul Dean. This is a collection of Dedera's dispatches from the field, accompanied throughout by photographs.

645 Dengler, Dieter. *Escape from Laos*. San Rafael, Calif.: Presidio Press, 1987.
Dengler, a German-born American naval pilot, was shot down over Laos in 1966 and captured by the Pathet Lao. Five months later,

he escaped. The abominable conditions and inhuman treatment are graphically described. Dengler was the only one of six escapees to survive.

646 Denton, Jeremiah A. *When Hell Was in Session*. New York: Reader's Digest Press, 1976.

Denton was a POW for over seven years after being shot down over North Vietnam on a bombing mission in 1965. Incarcerated in the Hanoi Hilton, he was tortured and managed to convey this fact during a staged press conference by blinking his eyes in morse code to spell "torture."

647 Donlan, Roger H. C., as told to Warren Rogers. *Outpost of Freedom*. New York: McGraw-Hill, 1965.

A Green Beret and Congressional Medal of Honor winner, Donlan tells his life story from his birth to his experiences in Vietnam. He commented that "the worst thing about serving in Vietnam is that you never see an American flag." He was honored for bravery during a surprise night attack by the Vietcong at Nam Dong. This book was written at the height of the war, which accounts for the self-effacing, patriotic tone.

648 Donovan, David. *Once a Warrior King: Memories of an Officer in Vietnam*. New York: McGraw-Hill, 1985.

The author was a U.S. Army lieutenant involved in the training of local militia–"Vietnamization." He describes the brutality he witnessed and in which he himself participated, his team members, the villagers with whom he worked, and his experiences in combat.

649 Dooley, Thomas A. *Deliver Us from Evil: The Story of Viet Nam's Flight to Freedom*. New York: Farrar, Straus & Cudahy, 1956.

Thomas Dooley was a Navy doctor who worked in the refugee camps of Southeast Asia in the late fifties after Indo-China fell to the Communists. He wrote a series of books relating his experiences which were very popular at the time. He gives an interesting view of Vietnam and Laos prior to major American involvement. Dooley died of cancer in 1961. Other books by Dooley include: *The Edge of Tomorrow* (New York: Farrar, Straus & Cudahy, 1958); *The Night They Burned the Mountain* (New York: Farrar, Straus & Cudahy, 1960); *Before I Sleep*

(New York: Farrar, Straus & Cudahy, 1961). Also of interest is the biography of Dooley by his mother Agnes W. Dooley, *Promises to Keep: The Life of Doctor Thomas A. Dooley*. (New York: Farrar, Straus & Cudahy, 1961).

650 Dougan, Clark, and Stephen Weiss. *The American Experience in Vietnam*. New York: Norton, 1988.

    Each of the eight chapters of *The American Experience in Vietnam* is written by eyewitnesses to the events described. The chapters trace the war from its beginnings to the fall of Saigon. Witnesses include Morris Udall, Walter Cronkite, Al Santoli, newsmen, soldiers, and Vietnamese. Bibliography, index, black and white and color photographs.

651 Downs, Frederick. *Aftermath: A Soldier's Return from Vietnam*. New York: Norton, 1984.

    Downs was a Second Lieutenant from Indiana who served in Delta Company, 3rd Brigade, in Duc Pho. He lost his left arm and suffered other severe injuries after stepping on a land mine in 1968–the story he told in *The Killing Zone* (see 652). This is the story of his recovery after many operations and how he rebuilt his life.

652 _____. *The Killing Zone: My Life in the Vietnam War*. New York: Norton, 1978.

    Downs tells the story of his life as a ground infantry lieutenant and leader of the first platoon of Delta Company, his efforts to keep his men safe, and his personal growth through the ordeal of combat. Downs won four Purple Hearts, the Bronze Star with Valor, and the Silver Star. He tells the story of the recovery from his war injuries in *Aftermath* (see 651).

653 Dramesi, John A. *Code of Honor*. New York: Norton, 1975.

    Dramesi describes his survival as a POW in North Vietnam after being shot down in his F-105D. He was held prisoner for six years. He described how he followed the military Code of Conduct demanded of prisoners of war by the U.S. government (Executive Order #10631), using mind tricks, and sheer courage, to prevent himself from giving in to torture.

654   Drury, Richard S. *My Secret War*. Fallbrook, Calif.: Aero, 1979.
        The author was a combat pilot in Vietnam who flew Douglas Skyraiders over Laos and the Ho Chi Minh Trail. He was awarded several medals for his service. Drury communicates the danger but also the love of flying.

655   Dudman, Richard. *Forty Days with the Enemy*. New York: Liveright, 1971.
        The author, a journalist for the *St. Louis Post-Dispatch,* entered Cambodia after Nixon announced its invasion by American troops in 1970. He and two other reporters were captured by Cambodian guerrillas. He describes their experiences during the forty days they were held, a time during which Americans were bombing Cambodia, and the relationship they developed with their captors.

656   Duncan, Donald. *The New Legions*. New York: Random House, 1967.
        Duncan was a Special Forces Trooper, a Green Beret, in Vietnam in 1964-65. He turned down a battlefield commission, resigned, returned to the U.S., and spoke out against the war. He describes missions he planned and executed into Vietcong territory and how he began to see the error of U.S. military policy.

657   Edelman, Bernard, ed. *Dear America: Letters Home from Vietnam*. New York: Norton, 1985.
        A book of letters home from those serving and working in Vietnam during the war in all areas from soldiers to donut dollies. The letters were gathered as part of a memorial to Vietnam veterans in New York City. 208 items (including poems) by 125 people were chosen from those that were gathered or donated. The last chapter, "last letters," is heartbreaking. This book was the basis for the made-for-cable-television film, "Dear America." Photographs.

658   Ehrhart, W. D. *Going Back: An Ex-Marine Returns to Vietnam*. Jefferson, N.C.: McFarland, 1987.
        Ehrhart, a major voice in Vietnam War literature, was an eighteen-year-old volunteer who served with distinction in Vietnam in 1967-68. He returned to Vietnam in 1985 at the Vietnam government's invitation. Ehrhart reports on Vietnam today, the effects of the war, and life under communism. The book ends with an epilogue that

stresses that Americans must learn from the experience of Vietnam in order to prevent being involved in another, similar tragedy. His combat experiences were related in *Vietnam Perkasie*.

659 ____. *Marking Time*. New York: Avon, 1986.
    Marking Time describes Ehrhart's experiences when he returns home from Vietnam, wounded and decorated, and enrolls as a student at Swarthmore where he attempts to come to terms with his experiences amid the campus antiwar protests. The insensitivity of those who didn't go is juxtaposed with the author's own doubts, nightmares, and emotional upheavals, against the backdrop of a war winding down. Eventually Ehrhart becomes a seaman on a oil tanker.

660 ____. *Vietnam Perkasie: A Combat Marine Memoir*. Jefferson, N.C.: McFarland, 1983.
    Ehrhart describes his Marine service in Vietnam, as well as his youth, basic training, and return home from the war. He notes in his prologue that the work is neither fiction or really a memoir. Every event described happened, but liberties were taken in sequence, speaker's participation, and characterization. Names were also changed. The Perkasie of the title is the town in Pennsylvania where the author was raised. Foreword by John Clark Pratt.

661 Eilert, Rick. *For Self and Country*. New York: Morrow, 1983.
    Eilert's narrative is subtitled, "For the wounded in Vietnam, the journey home took more courage than going into battle: a true story." The author was a Marine lance corporal who was severely wounded by a grenade in Vietnam, after which he spent a year in Great Lakes Naval Hospital in Illinois. This memoir chronicles not only combat experiences, but describes the physical rehabilitation process following a crippling injury and its attendant psychological and spiritual problems. As Eilert says "sometimes, the journey home required more bravery." Artwork throughout the book.

662 Elford, George Robert. *Devil's Guard*. New York: Delacorte, 1971.
    Elford presents the story of the French Foreign Legion in Vietnam, emphasizing the dehumanization of men in war.

663 Elkins, Frank. *The Heart of a Man*. New York: Norton, 1973.

A personal diary of Lieutenant Elkins's experience as an A-4 pilot bombing Vietnam in 1966, *The Heart of a Man* chronicles the daily life aboard an aircraft carrier during the war. The author, recipient of seven air medals and the Distinguished Flying Cross, was listed as MIA in 1966. The book was edited by his wife, whom he had married only eight months before he was listed as missing. She waited six years and was finally convinced of his death after numerous trips to the North Vietnamese delegation in Paris. Elkins is still listed as missing.

664 Emerson, Gloria. *Winners and Losers: Battles, Retreats, Gains, Losses and Ruins from the Vietnam War*. New York: Random House, 1976.

Emerson was a correspondent for the *New York Times* and visited Vietnam in 1956 and 1970-72. She discusses what she saw as the affect of the war on both America and Vietnam and the individuals involved on both sides based on her observations and numerous interviews with POW's, veterans, antiwar demonstrators, deserters, etc.

665 Esper, George, and the Associated Press. *The Eyewitness History of the Vietnam War: 1961-1975*. New York: Ballantine, 1983.

The author was an AP journalist who covered the Vietnam War from 1965 to 1975 and served as Saigon bureau chief. He remained in Vietnam after the fall of Saigon until he was expelled by the Communist government. His history is based on letters, diaries, and personal accounts, some of which are reproduced, as well as his own personal observations. Photographs.

666 Estes, Jack. *A Field of Innocence*. Portland, Ore.: Breitenbush Books, 1987.

This is the story of a teenaged boy who joined the Marines in 1968, leaving an unhappy home life and pregnant girlfriend behind. The author tells of his training, his special relationship with Vietnamese children, battles (in one instance he was protected by the dead body of another soldier), and R & R in Hawaii with his wife and child. Actual letters home are included. Estes served in Vietnam in 1968-69, close to the DMZ at Khe Sahn, Quang Tri, and Con Thien. He was wounded and decorated for heroism.

667 Falabello, Robert J. *Vietnam Memories: A Passage to Sorrow*. New York: Pageant Press International, 1971.

Falabello served in the infantry in Vietnam as a volunteer and provides a first-hand look at the Tet Offensive. He was a chaplain with various combat battalions, feeling a need to go into the field with the men, to understand what they faced.

668 Fall, Bernard. *Vietnam Witness, 1953-66.* New York: Praeger, 1966.

Fall spent a considerable amount of time in Vietnam under French control and through American involvement. He visited both the North and the South as a correspondent and had an influence on other reporters. He was killed by a land mine in Vietnam. This is a selection of his interpretive reporting of the war in which he claims that the war was not unavoidable. He describes the events he witnessed there and the mistakes that were made. Other books by Fall that combine personal narrative with the history of the war are *Street without Joy* (Harrisburg, Pa.: Stockpole, 1964); *The Two Viet Nams* (New York: Praeger, 1964); *Hell in a Very Small Place: The Siege of Dien Bien Phu* (New York: Lippincott, 1967); *Last Reflections on a War* (New York: Praeger, 1972).

669 Fallaci, Oriana. *Nothing, and So Be It*. Garden City, N.Y.: Doubleday, 1972.

Fallaci is an Italian journalist who describes her year as a combat correspondent in Vietnam. She relates not only what she saw at Dak To and Khe Sahn, but also how it changed her. She interviewed Vietcong prisoners.

670 Favreau, Dan. *Thumbs Up*. Minneapolis: Montage Books, 1981.

Favreau was a member of Charlie Company of the First Air Cavalry, 1966-67. He states that his objective is "to provide insight into the daily life, the activities, the thoughts and dreams of the infantry soldier in Vietnam," which he does through the retelling of his experiences. His platoon served near the Ia Drang Valley where he was wounded.

671 Flood, Charles Bracelen. *The War of the Innocents*. New York: McGraw-Hill, 1970.

Older than most, Flood was given the opportunity to enter the war as an attached member of a fighter-bomber wing rather than as a correspondent. He became a member of a dive-bomber unit that dropped napalm and spent a year in Vietnam, including three months in the jungles on the Cambodian border.

672 Franks, Linda. *Waiting Out a War: The Exile of Private John Picciano*. New York: Coward, McCann & Geoghegan, 1974.

John Picciano was a draftee who deserted the army in 1967. Horrified by newsreels and stories of the war, he went AWOL from Fort Dix, N.J., before being sent to Vietnam. He spent five years on the run in the United States and Canada, eventually ending up in Sweden. Franks tells his story.

673 *Front Lines: Soldiers' Writings from Vietnam*. Cambridge, Mass.: Indochina Curriculum Group, 1975.

A collection of personal narratives, letters and excerpts from diaries of Vietnam veterans used as a teaching tool for high school students. See also entry 1691.

674 Futrell, Robert Frank. *Aces and Aerial Victories: The United States Air Force in Southeast Asia, 1965-1973*. Washington, D.C.: U.S. Government Printing, 1976.

A collection of first person accounts by Air Force fighter crews, telling their experiences while bombing North Vietnam. Extensive appendix of individual crew members and fighter units included.

675 Gadd, Charles. *Line Doggie: Foot Soldier in Vietnam*. Novato, Calif.: Presidio Press, 1987.

Gadd was a "Screaming Eagle" of the 101st Airborne Division in Vietnam in 1967-68. He describes the horror of jungle fighting, the daily search and clear operations and patrols, and discusses the affect of killing in war on the conscience. "It's easy to kill in the din and confusion of a firefight – it's those long hours spent alone in a foxhole that gnaw at your guts."

676 Gaither, Ralph. *With God in a POW Camp*. Nashville: Broadman, 1973.

Gaither was a Navy F-4 fighter pilot shot down over North Vietnam and imprisoned in the Hanoi Hilton. He describes the interrogations and the humiliating march of prisoners through the streets of Hanoi where they were assaulted by by-standers, the food, the conditions, his relationship with other POW's, and his final release and return home. He emphasizes the role his religious faith played throughout his ordeal. The text includes several poems written while in prison.

677 Garland, Albert N., ed. *Combat Notes from Vietnam*. Fort Benning, Ga.: Infantry Magazine, 1968.

A collection of fourteen personal accounts of soldier's experiences in Vietnam with information about fighting techniques used there.

678 _____. *Infantry in Vietnam*. Fort Benning, Ga.: Infantry Magazine, 1967.

A collection of personal experiences describing small unit infantry combat.

679 Garms, David. *With the Dragon's Children*. New York: Exposition Press, 1973.

In 1967-68, Garms was a member of USAID in Vietnam assigned to win hearts and minds in the Mekong Delta area. He describes his experiences at the Chieu Hoi Center which re-indoctrinated deserters from the National Liberation Front. The title refers to the Vietnamese who sometimes refer to themselves as "children of the dragon."

680 Glasser, Ronald J. *365 Days*. New York: Braziller, 1971.

Dr. Ronald Glasser, a major in the U.S. Army Medical Corps and a draftee, relates his experiences in Zama Hospital in Japan in 1968–a hospital that saw six to eight thousand injured GI's a month. Glasser relates his own experiences as well as those of his patients. Glasser says "there is no novel in Nam, there is not enough for a plot, nor is there really any character development. If you survive 365 days without getting killed or wounded you simply go home and take up again where you left off. . . . As for me, my wish is not that I had never been in the Army, but that this book could never have been written." An important book in Vietnam War literature.

681 Goff, Stanley, and Robert Sanders, with Clark Smith. *Brothers: Black Soldiers in the Nam*. Novato, Calif.: Presidio Press, 1982.

The authors are two blacks who met at the Oakland California Army Induction Center in 1968 during the Tet Offensive and became friends. They describe military training and what it was like to be a black soldier in Vietnam.

682 Goldman, Peter, and Tony Fuller. *Charlie Company*. New York: Morrow, 1983.

A team of *Newsweek* reporters questioned the sixty-five infantrymen of Charlie Company about their experiences in Vietnam. The result is this history of the men of one combat company of 18-20 year olds, and of the silence that greeted their return home. At a reunion of the company, one of the reporters asked "How do you explain that so many of the guys are now talking? Not only talking, but it's–it's coming out of them like a waterfall." One of them, David Brown, responded, "Somebody asked us." Photographs.

683 Grant, Zalin. *Over the Beach: The Air War in Vietnam*. New York: Norton, 1986.

Grant tells the story of the air war over Hanoi and Haiphong told by the "voices" of pilots, a POW, and a MIA wife. The reader is told of the bombing of the same bridge on the same day in 1966, 1967, and 1972–a typical event in this war. Grant was an army intelligence officer in Vietnam and then a reporter for *Time* and the *New Republic*.

684 ____. *Survivors*. New York: Norton, 1975.

Survivors is the story of nine Americans captured in early 1968 and held in the jungle before being moved on foot to the Hanoi Hilton where they were imprisoned for five years. Each of the POWs tells his own story about life in prison and the reasons for the eventual antiwar activities of some of them as part of a POW "peace committee." Upon their return home, five were charged with misconduct, charges that were eventually dropped. One of the five, James Daly, tells his story more fully in *A Hero's Welcome*.

685 Groom, Winston, and Duncan Spencer. *Conversations with the Enemy: The Story of Pfc. Robert Garwood*. New York: Putnam, 1983.

Robert Garwood was a POW in Vietnam for an incredible fourteen years. He had been a nineteen year old Marine driver assigned to pick up a lieutenant from a reconnaissance company near Da Nang when he was captured. His prison experiences are harrowing to read and provides a clear picture of what it takes to survive in a prison camp. After his return to the United States, he was accused of being an enemy collaborator and was threatened with the possibility of death by firing squad. He was brought to trial and acquitted.

686 Halstead, Fred. *GI's Speak out against the War: The Case of the Ft. Jackson 8*. New York: Pathfinder, 1970.
This is the story of the organization called GI's United Against the War in Vietnam. The army tried to end the activities of the organization, imprisoning some of the men involved. The author interviewed members of the organization.

687 ____. *Out Now! A Participant's Account of the American Movement against the Vietnam War*. New York: Monad Press, 1978.
A personal history of the U.S. antiwar movement against the Vietnam Conflict written by a member of the Vietnam Peace Committee in New York. In 1968 he was a presidential candidate for the Socialist Workers Party and visited Japan, South Vietnam, and Germany to talk to American GI's. Halstead was also a member of a number of other antiwar committees including the National Coordinating Committee to End the War in Vietnam. He documents famous events from the 1960s including the SDS March on Washington, teach-ins, the 1968 Democratic National Convention in Chicago, and the Vietnam Moratorium. Photographs, index.

688 Hamill, Pete. *Irrational Ravings*. New York: Putnam, 1971.
A collection of articles and essays including many describing his experiences as a reporter in Vietnam in 1966.

689 Hamilton-Patterson, James. *The Greedy War: A Very Personal War*. New York: McKay, 1972.
First published as *A Very Personal War: The Story of Cornelius Hawkridge* (London: Hodder and Stoughton, 1971). Cornelius Hawkridge worked at a number of civilian jobs in Vietnam in 1966 and witnessed the large scale corruption and profiteering at the expense of

the U.S. He tried to get the U.S. government to see this and put a stop to it, but failed. He wanted the United States to let him investigate; they refused.

690 Hammer, Richard. *One Morning in the War: The Tragedy at Son My.* New York: Coward, McCann, 1970.

Two massacres took place on March 16, 1968: one at My Lai and the other at Son My. This is a description of those events and an attempt to explain how they happened. Interviews included.

691 Harris, J. D. *War Reporter.* New York: Manor Books, 1979.

Harris was a Hearst newspaper correspondent who covered stories in the hot spots all over the world including Northern Ireland, the Middle East, Cyprus, Africa, and Vietnam. Part of this account deals with his experiences in Vietnam in 1965 during which time he was in the field with Marines and paratroopers and flew combat missions with American pilots.

692 Hawthorne, Leslyanne, ed. *Refugee: The Vietnamese Experience.* New York: Oxford University Press, 1982.

The author, an Australian, relates her experiences in working with the flood of Vietnamese refugees that came into Australia beginning in 1978. The book is a series of interviews with refugees in which she tried to discover what their lives had been like before and after the fall of Saigon. She found that all her stereotypes were shattered and that "to be a refugee was a great leveller." She also explores the question the presence of the refugees raise – "to what extent people have the right to leave a situation they find intolerable and expect the rest of the world to take them in."

693 Helsop, J. N., and D. H. Van Orden. *From the Shadows of Death.* Salt Lake City: Desert Books, 1973.

This narrative is a collection of eight interviews with Mormon POWs and their families from Utah, Texas, Idaho, and California. The accounts emphasize each soldier's religious faith and Mormon beliefs and the role these played in their survival. Photographs.

694 Henderson, Charles. *Marine Sniper: 93 Confirmed Kills.* Briarcliff Manor, N.Y.: Stein & Day, 1986.

Henderson tells the story of Marine Sgt. Carlos Hathcock, famous top Marine sniper. He explains how he was trained, what his job was, and describes several missions in which Hathcock was involved. Hathcock was in his second tour when he saved several marines from a burning armored vehicle, suffering massive burns himself. The book concludes with his recovery and return to duty. Photographs, bibliography.

695 Hensler, Paul G., with Jeanne Houston. *Don't Cry, It's Only Thunder.* Garden City, N.Y.: Doubleday, 1984.

Hensler was a young recruit from the Midwest who eventually, with two nuns, fed, housed, and cared for 126 Vietnamese orphans during the war.

696 Herbert, Anthony B., and James T. Wooton. *Soldier.* New York: Holt, Rinehart & Winston, 1973.

The autobiography of a career army soldier. Herbert rose in the ranks, eventually training Special Forces troops. He commanded a battalion in Vietnam, and pressed for reform in the army. He was relieved of command and a report was filed that effectively ended any chance of promotion because of his activities. He appealed, the appeal was dismissed, and he resigned.

697 Herr, Michael. *Dispatches.* New York: Knopf, 1977.

Generally considered to be one of the best Vietnam books, *Dispatches* chronicles what it was like to fight in the Vietnam War. The book is graphic, surrealistic, terrifying. Herr first went to Vietnam in 1967 as a correspondent for *Esquire.*

698 Herrgesell, Oscar. *Dear Margaret, Today I Died: Letters from Vietnam.* San Antonio, Tex.: Naylor, 1974.

A collection of Lt. Herrgesell's letters to his wife from Vietnam, February 19, 1972, to July 25, 1972, compiled by his wife Margaret. Herrgesell died four days after the last letter was written when his helicopter was hit by enemy artillery. Also included is an unfinished poem by the author.

699 Herrington, Stuart A. *Peace with Honor? An American Reports on Vietnam, 1973-1975.* Novato Calif.: Presidio Press, 1983.

The author was a military intelligence officer assigned to the Defense Attache Office in Saigon. He describes his experiences there telling how the North Vietnamese continued to build for the war after the Vietnam Paris agreements. He describes the fall of Da Nang and Saigon and questions the conduct of the war. Herrington later worked on a MIA investigation team. This is a sequel to *Silence Was a Weapon* (see 700).

700 _____. *Silence Was a Weapon: The Vietnam War in the Villages – A Personal Perspective.* Novato, Calif.: Presidio Press, 1982.

Herrington tells of his job as an American advisor in Vietnam from 1971-72 locating and eliminating insurgency in the small villages – Operation Phoenix. He explains how this was done under conditions in which the villagers were silent from fear of retaliation and distrust of foreigners.

701 Higgins, Marguerite. *Our Vietnam Nightmare.* New York: Harper & Row, 1965.

The author, a noted journalist and correspondent, describes what she saw and experienced in pre-Tet Vietnam early in the war. Antoinette May's biography of Higgins, *Witness to War* (New York: Beaufort, 1983), also deals in part with Higgins's experiences in Vietnam.

702 Hope, Bob. *Five Women I Love: Bob Hope's Vietnam Story.* Garden City, N.Y.: Doubleday, 1966.

Hope describes his experiences on his trips to entertain the troops in Vietnam.

703 Hubbell, John G. *P.O.W.: A Definitive History of the American Prisoner-of-War Experience in Vietnam, 1964-1973.* New York: Reader's Digest Press, 1976.

P.O.W. is the product of interviews with over 200 American prisoners of war in Vietnam. It graphically presents their experiences in North Vietnam prison camps – the torture and punishments, humiliations – like being paraded through the streets of Hanoi – escape attempts, and their continuing efforts to communicate with and support each other, to stay alive and to remain human. Photographs, index, appendix of POWs returned to the U.S. in February-March, 1973.

704 Hughes, Larry. *You Can See a Lot Standing under a Flare in the Republic of Vietnam: My Year at War*. New York: Morrow, 1969.
　　　Hughes, a 1965 draftee, served as an Information Specialist for the Army in Vietnam from April 1966 to May 1967. His job was to write stories about the Combat Engineers in the Central Highlands, an area he traveled through observing both Americans and Vietnamese. He describes "the common man's look at the war."

705 Hurwitz, Ken. *Marching Nowhere*. New York: Norton, 1971.
　　　A member of the Vietnam Moratorium Committees describes life as an antiwar protester.

706 Hutchens, James. *Beyond Combat*. Chicago: Moody Press, 1968.
　　　The author was an army chaplain in Vietnam from 1965-66. He tells of his experiences with dying soldiers and in those moments before a battle. He stresses the value of religious belief for soldiers in combat.

707 Huynh Quang Nhuong. *The Land I Lost: Adventures of a Boy in Vietnam*. New York: Harper & Row, 1982.
　　　The author, a Vietnamese born in the Central Highlands, poignantly describes his life as a child in Vietnam that was disrupted and destroyed by the war. Black and white drawings. Designed for grades 4-7.

708 Jason, Alexander. *Heroes: The True Account of the Medal of Honor Winners, Southeast Asia, 1964-1975*. Pinole, Calif.: Anite Press, 1979.
　　　Jason tells the stories of the 236 Vietnam War Congressional Medal of Honor winners.

709 Jensen, Jay Roger. *Six Years in Hell: A Returned POW Views Captivity, Country, and the Nation's Future*. Bountiful, Utah: Horizon, 1974.

710 Johnson, Raymond W. *Postmark: Mekong Delta*. Westwood, N.Y.: Revell, 1968.

Johnson was a Navy chaplain, twice wounded. This is a collection of his letters home to his wife and children from Vietnam. Johnson served as chaplain to the men of River Assault Flotilla One.

711 Jones, Bruce E. *War without Windows: A True Account of a Young Army Officer Trapped in an Intelligence Cover-Up, Saigon*. New York: Vanguard, 1988.

Jones was an intelligence officer in Vietnam. He describes his own experiences in the war and also focuses on the military's attempt to conceal the strength of the Vietcong military, which led to many unnecessary American deaths. Bibliography.

712 Jones, James. *Viet Journal*. New York: Delacorte, 1973.

The *New York Times Magazine* asked James Jones, author of the famous war story *From Here to Eternity*, to go to both North and South Vietnam after the 1983 cease-fire to write what it was like there – "the sounds, the smells of Vietnam – after the end." The newspaper was seeking a novelist's viewpoint. These are his experiences.

713 Jury, Mark. *The Vietnam Photo Book*. New York: Grossman, 1971.

Jury was drafted and sent to Vietnam in 1969 where he served as an army photographer. The powerful black and white photographs are accompanied by narration, explanation, and personal accounts. The 1986 Vintage edition includes a preface by Bernard Edelman.

714 Just, Ward. *To What End: Report from Vietnam*. Boston: Houghton Mifflin, 1968.

Just writes of his experiences as a reporter in Vietnam and gives a warning about the progress of the war. Most interesting is a description of the atmosphere of South Vietnam from December 1965 to May 1967.

715 Keenan, Barbara Mullen. *Every Effort*. New York: St. Martin's, 1986.

The author's husband, Bill Keenan, was shot down over Laos in April 1966. As time went by, she became angry at the futile attempts by the U.S. to locate Bill and became a spokeswoman against the war and for the MIA families. Keenan tells of her life, her efforts to go on and raise her two children, and how she coped, caught between marriage and widowhood.

716 Kennerly, David Hume. *Shooter*. New York: Newsweek Books, 1979.
Kennerly is a Pulitzer-Prize-winning photographer. *Shooter* describes his experiences as a photographer in the Vietnam War as well as his later experiences as a White House photographer for President Ford. The text is liberally interspersed with photographs illustrating the various periods of his career.

717 Kerry, John, and Vietnam Veterans against the War. *The New Soldier*. New York: Macmillan, 1971.
The pictures and text of *The New Soldier* describe the veterans antiwar rally in Washington, D.C., on April 18, 1971. Fifty-four personal accounts of the war experiences of veterans are included. The book is edited by David Thorne and George Butler.

718 Ketwig, John. *. . . and a Hard Rain Fell: A GI's True Story of the War in Vietnam*. New York: Macmillan, 1985.
Ketwig went to Vietnam in 1967, a farm boy from upper New York. From his viewpoint as a private first class, he tells of what he saw, describes the change in his attitude from optimism to despair over the napalming of children and torture of women, the culture shock of Asia as well as the sense of alienation upon returning home. He fell in love with a Vietnamese prostitute whom he wanted to bring home. How he dealt with the end of the relationship is described.

719 Kimball, William R. *Vietnam: The Other Side of Glory*. Canton, Ohio: Daring Books, 1987.
Sixteen personal accounts of the Vietnam War by veterans who served there. Included are memoirs of a Green Beret, an army nurse, and a captured pilot.

720 Kirban, Salem. *Goodbye, Mr. President: The Story of One Man's Search for Peace*. Huntington Valley, Pa.: Salem Kirban, 1967.

Kirban's son enlisted in the army and went sent to Vietnam in 1967. The author wrote to President Johnson requesting a personal interview to discuss the war as an ordinary citizen. The president was unable to meet with him. Kirban then launched his own round-the-world citizen's fact-finding mission to Vietnam, Israel, Egypt, Jordan, and Russia on a search for peace. Photographs.

721   Kirk, Donald. *Tell It to the Dead: Memories of a War*. Chicago: Nelson-Hall, 1975.

Kirk was a correspondent from the *Chicago Tribune*. He came to concentrate more on the GI the longer he stayed in Vietnam. He describes his entry into Saigon in 1965, his experiences in the field, the low morale of the troops as the war drags on, racial and drug problems, and later the problems veterans encountered upon returning home. The theme that runs through his work is his shock at the incredible waste. At the conclusion, the author notes that bomber pilots never saw the damage they did. He tells of a former Marine speaking at a school who said "We negotiated a satisfactory conclusion. I am confident we achieved our aims. That's why we fought." Kirk says, "As a marine at Khe Sahn remarked, 'Tell it to the dead.'"

722   Klein, Joe. *Payback: Five Marines after Vietnam*. New York: Knopf, 1984.

Klein describes the readjustment experiences of five Vietnam veterans, one of which died in a berserk shootout with police in Illinois. This is a story of the difficulty of many veterans to readjust to life in peacetime and the confused attitudes of those who received them home.

723   Knoebl, Kuno. *Victor Charlie: The Face of War in Viet Nam*. New York: Praeger, 1967.

Knoebl was a Viennese journalist who had access to both sides in the war. He describes the North Vietnamese he met – in combat, behind the lines, and in villages – in an attempt to paint a more human face on the war. The book was translated by Abe Farbstein with an introduction by Bernard Fall.

724   Kovic, Ron. *Born on the Fourth of July*. New York: McGraw-Hill, 1976.

Kovic enlisted in the Marines in 1963, the year he graduated from high school. During his tour, he accidentally shot and killed a corporal in his outfit. Later he was wounded and paralyzed from the chest down. He was nineteen. Kovic describes his growing up in Long Island, his experiences in Vietnam on two tours, and the pain of his return home. He also tells of attending the Republican Convention and, with others, disrupting Nixon's acceptance speech.

725 Kukler, Michael A. *Operation Barooom*. Gastonia, N.C.: TPC, 1980.
Kukler was the Chief Information Non-Commissioned Officer in Vietnam where he served for thirty-two months. Operation Barooom was the code name used by the U.S. Military Assistance Command in Vietnam to parachute elephants into remote areas of South Vietnam to the mountain people, the Montagnards. The book is a series of short vignettes about the war, a collage of stories, interesting trivia, factual information and statistics in no particular order of arrangement. Drawings, maps, photographs. Interesting browsing. The book is subtitled "Saigon Tea Number One, Vietnam Number Ten."

726 Kunen, James Simon. *Standard Operating Procedure: Notes of a Draft-Age American*. New York: Avon, 1971.
This is a transcript of the proceedings of the national Veterans' Inquiry held in Washington, D.C., in 1970 in which veterans testified to the atrocities they had witnessed in Vietnam. Kunen provides a commentary on the testimony. He is the author of *The Strawberry Statement.*

727 Labin, Suzanne. *Vietnam: An Eyewitness Account*. Springfield, Va.: Crestwood Books, 1964.
The author, a noted French writer, describes the 1963 military coup in Vietnam and her experiences there. The account includes conversations with noted leaders including President Diem and Madame Nhu among others. She warns about the dangers of Communism and discusses the future of Vietnam.

728 Lane, Mark. *Conversations with Americans*. New York: Simon & Schuster, 1970.
Lane interviewed thirty-two Vietnam vets from deserters to decorated soldiers. He emphasizes the atrocities performed by

American soldiers in Vietnam and the war's ultimate affect on the men themselves as well as the moral fiber of the nation. The brutality of military training is shown. The stories are often told in a question/answer format with Lane and the interviewee. Accounts of torture and fragging abound. Eye-opening and definitely not a pleasant read, but this was more shocking at the time of its publication date (1970) than it is now.

729 Lang, Daniel. *Casualties of War*. New York: McGraw-Hill, 1969.

Lang, a writer, tells the story of a former private first class from Minnesota who he calls Sven Eriksson "to protect the identity of the real soldier for his safety." This soldier was ordered, with four others, to guard a young Vietnamese peasant girl in the Central Highlands in 1966. The others raped and killed her. Private Eriksson eventually instigated court martial proceedings against them. *Casualties of War* originally appeared in the *New Yorker*, 18 October 1969, 61-146, under the title "A Reporter At Large: Casualties of War." It was subsequently expanded to book length.

730 Lanning, Michael Lee. *The Only War We Had: A Platoon Leader's Journal of Vietnam*. New York: Ballantine, 1987.

Lanning's story is presented in the form of a journal which he kept in Vietnam where he served as an infantry platoon leader, reconnaissance platoon leader and company commander in 1969-70. The title comes from a well-used phrase among soldiers. Lanning went to war excited for the adventure, an attitude which quickly paled in the face of experience. An honest account of the horrors of the war and the responsibilities accepted by the platoon leaders for their men. The 1988 Ivy Books edition bears the subtitle "A Company Commander's Journal."

731 Larteguy, Jean. *The Face of War: Reflections on Men and Combat*. Indianapolis: Bobbs-Merrill, 1979.

Larteguy, French soldier, war correspondent, and novelist, presents his memories and reflections of the wars that affected his life, particularly his twenty-five years in Vietnam. Larteguy is one of the most important foreign writers to deal with the Vietnam War.

732 Levy, Charles J. *Spoils of War*. Boston: Houghton Mifflin, 1974.

Levy, a sociologist, interviewed Vietnam veterans and describes the violence Marines committed against Vietnamese villagers, South Vietnamese soldiers, their own officers, and each other. Accounts of court martial trials are included as well as the experiences of vets returning from Vietnam and the readjustment problems they encountered. Particular emphasis is placed on the violent behavior that often occurred back in the states.

733 Lifton, Robert Jay. *Home from the War: Vietnam Veterans – Neither Victims nor Executioners. New York: Simon & Schuster, 1973.*
Lifton presents a psychological study of the soldier in Vietnam and at home, particularly those involved in atrocities like My Lai. He notes that Vietnam veterans are more alienated than veterans of other wars. Personal narratives are included throughout. An important book.

734 Linedecker, Clifford L., with Michael and Maureen Ryan. *Kerry: Agent Orange and an American Family.* New York: St. Martin's, 1982.
In 1970 Maureen Ryan gave birth to a daughter, Kerry, who was born with multiple serious defects. Michael Ryan had been a draftee to Vietnam and was exposed to herbicides. This is the story of their struggle to keep their child alive and to win recognition and compensation from the government for the defects caused by the use of herbicides. Appendix of helpful organizations, transcript of Maureen Ryan's testimony before the Senate, and a bibliography.

735 Lovy, Andrew. *Vietnam Diary, October, 1967-July, 1968.* New York: Exposition Press, 1970.
A surgeon's daily record of his experiences in Vietnam.

736 Lowry, Timothy S. *And Brave Men, Too.* New York: Crown, 1985.
The author, who served two tours in Vietnam is a journalist who traveled across the U.S. interviewing recipients of the Congressional Medal of Honor. Included are stories of fourteen soldiers told in chronological order which create a complete picture of the war and its costs in human terms. "A History of the Medal of Honor" by F. E. Ferguson is also included.

737 Lucas, Jim G. *Dateline: Viet Nam.* New York: Award House, 1966.

An interesting early day-by-day account of the war. Lucas, winner of the Ernie Pyle and Pulitzer prizes, describes Vietnam and the war through his dispatches during 1964-66 when he was the first, and for the first six months, the only reporter assigned to American combat troops in the Mekong Delta. He was the first reporter allowed to fly north of the 17th parallel. Vivid descriptions of jungle combat. The book includes an introduction by Robin Moore, author of *The Green Berets*.

738   Luce, Don, and John Sommer. *Vietnam: The Unheard Voices*. Ithaca, N.Y.: Cornell University Press, 1969.
    The authors went to Vietnam as volunteers for International Voluntary Services (IVS). Their book is a composite of their separate and individual experiences in Vietnam and those of their friends and co-workers there during the war. The authors state that their purpose is "to demonstrate that understanding people is the key to successful policy, that failure to understand them and respond to their needs is to fail in one's goals, and finally that a great America cannot win hearts and minds by technology and material means alone. A concern for the human spirit is not a luxury; it is an essential." Forward by Edward M. Kennedy. Index.

739   Lunn, Hugh. *Vietnam: A Reporter's War*. New York: Stein & Day, 1985.
    Lunn, an Australian, was a Reuters correspondent in Vietnam in 1967 and describes his experiences and friendship with Pham Ngoc Dinh, a fellow reporter who survived the fall of Saigon.

740   Lynd, Alice, comp. *We Won't Go: Personal Accounts of War Objections*. Boston: Beacon Press, 1968.
    Twenty-four students who resisted the draft and protested the war relate their struggles with their consciences and their activities during the war. Those whose essays are included answered the questions provided by the authors:

1.   What did you do to resist or avoid military service?
2.   How did you decide what you would do? (What influenced you? What choices did you have to make? What pressures did you feel?)
3.   Were you part of a group concerned with the draft? If so, please describe and evaluate the group experience.

4. What happened to you as a result of acting on your beliefs?
5. How do you feel now about what you have been through?
6. What issues seem most important to you? What do you want your action to make people think about?
7. Is there anything you would like to say to others who are trying to decide what they should do about the draft or military service?

741 McAuley, Anna K. *Miles from Home*. Wakefield, Mass.: AKLM, 1984.

742 McCarthy, Mary. *The Seventeenth Degree*. New York: Harcourt Brace Jovanovich, 1974.

McCarthy reports her observations and commentaries on the Vietnam War. This book includes the previously published *Vietnam, Hanoi,* and *Medina* and the review of Halberstam's *The Best and the Brightest*, "Sons of the Morning" (see 1470).

743 McConnell, Malcolm. *Into the Mouth of the Cat: The Story of Lance Sijan, Hero of Vietnam*. New York: Norton, 1985.

Sijan, a soldier from Wisconsin, was ejected from his plane over the jungle mountains of Laos. Severely crippled, he evaded capture and dragged himself on his back through the terrain for 146 days until he was finally captured on Christmas Day. He escaped the Bamboo Prison Camp where he was held but was recaptured, tortured, and died in Hanoi of untreated wounds, pneumonia and malnutrition. His example inspired other American prisoners to resist torture. The title comes from the patch B-57 crews who flew night strikes over North Vietnam wore on their jacket – a yellow-eyed cat wearing a pirate's patch.

744 McDaniel, Eugene B., and James L. Johnson. *Before Honor*. Philadelphia: A.J. Holman, 1975.

McDaniel was a Navy pilot shot down over North Vietnam, captured and imprisoned for over six years in the Hanoi Hilton and eventually Zoo Annex. He was tortured after repeated attempts to escape. He stresses how his religious faith helped him. Photographs.

745 McDaniel, Norman A. *Yet Another Voice*. New York: Hawthorne Books, 1975.

McDaniel was shot down over North Vietnam and held prisoner for seven years. He describes how his faith sustained him both in the POW camp, where he and other POWs held secret religious services, and later at home during the readjustment to normal life. Photographs.

746 McDonald, Glenn. *Report or Distort*. Jericho, N.Y.: Exposition Press, 1973.

The author was an Army combat correspondent in Vietnam from 1966-69 and later a free-lance journalist there. He describes his experiences in combat and reports on how the war was being reported by the media at that time. McDonald devotes a chapter to the work of women journalists. Included is an appendix of newsmen killed, wounded, or missing and a selection of outstanding war writing. Photographs.

747 McDonough, James R. *Platoon Leader*. Novato, Calif.: Presidio Press, 1985.

McDonough, a West Point graduate, was an infantry platoon leader in Vietnam in 1970. He describes his arrival as an inexperienced soldier and how he learned to become a leader – the decisions involved, the battles, and how the life and death responsibilities changed him.

748 McGinnis, Joe. *Heroes*. New York: Viking Press, 1976.

The author ponders the question of what makes a hero and wonders why in our age heroism has become mere celebrity. He interviewed some of the heroes of the 1960s and 1970s including Daniel Berrigan, General Westmoreland, and Lt. Joe Hooper, the most decorated soldier of the Vietnam War.

749 McGrady, Mike. *A Dove in Vietnam*. New York: Funk & Wagnalls, 1968.

A reporter for *Newsday,* McGrady writes of his experiences in covering Vietnam, especially the use of herbicides, the battles and the men, and the corruption he saw in Saigon. He notes that it cost $500,000 to kill a single enemy soldier. He also tells of the effect of the war deaths on American families.

750 McGrath, John M. *Prisoner of War: Six Years in Hanoi*. Annapolis, Md.: Naval Institute Press, 1975.

McGrath was a Navy pilot captured in June, 1967. He graphically tells the story of life in a prison camp, feeling that these stories must be told to refute Communist claims that POWs were treated humanely. The text is accompanied by pen and ink drawings by the author that are as compelling and powerful as the text.

751 McKay, Gary. *In Good Company: One Man's War in Vietnam*. Sydney, Australia: Allen & Unwin, 1987.

McKay, who trained cadets at the Royal Military College in Duntroon, Australia, wrote this book to remind his young officers what a platoon commander's life is like in war. He was drafted and led a rifle platoon in Vietnam, returning home in 1971 after nearly losing the total use of his arm after a serious wound. In this thoughtful book, the author not only relates his experiences but discusses the draft, fear of and in combat, and delayed stress. Glossary, index.

752 McLeod, Jesse T. *Crew Chief*. Canton, Ohio: Daring Books, 1988.

The author relates his experiences in as a door gunner on an assault helicopter in Vietnam during the Tet Offensive. He witnessed incidents of fragging, American atrocities, and children who functioned as terrorists. Photographs, bibliography.

753 MacPherson, Myra. *Long Time Passing: Vietnam and the Haunted Generation*. Garden City, N.Y.: Doubleday, 1984.

Five hundred men and women were interviewed to determine the war's impact on the generation that came of age during the 1960s and 1970s. The stories come from soldiers, draft dodgers, protesters, and deserters among others. The authors stress the human cost of this war and who was asked to fight it and for what in view of an American apparently poised to do the same in Central America. The epilogue, "Requiem for a Generation," is a poignant summary. Glossary, notes, bibliography, index.

754 Mailer, Norman. *The Armies of the Night: History as a Novel, The Novel as History*. New York: New American Library, 1968.

Mailer chronicles his adventures over the four days of the October 1967 anti-Vietnam demonstration in Washington, D.C., a history of the March on the Pentagon. This is considered one of the first of the nonfiction novels. The title was suggested by a line from Matthew Arnold's poem "Dover Beach."

755 Mangiolardo, Michael. *My Days in Vietnam*. New York: Vantage, 1969.
  This is the diary of a young soldier in Vietnam, a day-to-day description full of the little details of his life, from going over by ship up to the time of his death while defending a bridge. Three poems at the end of the book are written by friends and family. Illustrated throughout by Mangiolardo's own photographs taken in Vietnam. Very personal and poignant.

756 Mangold, Tom, and John Penycate. *The Tunnels of Cu Chi*. New York: Random House, 1985.
  An explanation of the elaborate tunnel system utilized by the North Vietnamese, *The Tunnels of Cu Chi* contains some eyewitness accounts, but is more history than personal narrative. Included is the poem, "The Mother-the Native Land" by Duong Huong Ly.

757 Manning, Robert, ed. *The Vietnam Experience Series*. Boston: Boston Publishing Company, 1981-88.
  Manning is editor in chief of the twenty-five volume series, *The Vietnam Experience*, which provides a extensive overview of the war. Several of the volumes present personal accounts of war experiences: *America Takes Over: The Big Build-Up* (vol. 4); *The Contagion of War: The Way the War Was Fought, 1965-67* (vol. 5); *Nineteen Sixty-Eight: The Tet Offensive* (vol. 6); *A War Remembered: Voice from Vietnam* (vol. 19, see 861); *Words of War: An Anthology of Vietnam War Literature* (vol. 24, see 878).

758 Marks, Richard E. *The Letters of Pfc. Richard E. Marks, USMC*. Philadelphia: Lippincott, 1967.
  Richard Marks died in Da Nang in 1966. He was nineteen. These are the letters he wrote home to family and friends describing his experiences in boot camp, on Parris Island, and in Vietnam. The last letter is dated three days before his death.

759 Marshall, Kathryn. *In the Combat Zone: An Oral History of American Women in Vietnam, 1966-1975*. Boston: Little, Brown, 1987.

Marshall interviewed twenty women who tell of their experiences in the war. They discuss their many motives for going to Vietnam, their experiences, and the affect it had on their lives. It is only recently that books such as this have begun to tell the women's stories. The author notes the large number of women, military and civilian, who served, quoting statistics from the department of Defense and the Veterans Administration. These women include army nurses, Donut Dollies, American civilians living in Saigon; some were church affiliated. Bibliography.

760 Marshall, S. L. A. *Bringing up the Rear: A Memoir*. San Rafael, Calif.: Presidio Press, 1979.

At seventeen, Samuel Lyman Atwood Marshall was the youngest soldier ever to be commissioned in the U.S. Army, and he served from the days of Pancho Villa to Vietnam, retiring as a brigadier general. He also covered wars as a reporter. These are his memoirs of over fifty years in the military. He died in 1977. Also of interest are:

Ambush. New York: Cowles, 1969. The story of the battle of Dau Tieng. On site interviews with survivors included.

Battles in the Monsoon: Campaigning in the Central Highlands, Summer 1966. New York: Cowles, 1966. Small-unit combat is described through personal narratives.

Bird: The Christmastide Battle. New York: Cowles, 1968. An account of a battle at Binh Dinh.

The Fields of Bamboo. New York: Dial, 1971. Story of the battles of Dong Tre, Trung Luong, and Hoa Hoi in June and October, 1966. Published in 1982 as *Vietnam – Three Battles*.

Lessons Learned: A Vietnam Primer. Sims, Ark.: Lancer Militaria, 1967. Written with Lt. Col. David H. Hackworth. A critique of command practices and battle tactics in small-unit combat in Vietnam, May 1966-February 1967.

West to Cambodia. New York: Cowles, 1968. Describes a battle to stop infiltration along the Vietnamese/Cambodian border. The U.S.

4th and 25th Infantry Divisions and Special Forces fought three regiments of North Vietnamese.

761 Martin, Earl S. *Reaching the Other Side*. New York: Crown, 1978.
 Reaching the Other Side is the journal of an American who stayed in Vietnam, witnessing the postwar transition. A Mennonite, Martin had volunteered to go to help orphans during the war. He spent five years in Vietnam and describes the end and the aftermath.

762 Mason, Robert. *Chickenhawk*. New York: Viking Press, 1983.
 Robert Mason was one of the first assault helicopter pilots in Vietnam in 1965, flying over 1,000 combat missions in one tour. His memoir is a vivid description of the life of these pilots, the frustration of taking the same patch of jungle over and over again, as well as the psychological effects of the war and the shock of a hostile welcome home.

763 Meshad, Shad. *Captain for Dark Mornings*. Playa del Rey, Calif.: Creative Image Associates, 1982.
 Meshad was a human services officer in the army, at the 95th Evacuation Hospital in Da Nang, responsible for the psychological well-being of the 70,000 troops of I Corps in South Vietnam in 1970. He dealt with problems caused by racial tension, stress, drugs, low morale, alienation, fragging incidents, and suicides. Meshad also helicoptered to bases and fire stations. This account shows the affect of the war on everyone involved, including those at home.

764 Miller, Carolyn P. *Captured!* Chappaqua, N.Y.: Christian Herald Books, 1977.
 Miller was a member of the Wycliffe Bible Translators assigned to Vietnam in 1961 where she was preparing a translation of the Bible (and other literary materials) in the Bru language – the language of a Vietnamese tribe in the South. The author, her husband, and her daughter were captured by communists in Banmethuot in 1975 and held for nine months.

765 Miller, Melissa, and Phil M. Shenk. *The Path of Most Resistance: Stories of Mennonite Conscientious Objectors Who Did Not Cooperate with the Vietnam War Draft*. Scottsdale, Pa.: Herald Press, 1982.

A presentation of the stories of ten of the fifty plus young Mennonites who refused to be drafted. These were men who refused alternate service. The resisters came from Kansas, Pennsylvania, Ohio, Indiana, and Virginia. Some were imprisoned, some fled to Canada, some were sentenced to probationary service assignments, some were not prosecuted, and some were forced to comply by coercion or circumstance.

766 Miner, Ernest. *Vietnam by Those Who Served: The War that Was and Was Not*. Great Neck, N.Y.: Todd and Honeywell, 1985.

Miner volunteered for two tours in Vietnam and retired from the Army in 1976 after twenty years of service. The book is dedicated to Max Cleland and includes special pages recognizing the dead in Vietnam, MIAs, Bob Hope, and the POWs. The author interviewed veterans and asked them to give their views on the war, noting any changes in viewpoint they experienced, and to comment on the problems they faced upon returning home. The result is a collection of very brief remarks, unattributed to individual writers. Also included is a letter from a father who lost a son in the war and the author's response as well as a poem by the author.

767 Morris, Jim. *War Story*. Boulder, Colo.: Paladin Press, 1979.

Morris was a Green Beret. This is the story of the Beret's relationship and work with the Montagnards – Vietnamese primitive tribesman of the Central Highlands.

768 Mulligan, Hugh A. *No Place to Die: The Agony of Viet Nam*. New York: Morrow, 1967.

Mulligan was a correspondent for AP in Vietnam in 1965 for six months and in 1966 for another six months. He relates his experiences and stresses the dangers to reporters, recounting their deaths. He describes the battles and soldiers and compares them to other wars.

769 Mulligan, James A. *The Hanoi Commitment*. Virginia Beach, Va.: RIF Marketing, 1981.

Mulligan was shot down in 1966, captured by the North Vietnamese, and held for seven years in the Hanoi Hilton, forty-two months of which were spent in solitary confinement. He describes the torture, beatings, sanitation, starvation, loneliness, and includes copies of letters the Vietnamese allowed the author to write home. He was released in 1973.

770 Munson, Glenn. *Letters from Vietnam*. New York: Parallax, 1966.

This Week magazine published selections of letters from servicemen in Vietnam in a series of articles. This collection of letters was selected from those submitted to *This Week*. The letters are fascinating, ironic, and ultimately heart-breaking. All the names of the letter writers are listed on the last page, with no indication as to who returned and who didn't.

771 Murphy, Edward F. *Vietnam Medal of Honor Heroes*. New York: Ballantine, 1987.

The stories of the actions which gained the Congressional Medal of Honor for 132 soldiers of the Vietnam War. Also included is a history of the medal and a register of all Vietnam War Congressional Medal of Honor recipients.

772 Nasmyth, Virginia, and Spike Nasmyth. *Hanoi Release John Nasmyth: A Family Love Story*. Santa Paula, Calif.: V Parr Publishers, 1984.

John Nasmyth, shot down on a mission, was a POW at the Hanoi Hilton. His sister, Virginia, began the story in 1969 when he was declared MIA. He was released in 1973 and helped his sister finish the story by relating his experiences. Also described is the ordeal of the family as they waited first for news and then for his release. Virginia Nasmyth describes her efforts to alert Washington to the plight of the MIA's. A list of Nasmyth's friends who did not survive is included plus facsimiles of letters. Photographs.

773 Ngan Nguyen Ngan, and E. E. Richie. *The Will of Heaven: A Story of One Vietnamese and the End of His World*. New York: Dutton, 1982.

The author was a twenty-seven year old father and husband when Saigon fell to the North Vietnamese. He had lived a middle class life in a quiet residential area of Saigon and did not escape in 1975. He had been a school teacher, was inducted into the South Vietnamese army, and was twice wounded before being returned to Saigon prior to the fall. After the fall, he was compelled to serve a ten day "reeducation term" which became three years of forced labor in the jungle. After his return to Saigon, he realized he and his family would need to escape. They became boat people, eventually ending up in Malaysia. He was sponsored by the Canadian government and now lives in British Columbia.

774 Nguyen Cao Ky. *Twenty Years and Twenty Days*. New York: Stein & Day, 1976.

The autobiography of the famous former Prime Minister of the Republic of Vietnam from 1965-67. Ky describes the corruption in Saigon and within the American establishment and gives an indictment of the American character and our dealings with foreigners-an inability or unwillingness to deal with cultural differences. Ky gives his opinions on the handling of the war and why it was lost.

775 Nguyen Thi Dinh. *No Other Road to Take: Memoir of Mrs. Nguyen Thi Dinh*. Ithaca, N.Y.: Cornell University Press, 1976.

The author was the deputy commander of the NLF Armed Forces. She describes the early stages of the revolutionary movement in South Vietnam in 1959-60 and her activities in the movement, particularly the 1960 uprising against Diem's regime in Ben Tre province. Translated by Mai Van Elliott.

776 Nichols, John B., and Barrett Tillman. *On Yankee Station: The Naval Air War over Vietnam*. Annapolis, Md.: Naval Institute Press, 1987.

Nichols was a fighter pilot who flew 350 missions off a carrier in the Gulf of Tonkin. Tillman, an aviation historian, gives a "cockpit view of war"-what it was like to fly from *Yankee Station* (the carrier used for air strikes against North Vietnam), 1964-73. Tactics are discussed but also personal experiences. The book does lean to aviation history. Appendix includes air strike statistics and a chronology.

777 Noel, Chris, with Bill Tredwell. *Matter of Survival: The "War" Jane Never Saw*. Boston: Branden, 1987.

The author, a movie and television actress, entertained troops in Vietnam for four years, traveling across Vietnam and encouraging troops via radio. She survived a helicopter crash. Upon returning home, she experienced post traumatic stress, and spent three months in a mental hospital. She describes her experiences, the things she saw, and the way she was treated when she returned home. A chapter is devoted to Jane Fonda's activities. Noel's work with veterans organizations is described.

778 Noel, Reuben, and Nancy Noel. *Saigon for a Song: The True Story of a Vietnam Gig to Remember*. Phoenix: USC Press, 1987.

The authors, a comedy-singing team, entertained troops in Vietnam for six months between 1968 and 1969. They describe the corruption in Saigon, black market activities as well as the soldiers they met. The two authors take turns giving their impressions in the narrative.

779 O'Brien, Tim. *If I Die in a Combat Zone*. New York: Delacorte, 1973.

Considered one of the best books to come out of the war, *If I Die in a Combat Zone* is the story of one foot soldier's journey from safe, middle class America to the center of the nightmare of the Vietnam War. It is typical of the stories of so many of the soldiers in this particular war – the fear and the moral dilemmas are emphasized. The title of the book is derived from the song the soldiers sang as they marched. O'Brien served form 1968-1970 in the infantry. He won seven medals and a Purple Heart.

780 O'Connor, John J. *A Chaplain Looks at Vietnam*. New York: World, 1968.

The author was a military chaplain in Vietnam where he received a Legion of Merit decoration. He describes his experiences and explores the moral implications of the war.

781 Page, Tim. *Page after Page*. London: Sidgwick and Jackson, 1988.

An autobiography of a noted war photographer of the Vietnam War who was the model for one of the heroes of Herr's *Dispatches*.

782 _____. *Tim Page's Nam*. New York: Knopf, 1983.

A powerful photographic essay of the war. Page was a British photographer working in Vietnam and was wounded twice while working for Time-Life. Finally, a massive head wound left him paralyzed on the left side. The photographs were exhibited at the Institute of Contemporary Arts in London.

783 Palmer, Laura. *Shrapnel in the Heart: Letters and Remembrances from the Vietnam Memorial*. New York: Random House, 1987.

Since its dedication in 1982, the Vietnam Veterans Memorial in Washington, D. C. has attracted letters and other memorabilia from the loved ones whose names appear on the Wall. Palmer, a reporter who was assigned to Vietnam and covered the fall of Saigon, selected 100 letters left at the wall and traced the letter writers across the country to hear their stories. Photographs of the dead are included with the letters. A powerful but sad book to read.

784 Parks, David. *G.I. Diary*. Washington, D.C.: Howard University Press, 1984.

David Parks, son of the noted photographer/writer, Gordon Parks, kept a written and photographic record of his war experiences on the advice of his father. The resulting diary relates the experiences of a black soldier, from a relatively affluent background, in Vietnam. The author is as concerned about his conflict with white soldiers as he is with the enemy. He presents an interesting counterpoint to Terry's *Bloods*. The author uses fictitious names and places. Maps. Photographs.

785 Parrish, John. *Twelve, Twenty and Five: A Doctor's Year in Vietnam*. New York: Dutton, 1972.

Dr. John Parrish, fresh from an internal medicine residency at University Hospital in Ann Arbor, Michigan, served as a doctor at the Marine Base camp in Phu Bai. The title refers to the announcement by the corpsmen delivering the wounded by helicopter of the number of wounded, dying, and dead on arrival. This very readable narrative is written with compassion and humor and details the real horror and waste of war from a medical point of view.

786 Parry, Francis Fox. *Three-War Marines: The Pacific, Korea, Vietnam*. Pacifica, Calif.: Pacifica Press, 1987.

The author is a retired Marine artillery officer, a 1941 graduate of Annapolis, who served on General Westmorland's staff in Vietnam. He describes his experiences in several wars including Vietnam and comments on the errors that lead to the outcome of that war. Photographs, maps.

787 Patterson, Charles J., and G. Lee Tippin. *The Heroes Who Fell from Grace*. Canton, Ohio: Daring Books, 1985.

Patterson tells the story of Operation Lazarus – the attempt to free American POWs from Laos in 1982. He maintains that American POWs are still in Southeast Asia. The actor Clint Eastwood was involved in this operation.

788 Pickerell, James H. *Vietnam in the Mud*. New York: Bobbs-Merrill, 1966.

A photojournalist's view of the war, written in 1966, in which Pickerell gives his opinion of what mistakes are being made, based on his experiences while accompanying soldiers into battle.

789 Pilger, John. *The Last Day*. New York: Vintage, 1975.

Pilger has written a personal account of the fall of Saigon, told in a you-are-there style. The events of each hour are reported as the author, a reporter, saw them from the American embassy. Very effective. Photographs.

790 Plumb, Charles. *I'm No Hero: A POW Story as Told to Glen de Werff*. Independence, Mo.: Independence Press, 1973.

Plumb was captured in 1967 after being shot down near Hanoi and held in a prison camp called "the Plantation." The elaborate communication system the prisoners used is described as well as their transfer to the Hanoi Hilton. Plumb feels that he is no hero because "I have joined the ranks of millions of Americans who have applied heroic principles in overcoming hardships." He explains how he was able to survive – through faith in God, love of country, self-discipline, and pride. Drawings.

791 Polner, Murray. *No Victory Parades: The Return of the Vietnam Veteran*. New York: Holt, Rinehart & Winston, 1971.

Based on interviews with over 200 veterans, *No Victory Parades* is a study of the impact of the war on those who fought. The nine chosen to speak in this book are divided into three categories: Hawks,

Doves, and the Haunted. Although there is a recognition that long-range effects won't be known, this 1971 book seems optimistic. The positive effects of the war are noted, namely learning and personality growth. However, there is a discussion of early delayed stress symptoms, and the author makes note of a comment that Remarque's WWI veteran made in *All Quiet on the Western Front*: "The war has ruined us for everything." This may be even more true for the Vietnam War. It would be interesting to see a 1980s follow-up of these men. Bibliography.

792 Prashker, Ivan. *Duty, Honor, Vietnam: Twelve Men of West Point Tell Their Story*. New York: Arbor House/Morrow, 1988.

Twelve West Point career officers from the classes of 1950-1968 are interviewed to ascertain their opinions on the changes in the army, society, and their perspectives on Vietnam. The officer's wives also respond. This is an attempt to determine the affect of the military on the lives of the men involved in it as a career.

793 Pratt, John Clark. *Vietnam Voices: Perspectives on the War Years, 1941-1982*. New York: Viking, 1984.

Pratt is a retired lieutenant colonel, an English professor, and a Vietnam War archivist. His *Vietnam Voices* is history and personal narrative – the story of the Vietnam War told in chronological order by career military men, veterans, Vietnamese on both sides, and those on the home front. The author attempts to include all points of view. Official documents are included throughout, and the volume provides an excellent overview that is at once scholarly and personal. Comprehensive bibliography.

794 Ransom, Robert C., Jr. *Letters from Vietnam*. Bronxville, N.Y.: n.p., 1968.

Ransom was from Bronxville, New York. When he received his draft notice in 1966, he enlisted and eventually commanded a platoon of forty-three men after arriving in Vietnam in 1967. Ransom was wounded, returned to battle, was wounded a second time, and died of peritonitis and pneumonia on May 11, 1968, after major surgery. He was twenty-two. These are his letters home and those of his nurse describing his death to his parents. Also included are the letters announcing the two Bronze star medal he won. The book is introduced by the poem "The Young Dead Soldiers" by Archibald MacLeish.

795   Rausa, Rosario. *Gold Wings, Blue Sea: A Naval Aviator's Story.* Annapolis, Md.: Naval Institute Press, 1980.

   Rausa flew 150 combat missions of the deck of the *USS Coral Sea* as a career naval aviator. This book resulted from a series of articles on his experiences that he wrote for *Naval Aviation News* from 1973-80 under the title "Soliloquy."

796   Ray Michele. *The Two Shores of Hell: A French Journalist's Life among the Vietcong and the GI's of Vietnam.* New York: McKay, 1968.

   The author was a French journalist and photographer in Vietnam who was captured by Vietcong and taken into guerilla territory. She relates her experiences with the Vietcong, the American soldiers she interviewed, and the South Vietnamese she met, both soldiers and civilians, especially children. In this book, she is angrily opposed to the U.S. presence in Vietnam. The book was translated by Elisabeth Abbott.

797   Reed, David. *Up Front in Vietnam.* New York: Funk & Wagnalls, 1967.

   Reed was a correspondent who spent months in the field during the war. *Up Front in Vietnam* is a series of sixty-five stories about the infantryman. He shows what it's like to be in combat, a picture of "the man to whom the government of the U.S. turns when it decides to wage war." The stories also reflect the pain of the Vietnamese villagers.

798   Regan, David J. *Mourning Glory: The Making of a Marine.* Old Greenwich, Conn.: Devin-Adair, 1981.

   Regan came to Vietnam as a naive seventeen year old Midwesterner. Often coming into conflict with his superiors, he won seven medals, but he also was involved in two court martial trials. He describes his training, experiences, combat, and what war does to a individual.

799   Reston, James, Jr. *The Amnesty of John David Herndon.* New York: McGraw-Hill, 1973.

   John David Herndon, a high school drop-out, went AWOL from the army in 1970 and eventually got to Paris where he lived underground for two years. He returned to the U.S. voluntarily in 1972 under the sponsorship of Safe Return, a veterans' organization, to face charges as a test case. The army was reluctant to pursue this and dishonorably discharged him. This is his story.

800 Risner, Robinson. *The Passing of the Night*. New York: Random House, 1973.
     Although tortured and publicly humiliated by the North Vietnamese, Col. Risner writes that "the distinctive character of imprisonment in a North Vietnamese prison camp was the suffocating monotony . . . the pervasive sameness of the routine, over and over, day in and day out." Risner was shot down over North Vietnam in 1965 and spent seven years in Hoa Lo Prison, the Hanoi Hilton. Risner's faith in the future and appreciation for his country was strengthened by his ordeal.

801 Rowan, Stephen A. *They Wouldn't Let Us Die: The Prisoners of War Tell Their Story*. Middle Village, N.Y.: Jonathan David, 1973.
     The author, an American-based Canadian journalist, interviewed POWs to determine how they were able to survive the years of physical and mental torture and deprivation. He questioned them as to their feelings, psychological reactions to events and people, coping mechanisms, what they thought of their captors, those back home, and Jane Fonda. The result is a psychological portrait of a POW.

802 Rowe, James N. *Five Years to Freedom*. Boston: Little, Brown, 1971.
     Rowe was a Special Forces major captured by the Vietcong during a firefight in South Vietnam. He was held in a Vietcong POW camp in the South and subjected to incredible conditions while continually being pressured to "confess" to his "crimes." He tells of the terrible sanitary conditions and the deaths of other Americans. After two previous escape attempts failed, he finally escaped in 1968 and was picked up by American helicopters. The author emphasizes the need to bring home those who are still there. Photographs.

803 Russ, Martin. *Happy Hunting Ground*. New York: Atheneum, 1968.
     Russ wrote of his Marine experiences in Korea in *The Last Parallel* in 1957. Wanting to observe and experience Vietnam in the light of his own combat experiences, he went to Vietnam in 1966 as an unaffiliated correspondent, spending six months in the field with Vietnamese, American, and Australian troops. Russ's journal and his

letters home form the basis for this book which is subtitled, "An E-Marine's odyssey in Vietnam," The author's note indicates that fictitious names have been used throughout the book.

804 Rutledge, Howard, and Phyllis Rutledge. *In the Presence of Mine Enemies, 1965-1973*. Old Tappan, N.J.: Fleming H. Revell, 1973.

This is the story of Howard Rutledge, who parachuted into North Vietnamese hands after his plane exploded, and the seven years he was held prisoner in the Hanoi Hilton. Rutledge's wife chronicles her years of anguish, not knowing the fate of her husband. The book emphasizes the religious faith of the writers as a sustaining force for them.

805 Sack, John. *M*. New York: New American Library, 1966.

Sack was commissioned by *Esquire* to follow a U.S. army infantry company, M Company, from basic training through the first engagement in battle. The first battle resulted in the death of a seven year old girl. Although he was supposed to be impartial, Sack soon became involved in the lives of the men of the company. *M* is considered to be one of the major books of Vietnam War literature.

806 _____. *The Man-Eating Machine*. New York: Farrar, Straus & Giroux, 1967.

Sack writes of how elements in American society turn men into inhuman parts of a machine. He says "Vietnam was another front in the Armageddon of the machine against man." He presents four stories of such men, all of whom are Vietnam veterans: Varoujan Demirgian, who never killed a communist in Vietnam, Robert Melvin, a black veteran working his way up the corporate ladder on Madison Avenue, Vantee Thompson, who returns to the States to find himself on riot control duty, and William Calley. Sack notes that man is less responsible as systems grow more complex. He seems to ignore the concept of free will in his discussion of his theme.

807 Sadler, Barry. *I'm a Lucky One*. New York: Macmillan, 1967.

The soldier who wrote "The Ballad of the Green Berets" tells of his training to be a Green Beret, serving in Vietnam, being wounded by a punji stick that caused a massive leg infection, his return home, and his song-writing success.

808 Salisbury, Harrison E. *Behind the Lines – Hanoi, December 23, 1966–January 7, 1967*. New York: Harper & Row, 1967.

Salisbury was finally allowed to go to North Vietnam after eighteen months of effort. This is his account of how the war looked from the enemy's side, seen during the height of the war. Photographs.

809 ____, ed. *Vietnam Reconsidered*. New York: Harper & Row, 1984.

A group of more than eighty American newsmen, historians, diplomats, and military and intelligence officers met at a symposium held in 1983 at the University of California, Los Angeles, seeking to find some answers, some lessons from the Vietnam War. In this collection of papers from their discussion, journalists discuss the difficulty of covering such as war and the affect of the war on broadcast journalism. Military leaders discussed American involvement, desertion, and home front resistance. Veterans provided input, and several poems by Bruce Weigl are included. In a final section, Vietnamese speakers have a chance to relate their experiences. An appendix is included which lists the number of gallons of herbicide applied in South Vietnam between 1965 and 1971. A powerful, important book.

810 Santoli, Al, ed. *Everything We Had: An Oral History of the Vietnam War by Thirty-Three American Soldiers Who Fought It*. New York: Random House, 1981.

An oral history by thirty-three veterans that takes the reader from December 1962 to the fall of Saigon on April 29, 1975. Santoli wanted these soldiers to have a chance to speak of their experiences and the American people to know what these men were really like, what the war was like. The author, one of those who provides an account, fought in the 1968 Tet Offensive and received three Purple Hearts and a Bronze Star for valor. Photographs, glossary, biographies.

811 ____. *To Bear Any Burden: The Vietnam War and Its Aftermath in the Words of Americans and Southeast Asians*. New York: Dutton, 1985.

A companion to *Everything We Had, To Bear Any Burden* focuses on the human side of the war in a series of forty-eight personal accounts of experiences relating to the Vietnam War by Vietnamese, before, during, and after the war, and by Americans, soldiers, nurses, journalists, and many others, in an attempt to answer the need to discover the meaning of the war. Glossary, biography, chronology, photographs.

812   Schell, Jonathan. *The Military Half*. New York: Knopf, 1968.
     A first-hand account of the destruction of over 70 percent of the villages in Quang Ngai and Quang Tin provinces and the resultant devastation caused to a populace forced to live in refugee camps. The title comes from the military's schizophrenic nature – the ability to see only the "military half" of the "civilian half" of a problem, but never the two at the same time. *The Military Half* originally appeared in *The New Yorker*. Schell dealt with the destruction of a single village in his *The Village of Ben Suc*.

813   _____ . *The Real War: Classic Reporting on the Vietnam War*. New York: Pantheon, 1988.
     The Real War contains the author's *The Village of Ben Suc* and *The Military Half* as well as a new essay, *The Real War* in which he again discusses the major issues of the war, speculates on the reasons for our loss there, and explores the lessons of the war. Schell was a correspondent for the *New Yorker* in Vietnam.

814   _____ . *The Village of Ben Suc*. New York: Random House, 1967.
     Schell tells the story of the American destruction of an entire farming village thirty miles from Saigon on the edge of a Vietcong stronghold. On January 8, 1967, American forces arrived with orders to "envelope the village, seal it off, remove its inhabitants, destroy its every physical trace, and to level the surrounding jungle." The author accompanied the operation which removed 3,500 framers to a barren refugee camp. The village was destroyed to save it.

815   Schemmer, Benjamin F. *The Raid*. New York: Harper & Row, 1976.
     Schemmer tells the story of the Nixon approved helicopter raid on Son Tay Prison near Hanoi in 1970 to rescue sixty-one American POWs. There were no casualties, but there were no POWs there either Photographs, bibliography, list of participants and supposed prisoners, index.

816 Scholl-Latour, Peter. *Death in the Ricefields: An Eyewitness Account of Vietnam's Three Wars, 1945-1979*. New York: St. Martin's, 1985.

The author is a television journalist who has worked in Indochina since 1945. He describes the continual turmoil that has afflicted Vietnam, Laos, and Cambodia, from his own experiences in the area.

817 Schulze, Gene. *The Third Face of War*. Austin, Tex.: Pemberton Press, 1970.

Gene Schulze, a physician from Texas, volunteered to serve in Vietnam. He describes his fear of dying and his experiences there. Photographs.

818 Schuyler, Philippa Duke. *Good Men Die*. New York: Twin Circle, 1969.

Schuyler was a writer, composer, and concert pianist. She played concerts in many of the world's trouble spots and wrote of her experiences including entertaining troops in Vietnam. She delayed her trip home to help rescue nuns and children from an orphanage in Hue and died in 1967, with one of the children, when the helicopter in which she was riding crashed into the sea at Danang Harbor after a mechanical failure.

819 Schwinn, Monika, and Bernhard Diehl. *We Came to Help*. New York: Harcourt Brace Jovanovich, 1976.

The authors were two German hospital nurses working in hospitals run by the Catholic Aid Service of Malta in An Hoa, South Vietnam who were kidnapped and held by the North Vietnamese in 1969. After four years of captivity, only two survived of the five captured.

820 Shaplen, Robert. *Bitter Victory*. New York: Harper & Row, 1986.

Shaplen was an Asia reporter for forty years and one of the last to leave Saigon in 1975. In 1985, he returned to view life in Vietnam and Cambodia under the new regimes.

821 Sheehan, Neil. *The Arnheiter Affair*. New York: Random House, 1971.

Lieutenant Commander Marcus Arnheiter was relieved of his command of the *USS Vance* off the coast of Vietnam in 1966. Sheehan tells the story of what caused this to happen and in the process tells of a modern day *Caine Mutiny*.

822 ____. *A Bright Shining Lie: John Paul Vann and America in Vietnam*. New York: Random House, 1988.
John Paul Vann was an advisor to the South Vietnamese Army in the Mekong Delta area who was enraged over the way the war was being fought and all the "bright shining lies"–the false statistics–coming from the U.S. government. Ten years in preparation, Sheehan tells the story of John Vann, a flawed hero who became the "Lawrence of Arabia" of Vietnam, eventually dying in a helicopter crash in 1972. *A Bright Shining Lie* was serialized in the *New Yorker*, 20, 27 June, 4, 11, July 1988 and won the 1988 Pulitzer Prize.

823 Sheehan, Susan. *Ten Vietnamese*. New York: Knopf, 1977.
Sheehan's husband was a *New York Times* correspondent assigned to the Times bureau in Saigon. The author, a *New Yorker* writer, interviewed the ordinary people, "the ninety-five percent that don't count"–a peasant, landlord, refugee, politician, montagnard, orphan, Buddhist monk, a South Vietnamese soldier, a Vietcong, and a North Vietnamese prisoner.

824 Shepard, Elaine. *The Doom Pussy*. New York: Trident Press, 1967.
Shepard went to Vietnam for the Mutual Broadcasting System and the North American Newspaper Alliance where she concentrated on writing about the fighting men. The title refers to those fighter pilots who flew over North Vietnam, whose Vietnamese motto was "I have flown into the jaws of the cat of death," or as the fliers said,"I have seen the Doom Pussy." The author flew with these men and tells their stories based on her experiences with them.

825 Shook, John H. *One Soldier*. New York: Bantam, 1986.
The author, a microbiologist, describes being drafted, basic army and officer's training, and his harrowing experiences as a machine gunner in Delta Company.

826 Smith, George. *P.O.W.: Two Years with the Viet Cong*. Berkeley, Calif.: Ramparts Press, 1971.

Smith was a Special Forces Trooper who was a Vietcong POW. He described his terrible experiences to Donald Duncan on tape, maintaining that the lot of the Vietcong was terrible, too. Smith stresses throughout the lack of understanding Americans had – from officials to the ordinary GI – of who the Vietnamese were, both those from the North and the South.

827 Snepp, Frank. *Decent Interval: An Insider's Account of Saigon's Indecent End*. New York: Random House, 1977.

Snepp was the CIA's Chief Strategy Analyst and operative for the U.S. Embassy in Saigon. He tells of intelligence operations in Vietnam and of the fall of Saigon and how unprepared the Ambassador and the State Department were for this event. The evacuation of the embassy and the heroism involved is described.

828 Sontag, Susan. *Trip to Hanoi*. New York: Farrar, Straus & Giroux, 1968.

Sontag was invited to Hanoi. She accepted, convinced that she wasn't knowledgeable enough to write about it. This stance made her more able to experience what she saw and the cultural dislocation she felt. Sontag says that "being in Hanoi was far more mysterious, more puzzling intellectually, than I expected."

829 Spence, Ernest. *Welcome to Vietnam, Macho Man: Reflections of a Khe Sanh Vet*. N.p.: Corps Press, 1987.

Spencer was a commander of a Marine rifle company in Vietnam for eight months, 1967-68. In this autobiography, he describes the soldiers with whom he fought – their inner and outer lives. The book was written in an attempt to help the author deal with post traumatic stress disorder. Reprinted by Bantam Books in 1987.

830 Stanton, Shelby L. *Green Berets at War: U.S. Army Special Forces in Southeast Asia, 1956-1975*. Novato, Calif.: Presidio Press, 1985.

Stanton was a Special Forces officer. He describes the activities of the elite Special Forces in Vietnam – the Green Berets. An appendix details the circumstances surrounding each of the MIA Special Forces soldiers' disappearance and lists Special Forces Medal of Honor winners.

831 Steer, John, with Cliff Dudley. *Vietnam: Curse or Blessing?* Harrison, Ark.: New Leaf Press, 1982.

Steer lost his right arm in Vietnam after being wounded in a mistake bombing ordered by an American officer. Upon his return home, he was ridiculed for fighting in the war and eventually ended up in psychiatric care for four years for delayed stress reaction. The last part of the book is devoted to his religious conversion. Photographs.

832 Steinbeck, John, IV. *In Touch.* New York: Knopf, 1969.

Steinbeck describes the events that occurred the year he was twenty-one – his experiences in the army in Vietnam, his later arrest in Washington, D.C. for marijuana possession, his trial and acquittal, and testifying before the Senate Subcommittee on Juvenile Delinquency. He discusses how being the "son of the novelist" has affected his life.

833 Stockdale, James B. *A Vietnam Experience. Ten Years of Reflection.* Stanford, Calif.: Hoover Institution Press, 1984.

A collection of Stockdale's speeches, magazine articles, and other writings dating from his release from Hanoi in 1973 to 1983. He describes the torture he endured in the prison and how he was able to maintain his sanity; how valuable an education can be to one confined alone. He also ponders the subject of war.

834 Stockdale, James B., and Sybil Stockdale. *In Love and War: The Story of a Family's Ordeal and Sacrifice during the Vietnam Years.* New York: Harper & Row, 1984.

Jim Stockdale, a Navy pilot, was shot down over North Vietnam, his back broken during ejection from the plane, captured, and held for over seven years in Hanoi. He and his wife Sybil tell their stories in alternating chapters, giving readers a picture of the anguish of those at home who wait as well. Sybil played a leading role in the organization of the League of POW/MIA families. Stockdale is a Congressional Medal of Honor recipient.

835 Sully, Francois, ed. *We, the Vietnamese: Voices from Vietnam.* New York: Praeger, 1971.

Sully covered Vietnam as a reporter for twenty-two years until his death in a helicopter crash in 1971. Sully says "all facts of life in Vietnam must be viewed in the context of war." This is a collection of personal accounts, speeches, letters, and documents of people from both North and South Vietnam. Included are selections from Emperor Bao Dai, Ngo Dinh Diem, Ho Chi Minh, General Giap, and President Thieu. The book is divided into three sections: Land and People: Beliefs and Customs; A Turbulent History; and A Poetic People: Literature and Art. Bibliography, index.

836 Tauber, Peter. *The Sunshine Soldiers*. New York: Simon & Schuster, 1971.

Tauber joined the Army Reserves to avoid Vietnam or jail. He describes his eight-week training at Fort Bliss, Texas, including its brutality and persecution, the bureaucracy, and the change in the men's attitude about themselves.

837 Taylor, Maxwell D. *Swords and Plowshares*. New York: Norton, 1972.

The author is a general who graduated from West Point in 1922. He fought in World War II, served in Korea, and was Chairman of the Joint Chiefs of Staff under Kennedy and Johnson (and a key Johnson advisor), finally serving as ambassador to Vietnam for one year. A large part of the book concerns itself with his Vietnam-related experiences.

838 Terry, Wallace. *Bloods: An Oral History of the Vietnam War by Black Veterans*. New York: Random House, 1984.

Black soldiers made up a large percentage of those who fought in Vietnam, accounting for 23 percent of the American fatalities. Their story has remained largely untold. Wallace Terry relates the war experiences of twenty black soldiers–experiences which included ugly, racist incidents with white soldiers, even one on the battlefield. Terry reports that General William Westmoreland said "I have an intuitive feeling that the Negro servicemen have a better understanding than whites of what the war is about."

839 Terzani, Tiziano. *Giai Phong!: The Fall and Liberation of Saigon*. New York: St. Martin's, 1976.

An Italian journalist describes the last days of Saigon. Interviews were conducted with people all over the city to document the end. Terzani was the first western journalist to tour the Delta provinces after the fall. Translated by John Sheply. Maps, illustrations, glossary, photographs, index.

840   Thomas, Liz. *Dust of Life*. New York: Dutton, 1977.
      Thomas was a twenty year old nurse in Vietnam. She worked in a Saigon orphanage and later started a home for girls living on the streets. She describes the poverty and the incredible living conditions. Thomas stayed on after Saigon fell and thus can relate what life was like under the new regime.

841   Tiede, Tom. *Your Men at War*. New York: Newspaper Enterprise Association, 1966.
      A collection of the dispatches of the author while he was a reporter in Vietnam.

842   Tran Van Don. *Our Endless War: Inside Vietnam*. San Rafael, Calif.: Presidio Press, 1978.
      The author, a prominent military officer in Vietnam, describes thirty-five years of Vietnamese history through his own experiences. His characterization of major figures such as Thieu, Diem, and Madame Nhu is fascinating. He concludes, "As most of us have become expatriates in other lands far from our beloved Vietnam, our only satisfaction is that we did our best for our country."

843   Tregaskis, Richard. *Vietnam Diary*. New York: Holt, Rinehart & Winston, 1963.
      Tregaskis was a war correspondent in Vietnam early in the war. In diary-form he describes Marine helicopter missions in the Delta area, special forces operations, fighter pilots' activities, and seacoast patrol. He tells of his own experiences, but also those of the men he met.

844   Trembly, Diane L. *Petticoat Medic in Vietnam: Adventures of a Woman Doctor*. New York: Vantage, 1976.
      Dr. Trembly volunteered to serve in Vietnam in 1970 where she worked for eighteen months. She describes her daily life and the people she treated – not all of whom were war victims. She served with

volunteers of other nations in several South Vietnamese hospitals, rather than in field hospitals.

845 Trotti, John. *Phantom over Vietnam: Fighter Pilot, USMC.* Novato, Calif.: Presidio Press, 1984.

A personal account of Marine pilot John Trotti's experience as a pilot of a F4 Phantom. He flew 600 missions in Vietnam, serving two tours, 1965-70. He describes his personal growth as a result of the experience and also his growing pessimism as to the outcome of the war.

846 Troung Nhu Tang, with David Chanoff and Doan Van Toai. *A Vietcong Memoir.* New York: Harcourt Brace Jovanovich, 1985.

Troung Nhu Tang was the Minister of Justice for the Vietcong Provisional Revolutionary Government and a founder of the National Liberation Front. He tells the political story from the Vietcong point of view, noting that the new Vietnam is as unjust as the old. He was disappointed that neither the revolutions national nor their social ideals were truly served. He now lives in exile. The book is subtitled "An Insider's Account of the Vietnam War and Its Aftermath." Glossary of names, appendix, maps, photographs, index.

847 Tucker, James Guy, Jr. *Arkansas Men at War.* Little Rock: Arkansas Pioneer Press, 1968.

Tucker covered the war for *Time,* UPI, and was a staff writer for *The Saigon Post.* The book is a series of stories chronicling the experiences of soldiers from Arkansas from 1965 to 1967. Introduction by J. William Fullbright.

848 Turley, Gerald H. *Easter Offensive, Vietnam, 1972.* Novato, Calif.: Presidio Press, 1985.

Col. Turley describes a multiple division NVA attack on March 30, 1972 in the northern provinces of South Vietnam's Military Region I in which he participated.

849 Turpin, James W., with Al Hirshberg. *Vietnam Doctor: The Story of Project Concern.* New York: McGraw-Hill, 1966.

Project Concern was a medical mission, treating people in Hong Kong. Turpin, a doctor and minister with a wife and four children, gave up his safe life to begin this project. He eventually moved the project to Vietnam The book describes his experiences early in the war.

850 Van Buskirk, Robert, with Fred Bauer. *Tailwind: A True Story*. Waco, Tex.: Word Books, 1983.

The author, son of a career army officer, enlisted, went to officers' training school, and became a Green Beret. He describes ten years of his life, from Vietnam, where he was wounded, his reassignment to Germany, his arrest for armed robbery and dealing in illegal automatic weapons. He spent one year in a German prison before the charges were dismissed. Van Buskirk relates his subsequent religious commitment, his attendance at a divinity school, and his work in prison ministry. The title refers to the name of a battle in Laos.

851 Van Devanter, Lynda. *Home Before Morning: The Story of an Army Nurse in Vietnam*. New York: Beaufort Books, 1983.

Lynda Van Devanter describes her experiences during one tour of duty, her change from an idealist who once viewed the war as a chance to save a country from the yoke of communism, the decompression she felt upon returning home, her treatment by those who viewed her as "a murderer rather than a healer," and her experiences with post traumatic stress syndrome. One of the few personal narratives from a woman's point of view. Glossary of Viet-medical terms included.

852 Van Tien Dung. *Our Great Spring Victory: An Account of the Liberation of South Vietnam*. New York: Monthly Review Press, 1977.

Van Tien Dung was Chief of Staff of the Vietnam People's Army, a general in charge of the four month assault on Saigon. He recounts the planning involved in the task and the intelligence work necessary. Translated by John Spragens, Jr.

853 Vance, Samuel. *The Courageous and the Proud*. New York: Norton, 1970.

An account of a black soldier in Vietnam and a description of the relationships between black and white soldiers in that war. The author feels that the black soldier has not been recognized for his role in the Vietnam War and that the war was a chance for black soldiers to "make a stand," to prove themselves as good an any other soldier. Vance was a combat infantryman in Vietnam in 1965 and was twice wounded.

854   Vietnam Veterans Against the War. *The Winter Soldier Investigation: An Inquiry into American War Crimes*. Boston: Beacon Press, 1972.
     Highlights from the testimony of Vietnam veterans recorded at a hearing to investigate American war crimes held in Detroit in 1971. See also 728.

855   Vo Nguyen Giap. *Unforgettable Months and Years*. Ithaca, N.Y.: Cornell University, Southeast Asia Program, 1975.
     The author was a general responsible for some of the strategy that led to both French and American defeat. He gives a unique view of the war albeit heavy on bias and propaganda. Translated by Mai Van Elliott.

856   Vysotsky, Sergei, and Ilya Glazunov. *The Undaunted Heroes: A Vietnam Diary*. New York: Beekman, 1975.
     Originally published in 1973 in the Soviet Union, this propaganda piece begins with a condemnation of the U.S. and its Vietnam policy, noting that "Vietnam has won the esteem of all progressive mankind" for its courage and mass heroism. The authors, who traveled in North Vietnam in 1967, present their diary of the tour, charting the damage done by the United States and the heroism of the workers and soldiers. Translation by Katherine Judelson.

857   Wain, Barry. *The Refused: The Agony of the Indochina Refugees*. New York: Simon & Schuster, 1981.
     Wain, a diplomatic correspondent for the *Asian Wall Street Journal*, traveled through the refugee camps in Asia and writes his eyewitness account of the harrowing experiences of the "boat people," who were exploited, robbed, raped, murdered, and often refused admission by free countries.

858　Walker, Keith. *A Piece of My Heart: The Stories of 26 American Women Who Served in Vietnam*. Novato, Calif.: Presidio Press, 1985.

Fifteen thousand women were involved in the Vietnam War – nurses, WACS, USO and Red Cross workers, entertainers, and civilian volunteers. Walker has gathered twenty-six stories of a representative sample of these women in an attempt to bring the woman's experience to the public. It is noted that even for these women, no place was safe in Vietnam. An introduction by Martha Raye, the entertainer who spent two years entertaining in Vietnam, is included as well as a useful appendix of companies and agencies employing women in Vietnam, USO units, Red Cross units, hospital ships, women's Marine units, hospitals, etc.

859　Walt, Lewis W. *Strange War, Strange Strategy: A General's Report on Vietnam*. New York: Funk & Wagnalls, 1970.

Walt was a Marine Corps general who took command of Marine units in May, 1965. He describes the war as he saw it and the men he knew. Vietcong propaganda is discussed plus the qualities which made the Vietnamese a strange and difficult adversary for the U. S. Walt also recounts acts of heroism.

860　Webb, Kate. *On the Other Side: 23 Days with the Viet Cong*. New York: Quadrangle, 1972.

Kate Webb, a New Zealand born UPI reporter who was captured in Cambodia by the Vietcong in 1971 and held for twenty-three days, relates her experiences. Included is an introduction, "About the War in Cambodia," by Jerry Gold. Photographs.

861　Weiss, Stephen. *A War Remembered: Voices from Vietnam*. Boston: Boston Publishing Company, 1986.

A War Remembered is volume nineteen of *The Vietnam Experience* series. Weiss has collected stories told by twenty-five Vietnam veterans, policymakers, nurses, campus protesters, missionaries, relief workers, and clerical staff. Both American and Vietnamese are represented. Photographs of each contributor are included plus a brief biography. A two page section of poems is also included. Maps.

862　West, Francis J. *The Village*. New York: Harper & Row, 1972.

West tells the story of twelve Marines who volunteered to serve with the South Vietnam I (Eye) Corps. They were chosen because of their genuine sympathy for the Vietnamese people. Their job was to protect a village of 5,000 that had been dominated by the Vietminh and Vietcong since the French defeat.

863 Westmoreland, William C. *A Soldier Reports*. Garden City, N.Y.: Doubleday, 1976.

Westmoreland presents his personal account of his life and forty year career in the army. Of particular interest in his years, 1964-1968 as field commander in Vietnam and later as Army Chief of Staff, 1968-72. He describes and explains his Vietnam. Photographs.

864 Whitmore, Terry, as told to Richard Weber. *Memphis, Nam, Sweden: The Autobiography of a Black American Exile*. Garden City, N.Y.: Doubleday, 1971.

Whitmore, a black who grew up in a ghetto in Memphis, joined the Marine Corps and was wounded in Vietnam where he was decorated by a visiting President Johnson and President Ky. After experiencing the horror of combat, he fled with the help of Japanese peace activists when ordered to return to duty. He fled through the USSR, which gave him a month-long VIP tour of the country, to Sweden where he sought asylum. At the time of the book's writing, he was living in Stockholm.

865 Whittington, Ruben Benjamin. *Moonspinners, Viet Nam '65-'66*. New York: Vantage, 1986.

The author tells the story of his tour in Vietnam as if this were a novel and he were a character in it. After he arrives at Bein Hoa Airbase, one of the other men tells him, "There are a lot of bad tricks the VC pull that you'll learn before your year is up or you'll leave early, one way or another." He does learn and eventually volunteers for a special group trained to protect the air base. He agonizes over a friend who lost a foot, feeling guilty that it wasn't him, and over a Vietcong he killed who had just killed a New Zealander.

866 Willenson, Kim. *The Bad War: An Oral History of the Vietnam War*. New York: New American Library, 1987.

The author explains how the United States got involved in Vietnam, what we did there, what it did to us, why and how we got out, and what it has meant to both the U.S. and Vietnam since. The voices in the book that discuss these issues represent people on both sides, the ordinary and the famous. Military leaders and soldiers, civilian personnel, intelligence officers, battlefield chaplains, presidential advisors, Vietcong leaders, statesmen, peace activists are represented. Some of the famous include: Clark Clifford, Eugene McCarthy, Joan Baez, William Calley, James Schlessinger, Walter Cronkite, Nguyen Cao Ky, and William Fullbright among others. An excellent, useful book. Chronology, index.

867 Williams, Fenton A. *Just Before Dawn: A Doctor's Experiences in Vietnam*. New York: Exposition Press, 1971.

Williams spent one year in Vietnam from 1968-69 with the Medical Battalion of the 9th Infantry Division at Dong Tam in the Mekong Delta. He describes the constants of Vietnam – low morale, racial discrimination, exploitation by the Vietnamese, the black market, massacres, atrocities, the poverty of the peasants, disease, prostitution, waste. Williams maintains that "the average Vietnamese saw Americans as enemies and things to be used rather than liberators."

868 Willwerth, James. *Eye of the Last Storm: A Reporter's Journal of One Year in Southeast Asia*. New York: Grossman, 1972.

Willwerth, a *Time* magazine reporter, presents his journal of one year in Indochina. Life in Saigon, Bob Hope's staged Christmas shows, battles, the children, and the incongruity of normal life going on amidst the chaos of war are described. Very readable.

869 Wright, Eddie. *Thoughts about the Vietnam War: Based on My Experiences, Books I Have Read and Conversations with Other Veterans*. New York: Carlton Press, 1986.

Wright was a black sergeant in a communications squadron in Vietnam. As part of his Adult Degree Study Program, he transcribed conversations with six Vietnam combat veterans and gives his reactions to six books about the war: *M*; *Winners and Losers*; *Bloods*; *Nam*; *Cover-up*; and *Vietnam: Why?* The purpose of this study is an attempt to bring the war into perspective. He deals effectively with the black soldier's experience and its ironic edge. Also discussed is the widespread delayed stress reaction veterans are experiencing, and the poor leadership many of the solders worked under during the war.

870 Yezzo, Dominick. *A GI's Vietnam Diary, 1968-1969*. New York: Franklin Watts, 1974.

Yezzo's story of his tour of duty is effectively told in the form of short diary entries – a day-to-day account of a soldier in this war. He describes not only events, but his feelings of fear, his doubts, his questioning of his beliefs and what he was taught about his country, the kind of self-examination often caused by Vietnam. Yezzo says "I learned that it is each man's war as he sees it through his own eyes and as he thinks it to be though his own mind."

871 Young, Perry Deane. *Two of the Missing: A Reminiscence of Some Friends in the War*. New York: Coward, McCann & Geoghegan, 1975.

Young tells the story of two of his friends, Sean Flynn, son of the actor Erroll Flynn, and Dana Stone, journalists who, by the time of this book's writing, had not returned from Cambodia. The author calls the book "a book of memories, dreams, and nightmares, arranged in no particular chronology," It is an attempt to come to terms with the war. The author was a UPI reporter in Vietnam. Flynn and Stone have never been found.

872 Zumwalt, Elmo, III, and Elmo R. Zumwalt, Jr. *My Father, My Son*. New York: Macmillan, 1986.

Lieutenant Elmo Russell Zumwalt III volunteered for Vietnam rather than make use of his position. He served with distinction, returned home, married, and had two children. Lt. Zumwalt had been exposed to Agent Orange, which was sprayed along the rivers he and his crew patrolled. In 1983, he developed cancer, and his son was born with a birth defect called sensory integration dysfunction. The irony was that his father, Adm. Zumwalt, had given the order to spray the defoliant. The Zumwalts tell their story and describe their attempt to cope with the tragedy and its attendant guilt. Admiral Zumwalt's son died in 1988.

873 Zumwalt, Elmo R., Jr. *On Watch: A Memoir*. New York: Quadrangle, 1976.

Admiral Elmo Zumwalt, Chief of Naval Operations, presents his autobiography and discusses his experiences in the Vietnam War.

Anthologies

874 Anisfield, Nancy, ed. *Vietnam Anthology: American War Literature*. Bowling Green, Ohio: Bowling Green State University Popular Press, 1987.

  An anthology which includes seven novel excerpts, eight short stories, two drama excerpts, and twenty-five poems. Each section has an introduction and study questions. Time-line, statistics, glossary, and bibliography included.

875 Cass, Shirley, et al., eds. *We Took Their Orders and Are Dead: An Anti-War Anthology*. Sydney, Australia: Ure Smith, 1971.

  A contributors' statement notes that "The writers in Australia and the writers overseas who contribute to this anthology do so to register their opposition to the military involvement of Australia and her American and other allies in the war in Vietnam." The anthology contains fifty-nine poems plus novel excerpts, short stories and nonfiction.

876 Crapser, William. *Remains: Stories of Vietnam*. Old Chatham, N.Y.: Sachem Press, 1988.

  A collection of seventeen short stories, four poems, four letters home, and a personal narrative by the author who was a Marine Corps veteran who served in Vietnam in 1968-69 (see also 1069).

877   Greenberg, Martin H., and Augustus Norton, eds. *Touring Nam: The Vietnam Reader*. New York: Morrow, 1985.

The anthology follows a twelve-month tour of duty with selections illustrating aspects of life from arrival in Vietnam, living conditions, first combat, feelings of terror and boredom, to daily life in the jungle. Included are short stories, novel excerpts, and journalistic accounts.

878   Hardy, Gordon, comp. *Words of War: An Anthology of Vietnam War Literature*. Boston: Boston Publishing Company, 1988.

Volume twenty-four of *The Vietnam Experience* series, this anthology excerpts twenty-one novels and personal narratives by major Vietnam War writers including O'Brien, Ehrhart, Del Vecchio, Herr, Glasser, Caputo, Stone, and Mason. Also included are letters, speeches, and photographs – both actual photos from the war and movie stills.

879   Heath, G. Louis, ed. *Mutiny Does Not Happen Lightly: The Literature of the American Resistance to the Vietnam War*. Metuchen, N.J.: Scarecrow, 1976.

A compilation of literature from groups that opposed the Vietnam War. Creative literature is not included. Massive bibliography.

880   Horne, A. D., ed. *The Wounded Generation: America After Vietnam*. New York: Prentice-Hall, 1981.

Intended as a reassessment of the tumultuous events of the Vietnam War viewed from the 1980s, this anthology includes personal narratives, poetry, and novel excerpts from some of the major Vietnam works such as *Going After Cacciato, Dispatches, Fields of Fire*, and *A Rumor of War*.

881   Knight, Cranston Sedrick, ed. *Tour of Duty: Vietnam in the Words of Those Who Were There*. *Samisdat* 46 (1986).

The editor states that the purpose of the anthology is "to witness the war from the perspective of individual American military personnel and to rekindle many of the repressed conscious emotions of that time." Poems, short stories, personal narratives, and short prose vignettes are included.

882 Lester, Julius. *Search for the New Land: History as Subjective Experience.* New York: Dial, 1969.

An undisciplined, eclectic mixed-media approach to discussing American history from Hiroshima to 1969 with an emphasis on racism and the Vietnam War. The author has selected poems, newspaper story "clippings," and excerpts from autobiographies, letters, and journals, intending to show how we became what we are. The antiwar sentiment is obvious. The reader is impressed by the ugliness of the events of the last several decades as depicted.

883 Scott, L. E. *Time Came Hunting Time.* Cammeray, Australia: Saturday Centre Books, 1978.

An anthology of poems, two short stories, and prose selections by Lewis Scott, an American living in New Zealand.

884 Strahan, Jack, Peter Hollenbeck, and R. L. Barth. *Vietnam Literature Anthology, A Balanced Perspective: Three Views of Vietnam and a Chapter from a Forthcoming Novel.* Edited by John Tophan. New York: American Poetry and Literature Press, 1984.

A collection of poems by the three authors plus an excerpt from an as yet unpublished novel by Peter Hollenbeck called *The Lotus and the Night.*

885 Taylor, Clyde, ed. *Vietnam and Black America: An Anthology of Protest and Resistance.* Garden City, N.Y.: Anchor/Doubleday, 1973.

Poetry, essays, novel excerpts, short stories, and personal narratives dealing with the black American's experience in Vietnam comprise this anthology. Writers include Martin Luther King, Jr., James Baldwin, Julian Bond, Stokley Carmichael, and Huey P. Newton. Bibliography.

886 Truscott, Robert Blake, ed. "Wars and Rumors." *Stone Country* 10, no. 1-2 (Fall/Winter [October] 1982):40-86.

One-half of a double issue of *Stone Country*, a periodical literary magazine published by the Nathan Mayhew Seminars of Martha's Vineyard, Inc., Menemsha, Mass., this anthology is divided into four sections: Overture, In-Country, Homecoming, and Legacies. The selections are primarily poetry, but some vignettes and Arias-Misson's "Vietnam-Superfiction" are included.

887 Villani, Jim, et al., eds. *Vietnam Flashbacks: Pig Iron, no. 12.* Youngstown, Ohio: Pigiron Press, 1984.

One of an annual series of popular literary anthologies supported by the Ohio Arts Council, this anthology includes thirty-five poems, thirteen short stories, and five nonfiction selections.

888 Williams, Reese, ed. *Unwinding the Vietnam War: From War into Peace.* Seattle: Real Comet Press, 1987.

An anthology of poetry, personal narratives, and critical analyses by veterans, peace activists, and refugees all expressing a need to speak out against the war. The anthology is an attempt to understand how we became involved in the conflict and to determine the effect it has had on the U.S. as a nation and on its people. "As a nation, we have not yet taken responsibility for our role in the catastrophe of the Vietnam War, nor have we offered any apologies or significant gestures of good will to the people of Vietnam." Contributors include Adrienne Rich, W. D. Ehrhart, Bobbie Ann Mason, Noam Chomsky, and Robert Bly.

Poetry

889 Alley, Rewi. *The Mistake*. Christchurch, New Zealand: Caxton Press, 1965.

      An antiwar, anti-American collection of eleven poems with an introduction by "P.J.A." who is unidentified. No information about the author is given. P.J.A. states in his introduction that "the Americans have no real urge to fight the Vietnamese. . . . Their morale is low, whereas the Vietnamese are fighting for their country. Under such conditions there can only be one outcome. The Americans will have to get out or be driven out."

890 Andrews, Michael. *A Telegram Unsigned*. *Samisdat* 45, no. 1 (1986).

      Andrews programmed computers for MACV in Saigon from 1969 to 1971 for the Phoenix Project. Several of the poems in this collection are on Vietnam.

891 *Artists and Writers Protest against the War in Viet Nam: Poems*. New York: Artists and Writers Protest, 1967.

      A twenty-eight page collection of poems against the war produced in a limited edition of 500. Designed and produced by Rudi Bass.

892 Baka, Steve I. *Thunder Silence*. Annapolis, Minn.: Annapolis Works, 1984.

893 Baker, Richard E. *Shell Burst Pond*. Tacoma, Wash.: Rapier Press, 1980.

This collection of twenty poems by a Vietnam veteran are painfully graphic in their depiction of fragging, the wounding and death of friends, and the deaths of children. Black and white drawings throughout this short pamphlet are by Frank Boehm.

894 Balaban, John. *After Our War*. Pittsburgh: University of Pittsburgh, 1974.

A poetic picture of the affects of the Vietnam War on the Vietnamese people and their culture by a major poet in Vietnam War literature. Not all of the poems in the collection are on Vietnam.

895 ____. *Blue Mountain*. Greensboro, N.C.: Unicorn Press, 1979.

During the summer of 1978, Balaban hitch-hiked across the country to gather material for a writing project. The majority of poems reflect these experiences, but the second part of the collection, called "After the Judean Campaigns," includes seven Vietnam poems.

896 ____. *Vietnam Poems*. Oxford: Carcanet Press, 1970.

The biographical material on this sixteen-page pamphlet of five poems notes that the author was a conscientious objector who seved in Vietnam from 1967 to 1969 as a college instructor and later as a field representative for the Committee of Responsibility to Save War-Injured Children. The poems mainly present images of the lives of the Vietnamese peasants. The last poem, "The Dragonfish," describes "darting jets, F-105's," but other than that the war is not directly mentioned.

897 Barry, Jan. *Veterans Day*. Montclair, N.J.: East River Anthology, 1983.

Also published in *Samisdat* 36, no. 1, 141st release, 1983, *Veterans Day* is a small pamphlet of eight poems which were originally presented in a reading on November 11, 1982, at the New York Shakespeare Festival Public Theatre in association with the Veterans' Ensemble Theatre Company. The poems deal with the dead of the Vietnam War, the Veterans' Day holiday, the duty of a soldier, and the nature of peace. Barry was a private in Vietnam in 1962-63. He resigned an appointment to West Point and became a founder of the Vietnam Veterans against the War and other antidraft, antiwar organizations.

898   ____. *War Baby*. Montclair, N.J.: East River Anthology, 1983.
       War Baby, an eight-poem pamphlet, is the sequel to *Veterans Day*, and was originally presented in a reading on November 11, 1983, at the Colonnades Theatre in New York. The theme is the relationship between war and children. One poem describes an American child asking his father about patriotism. Vietnamese children are also poetic subjects. The poems were also published in *Samisdat* 39, no. 2, 154th release (1983).

899   ____, ed. *Peace Is Our Profession: Poems and Passages of War Protest*. Montclair, N.J.: East River Anthology, 1981.
       Designed to be "a sort of reader of revolt to hand to the next generation being wooed into witless war," this powerful antiwar anthology is mostly poetry but includes some prose in the form of letters, comments, short recollections, and diary excerpts as well as photographs and art work. The contributors are both Americans and Vietnamese, men and women, soldiers and civilians – all trying to come to an understanding of the reason for the insanity of war. The title of the anthology comes from the Strategic Air Command's cold war slogan. Biographical notes on the contributors included.

900   Barry, Jan, and W. D. Ehrhart, eds. *Demilitarized Zones*. Perkasie, Pa.: East River Anthology, 1976.
       A companion to *Winning Hearts and Minds*, this powerful collection contains 180 poems by one hundred veterans.

901   Barth, Robert L. *Forced Marching to the Styx: Vietnam War Poems*. Van Nuys, Calif.: Perivale Press, 1983.
       Barth was a long range reconnaissance in Vietnam for thirteen months, serving with the Marines from 1966 to 1969. He begins this collection of twenty-one poems with a quote from Graham Greene's *It's a Battlefield* that expresses the theme of the collection: "One did not question during the war why one fought; One waited till the war was over for that."

902 ____. *A Soldier's Time: Vietnam War Poems*. Santa Barbara, Calif.: John Daniel, 1988.

The title comes from Samuel Johnson who said, "A soldier's time is passed in distress and danger, or in idleness and corruption." The author was a Marine in Vietnam in 1968-69 in a reconnaisance battalion. This is an excellent collection of forty-five of the author's poems tracing the history of Vietnam's wars from Dien Bien Phu through American involvement.

903 Bates, Scott, ed. *Poems of War Resistance*. New York: Grassman, 1969.

An interesting introduction to the history of 4,000 years of anti-war poetry–from the Greeks to the specter of nuclear war–precedes this collection of antiwar poetry by the great poets of the ages. Of particular interest, is the chapter called "Where Is Vietnam?" containing seven poems on the war. The book includes two forewords by Louis Untermeyer and Kenneth Patchen.

904 Bauer, Bill. *The Eye of the Ghost: Vietnam Poems*. Kansas City, Mo.: BkMk Press, University of Missouri, 1986.

The author was in a National Guard unit activated during the 1968 riots. He went to Vietnam in 1969. This is a poetry collection that includes twenty-four poems about the war. In addition, a short glossary of terms relating to Vietnam and the war is added. The title comes from a comment made by Captain Thomas Falkenthal who, when told that some Marine troops wanted to forget what happened to the Marines in Lebanon replied, "That raises a caution flag, because then it becomes a ghost. Sometimes you have to look the ghost in the eye," a fitting beginning for this collection of poems which explore the author's memories, images and stories of the Vietnam War.

905 Berkhoudt, John C. *Vietnam: A Year before the "Peace."* New York: Carlton Press, 1975.

906 Berrigan, Daniel. *Night Flight to Hanoi: War Diary with 11 Poems*. New York: Macmillan, 1968.

Eleven poems on various aspects of the war and on Berrigan's experiences and observations in North Vietnam are included in this personal narrative of the author's trip to Hanoi. See also 1006.

907 Berry, D. C. *Saigon Cemetery*. Athens: University of Georgia Press, 1972.

David Chapman Berry was a medic in Vietnam. *Saigon Cemetery* is a collection of forty untitled poems, mostly brief and filled with images of pain and death. George Garrett, in his introduction, notes that in American war poetry, the medical officer is often the narrator, and an effective one, as ".... it is those who stand between the civilian and the committed common soldier who are best able to translate the experience of war into a sensible affective language."

908 Bingaman, H. W. *Reckonings: Stories of the Air War over North Vietnam*. New York: Vantage, 1988.

Bingaman was a jet fighter pilot in Vietnam in 1966-67. These twenty-nine poems describe the author's tour and are "poetic tales about jet fighter raids in America's air compaign called Rolling Thunder." Each section of poems is prefaced by a page or two of explanation of terms or historical events in the war which are important to the following group of poems. Glossary, chronology.

909 Bly, Robert. *The Teeth-Mother Naked at Last*. San Francisco: City Lights, 1970.

Robert Bly was one of the contemporary American poets who protested the war and participated in the antiwar poetry read-ins on college campuses. The title poem of this collection is one of his major Vietnam War poems. Other poems on the war may be found in his collection *Sleepers Joining Hands*, New York: Harper & Row, 1973.

910 Bly, Robert, and David Ray, eds. *A Poetry Reading against the Vietnam War*. Madison, Minn.: Sixties Press, 1966.

Twenty-nine poems published by the American Writers Against the Vietnam War with an introduction by Robert Bly, these poems were read as part of the national poetry read-ins held on college campuses in which noted poets displayed their opposition to the war. Poems by Whitman, Jeffers, and Sassoon are included with poems by contemporary poets such as Ferlinghetti, Kinnell, and Bly. Excerpts from speeches are also included. Several pages are cut out and blacked out with what appears to be magic marker "in mourning for the poems of e. e. cummings for which permission was refused by Harcourt Brace." An angry book.

911 Brokaw, Richard M. *Bits and Pieces: Poems*. New York: Exposition Press, 1971.

A collection of mostly antiwar poems by the author. Vietnam is not specifically mentioned in the poems.

912 Cantwell, James M. *Highway Number One: A Vietnam Odyssey in Verse*. New York: Exposition Press, 1980.

A collection of forty-four poems by the author. He and his wife have sponsored two refugee families in their hometown of Green Bay, Wisconsin. These poems describe the journey of the Vietnamese refugees from their decision to leave their beleaguered country, their struggles and hardships on the journey to the United States, to their experiences in this country.

913 Casey, Michael. *Obscenities*. New Haven, Conn.: Yale University Press, 1972.

Stanley Kunitz suggests in his introduction that the poems be read as if this were a novel or a play. The poems are described as anti-poetry – a rejection of the forms of ordinary war poetry since more conventional war poems often talk of the glory of war. The poet recognizes the lack of any glory in the Vietnam War. Casey served as a military policeman on Vietnamese National Highway One – the settings for most of the poems. *Obscenities* is considered to be one of the most effective poetry collections to come out of the war.

914 Chagon, Jacqui, and Don Luce, eds. *Of Quiet Courage: Poems from Vietnam*. Washington, D.C.: Indochina Mobile Education Project, 1974.

A collection of Vietnamese poems translated into English. The collection includes major Vietnamese poets as well as the poems of political leaders, students, soldiers, and folk singers. The editors note that "the intent has been to give the reader some appreciation for the historical continuity of the larger themes of Vietnamese poetry: loyalty to ancestors, devotion to family, love of country and the struggle against foreign domination." Pen names are often used for safety reasons as well as by tradition. Striking Vietnamese art work throughout. A poem by Ho Chi Minh is included as well as one by a student who later immolated himself in a peace protest. The acknowledgment and introduction are nearly identical in this collection and in the Indochina Mobile Project's *We Promise One Another* (see 962). Some of the poems appear in both collections.

174

915 Clover, Timothy. *The Leaves of My Trees, Still Green*. Chicago: Adams Press, 1970.

> Poems of a soldier killed in the war.

916 Connell, Robert. *Firewinds: Poems on the Vietnam War*. Sydney: Wentworth Press, 1968.

> Nine poems by the author. Some of the poems are about war in general while others describe combat. Illustrated by David Ogg and Chris Amitzboll.

917 Cross, Frank A. *Reminders*. Big Timber, Mont.: Seven Buffaloes Press, 1986.

> The author was a draftee who served in Vietnam in 1969. The nineteen poems in the collection are based on his experiences in Echo Company of the Eleventh Brigade stationed at Duc Pho near the South China Sea where he was in a reconaissance platoon, the purpose of which he explains in his introduction.

918 Curry, Richard. *Crossing Over: A Vietnam Journal*. Cambridge, Mass.: Apple-wood Press, 1980.

> Called a "poetic documentary," *Crossing Over* is a series of forty-six short, stark vignettes of the war-prose poems – that the author jotted down originally in letters and diary entries. Portions of this collection originally appeared in the anthology *First Person Intense Anthology*, edited by Sasha Newborn (Santa Barbara, Calif.: Mudborn Press, 1978).

919 DiPrima, Diane, ed. *War Poems*. New York: Poets Press, 1968.

> A poetry anthology of twenty-five poems by eleven poets including poems by the author, Allen Ginsberg, Leroi Jones, Robert Creeley, and Robert Duncan among others.

920 Eastlake, William. *A Child's Garden of Verses for the Revolution*. New York: Grove Press, 1970.

An anthology of 136 poems and fourteen prose selections with Vietnam being the major emphasis. The poems react to events of the 1960s and early 1970s such as hippies, assassinations, Indians, Blacks, and the war. Many of the poems were written when the author was a correspondent in Vietnam for the *Nation*. Eastlake calls himself "the poet of the revolution" in one of his poems.

921 Ehrhart, W. D. *The Awkward Silence*. Stafford, Va.: Northwoods Press, 1980.

Ehrhart, a major voice in Vietnam War literature, was a Marine in Vietnam during a thirteen-month tour of duty, 1967-68, during which he served in a combat unit and was wounded. This is his poetic description of how this experience changed him and made him redefine his concept of patriotism.

922 _____. *A Generation of Peace*. New York: New Voices, 1975.

This collection of twenty-seven poems was originally written for the author's senior thesis at Swathmore College. Half of the collection is Vietnam poetry, describing and evaluating his experiences in the war.

923 _____. "A Generation of Peace." *Samisdat* 14, no. 3 (1977).

Most of the thirty-one poems collected here have appeared in other anthologies. Topics include poetic descriptions of Bob Hope's tours, night patrols and guard duty, the deaths of friends, and the experience of returning home. The entire issue is devoted to Ehrhart's poems.

924 _____. "The Samisdat Poems of W. D. Ehrhart." *Samisdat* 24, no. 1 (1980).

Samisdat gathered Ehrhart's poems three times. This seventy-two page collection includes all of the poems of the three previous collections. Not all of the poems are on Vietnam.

925 _____. *To Those Who Have Gone Home Tired: New and Selected Poems*. New York: Thunder's Mouth, 1984.

Ehrhart describes these poems as poems of love and friendship after the madness of war. Scenes of war and images of the return home are described in the twenty-seven poems on the war included. Some of the poems are taken from *A Generation of Peace* and other collections of his work.

926 ____, ed. *Carrying the Darkness: American Indochina: The Poetry of the Vietnam War*. New York: Avon, 1985.

Ehrhart notes in his introduction that in researching this book, he discovered over 5,000 poems written between 1961 and 1984 – the greatest outpouring of poetry of any war. This collection includes the work of seventy-four poets – from soldiers to civilians, men and women, Asians and Americans – representative of the generation that was marked forever by the war.

927 Fletcher, Harvey D. *Visions of Nam*. 2 vols. Raleigh, N.C.: Jo-Ely, 1987.

The author is a retired Marine veteran of Korea and Vietnam. These short poems reflect the pain and horror of the war, describe the deaths of friends, and note the lack of understanding the vets received at home. One poem, "Gather Round Strangers," ends with the plea:

> I desire
> not your sympathy
> nor want rejection
> I ask not
> for your judgment.
>
> just understanding.

928 Floyd, Bryan. *The Long War Dead: An Epiphany. 1st Platoon, U.S.M.C.* New York: Avon, 1976.

The author was a marine in 1967-68. He describes a poetic platoon. Each of the forty-seven poems bears the name of a man. The poem is his story – or his epitaph. A painfully sad, Spoon River-like view of the war.

929 Freibert, Stuart. *Dreaming of Floods*. Nashville: Vanderbilt University Press, 1969.

A collection of poetry by the author that contains the Vietnam War poems, "Vietnam" and "The Gunners."

930 Gallagher, Michael, and C. A. Smith. *Forever: An Anthology of Peace Poems*. Cleveland: Peaceoets' Ink, 1972.

931 Gitlin, Todd, ed. *Campfires of the Resistance: Poetry from the Movement*. Indianapolis: Bobbs-Merrill, 1971.
      A collection of political poems about the major "movements" of the late 1960s – from civil rights to antiwar protest – written by those involved. Fifty-eight contributors are represented; Vietnam is emphasized. Reading this from the vantage point of the late 1980s is like looking at an old black and white snapshot.

932 Gray, Nigel. *Aftermath*. Lancaster, England: Lancaster University Students' Union, 1976.
      Seventeen poems by the author with drawings by Vo-Dinh.

933 ____, ed. "Phoenix County." *Fireweed* 6 (September 1976).
      A special issue of an English literature journal dedicated to the British Hospital in Vietnam. All poems deal with the war or the country.

934 Hamilton, Fritz. *A Father at a Soldier's Grave*. New York: Downtown Poets, 1980.
      A collection of effective poems, each one depicting a father talking to or about his dead son, killed in Vietnam.

935 Hertzler, Terry. *The Way of the Snake and Other Poems: Writings from the War in Vietnam*. San Diego: Caernarvon Press, 1985.

936 Hollenbeck, Peter. *War Poems*. New York: American Poetry Press, 1981.
      A thin paper pamphlet of seven poems describing his experiences in the war and in a hospital in Georgia. Three of the poems were also included in his *Toward the Grey Coasts*, which was privately printed in Philadelphia in 1975.

937 Hollis, Jocelyn. *Collected Vietnam Poems and Other Poems*. Philadelphia: American Poetry and Literature, 1986.

A collection of the author's poetry. Forty-seven of the poems are about the war in Vietnam from her previous books *Vietnam Poems: The War Poems of Today* and *Vietnam Poems II: A New Collection*.

938 ____. *Poems of the Vietnam War*. Philadelphia: American Poetry and Literature Press, 1985.

A collection of twenty-nine poems, some of which appear in other of the author's collections. This collection poetically follows a young soldier as he leaves his family, goes through induction and combat, and returns home. He remembers his dead comrades. This collection was first published in 1980 although only the editor's name, J. Topham, appeared on the title page of that edition. The table of contents of that collection and the 1985 edition listed here are identical. This collection was revised in 1987.

939 ____. *Vietnam Poems: The War Poems of Today*. New York: American Poetry Press, 1979.

A collection of twenty-three poems on the war. The poems are lyric, poignant, powerful, literate. The appeal is to the readers' heart and mind, not the gut.

940 ____. *Vietnam Poems II: The War Poems of Today; A New Collection*. Philadelphia: American Poetry Press, 1983.

A collection of twenty-four poems with war as a theme, all relating to Vietnam, but not necessarily dealing with it directly. One of the poems deals with the loss of the submarine *Thresher* while another is dedicated to the soldier poet Wilfred Owen, who is often referred to in discussions of Vietnam War poetry.

941 Hope, Warren. *An Unsuccessful Mission*. Florence, Ky.: Robert L. Barth, 1983.

One hundred signed and numbered copies of this short collection of fourteen brief poems were printed. Suggestions in the poems "Commuters" and "Thoi" indicate that the author is a Vietnam veteran who may have been a driver, a medic, or perhaps an ambulance driver during the war.

942 Igantow, David. *Rescue the Dead*. Middletown, Conn.: Wesleyan University Press, 1962.

  Igantow is a major contemporary poet who opposed the war. This collection includes two Vietnam War related poems, "All Quiet" and "Soldier." Other poems relating to the war may be found in the following collections by the author: *Facing the Tree* (Boston: Little, Brown, 1975); *Tread the Dark* (Boston: Little, Brown, 1978).

943 Johnson, C. P. *I Was Fighting for Peace, but Lord, There Was Much More*. Hicksville, N.Y.: Exposition Press, 1979.

  Johnson states that his purpose is to show what war is and why it is wrong. The seventy-one poems are divided into the themes of war, peace, God, and love. The author served in the infantry in Vietnam in 1968-69. The poet emphasizes his belief in God.

944 Jordan, William Reynier. *In the Darkness and the Shadow*. Philadelphia: Dorrance, 1975.

  A collection of thrity-nine poems by the author. Some describe the experiences of a soldier, the sounds and smells of war. Other poems ponder the idea of war.

945 Kiley, Frederick T., and Tony Dater. *Listen: The War; A Collection of Poetry about the Viet-Nam War*. Colorado Springs: U.S. Air Force Academy Association of Graduates, 1973.

  The editors of this collection of poetry advertised for submisssions in armed forces journals and eventually chose 115 poems out of the 3,000 submitted. The contributors are men who fought in Vietnam or civilians who were in some way affected by the war. All aspects of war and a wide range of emotions are presented. These are primarily private poems, written to express feelings, with no thought of publication at the time of composition. The proceeds from this publication were donated to charity.

946 Kilmer, Forest L., ed. *Boondock Bards*. Tokyo/San Francisco: Pacific Stars and Stripes, 1968.

  Anthology of poems first published by U.S. servicemen in Vietnam in the paper *Pacific Stars and Stripes*.

947 Kinnell, Galway. *Body Rags*. Boston: Houghton Mifflin, 1968.

One of the contemporary poets who opposed the war, this collection contains the poem "Vapor Trail Reflected in a Frog Pond." Other poems by this author related to the war may be found in his *The Book of Nightmares* (Boston: Houghton Mifflin, 1971), which contains "The Dead Shall Be Raised Incorruptible," a full length poem with echoes of Vietnam.

948 Larsen, Earnest, and Bill Larsen. *And Tomorrow We. . . .* Liguori, Mo.: Liguorian Books, 1970.

Earnest Larson is a Redemptorist priest who works with youth. At the conclusion of the collection he notes that this work could be used in religious classes designed for working with young people. *And Tomorrow We . . .* is a powerful collection of the poems of Private Bill Larson, a medic seriously wounded in the face in Vietnam. The poems, divided into chapters, are a personal narrative in verse. These are Larson's memories as he lies wounded, drifting in and out of consciousness, as his friend Currier, who saved him, lies dying, his body spread across the author's legs. Larson did survive the war. There is no indication in the book as to whether the two Larsens are related.

949 Larson, Wendy Wilder, and Tran Thi Nga. *Shallow Graves: Two Women and Vietnam*. New York: Random House, 1986.

Larson went to Vietnam in 1970 to join her husband, a reporter. Tran Thi Nga was the bookkeeper in her husband's office and her friend and guide. Nga fled after Saigon fell and came to the United States. Together, in poetry, they give the reader their observations and their feelings about what they saw and experienced. An interesting meeting of two views of a culture, a time, and an experience.

950 Lawson, Todd, S. J. *Patriot Poems of Amerikkka*. San Francisco: Peace and Pieces Books, 1971.

The author is a San Francisco writer who received his ordination papers by mail order from the Universal Life Church of Modesto, California. This is a collection of thirty-five poems that are full of the 1960s passion and concern for the issues of that day, characterized by anti-Nixon, anti-administration poetry accompanied by satiric drawings of all of the key figures. Folk heroes of the time, like Janis Joplin, also receive attention. Illustrated by William F. Samolis.

Readers who were part of the Vietnam generation will find this a real trip down memory lane.

951 Layne, McAvoy. *How Audie Murphy Died in Vietnam.* Garden City, N.Y.: Anchor/Doubleday, 1973.

In this "novel," actually a series of brief, sardonic, poetic vignettes, the reader follows an ordinary soldier, named after the famous World War II hero and movie star, from his early life, through basic training and his experiences in Vietnam. His friends, their deaths in combat, his capture, the awarding of the silver star, and a phone call to the President are described in the short poems.

952 Le, Nancylee. *Duckling in a Thunderstorm.* Colorado Springs: Rong-Tien Publishing, 1983.

The author explains in her preface that she first went to Vietnam because of her brother who apparently died there. She met and married a Vietnamese citizen. Le states that "when a person is walking about in the middle of events, as I was, but doesn't understand their meaning, the Vietnamesse say "You are like a duck in a thunderstorm." This collection of ninety-three poems, which includes some by her brother, Paul, are a personal, emotional outpouring of her feelings about her life, her experiences in Vietnam, and the war.

953 Levertov, Denise. *The Freezing of the Dust.* New York: New Directions, 1975.

The author visited North Vietnam in Fall 1972. Seven of the poems in this collection reflect this experience while other poems reflect the inner and outer turmoil America experienced during the late 1960s and early 1970s.

954 ____. *Out of the War Shadow: The 1968 Peace Calendar and Appointment Book: An Anthology of Current Poetry.* New York: War Resisters League, 1967.

This is actually an appointment calendar with poems on the left facing the calendar pages on the right. Sixty-two poems by contemporary poets are included with brief authors' identifications at the end of the collection. The poems are about war, peace, and the Vietnam War.

955 _____. *Poems, 1960-1967*. New York: New Directions, 1966.
   Denise Levertov was well known for her antiwar stand during the Vietnam War. This collection of poems contains four Vietnam poems: "Life at War," "What Were They Like," "Two Variations," and "The Altars in the Street."

956 _____. *Relearning the Alphabet*. New York: New Directions, 1966.
   Includes four Vietnam poems, "A Marigold from North Vietnam," "An Interim," "Tennebrae," and "Advent, 1966."

957 _____. *The Sorrow Dance*. New York: New Directions, 1967.
   Five Vietnam poems included: "Life at War," "Didactic Poem," "What Were They Like," "Two Variations," and "The Altars in the Street."

958 _____. *To Stay Alive*. New York: New Directions, 1965.
   This collection of Levertov's work deals primarily with the Vietnam War and those events in the United States that it inspired during the 1960s – the protests, marches, sit-ins, etc. Some of the poems also appear in other collections of her work.

959 Livingstone, Richard N. *Speak in Shame and Sorrow: Vietnam Verses*. Hampton, N.H.: Hampton House, 1971.
   Nine powerful poems accompanied by equally powerful photographs from the war.

960 Lowenfels, Walter, ed. *Where is Vietnam? American Poets Respond*. Garden City, N.Y.: Anchor/Doubleday, 1967.
   An anthology of contemporary poems containing the work of eighty-seven poets, some Vietnamese. These are war protest poems in which poets took a more public and political role during the 1960s.

961 _____. *Writing on the Wall: 108 American Poems of Protest*. Garden City, N.Y.: Doubleday, 1969.
   A collection of protest poems which includes five poems about Vietnam: Clarence Major's "Vietnam no. 4," Denise Levertov's "What

Were They Like?," Barbara Gibson's "Thinking the Unthinkable," Bob Allen's "Musical Vietnams," and Allen Ginsberg's "Pentagon Exorcism."

962 Luce, Don, John C. Schafer, and Jacqueline Chagnon, eds. *We Promise One Another: Poems from an Asian War*. Washington, D.C.: Indochina Mobile Education Project, 1971.

   A collection of ninety-eight Vietnamese poems, "poems of the young of Viet Nam," including those of major poets as well as poems by students, soldiers, and folksingers. The poems describe all aspects of Vietnamese life and the effect of the war on their country. Some of the poems were written while the poets were in jail. Illustrated with black and white drawings. See also Jacqui Chagon's *Of Quiet Courage* (914).

963 McCarthy, Gerald. *War Story: Vietnam War Poems*. Trumansburg, N.Y.: Crossing Press, 1977.

   The author, an ex-marine, has written a series of poems to describe the life of a soldier-from the battlefield to the readjustment to "normal" life at home.

964 McDonald, Walter. *After the Noise of Saigon*. Amherst: University of Massachusetts Press, 1987.

   McDonald writes of the hard area of Texas where he grew up and his tour in Vietnam, reflecting the aftermath of the horror of the war. The reader has the image of a man riding across Texas, viewing the land and remembering the past, juxtaposed with images, like flashbacks, of Vietnam, and sorting his thoughts. Nine of the poems are specifically on Vietnam and include "After the Noise of Saigon," "The Guilt of Survivors," and "For Friends Missing in Action." Powerful poems.

965 ____. *Burning the Fence*. Lubbock: Texas Tech Press, 1981.

   Five out of thirty-nine poems deal with Vietnam: "Taking Aim," "Measuring Time," "The Winter Before the War," "Al Croom," and "Veteran."

966 ____. *Caliban in Blue and Other Poems*. Lubbock: Texas Tech Press, 1976.

   Thirty-four poems of the war by an ex-soldier.

967 McGovern, Robert, and Richard Snyder, eds. *70 on the 70's: A Decade's History in Verse*. Ashland, Ohio: Ashland Poetry Press, 1981.

    The poems deal with 1970s subjects such as Love Canal, Nixon, the deaths of John Wayne, Hubert Humphrey, and Robert Lowell, Patty Hearst, Guyana, and eleven poems on the Vietnam War.

968 _____. *60 on the 60's: A Decade's History in Verse*. Ashland, Ohio: Ashland Poetry Press, 1970.

    Included are poems on the major events and people of the sixties. Eleven poems deal with the Vietnam War.

969 Martin, Earl E. *A Poet Goes to War*. Bozeman: Big Sky Books, Montana State University, 1970.

    Martin was a member of an armored unit near Cu Chi in 1968. He fought in the Tet Offensive where he was wounded. Two medics were killed saving him. *A Poet Goes to War* is divided into four sections: Training, Korea, Viet Nam, and Home.

970 Mason, Steve. *Johnny's Song*. New York: Bantam, 1986.

    The author, a former army captain and decorated Vietnam veteran, presents eleven, well-developed, powerful poems, recording his feelings about his experience. The Vietnam Veterans Memorial, "The Wall," is the central image in the work. The collection begins with "The Wall Within," which was read at dedication ceremonies at the Wall and read into the Congressional Record, and ends with "After the Reading of the Names."

971 Mberi, Antar S. K., and Como Pieterse. *Speak Easy, Speak Free*. New York: International, 1977.

    An anthology of poetry of black American poets – teachers and students at Ohio University, Athens, between September 1967 and June 1976. Subjects include apartheid, racism in the United States, etc., but many are on Vietnam. The plight of the Vietnamese is likened to that of the blacks.

972 Miller, Stephen P. *An Act of God: Memories of Vietnam*. Eureka, Calif.: Northcoast View Press, 1982.

The author was an army draftee who served a year in Vietnam. This collection includes fourteen poems describing his experiences on his tour with twelve short prose poems on the left facing pages. Reprinted in 1987.

973 Moore, Daniel. *Burnt Heart: Ode to the War Dead*. San Francisco: City Lights, 1971.

Burnt Heart is a single, long poem divided into eighteen parts inspired by seeing photographs of a defoliated forest in Vietnam in a newspaper and stories of babies being born deformed as a result of their parents' exposure to herbicides. The burnt heart of the title refers to the heart left intact after a Bhuddist monk's self-immolation. There is a religious emphasis in the poem.

974 Nemerov, Howard. *War Stories: Poems about Long Ago and Now*. Chicago: University of Chicago Press, 1987.

The majority of the poems deal with World War II, but there are applications to Vietnam. Three poems deal directly with Vietnam: "Ultima Ration Reagan," "Authorities," and "At Sixties and Seventies."

975 Nhat Hanh, Tich. *The Cry of Vietnam*. Santa Barbara, Calif.: Unicorn Press, 1968.

Fifteen powerful, poignant, poems translated by Helen Coutant and illustrated by drawings by Vo-Dinh. The author, a Buddhist monk whose brothers were killed in the war, has taught in the United States and traveled the world. He was nominated for the Nobel Peace Prize by Martin Luther King, Jr.

976 Oldham, Perry. *Vinh Long*. Meadows of Dan, Va.: Northwoods Press, 1976.

A pamphlet of thirty-nine poems that describe the life of a soldier from arriving at Tan Son Nhut, Saigon and base life, the Vietnamese people, sanitary conditions, and combat. The author spent a year in Vietnam.

977 Pick, Michael Robert. *Childhood – Namhood – Manhood: The Writings of Michael Robert Pick, a Vietnam Veteran*. San Gabriel, Calif.: Pizzuto , 1982.

The author is a Vietnam veteran struggling to accept and live with the memories of the war. There is a sense of the difficulty of readjustment for these men as they struggle to find a meaning in their experiences. The poems are brief, some only a couplet, untitled, and deal with Vietnam as well as the author's life before the war.

978 *Poetry against the War. Poetry Magazine* 70, no. 6 (September 1972):319-65.

The entire issue is devoted to poetry about the Vietnam War, twenty-eight poems by twenty-eight poets including David Ignatow, Maxine Kumin, and Denise Levertov.

979 *A Poetry Reading for Peace in Vietnam*. Santa Barbara: Community Council to End the War in Vietnam, 1967.

A collection of twelve antiwar poems from a poetry reading held on July 23, 1967, in the First Methodist Church in Santa Barbara, California.

980 *Quixote* 1, no. 7 (8).

A seventy-six page "peace issue" of a University of Wisconsin, Madison literary magazine edited by Morris Edelson. The issue is primarily poetry.

981 Ransome, Donald F. *Nothing but the 'Boo*. Portland, Ore.: Skydog Press, 1981.

982 Rottmann, Larry, Jan Barry, and Basil T. Paquet, eds. *Winning Hearts and Minds: War Poems by Vietnam Veterans*. New York: McGraw-Hill, 1972.

The is the first publication of the 1st Casualty Press, a publishing group formed by Vietnam veterans when finding an outlet for authors writing about war experiences was difficult. The poetry was collected by members of Vietnam Veterans Against the War. The 106 poems by thirty-three poets are arranged in chronological order to describe a tour of duty in Vietnam. The editors note that the poets, unlike poets of the past, see themselves as "agent-victims of their own atrocities" and comment that "this poetry is an attempt to grapple with a nightmare, an national madness. It is poetry written out of fire and under fire."

983 Schlosser, Robert. *The Humidity Readings. Samisdat* 29, no. 1 (1981).
Schlosser served in Thailand as a member of the military police from 1969 to 1970. These twenty-nine poems were written during this time and describe his experiences and observations.

984 Shea, Dick. *Vietnam Simply*. Coronado, Calif.: Pro Tem Publishers, 1967.
Shea volunteered for Vietnam after serving in Guantanamo Bay during the Cuban Crisis and later in Cyprus. He was trained as a parachutist, demolitionist, and diver with the SEALs, the group with whom he served in Vietnam. This large collection of his poems speak of his personal feelings about and his experiences in Vietnam. The poems are unpunctuated and untitled.

985 Sinke, Ralph, E. G., Jr. *Don't Cry for Us*. Dale City, Va.: REGS Enterprises, 1984.
Illustrated by effective black and white drawings by W. P. Wass, the thirty-two poems in this collection show the American soldier in Vietnam and his life upon returning home. The author, a Marine major, states that "It is my hope that this book will, in some small measure, assist both veteran and non-veteran alike in achieving a better understanding of the Vietnam soldier and of his sacrifice."

986 Stallworthy, Jon, ed. *The Oxford Book of War Poetry*. New York: Oxford University Press, 1984.
An anthology of war poetry beginning with selections from the Bible. Poetry about man's greatest wars by the greatest poets, including six poems about the Vietnam War and about nuclear war. Vietnam poems include Allen Ginsberg's "A Vow," Galway Kinnell's "Vapor Trail Reflected in the Frog Pond," Denise Levertov's "What Were They Like," Robert Mezey's "How Much Longer?," Margaret Atwood's "It Is Dangerous to Read Newspapers," and Adrian Mitchell's "To Whom It May Concern."

987 Topham, J., ed. *Poems of the Vietnam War: The First Best-Selling Book in American Poetry since the Last Century*. New York: American Poetry Press, 1980.
Jocelyn Hollis is the author of these poems, however, only the name of the editor, J. Topham, appears on this edition. See 938.

988 ____. *Vietnam Heroes: A Tribute – An Anthology of Poems by Veterans and Their Friends*. Claymont, Del.: American Poetry Press, 1982.

A short collection of nineteen poems divided into two sections: poems by veterans, and poems by their friends. Although nine poets are represented, the majority of the poems are by James F. Dawson and J. Hollis.

989 ____. *Vietnam Heroes II: The Tears of a Generation –An Anthology of Poems and Prose by Veterans and Their Friends; Poems and Prose on the Consequences of War*. New York: American Poetry Press, 1982.

Second in a series of anthologies meant to serve as "an open forum for veterans and their friends to be heard." The content appears to be typed. Fourteen authors contributed to the anthology which is divided into four sections: Poems by veterans (sixteen), Poems on World War II (five), Poems by friends of the veterans (nine), and two prose pieces. Revised in 1984.

990 ____. *Vietnam Heroes III: That We Have Peace-An Anthology of Poems by Veterans*. Philadelphia: American Poetry Press, 1983.

A collection of twenty-eight poems by twelve contributors, all but two of which are Vietnam veterans. The major contributors are J. Hollis, Chet Pederson, and Jere Joyner.

991 ____. *Vietnam Heroes IV: The Long Ascending Cry-Memories and Recollections in Story and Poem by Vietnam Veterans*. Philadelphia: American Poetry Press, 1985.

This collection is dedicated to the veterans who still suffer the effects of the war and was compiled on the tenth anniversary of the end of the war. The collection includes thirty-three poems by nine poets with the majority of the poems written by Jim Costilow.

992 Tuck, Alfred David. *Poems of David*. New York: Carlton Press, 1968.

993 *Vietnam in Poems*. McLean, Va.: POW-MIA Common Cause, 1987.

994 *Vietnam Poetry*. Fullerton, Calif.: Union of the Vietnamese in the United States, 1973.

Vietnamese poetry translated into English illustrating Vietnam's struggle with various enemies. The acknowledgement states that "this little book is a sincere attempt to present as much as possible the mainstream of Vietnamese lifestyles and thoughts in the spirit of today's struggle for freedom and national independence."

995 *Vietnam Voices. Overland*, no. 54 (Spring 1973).
A special number of an Australian literary magazine devoted to poetry about the Vietnam War by Australians. Editor R. H. Morrison states in his introduction that "the Australian presence in Vietnam was born in deceit. It was a shabby attempt to buy cheap insurance concealed behind a smoke screen of cold war rhetoric."

996 Weigl, Bruce. *The Monkey Wars*. Athens: University of Georgia Press, 1985.
A nineteen-page collection of poems, eight of which are about the Vietnam War and present graphic images of the horror of the war especially for the civilians. Peaceful images are disrupted violently in the poems in this collection.

997 ____. *A Romance*. Pittsburgh: University of Pittsburgh Press, 1979.
A collection of thirty-five poetic stories set in Vietnam and the American midwest. This collection was the author's doctoral dissertation from the University of Utah.

998 Weiss, Stephen, et al. *A War Remembered: Voices from Vietnam*. Boston: Boston Publishing Company, 1986.
A War Remembered is volume 24 in *The Vietnam Experience* series. Two sections, "Long Way from Home" (56-57) and "Vietnam Voices" (128-29) present twelve poems about the war by American soldiers and Vietnamese civilians.

POETRY IN PERIODICALS

999 Barton, Peter. "Little Tri and Power." *Saturday Review* 52 (26 July 1969):52.
A group of six poems about members of one Vietnamese family.

1000 Nguyen Ngoc Bich. "War Poems From the Vietnamese." *Hudson Review* 20, no. 3 (Autumn 1967):361-68.

Ten poems showing the effect of war on the Vietnamese.

1001 "Poetry of the Anti-War." *Nation* 206, no. 23 (3 June 1968):738-39.

Seven antiwar poems.

1002 "Poetry of the Read-in Campaign." *Nation* 202, no. 22 (30 May 1966):653-55.

Poetry read-ins against the war were held all over the country. The read-ins were organized by poets Robert Bly, Galway Kinnell and David Ray, among others. The participants are listed and four notable poems: "Johnson's Cabinet Watched By Ants," "American Dreams," "Where Is Vietnam?" and "On the War in Vietnam."

1003 "War: Poetic Impressions." *Christian Century* 85, no. 13 (27 March 1968):382-83.

Nine poems about the war without accompanying text.

1004 Vo Van Ai. "Twelve Poems." *Unicorn Journal* 3 (1969):37-52.

These twelve poems, translated from the French by journal editor Teo Savory, begin with a letter from the author to the translator about the poems and the plight of his country. The poems relate the affect of the war on the people of Vietnam.

Dramas

1005 Balk, H. Wesley. *The Dramatization of 365 Days*. University of Minneapolis: Minnesota Press, 1972.

Ronald Glasser's personal narrative, *365 Days*, adapted for the stage.

1006 Berrigan, Daniel. *The Trial of the Catonsville Nine*. Boston: Beacon Press, 1970.

Courtroom drama based on the actual trial of the Berrigan brothers and others for antiwar activities including the burning of selective service records.

1007 Berry, David. *G. R. Point*. New York: Dramatists Play Service, 1980.

The main character is assigned to process the bodies of Vietnam War dead at the graves registration unit (G.R.) where he faces the horror of the war. Two acts.

1008 Brook, Peter. *Us*. In *Tell Me Lies: The Book of the Royal Shakespeare Theater Production*. Indianapolis: Bobbs-Merrill, 1968.

Edited by Michael Kustow, Geoffrey Reeves, and Albert Hunt, this two-act play is an experimental, mixed media drama about the Vietnam War that explores American involvement in Vietnam and

England's reaction to it. This edition contains the text of the play plus background and production notes.

1009 Clark, Sean. *Eleven-Zulu*. New York: French, 1983.

1010 Cole, Tom. *Medal of Honor Rag*. New York: French, 1977.
   A psychiatrist, who is also a concentration camp survivor, tries to help a black Vietnam War veteran suffering the delayed stress caused by the war. A full-length play in one act.

1011 *Coming to Terms: American Plays and the Vietnam War*. New York: Theatre Communications Group, 1985.
   A collection of seven plays about the Vietnam War. The plays selected reflect a broad range of emotions generated by the war. James Reston, Jr., provides a very effective introduction. The plays included are: David Rabe's *Streamers*, Terrence McNally's *Botticelli*, Amlin Gray's *How I Got That Story*, Tom Cole's *Medal of Honor Rag*, Michael Weller's *Moonchildren*, Emily Mann's *Still Life*, and Stephen Metcalfe's *Strange Snow*.

1012 Cowan, Ron. *Summertree*. New York: Random House, 1968.
   A sentimental story of a dying soldier whose life is remembered at the moment of death.

1013 DiFusco, John, et al., eds. *Tracers*. New York: Hill & Wang, 1983.
   The play was written by a group of eight actor Vietnam veterans. The story takes place during and after the war and is based on the authors' own experiences. "Make the first two or three rounds tracers. That way, when you see two red streaks in a row you know you're runnin' outta ammo."

1014 Durang, Christopher. *The Vietnamization of New Jersey: An American Tragedy*. New York: Dramatists Play Service, 1978.
   A two-act play that acts as a reply to Rabe's *Sticks and Bones*. Durang presents his view of the Vietnam and the state of the American family.

1015 Eichman, Mark. *American Gothic*. Chicago: Dramatic Publishing Company, 1977.

    A one-act play in which a "typical" American family is shown. One of their sons was killed in Vietnam. They pretend he is still alive. Their other son was crippled in the war.

1016 Garson, Barbara. *Macbird*. New York: Grove Press, 1967.

    A satiric parody of Shakespeare's *Macbeth* in which Kennedy and Johnson engage in a political struggle.

1017 George, Rob. *Sandy Lee Live at Nui Dat*. Sydney, Australia: Currency Press, 1983.

1018 Gerould, Daniel. "Candaules, Commissioner." In *Drama and Revolution*. Edited by B. F. Dukore. New York: Holt, 1971.

    The legendary Greek story of Candaules updated to the Vietnam War.

1019 Gidding, Nelson R. *The Centurions*. Hollywood: Red Lion Productions, 1965.

    A screenplay based on the novel of the same title by Jean Larteguy. The title on the cover is *Lost Command*, the title under which the movie was released.

1020 Gonzalez, Gloria. "The New America." In *Moving On! Three One-Act Plays*. New York: French, 1971.

    The story of a Vietnam era draft dodger and his flight to Canada.

1021 Graves, Warren. "The Proper Perspective." In *"The Proper Perspective" and "Who's Looking after the Atlantic?" Two One-Act Plays*. Toronto: Playwrights Co-op, 1978.

    A Senate investigation of a commander's role in a My Lai-like massacre in Vietnam. A one-act improvisational drama. Also in *Contemporary Canadian Drama*, compiled by Joseph L. Shaver (Ottawa: Borealis Press, 1974).

1022 Gray, Amlin. *How I Got That Story*. New York: Dramatists Play Service, 1981.

A two-act play in which a journalist is sent to an imaginary country suspiciously like Vietnam during the war. As he sends back the reports of what he is seeing, he becomes more and more disillusioned.

1023 Guare, John. "Muzeeka." In *"Cop-Out," "Muzeeka," "Home Fires": Three Plays*. New York: Grove Press, 1971.

American middle class values and the presentation of the Vietnam War through the television medium are satirized.

1024 Hare, David. *Saigon: Year of the Cat*. London: Faber and Faber, 1983.

A drama depicting the fall of Saigon.

1025 Henderson, Nancy. "Honor the Brave." In *Celebrate America: A Baker's Dozen of Plays*. New York: Messner, 1978.

In a cemetery on Memorial Day, two Vietnam veterans try to convince two women that the only way to really honor the dead is to work to ensure peace.

1026 Jack, Alex. *Dragonbrood*. Brookline, Mass.: Kanthaka Press, 1977.

A verse play about a journalist in Hue, Vietnam at the beginning of the Tet Offensive.

1027 Kessler, Lyle. *The Watering Place*. New York: Vintage, 1969.

A Vietnam veteran moves in with the family of a friend who died in the war, proceeding to become a nightmare version of the man who came to dinner.

1028 Ketron, Larry. *Rib Cage*. New York: Dramatists Play Service, 1978.

The story of a Vietnam veteran and his relationships in a small South Carolina town.

1029 King, Bruce. *Dustoff*. Santa Fe: Institute of American Indian Arts Press, 1982.

Old military values conflict with the values of the new soldiers in the Vietnam War.

1030 Kopit, Arthur. *Indians*. New York: Hill & Wang, 1969.

A political allegory about Vietnam under the guise of the story of Buffalo Bill and Sitting Bull.

1031 Kubrick, Stanley, Michael Herr, and Gustav Hasford. *Full Metal Jacket*. New York: Knopf, 1987.

The screenplay from the movie that was based on Hasford's *The Short-Timers*.

1032 Kupferberg, Tuli. *Fuck Nam: A Morality Play*. New York: Birth Press, 1967.

A sexually graphic anti-Vietnam War play.

1033 Linney, Romulus. *The Love Suicide at Schofield Barracks*. New York: Dramatists Play Service, 1972.

The drama revolves around an inquiry into the ritualistic suicide of a general and his wife. A two-act play.

1034 McLure, James. *Lone Star*. New York: Dramatists Play Service, 1980.

A Texan relates his Vietnam exploits during a backyard gathering. This one-act comedy is a companion piece to the author's *Laundry and Bourbon* in which the same main character appears.

1035 ____. *Pvt. Wars*. New York: Dramatists Play Service, 1980.

One-act, black comedy set in a veterans hospital. The drama is based on the interactions of the patients, Vietnam veterans.

1036 McNally, Terrence. *Botticelli*. New York: Dramatists Play Service, 1968.

The play takes place in the mid-1960s in a jungle in Vietnam. Two soldiers, Wayne and Stu, are playing a guessing game about artists and writers outside a tunnel where they have a man cornered. He comes out – they kill him.

1037 ____. "Bringing It All Back Home." In *"Cuba Si!," "Bringing It All Back Home," "Last Gasps": Three Plays*. New York: Dramatists Play Service, 1970.

    The moral and emotional wasteland of an American family is shown by their lack of reaction to the death of their son in Vietnam and his body's arrival home.

1038 ____. "Tour." In *Apple Pie: Three One Act Plays*. New York: Dramatists Play Service, 1968.

    Mr. and Mrs. Wilson are touring Rome in this one act-play, but their thoughts return to their son, Chuck, in Vietnam. They send him a postcard, wondering if there is sky left in Vietnam and will he be home soon?

1039 Mann, Emily. *Still Life: A Documentary*. New York: Theatre Communications Group, 1979.

    Three characters speak to the audience from a platform. They are Mark, a Vietnam vet who killed a family of five in the war, his mad wife, Cheryl, and his current lover, the disgruntled Nadine.

1040 Metcalfe, Stephen. *Strange Snow*. New York: Theatre Communications Group, 1982.

    Dave's old Vietnam buddy, Megs, comes to his home to take him fishing on opening day. Dave holds him responsible for the death of their friend Bobby in Vietnam as Bobby had died saving Megs, who was wounded. Dave hadn't wanted Bobby to go back for Megs. As the play unfolds, Megs and Dave's sister Martha, an unmarried school teacher, fall in love.

1041 Moody, M. D. *The Shortchanged Review*. New York: Dramatists Play Service, 1976.

    An Irish FM radio station owner, selfishly borrows his Vietnam veteran son's legacy to back a rock group.

1042 Orr, Mary. *Women Still Weep*. New York: Dramatists Play Service, 1980.

    In the author's earlier play, *Women Must Weep*, the women of a family cope with life after their men have gone to fight in the Civil

War. In the sequel, women descendents of those in the first play cope with the affects of the Vietnam War.

1043 Parkinson, Thomas. *What the Blindman Saw; or 25 Years of the Endless War.* Berkeley, Calif.: Thorp Springs Press, 1970.

A two-act anti-Vietnam play in which Sophocles' Thebes is a metaphor for the United States.

1044 Patrick, Robert. "La Repetition." In *Robert Patrick's Cheep Theatricks.* New York: French, 1969.

The rehearsal of a play about the Vietnam War is disrupted by an actor.

1045 _____. *Kennedy's Children.* New York: Random House, 1976.

The main character is Mark, a Vietnam vet, who reads aloud letters he never sent home from Vietnam at a bar in New York.

1046 Rabe, David. *"The Basic Training of Pavlo Hummel" and "Sticks and Bones."* New York: Viking Press, 1973.

Two of the major Vietnam plays. *The Basic Training of Pavlo Hummel* tells the story of the basic training, army life, and death of a U. S. soldier in Vietnam, told either in flashback or remembered in the last moments of his life. His *Streamers* completes the trilogy. In *Sticks and Bones*, David, a blind Vietnam veteran is goaded into suicide by his mother and father, Ozzie and Harriet, and his brother Ricky. A sad commentary on the American family.

1047 _____. *Streamers.* New York: Knopf, 1975.

Set in an army barracks early in the war, six very different soldiers, awaiting orders to Vietnam, fight over various things including the homosexuality on one of them. The title comes from a blackly humorous song one of the sergeants sings about parachutes that fail to open:

Beautiful streamer,
Open for me,
The sky is above me,
But no canopy---

1048 Ragni, Gerome, and James Rado. *Hair*. New York: Pocket Books, 1966.

First presented in 1967 and billed "the American tribal love-rock musical," *Hair* was one of the first rock musicals and reflected the concerns of the era including the Vietnam War. Experimental. Original sound recording was by RCA Victor in 1967 with music by Galt MacDermot. Also in Richards, Stanley, ed., *Great Rock Musicals* (New York: Stein & Day, 1979), 379-478.

1049 Ribman, Ronald. "The Burial of Esposito." In *Best Short Plays, 1971*. Edited by Stanley Richards. Radnor, Pa.: Chilton, 1971, 157-70.

A father confronts the death of his son in Vietnam.

1050 ____. "The Final War of Ollie Winter." In *CBS Playhouse Presents "The Final War of Ollie Winter."* New York: CBS Television Network, 1967.

A play written for television in which a black soldier tries to remain human – and humane – within the horror of the Vietnam War. As the play progresses, the audience comes to understand how he has been treated in his own country. The play may also be found in *Great Television Plays*, edited by William I. Kaufman (New York: Dell, 1969), 259-301.

1051 Sha, Seh, et al. "Letters from the South." In *Modern Drama from Communist China*. Edited by Walter J. Meserve and Ruth I. Meserve. New York: New York University Press, 1970.

The heroic resistance of the South Vietnamese against foreign invaders is presented in this Chinese version of the war.

1052 Sheridan, Phil. "O'er the Land of the Free." In *Stage 12: Playscripts for Young Actors*. Philadelphia: Westminster Press, 1971.

A two-act play in which the oldest son of the Simpson family, Jim, is home on leave from Vietnam. The family performs a little Flag Day ceremony and are subsequently ridiculed by two young girls on the sidewalk. A discussion ensues in which the sacrifices of World War II and Vietnam soldiers are compared. The girls end up pledging allegiance to the flag. A heavily patriotic, one-dimensional play designed for young people.

1053 Stone, Oliver, and Richard Boyle. "Platoon." In *Oliver Stone's "Platoon" and "Salvador": The Original Screenplays*. New York: Vintage, 1985. Screenplay from the movie *Platoon*. See also 135.

1054 Szanto, George. *After the Ceremony*. Toronto: Playwright's Co-op, 1977. A depiction of the stresses undergone by a Vietnam vet upon returning home to Canada. His difficulties are compounded by the appearance of an old army friend.

1055 Terry, Megan. "Viet Rock." In *"Viet Rock," "Comings and Goings," "Keep Tightly Closed in a Cool Dry Place," "The Gloaming Oh My Darling": Four Plays*. New York: Simon & Schuster, 1967.
    Viet Rock, an antiwar satire, was developed in the author's playwright's workshop for the Open Theatre. The play was created through improvisation and later "solidified" into a script. At the time the play was being written, the war was at its height. Constant revision during production was the norm. During the play's presentation, there is singing and audience involvement. *Viet Rock* has been called a folk war movie. It is a montage of images and feelings, often violent. Act One ends with a Senate hearing investigating the many different attitudes toward the war. Among those called to testify are Jesus Christ, Eleanor Roosevelt, and Cassius Clay.

1056 Valdez, Luis, and El Teatro Campesino. "Dark Root of a Scream." In *From the Barrio: A Chicano Anthology*. Edited by Luis Omar Salinas and Lillian Faderman. San Francisco: Canfield, 1973, 79-98.
    The story of a Chicano woman whose third son was killed in Vietnam and won the Congressional Medal of Honor. It is the third Medal of Honor she owns. Her first son was killed in France. Her second son was killed in Korea. El Teatro Campesino was a theater group of field hands in Delano, California's San Joaquin Valley organized by Luis Valdez to support his union's organizational efforts.

1057 ____. "Soldado Razo." In *Actos*. San Juan Bautista: Menyah Productions, 1971, 131-45.
    The effect of the Vietnam War on Mexican-Americans. Spanish and English mixed throughout the play.

1058 ____. "Vietnam Campesino." In *Actos*. San Juan Bautista: Menyah Productions, 1971, 104-30.

Effect of the Vietnam War on Mexican-Americans.

1059 Weiss, Peter. *Discourse on Viet Nam*. London: Calder & Boyars, 1971.

Translated from the German by Geoffrey Skelton, this experimental play concentrates on presenting Vietnamese history up to Dien Bien Phu.

1060 Weller, Michael. *Moonchildren*. New York: Delacorte, 1971.

A view of the flower-children of the 1960s, their lifestyles, concerns, and values. The scene is a student apartment of a university town.

1061 Wenckheim, Nicholas. *Twelve Hundred Hostages*. Hicksville, N.Y.: Exposition, 1978.

A powerful antiwar play in seven scenes in which two American soldiers, Joel Fenwick and Ned Thompson, are still POWs four years after the end of the war. This play describes their captivity. By 1978, Joel, nearly mad, is in love with a Vietnamese medic Thi-Khim, and foiled in his escape attempts by her illegitimate son, Dao.

1062 Wilson, Lanford. *The 5th of July*. New York: Dramatists Play Service, 1982.

The first play in the Talley Family trilogy and set over the 4th of July holiday finds the legless Vietnam veteran, Ken Talley, hosting a party for ex-Berkeley radicals from the 1960s. All have been scarred in some way by their experiences during that turbulent decade.

1063 *Xa: A Vietnam Primer*. N.p.: Pacifica Tape Library, n.d. Sound Recording.

The Provisional Theatre's dramatization of the history and culture of Vietnam using readings from original narratives and writings of both Vietnamese and French authors. Experimental theater.

Short-Story Collections

1064 Abbott, Lee K. *Love Is a Crooked Thing: Stories*. Chapel Hill, N.C.: Algonquin Books, 1982.

A collection of his short stories that includes three relating to Vietnam:

    a.   "Stand in a Row and Learn," 129-39.
    b.   "We Get Smashed and Our Endings Are Swift," 99-127.
    c.   "When Our Dream World Finds Us, and These Hard Times Are Gone," 1-12.

1065 _____. *Strangers in Paradise*. New York: Putnam, 1985.

A collection of his short stories that includes four relating to Vietnam:

    a.   "Category Z," 111-23.
    b.   "I'm Glad You Asked," 225-31.
    c.   "Rolling Thunder," 57-167.
    d.   "Where Is Garland Steeples Now?" 211-23.

1066 Algren, Nelson. *The Last Carousel*. New York: Putnam, 1973.

A collection of his short stories that includes four relating to Vietnam:

    a.   "I Know They'll Like Me in Saigon," 111-16.
    b.   "Letter From Saigon," 131-37.

    c.   "Police and Mama-Sans Get It All," 144-50.
    d.   "What Country Do You Think You're In," 138-43.

1067 Bejarano, Arthur T. *Bring Back the Boys: U.S. Armed Forces in Indochina.* New York: Vantage, 1977.

1068 Che Lan Vien. *The Fire Blazes.* Hanoi: Foreign Languages Publishing House, 1965.
        The authors are North Vietnamese "writing under the threat of U.S. napalm bombs," as the editor states in the acidly anti-American preface. A collection of twelve short stories relating the Vietnamese experience.

    a.   Anh Duc, "Smoke Screen," 156-70.
    b.   Hoang Le, "Y Moi," 86-96.
    c.   Lam Dong, "The First Days," 131-44.
    d.   Nguyen Thieu Nam, "Rapong Village," 97-116.
    e.   Phan Tu, "Awakened," 26-46.
    f.   Phan Tu, "Fires in the Night," 55-68.
    g.   Phan Tu, "Return to the Village," 69-85.
    h.   Phan Tu, "Two Brothers," 145-55.
    i.   Thanh Giang and Luu Ngo, "An American Sees the Light," 171-81.
    j.   Thuy Thu, "The Little Wooden Sandal," 15-25.
    k.   Van Tranh, "Y Hoa," 117-30.
    l.   Vo Tran Nha, "The Fire Blazes," 47-54.

1069 Crapser, William. *Remains: Stories of Vietnam.* Old Chatham, N.Y.: Sachem Press, 1988.
        See also 874. Short stories include:

    a.   "Baptism of Fire," 21-26.
    b.   "Billy Sunday," 39-43.
    c.   "The Descent," 4-8.
    d.   "Education of a Pointman," 44-48.
    e.   "For Timothy Baer," 74-80.
    f.   "Hungers," 27-34.
    g.   "Land of the Free, Home of the Brave," 96-101.
    h.   "Let It Be," 165-69.
    i.   "New Man," 19-20.
    j.   "Nicky Martinez," 49-57.
    k.   "Proud," 13-18.
    l.   "R & R," 58-70.

    m. "The Rest," 81-82.
    n. "Remains," 83-90.
    o. "The Wall: Michael Bowle," 11-12.
    p. "The War Enters," 9-10.
    q. "Wild Child," 102-64.

1070 Dann, Jean Van Buren, and Jack Dann. *In the Field of Fire*. New York: Tor, 1987.

An anthology of twenty-two science fiction short stories expressing the horror of the Vietnam experience through fantasy. Contributors include the well-known in the science fiction world as well as some lesser-known writers. An excellent introduction focusing on post-traumatic stress is included. The authors feel that the truth of war is often best told through dreams.

1071 De Grazia, Emilio. *Enemy Country*. St. Paul, Minn.: New Rivers Press, 1984.

A collection of eleven short stories on the Vietnam War by the author.

    a. "Brothers of the Tiger," 59-94.
    b. "The Cat-Hater," 95-108.
    c. "The Death of Sin," 9-19.
    d. "The Enemy," 41-48.
    e. "Enemy Country," 49-58.
    f. "The Girl and Two Old Men," 30-41.
    g. "Light At the End of the Tunnel," 133-45.
    h. "The Man Who Cursed and the Good Lutheran Boy," 116-20.
    i. "The Mask," 20-29.
    j. "The Sniper," 121-32.
    k. "Zabel and Cholez," 109-15.

1072 *Distant Stars*. Hanoi: Foreign Languages Publishing House, 1976.

A collection of North Vietnamese short stories that show the affect of the war.

    a. Chu Van, "The Perfume of the Areca Palm," 52-73.
    b. Do Chu, "The Wind in the Valley," 109-27.
    c. Le Minh Khu, "Distant Star," 9-34.
    d. Ma Van Khang, "The Young Meo Wife," 74-95.
    e. Nguyen Minh Chau, "Moonlight in the Forest," 156-76.
    f. Nguyen Thi Nhu Trang, "Rain," 35-51.

g. Tran Kim Thanh, "Story on the Bank of the River," 177-91.
h. Vu Le Mai, "The Heart of a Mother," 128-42.
i. Vu Thi Thuong, "The Drama of a Director of a Cooperative," 192-223.
j. Xuan Cang, "The Sparks," 143-55.
k. Xuan Trinh, "On the Long Road," 96-108.

1073 Duncan, H. G. *Brown Side Out: More Marine Corps Sea-Stories*. San Diego: James H. Gregory, 1983.
    Seventy-three short vignette, letter-style stories from Gene to Tom which tell of the men of the Marine Corps from 1950 to 1979, with the major emphasis on Vietnam. The author served two tours in Vietnam and was twice wounded. Glossary of terms.

1074 Goodman, Charles. *Hell's Brigade*. New York: Magnum/Prestige, 1966.
    A collection of men's magazine adventure stories.

1075 Gray, Nigel, ed. *Phoenix Country*. A special issue of *Fireweed*. September 1976.

1076 Gulassa, Cyril M. *The Fact of Fiction: Social Relevance in the Short Story*. San Francisco: Canfield Press, 1972.
    Thirty stories that, according to the introduction, "explore universal human problems within the context of today's social issues." Six of the stories deal with Vietnam.

1077 *Hair-Trigger III: A Story Workshop Anthology*. Chicago: Columbia College Writing Department, 1979.
    An anthology by advanced writing students and faculty at Columbia College that includes short stories and poetry. Five stories are on Vietnam.

1078 Henschel, Lee, Jr. *Short Stories of Vietnam*. Guthrie, Minn.: Guthrie Publishing Company, 1981.
    A collection of ten short stories by a former high school teacher.

    a. "The Desertion of Wiley Blooms," 40-107.
    b. "Ferguson and the Old Mama-San from Song Mao," 21-25.

    c.   "The First Day," 1-4.
    d.   "The 5:50 News," 16-19.
    e.   "The Game," 6-9.
    f.   "Going Back," 147-54.
    g.   "Psychadelic 'Nam: The World," 27-38.
    h.   "Psychadelic 'Nam: Karma," 128-45.
    i.   "The 'Reb,'" 11-14.
    j.   "Yobo Shibo," 109-26.

1079 *The Ivory Comb*. South Vietnam: Giai Phong Publishing House, 1968.
       A collection of short stories with an anti-American tone. Vietnamese forces are seen fighting for freedom as American forces burn down villages and kill innocent people who have not harmed the American people. The seven stories included are:.

    a.   Anh Duc, "Mr. Fourth's Dream," 41-62.
    b.   Anh Duc, "The Native Land," 25-40.
    c.   Anh Duc, "The Son," 9-24.
    d.   Giang Nam, "Crossing the Chu Lay Mountain," 63-84.
    e.   Nam Ha, "The Soil," 137-53.
    f.   Nguyen Sang, "The Ivory Comb," 113-36.
    g.   Nguyen Trung Thanh, "The Xanu Forest," 85-112.

1080 Jenks, Tom. *Soldiers and Civilians: Americans at War and at Home – Short Stories*. New York: Bantam Books, 1986.
       Vietnam is the core of the collection with nine stories. Jenks notes that the stories "redefine traditional military values and show the dark side – the consequences of war." The anthology ends with "Human Moments in World War III," by Don DeLillo, which meditates on man's future.

1081 Karlin, Wayne, Basil T. Paquet, and Larry Rottmann, eds. *Free Fire Zone: Short Stories by Vietnam Veterans*. New York: McGraw-Hill, 1973.
       A major collection of twenty-six Vietnam short stories.

1082 Klinkowitz, Jerome, and John Somer, eds. *Writing under Fire: Stories of the Vietnam War*. New York: Delta, 1978.
       A major collection of twenty stories with a chronology of the war and a bibliography.

1083 Ly Qui Chung, ed. *Between Two Fires: The Unheard Voices of Vietnam*. New York: Praeger, 1970.

    Nine short stories originally published in *Tieng Noi Dan Toc* (The people's voice), a Saigon newspaper, in 1969. Four of the stories are about the war.

    a.   Chu Thao, "Resuscitation of Dead Earth," 53-61.
    b.   Nguyen Pham Ngoc, "House for Rent," 63-73.
    c.   Nguyen Tan Bi, "When the Americans Came," 3-14.
    d.   Thanh Chau, "The Tears of Tan Qui Dong," 21-41.

1084 Mayer, Tom. *The Weary Falcon*. Boston: Houghton Mifflin, 1971.

    Five short stories about the war by the author.

    a.   "A Birth in the Delta," 149-74.
    b.   "Kafka for President," 111-47.
    c.   "The Last Operation," 79-10.
    d.   "A Walk in the Rain," 55-57.
    e.   "The Weary Falcon," 1-54.

1085 Moore, Robin. *Combat Pay*. New York: Manor Books, 1976.

    A collection of twenty-six short stories. Three are about Vietnam.

    a.   "Combat Pay," 13-41.
    b.   "We Have Met the Enemy," 181-86.
    c.   "Welcome Home," 220-27.

1086 Moore, Robin. *The Green Berets*. New York: Crown, 1965.

    This collection of eight short stories tells the story of the Special Forces fighting in Indo-China in 1964. The authors note that the stories are fact-based fiction. Each story intends to show a different facet of the Forces.

    a.   "The Cao-Dai Pagoda," 97-111.
    b.   "Coup de Grace," 149-73.
    c.   "Fourteen VC POW's," 232-50.
    d.   "A Green Beret – All the Way," 26-75.
    e.   "Hit 'Em Where They Live," 270-346.
    f.   "Home to Nanette," 174-231.
    g.   "The Immodest Mr. Pomfret," 251-69.
    h.   "The Immortal Sergeant Hanks," 76-96.
    i.   "Two Birds With One Stone," 112-48.

1087 Mort, John. *Tanks: Short Fiction*. Kansas City, Mo.: BkMk Press, University of Missouri, 1986.
>Eight short stories about the war by the author.

>a. "Called to God," 7-15.
>b. "Gomez," 69-78.
>c. "Good Blood," 1-5.
>d. "Hot," 55-60.
>e. "Human Wave," 17-26.
>f. "Lisa," 69-78.
>g. "The New Captain," 61-68.
>h. "Tanks," 27-54.

1088 *The Mountain Trail*. Hanoi: Vietnam Women's Union, 1970.
>A collection of seven stories emphasizing the North Vietnamese women who fought against the U.S.

>a. Bich Thuan, "The Red Tie," 9-24.
>b. Bich Thuan, "Women Gunners in Quang Binh," 25-40.
>c. Huu Mai, "The Mountain Trail," 117-36.
>d. Ma Van Kang, "Sung My," 77-99.
>e. Nguyen Kien, "A Moonlit-Night in the Forest," 41-56.
>f. Nguyen Thi Nhu Trang, "Drizzling," 101-16.
>g. To Hoang, "The Intermediate Post," 57-75.

1089 Primm, Sandy. *Short Time: Stories*. St. Louis, Mo.: Cauldron Press, 1977.
>A collection of thirty-seven short vignettes, some less than a paragraph. The author was a military correspondent, drafted and based in Saigon from October, 1968 to June, 1969. The vignettes give the reader a view of war experienced by those in Vietnam and those at home.

1090 Suddick, Tom. "A Few Good Men." *Samisdat* 4, no. 1 (1974).
>A collection of eight stories of Marines in Vietnam by the author. The title is taken from the ubiquitous bumper sticker "The Marines are looking for a few good men." The author states in his preface, "On Beating Dead Horses," that the purpose of this collection is a self-purging of demons and says ". . . for a long time I beat dead horses – tried to come to grips with my involvement in what must be the biggest mistake we've ever made. But that's all over now, like the war; I

can wash my hands of the whole matter. Finally, the damn thing is over."

- a.   "Caduceus," 8-20.
- b.   "The Diehard," 108-16.
- c.   "A Hotel on Park Place," 21-34.
- d.   "If a Frog Had Wings," 35-45.
- e.   "It Was a Great Fight, Ma," 46-66.
- f.   "A Shithouse Rat," 69-78.
- g.   "Totenkopf," 79-88.
- h.   "The Two Hundredth Eye," 89-107.

1091 Tam, H. T. *Saigon Seven*. Saigon: Damson, 1968.
Seven short stories by the author.

- a.   "Black Jack Won't Make It Home," 101-18.
- b.   "A Footsoldier in Town," 65-82.
- c.   "Here is the Kill Road," 23-41.
- d.   "Operation Hang Xanh," 119-73.
- e.   "Pfc Report," 43-63.
- f.   "The PMA Guy," 83-100.
- g.   "Silver Bird Slave," 6-21.

1092 "War Stories." *TriQuarterly* 45 (Spring 1979).
Edited by Elliot Anderson and Robert Onopa of Northwestern University, Evanston, Illinois, which publishes *TriQuarterly*, this collection of fourteen short stories includes five about Vietnam.

1093 Wongar, B. *The Sinners: Stories of Vietnam*. Greensborough, Victoria, Australia: Greensborough Press, 1972.
B. Wongar is a pseudonym for a mulatto American who served in the Army in Vietnam and deserted, fleeing to the bush while on leave in Australia. He lives with the Aborigines. Alan Marshall explains in his introduction that he received these stories through an intermediary.

- a.   "At Half Mast," 29-38.
- b.   "Boomerang Bullets," 21-28.
- c.   "The Charge at Dawn," 53-59.
- d.   "Hole," 13-20.
- e.   "Hot Ace," 47-52.
- f.   "Khe Sanh," 39-52.
- g.   "The Soldier That Died of Glory," 61-76.

Individual Short Stories

1094 Abbott, Lee K. "The Viet Cong Love of Sgt. Donnie T. Bobo." In
 − *The Heart Never Fits Its Wanting*. Edited by Lee K. Abbott. Cedar
 Falls, Iowa: North American Review, 1980, 26-34.

 − *North American Review* 264, no. 3 (Winter 1979):43-47.

 − *Touring Nam*. Ed. Greenburg. 181-92. (877).

1095 Aitken, James. "Lederer's Legacy." In *Free Fire Zone*. Ed. Karlin. 80-96.
 (1081).

1096 Alberts, Laurie. "Veterans." In *Love Stories/Love Poems*. Edited by Joe
 David Bellamy and Roger Weingarten. Canton, N.Y.: Fiction
 International, no. 14, 1982, 56-64.

1097 Aldiss, Brian. "My Country 'Tis Not Only of Thee." In *In the Field of
 Fire*. Ed. Dann. 370-92. (1070).

1098 Anderson, Kent. "Sympathy for the Devil." In
 − *Touring Nam*. Ed. Greenburg. 117-79. (877).

 − "War Stories." *TriQuarterly*. 99-150. (1092).

1099 Anderson, S. E. "Soldier Boy." In *Vietnam and Black America*. Ed.
 Taylor. 195-99. (885).

1100 Arias-Misson, Alain. "Vietnam-Superfiction." In
      – Chicago Review 23, no. 2 (Autumn 1971):5-23.

      – Stone Country, (Fall/Winter 1982):63-67.

      – Writing under Fire. Ed. Klinkowitz. 239-52. (1082).

1101 Asimov, Isaac. "The Thirteenth Page." In *The Union Club Mysteries*.
New York: Doubleday, 1983, 86-92.

1102 Baber, Asa.
    a. "The Ambush" (also known as "Ambush: Laos, 1960"). In

      – The Falcon, no. 4 (March 1972):39-42.

      – Touring Nam. Ed. Greenburg. 94-101. (877).

      – Tranquility Base and Other Stories. Canton, N.Y.: Fiction
      International, 1979, 14-20.

      – Vietnam Anthology. Ed. Anisfield. 45-49. (874).

      – "War Stories." *TriQuarterly*. 165-71. (1092).

      – Writing under Fire. Ed. Klinkowitz. 130-35. (1082).

    b. "The French Lesson." *Playboy* 28, no. 3 (March 1961):98-100, 108,
      202, 205-6, 208.

    c. "How I Got Screwed and Almost Tattooed, by Huck Finn." In
      Tranquility Base and Other Stories. Canton, N.Y.: Fiction
      International, 1979, 95-108.

1103 Ballard, J. G. "The University of Death." In
      – Transatlantic Review, no. 29 (Summer 1968):68-79.

      – Writing under Fire. Ed. Klinkowitz. 227-38. (1082).

1104 Bambara, Toni Cade. "The Sea Birds Are Still Alive." In *The Sea Birds
Are Still Alive: Collected Stories*. New York: Random House, 1974, 71-
93.

1105 Banks, Russell. "The Fish." In *Success Stories*. New York: Harper &
Row, 1986, 40-48.

1106 Barrus, Tim. "Tunnel Rats." *Christopher Street* 9, no. 105, 22-30.

1107 Baxter, Charles. "Xavier Speaking." In *Harmony of the World: Stories*. Columbia: University of Missouri Press, 1984, 17-35.

1108 Beal, M. F. "Survival." In
  –*The Fact of Fiction*. Ed. Gulassa. 122-32. (1076).

  –*New American Review,* no. 3. New York: New American Library, 1968, 188-200.

1109 Belanger, Charles A. "Once upon a Time When It Was Night." In *Angels in My Oven: A Story Workshop Anthology*. Edited by John Schultz. Chicago: Columbia College, 1976, 76-86.

1110 Bennett, Curtis D. "Khe Sahn Resupply: A Short Story." In *Aerospace Historian* 23, no. 4, Winter (December 1976):189-96.

1111 Blake, George."The Expatriate." *Literary Review* 16 (Fall 1972):67-82.

1112 Blei, Norbert. "An American Presence." In *The Ghost of Sandburg's Phizzog and Other Stories*. Peoria, Ill.: Ellis Press, 1986, 41-62.

1113 Bobrowsky, Igor. "The Courier." In *Free Fire Zone*. Ed. Karlin. 98-107. (1081).

1114 Bonazzi, Robert. "Light Casualties." *Transatlantic Review,* no. 28 (Spring 1969):46-51.

1115 Boswell, Robert. "The Right Thing." In *Dancing in the Movies*. Iowa City: University of Iowa Press, 1986, 127-44.

1116 Bova, Ben. "Brothers." In *In the Field of Fire*. Edited by Dann. 211-23. (1070).

1117 Boyd, William. "On the Yankee Station." In *On the Yankee Station: Stories*. New York: Morrow, 1984, 104-29.

1118 Boyle, Kay. "You Don't Have to Be a Member of the Congregation." In *Little Victories, Big Defeats: War as the Ultimate Pollution*. Compiled by George S. McHargue. New York: Delacorte, 1974, 11-18.

1119 Brunner, John. "The Inception of the Epoch of Mrs. Bedonebyasyoudid." In *From This Day Forward*. Garden City, N.Y.: Doubleday, 1972, 215-22.

1120 Bunting, Josiah. "The Lionheads" (excerpt). In *Touring Nam*. Ed. Greenburg. 223-62. (877).

1121 Burdick, Eugene. "Cold Day, Cold Fear." In *A Role in Manila: Fifteen Tales of War, Postwar, Peace and Adventure*. New York: New American Library, 1966, 40-51.

1122 Camoin, Francois. "Home Is the Blue Moon Cafe." In *Why Men Are Afraid of Women*. Athens: University of Georgia Press, 1984, 79-91.

1123 Carper, Charles. "The Land of the Free." In *Story: The Yearbook of Discovery, 1969*. Edited by Hallie Burnett and Whit Burnett. New York: Four Winds Press, 1969.

1124 Carr, Jess. "A Flicker of the Torch." In *A Creature Was Stirring and Other Stories*. Radford, Va.: Commonwealth Press, 1970, 103-25.

1125 Caspar, Susan. "Covenant with a Dragon,." In *In the Field of Fire*. Ed. Dann. 305-24. (1070).

1126 Chatain, Robert.
    a. "The Adventure of the Mantises." In

    –*The Fact of Fiction*. Ed. Gulassa. 104-11. (1076).

    –*New American Review*, no. 7. New York: New American Library, 1969, 150-58.

    b. "The Appointment." In *Ship Ride down the Spring Branch and Other Stories*. Edited by Jess Carr. Durham, N.C.: Moore, 1978, 117-26.

    c. "On the Perimeter." In

    –*New American Review*, no. 13. New York: Simon & Schuster, 1971, 112-31.

    –*Touring Nam*. Ed. Greenburg. 302-23. (877).

    –*Writing under Fire*. Klinkowitz. 209-26. (1082).

1127 Ch'en, Ying-Chen. "A Rose in June." In *Born of the Same Roots: Stories of Modern Chinese Women*. Edited by Vivian Ling Hsu. Bloomington: Indiana University Press, 1981, 210-26.

1128 Chiverton, William S., Jr. "Welcome to the World." In *Vietnam Flashbacks*. Ed. Villani. 62-63. (887).

1129 Clifton, Merritt. "Betrayal." *Samisdat* 24, no. 4 (1980):2-31.

1130 Clodfelter, Michael D. "The Mountain." In "Tour of Duty." *Samisdat* 46, no. 2 (1986):93-95.

1131 Coe, Charles. "First Combat." In *Story: The Yearbook of Discovery, 1968.* Edited by Hallie Burnett and Whit Burnett. New York: Four Winds Press, 1968, 277-81.

1132 Coetzee, J. M. "The Vietnam Project." In *Dusklands.* Johannesburg: Ravan Press, 1982, 1-49.

1133 Cohen, Stanley, "I'm Sorry, Mr. Griggs." In
   − *Best Detective Stories of the Year, 1975.* New York: Dutton, 1975, 215-23.

   − The Mystery Writers of America. *A Special Kind of Crime.* Garden City, N.Y.: Doubleday, 1982, 1-9.

1134 Cole, Duff.
   a. "Got Some Religion." In "Tour of Duty." *Samisdat* 46, no. 2 (1986):27-28. (881).

   b. "Two Jokers." In "Tour of Duty." *Samisdat* 46, no. 2 (1986):102-9. (881).

1135 Coleman, Charles A. "In Loco Parentis." In "War Stories." *TriQuarterly.* 189-98. (1092).

1136 Cross, Ronald Anthony. "The Heavenly Blue Answer." In *In the Field of Fire.* Ed. Dann. 258-69. (1070).

1137 Curley, Daniel. "Billy Will's Song,." In *Living with Snakes: Stories.* Athens: University of Georgia Press, 1985, 107-19.

1138 Currer, Barney. "The Rabbi." In *Free Fire Zone.* Ed. Karlin. 188-201. (1081).

1139 Dann, Jack. "Among the Mountains." In *Timetripping.* Garden City, N.Y.: Doubleday, 1980, 142-69.

1140 Davis, George.
   a. "Ben." In *Free Fire Zone.* Ed. Karlin. 183-86. (1081).

b. "Ben" (different story from the above). In *Free Fire Zone*. Ed. Karlin. 187-88. (1081).

c. "Coming Home" (excerpt). In *Vietnam and Black America*. Ed. Taylor. 185-94. (885).

1141 Dawson, Fielding. "The Triangle on the Jungle Wall." In *Krazy Kat, the Unveiling and Other Stories*. Los Angeles: Black Sparrow Press, 1969, 209-11.

1142 DeGrazia, Emilio.
a. "Brothers of the Tiger." In

   −*Enemy Country*. Ed. DeGrazia. 58-94. (1071).

   −*Likely Stories: A Collection of Untraditional Fiction*. Edited by Bruce R. McPherson. New Paltz, N.Y.: Treacle Press, 1981, 9-46.

b. "The Sniper." In

   −*Enemy Country*. Ed. DeGrazia. 121-32. (1071).

   −*Samisdat* 17, no. 1 (Spring 1978):29-42.

1143 Deighton, Len. "First Base." In *Eleven Declarations of War*. New York: Harcourt Brace Jovanovich, 1971, 98-115.

1144 Dempsey, Hank. "The Defensive Bomber." In *Nova 3*. Edited by Harry Harrison. New York: Walker, 1973, 93-111.

1145 Dick, Philip K. "Faith of Our Fathers." In *Dangerous Visions*. Edited by Harlan Ellison. Garden City, N.Y.: Doubleday, 1967, 181-215.

1146 Dinh Phong. "A Surgical Operation." South Vietnam: Giai Phong Publishing House, 1969, 22 pp.

1147 Domini, John. "Over 4,000 Square Miles." In *Bedlam: Short Stories*. Canton, N.Y.: Fiction International, 1976, 9-30.

1148 Dorris, James R. "The Accident." In *Free Fire Zone*. Ed. Karlin. 21-27. (1081).

1149 Dozois, Gardner R. "A Dream at Noonday." In
   −*In the Field of Fire*. Ed. Dann. 224-36. (1070).

- *Orbit* 7. Edited by Damon Knight. New York: Putnam, 1970, 127-39.

- *The Visible Man*. Edited by Gardner R. Dozois. New York: Berkley, 1977, 119-32.

1150 Drake, David.
- a. "Contact!" In *Body Armor: 2000*. Edited by Joe Haldeman, with Charles G. Waugh and Martin Harry. New York: Ace Science Fiction Books, 1986, 5-20.

- b. "Firefight." In *Frights: New Stories of Suspense and Supernatural Terror*. Edited by Kirby McCauley. New York: St. Martin's, 1976, 181-204.

1151 Dubbs, Chris. "My Fear in Little Cages." In *Vietnam Flashbacks*. Ed. Villani. 44-45. (887).

1152 Dubus, Andre. "Dressed Like Summer Leaves." In
- *The Last Worthless Evening: Our Novellas and Two Stories*. Edited by Andre Dubus. Boston: Godine, 1986, 65-78.

- *Sewanee Review* 94 (Fall 1986):541-54.

1153 Dwan, Kevin. "War Chips." In *Intro 6: Life as We Know It, and Other Original Fiction and Poetry with a Symposium on the First Novel Before and After*. Edited by George Garrett. Garden City, N.Y.: Anchor/Doubleday, 1974.

1154 Eastlake, William. "The Biggest Thing Since Custer." In
- *Atlantic Monthly* 222, no. 3 (September 1968):92-97.

- *Fifty Years of the American Short Story*, vol. 1. Edited by William Abrahams. Garden City, N.Y.: Doubleday, 1970, 243-53.

- *Killing Time: A Guide to Life in the Happy Valley*. Edited by Robert Disch and Barry Schwartz. New York: Prentice-Hall, 1972, 219-28.

- *Prize Stories, 1970: The O. Henry Awards*. Edited by William Abrahams. Garden City, N.Y.: Doubleday, 1970, 17-28.

- *Writing under Fire*. Ed. Klinkowitz. 58-68. (1082).

1155 Edelson, Morris. "A Mission in Vietnam." *Quixote* 1, no. 7 (June 1966):40-43.

1156 Ehrhart, W. D.
    a. "The Arrival." *Samisdat* 21, no. 1, 79th release, 47-54.
    b. "I Drink My Coffee Black." In

        – *Vietnam Flashbacks*. Ed. Villani. 42-43. (887).

        – "War Stories." *TriQuarterly*, 172-77. (1092).

1157 Ellison, Harlan.
    a. "The Basilisk." In

        – *Deathbird Stories*. Edited by Harlan Ellison. New York: Dell, 1975, 94-113.

        – *In the Field of Fire*. Ed. Dann. 350-69. (1070).

        – *Study War No More: A Selection of Alternatives*. Edited by Joe Haldeman. New York: St. Martin's, 1977, 7-25.

    b. "Night of Black Glass." In *Stalking the Nightmare*. Bloomfield, Mich.: Phantasia Press, 1982, 159-70.

1158 Elonka, Stephen Michael. "Marmy's Etched Teeth." In *Marmaduke Surfaceblow's Salty Technical Romances*. Huntington, N.Y.: Krieger, 1979, 75-77.

1159 Epstein, Leslie. "Lessons." In *The Steinway Quintet, Plus Four*. Boston: Little, Brown, 1976, 67-106.

1160 Erhart, Stephen. "As the Hippest Doctor Almost Grooved." *Harper's* 242, no. 1452 (May 1971):82-86.

1161 Etchinson, Dennis. "Deathtracks." In *In the Field of Fire*. Ed. Dann. 247-57. (1070).

1162 Fabian, Stephen E. "Dat-Tay-Vao." *Amazing Stories* 81, no. 6 (March 1987):16-33.

1163 Ferlinghetti, Lawrence. "Where Is Vietnam." In *New Directions in Prose and Poetry 19*. Edited by J. Laughlin. New York: New Directions, 1966, 201-2.

      A very short vignette.

1164 Ferrandino, Joseph. "Saddleback Ridge." In *Vietnam Flashbacks*. Ed. Villani. 26-29. (887).

1165 Ferry, James. "Dancing Ducks and Talking Anus." In
    – *The Best American Short Stories, 1982*. Edited by John Gardner, with Shannon Ravenel. Boston: Houghton Mifflin, 1982, 18-36.

    – *Literary Review* 25, no. 1 (Fall 1981):35-56.

1166 Flanagan, Robert.
    a. "A Game of Some Significance." *Phoebe* 8, no. 3 (July 1979):52-57.

    b. "Mayday." *Phoebe* 10, no. 4 (Summer 1981):71-75.

    c. "An Ordinary Imperative." *Phoebe* 10, no. 1 (Fall 1980):68-73.

1167 Flynn, Robert.
    a. "The Feelings of the Dead." In *Seasonal Rain and Other Stories*. San Antonio, Tex.: Corona/David Bowen, 137-44. (1086).

    b. "The Killer." In

    – *Seasonal Rain and Other Stories*. San Antonio, Tex.: Corona/David Bowen, 1986, 129-36.

    – *Vietnam Flashbacks*. Ed. Villani. 48-49. (887).

1168 Ford, Richard. "Communist." In *Soldiers and Civilians*. Ed. Jenks. 64-79. (1080).

1169 Fowler, Karen Joy.
    a. "The Lake Was Full of Artificial Things." *Isaac Asimov's Science Fiction Magazine*, October 1985.

    b. "Letters from Home." In *In the Field of Fire*. Ed. Dann. 70-89. (1070).

1170 Frazier, Robert. "Across Those Endless Skies." In *In the Field of Fire*. Ed. Dann. 90-106. (1070).

1171 Friedman, Paul. "Portrait: My American Man, Fall 1966." In
    – *New Directions in Prose and Poetry* 20. New York: 1968, 63-69.

    – *Writing under Fire*. Ed. Klinkowitz. 146-11. (1082).

1172 Gains, Timothy Southerly. "The Deserter." *North American Review* 259, no. 4 (Winter 1974):53-60.

1173 Garry, Allan. "Two Looks at the Funeral Business." *Red Fox Reviews* 1, no. 5 (1977):51-56.

1174 Geller, Ruth. "Pat's Friend Norm." In *Pictures from the Past and Other Stories*. Buffalo, N.Y.: Imp Press, 1978, 187-94.

1175 Gerald, John Bart
    a.   "Blood Letting." In

        – *Atlantic Monthly* 113, no. 5 (May 1969):88-90.

        – *The Best American Short Stories, 1970*. Edited by Martha Foley and David Burnett. Boston: Houghton Mifflin, 1970, 108-14.

    b.   "Walking Wounded." In

        – *The Best American Short Stories, 1969*. Edited by Martha Foley and David Burnett. Boston: Houghton Mifflin, 1969, 37-48.

        – *The Fact of Fiction*. Ed. Gulassa. 112-21. (1076).

        – *Harper's* 237, no. 1419 (August 1968):45-50.

1176 Gibson, John. *Nothing Could Happen*. Burnsville, N.C.: AMS/RGW, 1987, 41 pp.

1177 Gibson, Margaret. "All Over Now." In *Considering Her Condition*. New York: Vanguard, 1978, 53-68.

1178 Glasser, Ronald, J. "A Simpler Creed." In *Writing under Fire*. Ed. Klinkowitz. 69-70. (1082).

1179 Grajewski, Julian. "The Meeting." In *The Fire Zone*. Ed.Karlin. 14-16. (1081).

1180 Grant, Charles L.
    a. "Come Dance with Me on My Pony's Grave." *Magazine of Fantasy and Science Fiction* 45, no. 1 (July 1973):72-84.

    b. "The Sheeted Dead." In *In the Field of Fire*. Ed. Dann. 95-106. (1070).

1181 Grant, John. "Polyorific Enterprises." *Penthouse* 6, no. 5 (January 1975):64-66, 146-48.

1182 Grau, Shirley Ann. "Homecoming." In
    –*Vietnam Anthology*. Ed. Anisfield. 56-65. (874).

    –*The Wind Shifting West*. New York: Knopf, 1973, 41-54.

1183 Grinstead, David. "A Day in Operations." In
    –*The Fact of Fiction*. Ed. Gulassa. 86-98. (1076).

    –*Literary Review* 12, no. 1 (Autumn 1968):103-15.

    –*Prize Stories, 1970: The O. Henry Awards*. Edited by William Abrahams. Garden City, N.Y.: Doubleday, 1970, 205-18.

1184 Guidera, Mark. "Tiger in the Rain." *North American Mentor Magazine* 22, no. 1 (Spring 1984):22-29.

1185 Haldeman, Joe W.
    a. "Counterpoint." In

    –*Infinite Dreams*. Edited by Joe W. Haldeman. New York: St. Martin's, 1978, 1-12.

    –*Orbit 11: An Anthology of New Stories*. Edited by Damon Francis Knight. New York: Putnam, 1972, 168-78.

    b. "DX." In *In the Field of Fire*. Ed. Dann. 393-401. (1070).

    c. "The Monster." In *Cutting Edge*. Edited by Dennis Etchison. Garden City, N.Y.: Doubleday, 1986, 56-66.

1186 Hall, James B. "God Cares, but Waits." In
    –*New Directions in Prose and Poetry 22*. New York, 1970, 1-18.

    –*Writing under Fire*. Ed. Klinkowitz. 253-70. (1082).

1187 Hamil, Ralph E. "The Vietnam War Centennial Celebration." *Analog* 90, no. 2 (October 1972):94-107.

1188 Hannah, Barry. "Midnight and I'm Not Famous Yet." In
   −*Airships*. New York: Knopf, 1978, 105-18.

   −*Esquire* 84, no. 1 (July 1975):58-60, 134-36.

1189 Hardy, Frank.
   a. "A Friend Today Is an Enemy of Tomorrow." In *We Took Their Orders and Are Dead*. Ed. Cass. 52-61. (875).

   b. "How I Met General Pau." In *We Took Their Orders and Are Dead*. Ed. Cass. 62-68. (875).

1190 Harrington, Joyce. "A Letter to Amy." In *The Year's Best Mystery and Suspense Stories, 1986*. Edited by Edward D. Hoch. New York: Walker, 1986, 83-102.

1191 Harrison, Harry. "Commando Raid." In *Study War No More: A Selection of Alternatives*. Edited by Joe Haldeman. New York: Avon, 1977, 101-10.

1192 Hasford, Gustav.
   a. "Is That You, John Wayne? Is This Me?" *Mirror Northwest* 3 (1972):58-59.

   b. "The Short-Timers" (excerpt). In *Yesterday's Tomorrows*. Edited by Frederick Pohl. New York: Berkley, 1982, 425-30.

1193 Hauley, D., Jr. "Two Separate Men Sharing the Same Seat On a Train." *Mirror Northwest* 2 (1971):56-60.

1194 Heinemann, Larry.
   a. "By the Rule." In *It Never Stopped Raining*. Edited by John Schultz. Chicago: Columbia College, 1971, 15-18.

   b. "Cole." In *It Never Stopped Raining*. Edited by John Schultz. Chicago: Columbia College, 1971, 9-14.

   c. "Coming Home High" (excerpt from *Close Quarters*). In
   −*Penthouse*, December 1974, 92-94, 160, 175-76.

–*The Story Workshop Reader.* Edited by John Schultz. Chicago: Columbia College, 1982, 29-55.

d. "Do You Know What an Ambush Is?" In *Don't You Know There's a War On?* Edited by John Schultz. Chicago: Columbia College, 1969, 13.

e. "The Firefight." *Penthouse* 7, no. 2 (October 1975):100-102, 115-17.

f. "The First Clean Fact." In

–*The Best American Short Stories, 1980.* Edited by Stanley Elkin and Shannon Ravenel. Boston: Houghton Mifflin, 1980, 210-20.

–*The Best of TriQuarterly.* Edited by Jonathan Brent. New York: Washington Square Press, 1982, 203-13.

–*Vietnam Anthology.* Ed. Anisfield. 66-74. (874).

–"War Stories," *TriQuarterly*, 178-88. (1092).

g. "Gallagher's Old Man." In *Chicago*, edited by Reginald Gibbons, a special issue of *TriQuarterly* 60 (Spring/Summer 1984):380-85.

h. "God's Marvelous Plan." *Harper's* 263, no. 1575 (August 1981):54-60.

i. "Good Morning to You, Lieutenant." In

–*Harper's* 260, no. 1561 (June 1980):59-60, 64, 66-69.

–*Soldiers and Civilians.* Ed. Jenks. 155-68. (1080).

j. "The Mission." In *Don't You Know There's a War On?* Edited by John Schultz. Chicago: Columbia College, 1969, 14-17.

k. "Suddenly the Sun." In *Don't You Know There's a War On?* Edited by John Scultz. Chicago: Columbia College, 1969, 18-23.

1195 Herd, Dale. "Girls." In *Wild Cherries*. Bolinas, Calif.: Tombouctou, 1980, 33-34.

1196 Herr, Michael.
a. "The Hook: A Love Note from Downtown." *Rolling Stone* 249 (6 October 1977):78-79.

b. "Illumination Rounds." In

 −*New American Review,* no. 7. New York: New American Library, 1969, 64-85.

 −*Writing under Fire.* Ed. Klinkowitz. 112-29. (1082).

 c. "Lz Loon" (excerpt from *Dispatches*). *Rolling Stone* 251 (3 November 1977):68-71.

1197 Hobson, Gerald. "The CO." *A Journal of Contemporary Literature* 1, no. 1 (Fall 1976).

1198 Hoch, Edward D. "The Nine Eels of Madame Wu." In *Mystery Writers of America: A Special Kind of Crime.* Garden City, N.Y.: Doubleday, 1982, 59-73.

1199 Hogdin, D. Wayne. "Interrogation." In *Vietnam Flashbacks.* Ed. Villani. 46-47. (887).

1200 Hollenbeck, Peter. "The Lotus and the Night" (chapter from a forthcoming novel). In *Vietnam Literature Anthology.* Ed. Strahan. 67-77. (884).

1201 Howe, John F.
 a. "From Danang to An Hoa." In *Hair-Trigger III: A Story Workshop Anthology,* 23-25. (1077).

 b. "The Land." In *Hair-Trigger IV: A Story Anthology.* Chicago: Columbia College, 1980, 145-46.

 c. "Impaled Man." In

 −*The Best of Hair-Trigger.* Edited by John Schultz. Chicago: Columbia College, 1983, 389-93.

 −*Hair-Trigger IV: A Story Anthology.* Chicago: Columbia College, 1980, 147-153.

 d. "K.I.A." In *Hair-Trigger III: A Story Workshop Anthology.* 20-22. (1077).

1202 Howerton, Walter. "The Persistence of Memory." In *Writing Fiction: A Guide to Narrative Craft.* Edited by Janet Burroway. Boston: Little, Brown, 1987, 135-50.

1203 Huddle, David.

a. "The Interrogation of the Prisoner Bung by Mr. Hawkins and Sergeant Tree." In

    −*A Dream with No Stump Roots in It*. Columbia: University of Missouri Press, 1975, 17-26.

    −*Esquire* 75, no. 1 (January 1971):128-29, 156, 158, 160, 162.

    −*Free Fire Zone*. Ed. Klinkowitz. 59-67. (1082).

    −*The Secret Life of Our Times: New Fiction from Esquire*. Edited by Gordon Lish. Garden City, N.Y.: Doubleday, 1973, 265-78.

    −*Vietnam Anthology*. Ed. Anisfield. 37-44. (874).

b. "Rosie Baby." In *A Dream with No Stump Roots in It*. Columbia: University of Missouri Press, 1975, 35-58.

1204 Ireland, David. "The Wild Colonial Boy." In *Winter's Tales* 25. Edited by Caroline Hobhouse. New York: St Martin's, 1980, 71-84.

1205 Ivey, Ross. "Major Little's Last Stand." *Penthouse* 11, no. 2 (October 1979):144-47.

1206 Jacobs, Harvey. "The Negotiators." In
    −*Esquire* 71, no. 4 (April 1969):28, 44, 48, 50, 52, 54.

    −*Writing under Fire*. Ed. Klinkowitz. 185-95. (1082).

1207 James, Joseph. "Back in the World." *Penthouse* 6, no. 8 (April 1975):65-66, 92, 94, 108.

1208 Jorgenson, Kregg P. J. "Red, White and Tutti Frutti." *Stonecloud*, no. 6 (1976):61-65.

1209 Jorgensen, Erik. "Typhoon." In *Angels in My Oven: A Story Workshop Anthology*. Edited by John Schultz. Chicago: Columbia College, 1976, 294-312.

1210 Jose, Nicholas. "Outstretched Wings and Orient Light." In *The Possession of Amber*. St. Lucia, Queensland, Australia: University of Queensland Press, 1980, 208-48.

1211 Just, Ward.
    a. "The Congressman Who Loved Flaubert." In

−*Atlantic Monthly* 230, no. 4 (October 1972):109-19.

−*The Congressman Who Loved Flaubert and Other Stories*. Boston: Little, Brown, 1973, 1-32.

−*Writing under Fire*. Ed. Klinkowitz. 165-84. (1082).

b.   "Dietz at War." In

−*Best American Short Stories 1976*. Edited by Martha Foley. Boston: Houghton Mifflin, 1976, 133-44.

−*Honor, Power, Riches, Fame and the Love of Women*. New York: Dutton, 1979, 73-86.

−*Virginia Quarterly Review* 51, no. 4 (Autumn 1975):587-600.

c.   "Journal of a Plague Year." In

−*Atlantic Monthly* 232, no. 2 (August 1973):87-90.

−*Honor, Power, Riches, Fame and the Love of Women*. New York: Dutton, 1979, 87-97.

d.   "A Man at the Top of His Trade." In *Honor, Power, Riches, Fame and the Love of Women*. New York: Dutton, 1976, 98-108.

e.   "Prime Evening Time." In *The Congressman Who Loved Flaubert*. Boston: Little, Brown, 1973, 95-114.

1212 Juvik, Tom Miller. "Pulling Guard." In *Vietnam Flashbacks*. Ed. Villani. 51-53. (887).

1213 Kalpakian, Laura. "Veterans' Day." In *Stand One: Winners of the Stand Magazine Short-Story Competition*. Edited by Michael Blackburn, Jon Silkin, and Lorna Tracy. London: Gollancz, 1984, 9-30.

1214 Kaplan, Johanna. "Dragon Lady." In
−*Harper's* 241, no. 1442 (July 1970):70-34.

−*Other People's Lives*. New York: Knopf, 1975, 155-71.

−*Writing under Fire*. Ed. Klinkowitz. 22-34. (1082).

1215 Karlin, Wayne.
a.   "Extract." In *Free Fire Zone*. Ed. Karlin. 177-82. (1081).

b.   "Medical Evacuation." In *Free Fire Zone*. Ed. Karlin. 17-19. (1081).

   c. "R & R." In *Free Fire Zone*. Ed. Karlin. 136-43. (1081).

   d. "Search and Destroy." In *Free Fire Zone*. Ed. Karlin. 51-54. (1081).

   e. "The Vietnamese Elections." In *Free Fire Zone*. Ed. Karlin. 56-58. (1081).

1216 Kelly, F. J. "The Vietnam Circle." In *Alfred Hitchcock's Tales to Fill You with Fear and Trembling*. Edited by Eleanor Sullivan. New York: Dial, 1980, 308-18.

1217 Kerr, Baine. "Rapture." In *Jumping Off Place: Stories*. Columbia: University of Missouri Press, 1981, 47-64.

1218 Kessell, John. "Credibility." In *In the Field of Fire*. Ed. Dann. 329-49. (1070).

1219 Kidder, Tracy. "In Quarantine." *Atlantic Monthly* 246, no. 3 (September 1980):92-100.

1220 Kimpel, John M. "And Even Beautiful Hands Cry." In *Free Fire Zone*, Ed. Karlin. 69-79. (1081).

1221 Kissinger, Gerald. "Grave Trade." *Transatlantic Review*, no. 39 (Spring 1971):64-76.

1222 Kolpacoff, Victor. "The Room." In
    –*New American Review*, no. 1. New York: New American Library, 1967, 7-27.

    –*Writing under Fire*. Ed. Klinkowitz. 71-89. (1082).

1223 Koons, George. "Extra Man." In *Angels in My Oven: A Story Workshop Anthology*. Edited by John Schultz. Chicago: Columbia College, 1976, 140-44.

1224 Kumin, Maxine.
   a. "The Missing Person." In

    –*The Best American Short Stories 1979*. Edited by Joyce Carol Oates and Shannon Ravenel. Boston: Houghton Mifflin, 1979, 234-42.

- *The Best of TriQuarterly*. Edited by Jonathan Brent. New York: Washington Square Press, 1982, 152-60.

- *Why Can't We Live Together Like Civilized Human Beings?* New York: Viking Press, 1982, 127-38.

  b. "These Gifts." In *Why Can't We Live Together Like Civilized Human Beings?* New York: Viking Press, 1982, 149-75.

1225 Kunen, James S. "Pieces of War." *True* 52 (May 1971):91-92, 94, 96-97.

1226 Lake, Larry. "Dumb Slumbo." In *5000' and Closing*. Denver: Bowery Press, 1981, 13-27.

1227 Landis, John. "Bill." In *Twilight Zone: The Movie*. Edited by Robert Block. New York: Warner, 1983, 7-55.

1228 Larner, Jeremy. "They Are Taking My Letters." *Harper's* 237 (October 1968):45-57.

1229 Laufer, William. "Prospects and Abysses." In *North American Mentor Magazine* 18, no. 31 (Spring 1980):47-54.

1230 Leonardy, Peter. "The Dust Off." In *Hair-Trigger VI and VII*. Chicago: Columbia College, 1984, 171-73.

1231 Linhein, K. J. "A Sort of an Occulation." *Reed* (Spring/Summer 1974):23-27.

1232 Little, Loyd. "Out with the Lions." In *Free Fire Zone*. Ed. Karlin. 41-50. (1081).

1233 Loewald, Uyen. "Prosperity." *Short Story International* 9, no. 49. Great Neck, N.Y.: International Cultural Exchange, 1985, 150-58.

1234 Lowell, Susan. "David." *Southern Review* 7 (Winter 1971):254-64.

1235 Lupack, Alan. "Miss America and the Strippers." In *Vietnam Flashbacks*. Ed. Villani. 67-69. (887).

1236 McAllister, Bruce. "Dream Baby." In *In the Field of Fire*. Ed. Dann. 270-304. (1070).

1237 McCammon, Robert R. "Nightcrawlers." In *Masques: All New Works of Horror and the Supernatural*. Edited by J. N. Williamson. Baltimore: Maclay, 1984, 11-36.

1238 McCluskey, John A. "John Henry's Home." In
- *The Best American Short Stories 1976*. Edited by Martha Foley. Boston: Houghton Mifflin, 1976, 145-55.

- *On the Job: Fiction about Work by Contemporary American Writers*. Edited by William O'Rourke. New York: Vintage, 1977, 93-104.

1239 McCord, Howard. "Sharing a Little Heat With the Pathet Lao." In *Vietnam Flashbacks*. Ed. Villani. 18-19. (887).

1240 McDonald, Walter.
   a. "Bien Dien." *Sam Houston Literary Review* 2, no. 2, November 1977, 46-53.

   b. "Lebowitz." *Re: Artes Liberales* 3, no. 1 (Fall 1976):75-80.

   c. "New Guy." In *New and Experimental Literature*. Edited by James P. White. Midland: Texas Center for Writers Press, 1975, 43-50.

   d. "The Sendoff." In *The Bicentennial Collection of Texas Short Stories*. Edited by James P. White. Dallas: Texas Center for Writers Press, 1975, 74-80.

   e. "Snow Job." *Quartet* 7, no. 51-53 (Summer/Fall/Winter 1975-76):75-84.

   f. "The Track." *Sam Houston Literary Review* 1, no. 1 (April 1976):45-48.

   g. "Waiting for the End." *Descant* 20, no. 3 (1976):2-10.

1241 McNamara, Brian W.
   a. "Dust." *Assay* 29, no. 2 (Winter 1974):27-28.

   b. "Swanson." *Assay* 29, no. 2 (Winter 1974):5-7.

1242 Madden, David. "No Trace." In *The Best American Short Stories 1971 and the Yearbook of the American Short Story*. Edited by Martha Foley and David Burnett. Boston: Houghton Mifflin, 1971, 134-55.

1243 Major, Clarence.

a. "Dossy O." In *Writing under Fire*. Ed. Klinkowitz. 108-10. (1082)

b. "We Is Grunts." In

   - *All-Night Visitors*. New York: Olympia Press, 1969, 71-78.

   - *19 Necromancers from Now*. Edited by Ishmael Reed. Garden City, N.Y.: Anchor, 1970, 177-83.

1244 Malamud, Bernard. "My Son the Murderer." *Esquire* 70, no. 5 (November 1968):102-4, 152.

1245 Malzberg, Barry N.
   a. "Final War." In *Final War and Other Stories*. New York: Ace, 1969.

   b. "The Queen of Lower Saigon." In *In the Field of Fire*. Ed. Dann. 236-46. (1070).

1246 Mason, Bobbie Ann. "Big Bertha Stories." In
   - *Soldiers and Civilians*. Ed. Jenks. 202-16. (1080).

   - *Prize Stories 1986: The O. Henry Awards*. Edited by William Abrahams. Garden City, N.Y.: Doubleday, 1986, 80-94.

   - *Mother Jones* 10, no. 3 (April 1985):10-18.

1247 Mauser, Harold Q. "Dead Game." In
   - *Alfred Hitchcock Presents: Stories that Go Bump in the Night*. Edited by Alfred A. Hitchcock. New York: Random House, 1977, 219-32.

   - *Alfred Hitchcock's Mortal Errors*. Edited by Cathleen Jordan. New York: Dial, 1983, 35-46.

1248 Mayer, Tom.
   a. "Anson's Last Assignment." In

   - *Playboy* 14, no. 8 (August 1967):97, 131-34, 136-37.

   - *The Weary Falcon*, 79-110 (called "The Last Operation"). (1084).

   b. "A Birth in the Delta." In

   - *Touring Nam*. Ed. Greenburg. 339-57. (877).

   - *The Weary Falcon*, 149-74. (1084).

–*Writing under Fire*. Ed. Klinkowitz. 43-57. (1082).

1249 Meisinger, Richard. "Taps." In *Vietnam Flashbacks*. Ed. Villani. 56-60. (887).

1250 Menzies, H. N. "About March!" In *Festival and Other Stories*. Edited by Brian Buckley and Jim Hamilton. London: David & Charles, 1974, 90-94.

1251 Metcalfe, Barry. "Black Cat." In *The Oxford Book of New Zealand Writing Since 1945*. Edited by P. Jackson MacDonald and Vincent O'Sullivan. Auckland, New Zealand/New York: Oxford University Press, 1983, 446-48.

1252 Meyer, Mike. "Klein's Wedding." In *The Story Workshop Reader: A Story Workshop Anthology*. Edited by John Schultz. Chicago: Columbia College, 1976, 76-83.

1253 Minick, Jeffrey. "Old Men." *Samisdat* 19, no. 1, 72d release (1979):35-48.

1254 Moorcock, Michael.
    a. "Crossing into Cambodia." In

      –*Light Years and Dark*. Edited by Michael Moorcock. New York: Berkley, 1984, 244-58.

      –*My Experiences in the Third World War*. London: Savoy Books, 1980, 47-64.

    b. "So Long Sonn Lon: 1968: Babies." In *Breakfast in the Ruins*. New York: Random House, 1971, 156-66.

1255 Moriarity, Tom H.
    a. "Condition Red in Saigon." *Man From U.N.C.L.E. Magazine* 4, no. 2 (September 1967):106-23.

    b. "Murder in Saigon." *Man From U.N.C.L.E. Magazine* 2, no. 2 (September 1966):60-90.

    c. "The Saigon Charade." *Man From U.N.C.L.E. Magazine* 2, no. 5 (December 1966):88-118.

1256 Mort, John.

    a.   "Called to God." In

      – *Gentlemen's Quarterly* 55, no. 3 (March 1985):299-301, 323-24.

      – *Tanks*. Ed. Mort. 7-15. (1087).

    b.   "Incubation Period." *Gentlemen's Quarterly* 56, no. 7 (July 1986):172-74, 184, 186, 188.

    c.   "The New Captain." In

      – *Missouri Review* 8, no. 2 (1985):45-51.

      – *Tanks*. Ed. Mort. 61-68. (1087).

    d.   "Tanks." In

      – *Soldiers and Civilians*. Ed. Jenks. 169-81. (1080).

      – *Tanks*. Ed. Mort. 27-54. (1087).

1257 Mueller, Quentin. "Children Sleeping–Bombs Falling." In *Free Fire Zone*. Ed. Karlin. 202-4. (1081).

1258 Nash, Jay Robert. "Getting the Count." In *On All Fronts*. Western Springs, Ill.: December Press, 1974, 137-39.

1259 Neimark, Paul G. "The Boy Who Did a Man's Job." In *Combo*, no. 3: *An Ace Anthology*. Edited by John Cooper. Glenview, Ill.: Scott, Foresman, 1968, 17-19.

1260 Newman, Charles. "There Must Be More to Love Than Death." *Antioch Review* 31, no. 3 (Summer 1971):151-98.

1261 Nguyen Sang. "The Ivory Comb." In

      – *Fragment from a Lost Diary and Other Stories: Women of Asia, Africa, and Latin America*. Edited by Naomi Katz and Nancy Milton. New York: Pantheon Books, 1973, 229-43.

      – *The Ivory Comb*, 113-36. (1079).

      – *Phoenix Country*, 2-15. (1075).

1262 Nguyen Trung Thanh.

    a.   "The Village in the Forest." In *Phoenix Country*, 132-45. (1075).

    b.   "The Xanu Forest." In *The Ivory Comb*, 85-112. (1079).

1263 Nhat Hanh. "The Return Path of Thoughts," (excerpts from a novel translated by Vo-Dinh). *Unicorn Journal*, no. 3 (1969):17-36.

1264 Oates, Joyce Carol. "Out of Place." In *The Seduction and Other Stories*. Los Angeles: Black Sparrow Press, 1976, 154-64.

1265 O'Brien, Tim.
    a. "The Ghost Soldiers." In

    –*Esquire* 95, no. 3 (March 1981):90-100.

    –*Great Esquire Fiction: The Finest Stories*. Edited by Rust Hills. New York: Viking Press, 1983.

    –*Prize Stories, 1982: The O. Henry Awards*. Edited by William Abrahams. Garden City, N.Y.: Doubleday, 1982, 206-28.

    –*Soldiers and Civilians*. Ed. Jenks. 182-201. (1080).

    b. "Going After Cacciato" (excerpt). In

    –*The Best American Short Stories 1977*. Edited by Martha Foley. Boston: Houghton Mifflin, 1977, 256-74.

    –*Ploughshares* 3, no. 1 (Winter 1973):42-65.

    c. "How to Tell a True War Story." *Esquire* 108, no. 4 (October 1987):208-15.

    d. "Keeping Watch by Night" (excerpt from *Going After Cacciato*). *Redbook* 148, no. 2 (December 1976):65-68.

    e. "Landing Zone Bravo." *Denver Quarterly* 4, no. 3 (Autumn 1975):72-77.

    f. "Night March" (also called "Where Have You Gone, Charming Billy?" excerpt from *Going After Cacciato*). In

    –*Lessons of the Vietnam War: A Modular Textbook*. Ed. Starr. Unit 7, 12-16. (1721).

    –*Phoenix Country*. Ed. Gray. 80-86. (1075).

    –*Prize Stories, 1974: The O. Henry Awards*. Edited by William Abrahams. Garden City, N.Y.: Doubleday, 1976, 211-19.

    –*Prize Stories of the Seventies: From the O. Henry Awards*. Garden City, N.Y.: Doubleday, 1981, 258-65.

    –*Redbook* 145 (May 1975):81, 127-28, 130, 132.

g. "Speaking of Courage" (excerpt from *Going After Cacciato*). In

– *Massachusetts Review* 17, no. 2 (Summer 1976):243-53.

– *Prize Stories, 1978: The O. Henry Awards*. Edited by William Abrahams. Garden City, N.Y.: Doubleday, 1978, 159-68.

h. "The Things They Carried." In

– *The Best American Short Stories 1987*. Edited by Ann Beattie. Boston: Houghton Mifflin, 1987, 287-305.

– *The Bread Loaf Anthology of Contemporary American Short Stories*. Edited by Robert Pack and Jay Parini. Hanover, N.H.: University Press of New England, 1987, 227-46.

– *Esquire* 102, no. 2 (August 1986):76-81.

– *Vietnam Anthology*. Ed. Anisfield. 79-94. (874).

i. "The Way It Mostly Was" (excerpt from *Going After Cacciato*). *Shenandoah* 27, no. 2 (Winter 1976):35-45.

j. "Where Have You Gone, Charming Billy?" see "Night March."

1266 Oestreich, Jerry.
   a. "Perimeter Guard," In *Hair Trigger III*. Ed. Columbia College Writing Department. 27-28. (1077).

   b. "Poetry at Parade Rest," In *Hair Trigger III*. Ed. Columbia College Writing Department. 29-33. (1077).

   c. "To Do Street," In *Hair Trigger III*. Ed. Columbia College Writing Department. 26. (1077).

1267 Pak, Si-jong. "Ten Minutes to Seven." In *Early Spring, Mid-Summer and Other Korean Stories*. Edited by Korean National Commission for UNESCO. Cape, Ore.: Si-sa-yong-o-sa/Pace International Research Seoul/Arch 1983, 176-91.

1268 Palladine, Michael. "Khong Biet." In *Vietnam Flashbacks*. Ed. Villani. 30-35. (887).

1269 Pancake, Breece D'J. "The Honored Dead." In
   – *Atlantic Monthly* 247, no. 1 (January 1981):49-53.

   – *Soldiers and Civilians*. Ed. Jenks. 98-106. (1080).

– *The Stories of Breece D'J Pancake*. Boston: Little, Brown, 1983.

1270 Paquet, Basil T. "Warren." In *Free Fire Zone*. Ed. Karlin. 154-75. (1081).

1271 Parker, Thomas. "Troop Withdrawal – The Initial Step." In
– *The Fact of Fiction*. Ed. Gulassa. 67-85. (1076).

– *Harper's* 239, no. 1431 (August 1969):61-68.

– *Prize Stories, 1971: The O. Henry Awards*. Edited by William Abrahams. Garden City, N.Y.: Doubleday, 1971, 148-67.

– *Touring Nam*. Ed. Greenburg. 389-411. (877).

– *Writing under Fire*. Ed. Klinkowitz. 90-107. (1082).

1272 Pascoe, Bruce.
   a. "Friday Night." In *Night Animals*. New York: Penguin, 1986, 77-83.

   b. "Soldier Goes to Ground." In *Night Animals*. New York: Penguin, 1986, 125-30.

1273 Pelfrey, William. "Bangalore." In *Free Fire Zone*. Ed. Karlin. 3-12. (1081).

1274 Perea, Robert L.
   a. The Battle of Engineer Hill." *Americas* 14, no. 2 (Summer 1986):15-20.

   b. "Dragon Mountain." In

      – *Mestizo: Anthology of Chicano Literature*. Albuquerque, N.M.: Parjarito Publications, 1978, 33-41. A special issue of *De Colores: Journal of Chicano Expression and Thought* 4, nos. 1 & 2.

      – *The Remembered Earth: An Anthology of Contemporary Native American Literature*. Edited by Geary Hobson. Albuquerque: University of New Mexico Press, 1981, 358-65.

   c. "Small Arms Fire." In *Cuentos Chicanos: A Short Story Anthology*. Edited by Rudolfo A. Anaya and Antonio Marques. Albuquerque: New America/University of New Mexico Press, 1984, 119-24.

    d. "Trip to Da Nang." *Bilingual Review* 12, nos. 1 & 2 (January-August 1985):97-102.

    e. "A War Story." *Thunderbird* 23, no. 2 (December 1973):24-25.

1275 Pfundstein, Roy. "An Odd Coin." *Ball State University Forum* 13, no. 32 (Spring 1972):52-56.

1276 Phillips, Jayne Anne. "November and December: Billy, 1969." In *Soldiers and Civilians*. Ed. Jenks. 126-54. (1080).

1277 Pittman, Luther. "A Day in Camp." *Mirror Northwest* 3 (1972):60-63.

1278 Pitts, Oran R. "Temporary Duty." In *Free Fire Zone*. Ed. Karlin. 126-34. (1081).

1279 Pitzen, Jim. "The Village." In

    -*Fiction Network*. Spring/Summer 1986, 13-17.

    -*Prize Stories, 1987: The O. Henry Awards*. Edited by William Abrahams. Garden City, N.Y.: Doubleday, 1987, 132-43.

1280 Porsche, Don.
    a. "Evenings in Europe and Asia." In

    -*Prairie Schooner* 46, no. 2 (Summer 1972):96-104.

    -*Touring Nam*. Ed. Greenburg. 20-29. (877).

    -*Writing under Fire*. Ed. Klinkowitz. 35-42. (1082).

    b. "The Hump." *Samisdat* 4, no. 4 (Summer 1975, 19th release):72-78.

1281 Poyer, Joe. "Null Zone." *Analog* 81, no. 5 (July 1968):54-72.

1282 Prager, Emily. "The Lincoln-Pruitt Anti-Rape Device: Memoirs of the Women's Combat Army in Vietnam." In *A Visit from the Footbinder and Other Stories*. New York: Simon & Schuster, 1982, 103-80.

1283 Presley, John. "The Soldier." *Kansas Quarterly* 2, no. 1 (Winter 1969/70):86-101.

1284 Price, Bill. "Jimmy's Home." *Evergreen Review* 77, no. 14 (April 1970):23-24.

1285 Rascoe, Judith. "Soldier, Soldier." In *Yours, and Mine: Novella and Stories*. Boston: Little, Brown, 1973, 164-79.

1286 Richie, Mary. "Hunt and Destroy." In
    – *The Fact of Fiction*. Ed. Gulassa. 99-103. (1076).

    – *New American Review*, no. 6. New York: New American Library, 1969, 64-68.

1287 Robinson, Kim Stanley. "The Memorial." In *In the Field of Fire*. Ed. Dann. 19-23. (1070).

1288 Robinson, Spider. "Unnatural Causes." In *Callahan's Crosstown Saloon*. New York: Ace Books, 1977, 129-61.

1289 Rossman, Michael. "The Day We Named Our Child We Had Fish for Dinner." In
    – *New American Review*, no. 11. New York: Simon & Schuster, 1971, 33-47.

    – *Writing under Fire*. Ed. Klinkowitz. 196-208. (1082).

1290 Rottmann, Larry. "Thi Bong Dzu." In
    – *Free Fire Zone*. Ed. Karlin. 119-25. (1081).

    – *Lessons of the Vietnam War: A Modular Textbook*. Ed. Starr. Unit 7, 19-23. (1721).

    – *Vietnam Anthology*. Ed. Anisfield. 50-55. (874).

1291 Russo, Richard Paul. "In the Season of the Rains." In *In the Field of Fire*. Ed. Dann. 107-21. (1070)

1292 Ryman, Geoff. "The Unconquered Country." In *Interzone 4*. St. New York: St. Martin's, 1987.

1293 Sack, John.
    a. "M" (excerpt from the novel). *Esquire* 66, no. 4 (October 1966):79-86, 140, 142, 144-45, 147, 150, 152, 154, 158, 160, 162.

b. "When Demirgian Comes Marching Home Again, Hurrah? Hurrah?" (excerpt from *M*). *Esquire* 69, no. 1 (January 1968):56-59, 124-27.

1294 Sayles, John. "Tan." In

– *The Anarchists' Convention*. Boston: Little Brown, 1979, 257-81.

– *Soldiers and Civilians*. Ed. Jenks. 107-25. (1080).

1295 Schmidt, Warren. "A War Dream." In *Believing Everything*. Edited by Mary Mary Logue and Lawrence Sutin. Minneapolis: Holy Cow! Press, 1980, 63-66.

1296 Scotellaro, Robert. "Ti-Ti." In *Tour of Duty*. Ed. Knight. 77-89. (881).

1297 Scott, L. E.
a. "Three Hearts," In *Time Came Hunting Time*. Ed. L. E. Scott. 38-50. (883).

b. "Vietnam – April 4, 1968," In *Time Came Hunting Time*. Ed. L. E. Scott. 51-55. (883).

1298 Shaplen, Robert. "The Lovemaking of Max-Robert." In *A Corner of the World*. New York: Knopf, 1949, 97-130. Saigon during the time of the French.

1299 Shedivy, Charles.
a. "The Kid and Victor Charlie." In *Hair-Trigger* 6 & 7. Chicago: Columbia College, 1984, 31-38.

b. "The Virgin French Nurse." In *Hair-Trigger* 6 & 7. Chicago: Columbia College, 1984, 23-30.

1300 Shepard, Lucius.
a. "Delta Sly Honey." In *In the Field of Fire*. Ed. Dann. 24-43. (1070).

b. "Fire Zone Emerald." *Playboy* 33, no. 2 (February 1986):100, 164-66, 167-70. The story takes place in Belize but reads like Vietnam.

c. "R & R." *Isaac Asimov's Science Fiction Magazine* 10, no. 4 (April 1986).

    d.   "Salvador." *Magazine of Fantasy and Science Fiction* 66, no. 4 (April 1984):8-23. The story takes place in Central America but, like "Fire Zone Emerald," reads like Vietnam.

    e.   "Shades." In *In the Field of Fire*. Ed. Dann. 122-57. (1070).

1301 Shields, James. "The Candidate." In
     – *Carolina Quarterly* 25, no. 1 (Spring 1972).

     – *Free Fire Zone*. Ed. Karlin. 108-17. (1081).

1302 Shiner, Lewis. "The War at Home." In
     – *In the Field of Fire*. Ed. Dann. 325-28. (1070).

     – *Isaac Asimov's Science Fiction Magazine* 9, no. 5 (May 1985):74-76.

     – *The Year's Best Science Fiction: 3rd Annual Collection*. Edited by Gardner Dozois. Chappaqua, N.Y.: Bluejay Books, 1986, 522-25.

1303 Sloan, James Park. "Vietnam No Big Deal." In *Moral Fiction: An Anthology*. Edited by Joe David Bellamy. Canton, N.Y.: Fiction International, 1980, 201-8.

1304 Smeds, Dave. "Goats." In *In the Field of Fire*. Ed. Dann. 169-210. (1070).

1305 Smith, Kathleen R. "Letters from Vietnam." In *The Fallen Angel and Other Stories*. Edited by Mel Cebulash. New York: Scholastic Book Services, 1970, 155-70.

1306 Smith, M. H. "A Rebellion." *Samisdat* 25, no. 2, 98th release (1980):34-38.

1307 Smith, Steve. "First Light." In *Free Fire Zone*. Ed. Karlin. 28-39. (1081).

1308 Stanford, Dan. "Little Miss Tiger." *Redbook* 131 (June 1968):141-64.

1309 St. Denis, Bake. "With Only One Shot." In *Vietnam Flashbacks*. Ed. Villani. 6-16. (887).

1310 Steel, Rodger. "Just Another War Story." *Assay* 29, no. 3 (Spring 1974):25-28.

1311 Steiber, Raymond. "The Lost Indemnity." *Trace* 53 (1964):166-72.

1312 Stone, Robert. "Fear." *Place: Neon Rose* 3, no. 1 (June 1973):126-35.

1313 Strete, Craig Kee. "The Game of Cat and Eagle." In *In the Field of Fire*. Ed. Dann. 44-69. (1070).

1314 Suddick, Tom.
    a. "Caduceus." In

        – *A Few Good Men*. Ed. Suddick. 8-20. (1090).

        – *Touring Nam*. Ed. Greenburg. 206-221. (877).

    b. "The Diehard." In

        – *Berkley Samisdat Review* 1, no. 1 (June 1973):3-12.

        – *A Few Good Men*. Ed. Suddick. 108-16. (1090).

        – *The Tower Anthology of the San Jose Movement in Fiction*. San Jose, Calif.: The Brothers of Tau Delta Phi Fraternity, San Jose State University, 1974, 1-7.

    c. "1965." *Samisdat* 25, no. 2, 98th release (1980).

    d. "On Making the Same Mistake Twice." In

        – *Samisdat* 26, no. 2, 102d release (1980):18-23.

        – *Tour of Duty*. Ed. Knight. 13-23. (881).

    e. "A Shithouse Rat." In

        – *Samisdat* 2, nos. 2, 3 (Summer/Fall 1974).

        – *Touring Nam*. Ed. Greenburg. 325-36. (877).

1315 Tavela, John. "The Souvenir." In *Free Fire Zone*. Ed. Karlin. 148-53. (1081).

1316 Taylor, Harry H. "Up at the Front." *South Dakota Review* 4, no. 3 (Fall 1966):57-64.

1317 Taylor, Robert. "Where Are Our M.I.A.'s." In *The Roots Grow Deeper than We Know: Pennsylvania Writers, Pennsylvania Life*. Edited by Lee Gutkind. Pittsburgh: University of Pittsburgh Press, 1985, 73-84.

1318 Thacker, Julia. "A Civil Campaign." In *New Directions in Prose and Poetry* 44. Edited by J. Laughlin. New York: New Directions, 1982, 83-88.

1319 Tipton, Paul W. "A Day for No Letters." In *Tour of Duty*. Ed. Knight. 44-46. (881).

1320 Tiptree, James, Jr. "Beam Us Home." In *Ten Thousand Light Years from Home*. Boston: Gregg Press, 1976, 296-312.

1321 Vargas, Ernesto. "The Excuse." *Mirror Northwest* 3 (1972):53-57.

1322 Viorel, George. "The Haint." *Vietnam Flashbacks*. Ed. Villani. 37-39. (887).

1323 Weaver, Gordon.
   a. "Canavan's Knee." In *Morality Play*. Kirksville, Mo.: Chariton Review Press, 1985, 35-46.
   b. "Under the World." *Western Humanities Review* 41, no. 3 (Autumn 1987):193-257.

1324 West, Paul. "He Who Wears the Pee of the Tiger." *TriQuarterly* 55 (Fall 1982):5-13.

1325 West, Thomas A., Jr. "Gone Are the Men." In
   – *Transatlantic Review*, no. 41 (Winter/Spring 1972):35-45.
   – *Writing under Fire*. Ed. Klinkowitz. 136-45. (1082).

1326 Wilbur, Ellen. "Wind Birds and Human Voices." In *Wind Birds and Human Voices and Other Stories*. New York: New American Library, 1984, 5-34.

1327 Wilhelm, Kate. "The Village." In *In the Field of Fire*. Ed. Dann. 158-68. (1070).

1328 Wolfe, Gene. "Feather Tigers." In *The Island of Doctor Death and Other Stories*. New York: Pocketbooks, 1980.

1329 Wolfe, Tom. "The Truest Sport: Jousting with Sam and Charlie." In *Mauve Gloves and Madmen, Clutter and Vine*. New York: Farrar, Straus & Giroux, 1976, 26-65.

1330 Wolff, Tobias.
    a. "Soldier's Joy." In

      – *Back in the World*. Boston: Houghton Mifflin, 1985, 95-119.

      – *Esquire* 104, no. 4 (1985):210-12, 214-19.

      – *Soldiers and Civilians*. Ed. Jenks. 26-43. (1080).

    b. "Wingfield." In

      – *Encounter* 55, no. 1 (July 1980):3-5.

      – *In the Gardens of the North American Martyrs*. New York: Ecco Press, 1981, 101-5.

      – *Vietnam Anthology*. Ed. Anisfield. 75-78. (874).

1331 Woods, William Crawford. "He That Died of Wednesday." In
    – *Esquire* 71, no. 6 (June 1969):115, 213-17.

      – *Writing under Fire*. Ed. Klinkowitz. 152-64. (1082).

1332 Yates, Ethel M. "Seeds of Time." In *Alabama Prize Stories, 1970*. Edited by D. B. Emerson. Huntsville, Ala.: Strode, 1970, 262-73.

Literary Criticism/Secondary Sources

1333 Adler, Thomas P. "Blind Leading the Blind: Rabe's *Sticks and Bones* and Shakespeare's *King Lear.*" *Papers on Language and Literature* 15, no. 2 (Spring 1979):203-6.
    Adler discusses the pervasive verbal and visual images of reason in madness and sight in blindness in *Sticks and Bones* and compares it to the same imagery in *King Lear*.

1334 Aiken, William. "Denise Levertov, Robert Duncan, and Allen Ginsberg: Modes of the Self in Projective Poetry." *Modern Poetry Studies* 10, no. 2/3 (1981):200-240.
    A comparison of the work of the three poets of the title and a selection of their Vietnam War poems.

1335 Aldridge, John W. "From Vietnam to Obscenity." *Harper's* 236, no. 1413 (February 1968):91-97.
    A discussion of Mailer's *Why Are We in Vietnam?* and the role of obscenity in the novel.

1336 Allott, Miriam. "The Moral Situation in *The Quiet American*." In *Graham Greene: Some Critical Considerations*. Edited by Robert O. Evans. Lexington: University Press of Kentucky, 1963, 188-206.

Allott discusses the moral factors and themes in *The Quiet American* and its relationship to Greene's other "Catholic" novels. This essay provides an interesting counterpoint to Nathan Scott's article in *Christian Century* (1 August 1956):901-2.

1337 Arens, Werner. "Trends in Contemporary Australian Poetry." In *Voices from Distant Lands: Poetry in the Commonwealth*. Edited by Konrad Gross and Wolfgang Kloos. Wurzburg: Konigshausen and Neumann, 1983, 34-49.

Australian poetry from 1960 to 1968 (a transitional phase) is discussed through the modernist phase (1968-1978) to the phase of consolidation. The section on the modernist phase discusses the social, political, and cultural upheaval of the Vietnam War period and its affect on Australian poetry and Australia's part in the war.

1338 Ariizumi, Norioki. "Vietnam War Plays." In *The Traditional and the Anti-Traditional: Studies in Contemporary American Literature*. Tokyo: Tokyo Chapter of the American Literature Society, 1980, 191-200.

The author compares the plays of World War II and Korea to Vietnam War plays by David Rabe, Daniel Berrigan, and Terrence McNally and notes that the protagonists become symbols of the American nightmare in Vietnam – a reflection on the image of the American Dream. The value of survival is emphasized and an overwhelming discontent with war.

1339 Asahina, Robert. "Basic Training of American Playwrights: Theater and the Vietnam War." *Theater* 9 (Spring 1978):30-37.

The Vietnam War's delayed appearance on the stage as a dramatic subject, six years after the escalation of the war, in 1971, is discussed, particularly Megan Terry's *Viet Rock*.

1340 Ashmore, Harry S. "A Limited Revulsion." *Center Magazine* 11, no. 4 (July/August 1978):27-33.

Ashmore responds to Capp's discussion (see 1369) and questions the long-term effects of the Vietnam War on future generations, viewing particularly the war protesters as they approach middle-age. Following this, is a discussion between the two authors and Donald McDonald, magazine editor, on the moral and spiritual implications of the war.

1341 Austin, Jacquelin. "Women Watching War." *Women's Review of Books* 1, no. 12 (September 1984):8-9.

Austin says there are three truisms about women in the Vietnam War: No one forced the women to go, they were protected from combat, and they recorded very little history at the time. The press was not kind to the women in Vietnam. Now women are beginning to write of their experiences. Austin discusses how women's perspective of the history of the time is different. The major books by women are examined including *Witness to War, Long Time Passing,* and *Home Before Morning.* Bibliography.

1342 Baldwin, Neil. "Going After the War." *Publishers Weekly* 223 (11 February 1983):34-38.

Baldwin discusses the major Vietnam novels and plays, charting the increasing interest in the subject by readers and publishers. He compares the novels and includes a list of "Best of the Lost Books,"–those currently out of print, and emphasizes the need for books such as these to continually remind and help Americans to understand the Vietnam experience.

1343 Barnes, Barbara. "William Eastlake." In *Postmodern Fiction: A Bio-Bibliographical Guide.* Edited by Larry McCaffery. New York: Greenwood Press, 1986, 345-48.

A short biography and critique of William Eastlake and his work with a brief bibliography of primary and secondary sources.

1344 Begiebing, Robert J. "Norman Mailer's *Why Are We in Vietnam?*: The Ritual of Regeneration." *American Imago* 37, no. 1 (Spring 1980):12-37.

A discussion of *Why Are We in Vietnam?* emphasizing the use of metaphor and myth. The author notes the significance of the setting and the nature of the hero's guilt.

1345 Beidler, Philip D. *American Literature and the Experience of Vietnam.* Athens: University of Georgia Press, 1982.

A major historical survey of the literature of the Vietnam War. Beidler calls it "a case study in literature and literary consciousness considered in relation to the larger process of cultural myth-making. . . ." The five major chapters are: "Situation Report: The Experience of Vietnam"; "American Literature: Prophecy and Content";

"Early Vietnam Writing, 1958-1970"; "In the Middle Range, 1970-1975"; and "The New Literature of Vietnam, 1975-present."

1346 _____. "Raging Joys, Sublime Violations: The Vietnam War in the Fiction of Chandler Brossard." *Review of Contemporary Fiction* 7, no. 1 (Spring 1987):166-75.

A discussion of the style, form, theme, and characterization employed by Brossard in his *Raging Joys, Sublime Violations*.

1347 _____. "Truth-Telling and Literary Values in the Vietnam Novel." *South Atlantic Quarterly* 78 (Spring 1979):141-56.

Beidler discusses the ways employed in telling the truth of the war in Vietnam War novels. Halberstam and Bunting use "traditional" methods while Eastlake uses surrealism. Charles Durden's technique, employed in *No Bugles, No Drums* is contrasted to the others.

1348 _____. "The Vietnam Novel: An Overview with a Brief Checklist of Vietnam War Narrative." *Southern Humanities Review* 12, no. 1 (Winter 1978):45-55.

Beidler reviews the depiction of the American soldier in Vietnam novels – tired men, morally and spiritually exhausted – that suggests a new way of looking at America's moral and spiritual assumptions. A checklist of novels, written in bibliographic essay form, is included.

1349 Bell, Pearl K. "Writing About Vietnam." *Commentary* 66, no. 4 (October 1978):74-77.

Bell describes Vietnam, "that wasted and unavailing conflict . . . the one war we could not win," and its affects on literary attempts to describe and explain it. She critiques both novels and personal narratives, particularly *A Rumor of War, Dispatches, Better Times Than These*, and *Going After Cacciato*.

1350 Bellhouse, Mary L., and Lawrence Litchfield. "Vietnam and Loss of Innocence: An Analysis of the Political Implications of the Popular Literature." *Journal of Popular Culture* 16 (Winter 1982):157-74.

The concept of innocence, as it relates to the United States and its dealings with Vietnam, its conduct of the war, and its evaluation of itself afterward, is discussed in this essay. Significant works, both fiction and nonfiction, written by those with first-hand combat experience (soldiers and journalists) are used to exemplify the true nature of the war. The author concludes that "what Vietnam literature teaches us is that our moral credibility is severely damaged."

1351 Bergonzi, Bernard. "Vietnam Novels: First Draft." *Commonweal* 49 (27 October 1972):84-88.

Six major novels are discussed: *To Defend, To Destroy, Limbo, The Weary Falcon, The Lionheads, War Year,* and *War Games.* The author comments on the well-educated soldier-novelist and compares Vietnam novels to the great war novels of the past from *War and Peace* to *The Red Badge of Courage* to *Catch 22.*

1352 Berkvist, Robert. "If You Kill Somebody . . ." *New York Times* (12 December 1971):3, 22.

A useful discussion and comparison of David Rabe's *Sticks and Bones* and *The Basic Training of Pavlo Hummel.*

1353 Bernstein, Samuel J. *The Strands Entwined: A New Direction in American Drama.* Boston: Northeastern University Press, 1980, 17-36.

Bernstein reviews the criticism and discusses Rabe's *Sticks and Bones.*

1354 Bock, Hedwig, and Albert Wertheim, eds. *Essays on Contemporary American Drama.* Munich: M. Hueber, 1981.

A collection of essays written by scholars in Europe and the United States meant to be an introduction to the playwrights and dramas of the U. S. during the last twenty years. Three of the seventeen essays deal with Vietnam War literature: "Arthur Kopit" by Jurgen Wolter, "David Rabe" by Janet Hertzback, and "Ronald Ribman" by Gerald Weales.

1355 Boheemen-Saaf, Christel van. "The Artist as Con Man: The Reaction against the Symbolist Aesthetic in Recent American Fiction." *Dutch Quarterly Review of Anglo-American Letters* 7 (1977):305-18.

A discussion of how postmodern contemporary fiction relates to the modernist novel, focusing on Mailer's *Why Are We in Vietnam?,*

Pynchon's *V*, and Barth's *Lost in the Funhouse*. *The Armies of the Night* is compared to *Why Are We in Vietnam?*

1356 Boyd, William. "War in Fiction." *London Magazine* 19, no. 5/6 (August/September 1979):124-29.
    Boyd notes in his discussion of major Vietnam war novels that it is this war that forces a reexamination of all previous war fiction and makes obvious their inadequacies. In explaining the relatively few good novels in existence on the Vietnam War by 1979 he says "Vietnam, having exposed the redundancy of war fiction, has literally left writers wordless."

1357 Boyer, Jay. "Why You Will Never Read the Novel You Might Like To." In *The 60s without Apology*. Edited by Sohnya Sayres, Anders Stephanson, Stanley Aronowitz, and Frederic Jameson. Minneapoplis: University of Minnesota Press, 1984, 309-10.
    The author maintains that it is impossible to write a novel of the Vietnam War that really describes what it was like.

1358 Bradley, David. "War in an Alternate Universe." *New York Times Book Review*, (3 May 1987):25, 49.
    An excellent appraisal of Dann's *In the Field of Fire* which emphasizes the surreal nature of the Vietnam War and its appropriateness for science fiction literature.

1359 Braestrup, Peter. "Vietnam as History." *Wilson Quarterly* 2, no. 2 (Spring 1978):178-87.
    A survey of the Vietnam works in progress and a discussion of the existing literature to note which break new ground and will survive the test of time. Fiction, personal narratives, and histories are discussed.

1360 Breslin, James E. "Style in Norman Mailer's *The Armies of the Night*." *Yearbook of English Studies* 8 (1978):157-70.
    An examination of Mailer's literary achievements, particularly in *The Armies of the Night*, and the controversies surrounding them. Use of language is discussed in detail.

1361 Breslin, John B. "The Three Faces of War." *America* 125 (23 October 1971):314-16.

A comparison of three books that, from their differing viewpoints, illustrate the causes, meaning, and results of war: *The Pentagon Papers*, Glasser's *365 Days*, and J. Glenn Gray's *The Warriors: Reflections on Men in Battle*.

1362 Brien, Alan. "US – A Convulsion of Anger." *Atlas* 12, no. 6 (December 1966):24-25.

Brien reviews Peter Brook's *US*, "a documentary act-in" of Vietnam history, that analyzes the play's basic assumptions that the theater is fact, the director is the historian, and the newspaperman is the villain. The author questions the playwright's concept of truth – we are bad and the enemy is good – but applauds the form of the play.

1363 Brinkmeyer, R. H. "Finding One's History: Bobbie Ann Mason and Contemporary Southern Literature." *Southern Literary Journal* 19 (Spring 1987):20-33.

Mason's place in recent Southern literature is discussed with attention given to *In Country*, which is called her "most significant and forceful statement of personal growth through the challenge of history."

1364 Brown, Edward G. "The Teatro Campesino's Vietnam Trilogy." *Minority Voices*, 4 no. 1 (Spring 1980):29-38.

A discussion of the Teatro Campesino of Delano in the San Joaquin Valley which in 1970 presented the play *Vietnam Campesino* dealing with the impact of the war on the Chicano. Two further plays were written on this theme to form a Vietnam trilogy – *Soldado Razo* (1971) and *Dark Root of a Scream* (1971).

1365 Bryan, C. D. B. "Barely Suppressed Screams: Getting a Bead on Vietnam War Literature." *Harper's* 268, no. 1609 (June 1984):67-72.

Bryan, the author of *Friendly Fire*, discusses his idea of the basic, archetypical Vietnam war story, as he calls it "the generic Vietnam war narrative." Specific books are critiqued: *Meditation in Green*, *Fragments*, *A Rumor of War*, *365 Days*, *Born on the Fourth of July*, *Nam*, *Winners and Losers*, and *Dispatches*.

1366 Bunting, Josiah. "The Military Novel." *Naval War College Review* 26 (November/December 1973):30-38.

Bunting, author of *The Lionheads*, discusses the literary technique of writing war novels – from Thucydides' *The Peloponnesian War* to Halberstam's *The Best and the Brightest*.

1367 Burnside, Gordon. "Death Valley." *St. Louis Magazine* 15 (January 1983):38-39.

Burnside discusses Vietnam War novels and compares them to World War II novels with emphasis on *The 13th Valley* and *The Naked and the Dead*.

1368 Busby, Mark. "Tim O'Brien's *Going After Cacciato*: Finding the End of the Vision." *CCTE Proceedings* (Conference of College Teachers of English of Texas) 47 (September 1982):63-69.

Busby, in discussing *Going After Cacciato*, emphasizes that O'Brien does draw on traditional American fiction modes, for which he has received some criticism, but this technique only emphasizes his "break from the past." Busby calls the book an anti-antiwar novel in that it "denies the possibility of individual fulfillment as presented by Hemingway and Heller." Echoes of Heller and Hemingway are traced in O'Brien's work and comparisons are made to Vonnegut and other major American writers. Throughout, Busby defends O'Brien's use of traditional elements.

1369 Capps, Walter H. "The War's Transformation." *Center Magazine* 11, no. 4 (July/August 1978):18-26.

Capps discusses how the use of the A-bomb at Hiroshima changed fundamental attitudes toward life and toward governments and power. Capps states that "In many respects, Hiroshima created Vietnam." The revised understanding of the implications of warfare affected the way the Vietnam war was perceived – winning and losing could not be defined in the same way as before. The author discusses the books which reflect this change, particularly Caputo's *Rumor of War*. See also 1340.

1370 Champoli, John D. "Norman Mailer and *The Armies of the Night*." *Massachusetts Studies in English* 3, no. 1 (Spring 1971):17-21.

Champoli feels that *The Armies of the Night* is "the fullest embodiment of its author's persistent refusal to adopt the comforting banalities of moral seriousness or the comic cynicisms of black humor." He discusses form and Mailer's "verbal pyrotechnics," as well as his attempt to create a style which reflected the tensions and ambiguities of the culture and politics of the time.

1371 Clark, Michael. "Remembering Vietnam." *Cultural Critique* 3 (Spring 1986):46-78.

Clark states, "Since the withdrawal of American troops from Vietnam in 1975, the media industry in the United States has worked doggedly to represent that war and its veterans in a form compatible with the traditional norms of popular culture, and the various events surrounding the tenth anniversary of the fall of Saigon testify to the complete success of that program." He discusses how the war is portrayed in TV (*Murder, She Wrote, Magnum P.I.*), films (*The Deer Hunter, Memorial Day*), and literature including the major novels, personal narratives, and dramas. Photographs.

1372 Clements, Robert J. "Patterns of 20th Century Anti-War Poetry in World Literature." *Contemporary Literature Studies* 18 (September 1981):353-61.

1373 Cobley, Evelyn. "Narrating the Facts of War: New Journalism in Herr's *Dispatches* and Documentary Realism in First World War Novels." *Journal of Narrative Technique* 16, no. 2 (Spring 1986):97-116.

Narrative strategy and the role of documentary prose—the new journalism—is compared to the documentary realism of World War I novels. Cobley discusses the difficulty of translating experience into a literary work—a special problem in writing about the Vietnam War and thus the reason for the evolution of the new journalism. Herr's *Dispatches* is discussed as an example of this technique.

1374 Cooper, Pamela. "David Rabe's *Sticks and Bones:* The Adventures of Ozzie and Harriet." *Modern Drama* 29 (December 1986):613-25.

Cooper discusses David Rabe and his Vietnam trilogy with a full critique of *Sticks and Bones*.

1375 Cooperman, Stanley. "American War Novels: Yesterday, Today, and Tomorrow." *Yale Review* 61 (June 1972):517-29.

Cooperman states "everything I have seen or witnessed . . . has convinced me . . . that war has become the single, universal quality of existence in America. What aspect of American life today could not – and does not – produce war novels?" The author compares war writing of the past, especially Hemingway's work, with the writing of Vietnam, particularly *The Prisoners of Quai Dong* and *Why Are We in Vietnam?*

1376 Couch, William, Jr. "The Image of the Black Soldier in Selected American Novels." *CLA Journal* (College Language Association) 20, no. 2 (December 1976):176-84.

"War is a mirror reflecting the black struggle for liberation in America." With that statement Couch begins a discussion of the black soldier in other wars' novels and in *Captain Blackman*. This article was written too early to include some of the more recent novels with black soldiers as characters.

1377 Couser, G. Thomas. "*Going After Cacciato*: The Romance and The Real War." *Journal of Narrative Technique* 13, no. 1 (Winter 1983):1-10.

The author notes that the Vietnam War defies conventional literary precedents and thus personal narratives have been the most popular form used to relate war experience. *Going After Cacciato* is important because it has at its center an inquiry as to what is the most appropriate way to convey the truth of this particular war. The three elements of experience are delineated: "the real war," "war stories," and "simple facts."

1378 Cronin, Cornelius A. "Historical Background to Larry Heinemann's *Close Quarters*." *Critique* 24, no. 2 (Winter 1983):119-30.

Cronin uses *Close Quarters* as a representative novel to show the differences between the kind of war Vietnam was and other wars, i.e., no front lines, a one-year tour of duty, ground fought for and then abandoned, body counts, and kill ratios.

1379 Cushman, John H., Jr. "James Webb's New 'Fields of Fire.'" *New York Times Magazine*, 28 February 1988, 28-31, 84.

James Webb, author of *Fields of Fire, A Country Such as This,* and *A Sense of Honor,* was named Secretary of the Navy. Cushman profiles Webb and discusses his views on Vietnam, events in the Persian Gulf, and his books. Webb states "I really learned how Vietnam got so screwed up by watching the way decisions were made on the Persian Gulf."

1380 Dickstein, Morris. *Gates of Eden: American Culture in the Sixties.* New York: Basic Books, 1977.

A study of the cultural upheaval of the 1960s, *Gates of Eden* provides an intellectual and literary history of what was going on on the homefront during the Vietnam War. Related to Vietnam War literature is a discussion of the work of Norman Mailer from this period – *The Armies of the Night.* A suggested reading list and photos are included.

1381 Dong, Stella. "The Cinderella Story of *The Alleys of Eden.*" *Publishers Weekly* 221 (1 January 1982):25-26.

Dong relates the publishing history of Butler's *The Alleys of Eden.*

1382 Dudman, Richard. "Daybooks from the Battlefield." *Saturday Review* 51 (15 June 1968):36-37.

A discussion and comparison of four Vietnam diaries: Park's *GI Diary,* Russ' *Happy Hunting Ground,* Just's *To What End: A Report from Vietnam,* and Ray's *The Two Shores of Hell.* Dudman is the author of the personal narrative *Forty Days With the Enemy.*

1383 Ehrhart, W. D. "Soldier-Poets of the Vietnam War." *The Virginia Quarterly Review* 63 (Spring 1987):246-65.

Ehrhart, a Vietnam poet himself, outlines the history of the poetic response to the Vietnam Conflict as expressed in the poems collected in 1972 *Winning Hearts and Minds* anthology. Three Ehrhart poems follow the article on pages 266-68.

1384 Emerson, Gloria. "Our Man in Antilles: Graham Greene." *Rolling Stone,* no. 260 (9 March 1978):45-49.

Emerson comments on the importance of Graham Greene to the literature of the Vietnam War, even though he left Vietnam before the war began, and his lingering presence there. Emerson interviews Greene and discusses his career and his activities during the Vietnam War.

1385 ____. "The Children in the Field." *TriQuarterly* 65 (Winter 1986):221-28.

A discussion of the relationship between soldiers, children, and war and the particular relationship between the Vietnamese children and the American platoons during the war. Emerson gives graphic examples of the American soldier's cruelty to Vietnamese children – the love/hate relationship that found voice in *The Winter Soldier Investigation* and also in Ballard's *The Empire of the Sun* about WWII.

1386 Evans, Patrick. "The Provincial Dilemma, 3: New Zealand as Vietnam in Fiction: The World's Wars in New Zealand." *Landfall: A New Zealand Quarterly* 31, no. 1 (March 1977):9-22.

Evans says that New Zealanders have always tried to keep themselves apart from the world's problems in order to continue to live a serene existence. He discusses the Vietnam War and the impact it had on how New Zealanders viewed New Zealand. Vietnam War literature by New Zealanders is discussed in which New Zealand is seen *as* Vietnam by noting the similarities between the two countries – the isolation and foreign influence. This was the third in a series of articles on how outside influences affect New Zealand writing.

1387 Farish, Terry. "If You Knew Him, Please Write Me: Novels About the War in Vietnam." *School Library Journal* 35, no. 3 (November 1988):52-53.

The author served a tour in Cu Chi and Qui Nhon, 1969-70, as a Red Cross worker. She discusses how the war is portrayed in books for children and young adults. Major titles are compared.

1388 Felstiner, John. "American Poetry and the War in Vietnam." *Stand* 19, no. 2 (1978):4-11.

Vietnam war poems from 1965 to 1972 are discussed as a "seismic record" of what Americans were feeling. The author also comments on the apparent collective amnesia the followed the end of the war. "For many writers, the wholeness, harmony, and joy that lyric poetry often vouches for were blocked by their knowledge of what was happening in Vietnam." The works of Kinnell, Griffin, Levertov, Casey, Ginsberg, and Levine are profiled.

1389 ____. "Bearing the War in Mind." *Parnassus: Poetry in Review* 6, no. 2 (Spring/Summer 1978):30-37.
    A discussion of Vietnam War poetry, particularly the anthology *Demilitarized Zones*. Individual poems within the anthology and the anthology's place in Vietnam War poetry are critiqued and noted.

1390 Frazier, J. Terry. "Vietnam War Stories Looking at the Heart of Darkness." *Studies in Popular Culture* 5 (1982):1-6.

1391 Fuller, Jack. "The War in Words." *Chicago Tribune Magazine*, 19 September 1982, 58-59, 61-63, 65, 68.
    Histories, fiction, and poetry, written eight years after the end of the war, are discussed. A short bibliography is included.

1392 Fuson, Ben W. "*White the Bones of Men*: Asian Poets React to War." *New Letters* 38, no. 4 (July [Summer] 1972):47-63.
    The poems of Thich Nhat Hanh are discussed among those by other Asian poets reacting to war. A longer version of this article may be found in the author's "Anti-War Poems by Asian Writers: *White the Bones of Men*" in *Kobe College Studies* 20 (March 1974):39-90.

1393 Gaston, G. M. "Structure of Salvation in *The Quiet American*." *Renascence* 31 (Winter 1979):93-106.
    Gaston maintains that *The Quiet American* is primarily a book about the quest for personal salvation – a major Greene theme – rather than a strictly political and antiwar novel.

1394 Gelman, David. "Vietnam Marches Home." *Newsweek* 91 (13 February 1978):85-86.
    A discussion of the early, tentative appearance of Vietnam War stories and films. The major books are compared and publisher's reactions noted.

1395 Gilman, Owen W., Jr. "Ward Just's Vietnam: Where Word and Deed Did Not Meet." *South Atlantic Quarterly* 84 (Autumn 1985):356-67.

Gilman examines the narrative technique in Vietnam War literature and explores why people are compelled to write about war, the affect of Vietnam on the American people, and the purpose of the Vietnam War novel. The major emphasis is on a discussion of Ward Just's *Stringer* and *In the City of Fear*.

1396 Gitlin, Todd. "Notes on War Poetry." *Confrontation*, no. 8 (Spring 1974):145-47.

Vietnam War poetry and that of World War I are compared and differences noted. The author says that "the best Vietnam War poetry . . . is that which lucidly expresses the relationship between the victim and the executioner."

1397 Goldstein, William. "Three Splendid First Novels Examine the Vietnam War." *Publishers Weekly* 224, no. 17 (21 October 1983):39,42.

A discussion of *Gardens of Stone*, *Tiger the Lurp Dog*, and *Meditations in Green*.

1398 Gordon, Andrea. "Why Are We in Vietnam?: Deep in the Bowels of Texas." *Literature and Psychology* 24, no. 2 (1974):55-65.

Gordon discusses images of castration and evisceration in *Why Are We in Vietnam?*

1399 Grant, Zalin. "Vietnam as Fable." *New Republic* 178 (25 March 1978):21-24.

Grant was an Army intelligence officer and Vietnamese linguist and later a reporter for *Time* and the *New Republic*. He discusses films about the war (*Apocalypse Now*) and traces the history of writing about the Vietnam War including the reactions of publishers and the reading public. Both fiction and nonfiction are considered. Grant notes that Vietnam is often considered as "simply a time of temporary national madness" and that the "dope-and-dementia" interpretation of Vietnam will continue to be our image of it.

1400 Gray, Paul. "Secret History." *Time* 110 (7 November 1977):119-20.
Gray discusses Herr's *Dispatches* and notes that Herr tells his story because it has to be told, knowing full well that it (war) will happen again.

1401 Hampl, Patricia. "The Mayflower Moment: Reading Whitman During the Vietnam War." In *Walt Whitman: The Measure of His Song*. Edited by Jim Perlman, Ed Folsom, and Dan Campion. Minneapolis: Holy Cow!, 1981, 300-13.
The author, a student and fledgling writer during the Vietnam years, discusses the effect of reading poetry, particularly Walt Whitman's poetry, at a time of national loss of identity and shame.

1402 Harris, Norman. "Blacks in Vietnam: A Holistic Perspective Through Fiction and Journalism." *Western Journal of Black Studies* 10, no. 3 (Fall 1986):121-31.
Harris studies what the Vietnam War meant to black soldiers as viewed through *Coming Home*, *Tragic Magic*, and *Captain Blackman*, as well as the nation's attitude toward the black soldier in Vietnam.

1403 _____. *Connecting Times: The Sixties in Afro-American Fiction*. Jackson: University Press of Mississippi, 1988.
The war in Vietnam, the civil rights movement, and the black power movement were key events from 1960 to 1973. Part I of the book deals with the novels of the war and what the war meant to Afro-American soldiers and civilians, as seen in *Coming Home*, *Tragic Magic*, and *Captain Blackman*. He notes the effects of the war occurring in three stages shown in the novels:

1. The soldiers are thrilled at the opportunity to prove their fighting skills.
2. They become disillusioned by the discriminatory practices of white peers and commanding officers.
3. Finally, they begin a cultural-historical search for precedents that can help them make sense of their involvement.

1404 Hassan, Ihab. "Focus on Norman Mailer's *Why Are We in Vietnam?*" In *American Dreams, American Nightmares*. Edited by David Madden. Carbondale: Southern Illinois University Press, 1970, 197-203.

Hassan discusses Mailer's work and legend, and the confusion that often arises between the two, focusing particularly on the tone, themes, narrative style, and use of obscenity in *Why Are We In Vietnam?*

1405 Hayashi, Tetsumaro. *John Steinbeck and the Vietnam War*. Muncie, Ind.: Ball State University, 1986.

The author, a teacher at Ball State University, discusses John Steinbeck's reaction to the Vietnam War as the first part of a larger research project in preparation. Hayashi points out that Steinbeck's changing views through the era paralleled America's changing views – he first supported the war and then opposed it. The political aspects of Steinbeck's novels are noted as is his relationship with Lyndon Johnson. Bibliography.

1406 Hellman, John. *American Myth and the Legacy of Vietnam*. New York: Columbia University Press, 1986.

Using American literature, especially works about the Vietnam era, the book "traces the relationship of America's mythic heritage to its experience in Vietnam." Hellman says that "Vietnam is an experience that has severely called into question American myth."

1407 ____. *Fables of Fact: The New Journalism as New Fiction*. Urbana: University of Illinois Press, 1981.

A discussion of the new journalism – the nonfiction novel – that emerged after 1965, paying particular attention to Mailer's *The Executioner's Song*, Thompson's *Fear and Loathing: On the Campaign Trail '72*, Wolfe's *Electric Kool-Aid Acid Test*, and Herr's *Dispatches*. See 1408 and 1635.

1408 ____. "Memory, Fragments and 'Clean Information' in Michael Herr's *Dispatches*." In *Fables of Fact: The New Journalism as New Fiction*. Urbana: University of Illinois Press, 1981.

Hellman describes the advantages of Herr's use of the new journalistic style – the nonfiction novel – in *Dispatches* to present the war in a way that is more understandable than either more traditional reporting or traditional fiction writing styles would allow. Examples of Herr's style are presented and discussed. The book, of which this essay is a part, is a thorough explanation and discussion of the new journalism as a writing style. Bibliography.

1409 ____. "New Journalism and Vietnam: Memory as Structure in Michael Herr's *Dispatches*." *South Atlantic Quarterly* 79 (Spring 1980):1-51.

A discussion of Herr's *Dispatches* and the rise of the new journalism. Neither journalistic accounts nor fiction of the conventional type can tell the truth of the Vietnam experience. Herr utilized a form that would present the actual experience and allow a way to explore its meaning.

1410 Hendin, Josephine. *Vulnerable People: A View of American Fiction Since 1945*. New York: Oxford University Press, 1978.

This source contains brief references to Vietnam and a short discussion of *Dog Soldiers*.

1411 Herring, George C. "Vietnam Remembered." *Journal of American History* 73, no. 1 (June 1986):152-64.

A discussion and review of the major personal narratives of the Vietnam War including . . . *And A Hard Rain Fell, Dear America: Letters Home from Vietnam, Once A Warrior King, Platoon Leader, To Bear Any Burden, The Tunnels of Cu Chi*, and *Vietcong Memoir*.

1412 Hertzbach, Janet S. "David Rabe." In *Critical Survey of Drama* (English Language Series). Edited by Frank N. McGill. Englewood Cliffs, N.J.: Salem Press, 1985, 4:1545-54.

A reference work discussion of Rabe's plays that includes biographical data, achievements, a list of principal dramas, analysis of his work, and a short bibliography.

1413 ____. "The Plays of David Rabe." In *Essays on Contemporary American Drama*. Edited by Hedwig Bock and Albert Wertheim. Munich: Max Hueber Verlag, 1981, 173-86.

Hertzbach discusses Rabe's plays with special emphasis on the Vietnam trilogy. Rabe's depiction of contemporary American life as a battlefield as real as Vietnam is explored.

1414 Herzog, Tobey C. "*Going After Cacciato*: The Soldier-Author-Character Seeking Control." *Critique* 24, no. 2 (Winter 1983):88-96.

This essay is based on a paper delivered at the 1981 MLA Convention for a panel on "The Consciousness of a Nation: Vietnam in American Literature and Film." The author notes that all wars are chaotic, but Vietnam was especially so with no decisive battles, no center, no land taken and held, no sense of progress. The author discusses the ways Paul Berlin, the main character in *Going After Cacciato*, must continually seek some kind of control over his world – the focal point of this discussion.

1415 _____. "Writing About Vietnam: A Heavy Heart-of-Darkness Trip." *College English* 41 (February 1980):680-95.

The author, a Vietnam veteran and English teacher at Wabash College, reviews the early fiction and nonfiction of Vietnam including *The Killing Zone*, *Friendly Fire*, *A Rumor of War*, *Better Times Than These*, *Fields of Fire*, and *Going After Cacciato*. He points out the unique qualities of Vietnam War writing. See also 1454 for John Leland's response to this article.

1416 Hidesaki, Yasuro. "American Conscience and Vietnam War Literature." *Kyushu American Literature* 25 (July 1984):46-53.

Hidesaki notes that when the soldier merges himself into larger military structures he loses his conscience and humanity as can be seen in several works including Daniel Lang's personal narrative *Casualty of War* and several novels as well as in Sontag's *Trip to Hanoi*, Mailer's Vietnam novels, and the works of Mary McCarthy.

1417 _____. "Black Humor and Vietnam War Novels." *Kyushu American Literature* 27 (1986):97-106.

The differences between Vietnam War novels and personal narratives and those of World War II are illustrated in a discussion of Kovic's *Born On the Fourth of July* and Caputo's *A Rumor of War*. Both authors tell their readers that "once a man's reason awakes and his conscience revives him he is naturally led to one conclusion: returning to peace." The author feels that the true worth of the Vietnam War is that it clarifies the line between justice and injustice.

1418 ____. "The Peculiarity and Background of Vietnam War Literature."
Kyushu American Literature 24 (July 1983):60-69.

The Vietnam War is unique in that it was fought in what the
author describes as a "technological blizzard and a moral vacuum" thus
giving rise to a prevailing mood of futility and despair among the
troops. He discusses how this is expressed in the black humor of such
novels as Burke's *Laughing War*, Hasford's *The Short-Timers*, Roth's
Sand in the Wind, and Caputo's *Rumor of War*.

1419 Holdstein, Deborah H. "Vietnam War Veteran-Poets: The Ideology of
Horror." *USA Today* 112, no. 2460 (September 1983):59-61.

A discussion of Vietnam veteran poetry which reflects the
struggle to find a reason for fighting. Specific collections and poems are
discussed (*Winning Hearts and Minds* and *Obscenities*) and the specific
style of the Vietnam vet is noted.

1420 Hollowell, John. *Fact and Fiction: The New Journalism and the
Nonfiction Novel*. Chapel Hill: University of North Carolina Press,
1977.

Fact and Fiction reviews the social changes of the 1960s and
the response of novelists and journalists that resulted in "the form of
nonfiction that relies upon the narrative technique and intuitive insights
of the novelist to chronicle contemporary events." Specifically discussed
are Truman Capote's *In Cold Blood*, Norman Mailer's *The Armies of
the Night* and Tom Wolfe's *The Electric Kool-Aid Acid Test*. This work
has relevance for a study of the personal narratives and the journalistic
accounts of the Vietnam War. Bibliography.

1421 Homan, Richard L. "American Playwrights in the 1970's: Rabe and
Shepard." *Critical Quarterly* 24, no. 1 (Spring 1982):73-82.

Homan discusses the work of Sam Shepard and David Rabe
and explores the question of whether their successes will be enduring.

1422 Hooker, Jeremy. "The Boundaries of Our Distances: On 'Of Being
Numerous.'" *Ironweed* 13, no. 2 (Fall 1985):81-103.

A brief discussion of poet George Oppen's Vietnam War
imagery in his poem *Of Being Numerous*. The poem was written at the
height of the war and is an indictment of America's involvement.

1423 Hughes, Catherine. "David Rabe." In *American Playwrights, 1945-1975*. London: Pitman, 1976, 81-87.
      The Basic Training of Pavlo Hummel and *Sticks and Bones* are studied in this discussion of the works of David Rabe.

1424 _____. "The Theatre Goes to War." *America* 116 (20 May 1967):759-61.
      Hughes compares the thirty-five year old anti-war play *The Green Table* by Kurt Jooss with Megan Terry's *Viet Rock* and Peter Brook's *US*.

1425 Hurrell, Barbara. "American Self-Image in David Rabe's Vietnam Trilogy." *Journal of American Culture* 4, no. 2 (Summer 1981):95-107.
      Hurrell shows how Rabe's trilogy of Vietnam plays force American audiences to confront the returning veteran and the questions he brings with him as to who we are as Americans.

1426 Jerome, Judson. "Poetry: How and Why." *Writer's Digest* 49 (February 1969):16-23.
      Jerome poses the question "Does poetry make things happen? Can it help us out of Viet Nam?" The author discuss the poetry of Denise Levertov in searching for an answer.

1427 Johnson, Diane, ed. "The Loss of Patriotic Faith: C. D. B. Bryan's *Friendly Fire*." In *Terrorists and Novelists*. New York: Knopf, 1982, 179-92.
      The story of Peg and Gene Mullen's attempt to learn more about the death of their son in Vietnam and Bryan's writing of their story is told. The struggle of the Mullen family to reconcile the America they thought they knew with the America they found and their struggle to maintain their image of America is recounted.

1428 Johnson, Mark. "History, the Body's Prison: American Poetry During and After Vietnam." *Publications of the Missouri Philological Association* 8 (1983):25-30.
      Johnson discusses four long poems written during the late 1960s to early 1980s: Robert Kelly's *The Common Shore*, Allen Ginsberg's *The Fall of America*, Robert Pinsky's *An Explanation of America*, and Daniel Hoffman's *Brotherly Love*. The author shows that

these poems illustrate a cultural and literary shift from "polarization to fragmentation" as a result of the Vietnam War.

1429 Jones, Dale W. "The Vietnams of Michael Herr and Tim O'Brien: Tales of Disintegration and Integration." *Canadian Review of American Studies* 13, no. 3 (Winter 1982):309-20.
      Jones feels that *Dispatches* and *Going After Cacciato* are the two most important books to emerge from the Vietnam War. He notes the different techniques used by each author. Form is emphasized.

1430 Jones, Peter G. *War and the Novelist: Appraising the American War Novel*. Columbia: University of Missouri Press, 1976.
      This interesting study of war and literature focuses on literary form, internal politics of war organization, psychological processes, and the relationship of sexuality and violence to the psychology of combat. There are allusions to Vietnam but other wars are emphasized. Halberstam's *One Very Hot Day* and John Sack's *M* are discussed. Bibliography of primary and secondary sources.

1431 Jordan, Clive. "Vietnam Connection: New Novels." *Encounter* 45 (September 1975):71-76.
      A discussion and review of Robert Stone's *Dog Soldiers*.

1432 Just, Ward. "Vietnam: Fiction and Fact." *TriQuarterly* 65 (Winter 1986):215-20.
      Just discusses the war and why it is important to write about it even if no one seems to learn from wars. For the writer, there is a need to come to terms with the experience. Just states that "the writer comes closest to the heart of war, its infinitely still center, when he begins to invent Vietnam." He comments that seeing the events on television does not simulate the experience of being there.

1433 Kakutani, Michiko. "Novelists and Vietnam: The War Goes On." *New York Times Book Review*, 15 April 1984, 1, 39-41.
      Kakutani points out that thus far (1984) Vietnam has remained as resistent to fictional treatment as it did to journalistic reporting at the time. "It has proved difficult to transmute the experiences into fully imagined works of art." He maintains that "both the difficulties Vietnam

poses as a fictional subject and its lasting effects on writing are inextricably tied up with its anomalous moral, political, and military nature."

1434 Kamla, Thomas A. "Remobilization from the Left: Peter Weiss' *Viet Nam Discourse." Modern Drama* 18 (December 1975):337-48.

   The form, theme, and presentation of German writer Peter Weiss' *Viet Nam Discourse* are discussed as well as its place in German documentary theater.

1435 Karagueuzian, Maureen. "Interview with Robert Stone." *TriQuarterly* 53 (Winter 1982):248-58.

   The author interviewed Robert Stone in the summer of 1980. He describes how he writes, his writing style, and the reasons for the settings of his novels. He comments on the making of *Dog Soldiers* into a film. Specific discussion of his three novels is brief.

1436 ____. "Irony in Robert Stone's *Dog Soldiers." Critique* 24, no. 2 (Winter 1983):65-73.

   The source of ironic tension in *Dog Soldiers* and Stone's use of Hemingway's world as a standard against which the Vietnam War can be measured are explained.

1437 Karl, Frederick R. "Vietnam as a Metaphor for Life." In *American Fictions, 1940-1980*. New York: Harper & Row, 1983, 113-18.

   American Fictions is a comprehensive history and critical evaluation of American fiction with references to Vietnam throughout. Chapter Four, "The War and the Novel – Before and After" (75-128) includes a section called "Vietnam as a Metaphor for Life" in which *Dog Soldiers*, *Going After Cacciato*, and *A Flag for Sunrise* are discussed. Chapter Twelve, "The Nonfiction Novel" (560-90) mentions and briefly discusses the work of Norman Mailer.

1438 Kaufman, Donald L. "Catch 23: The Mystery of Fact (Norman Mailer's Final Novel?)" *Twentieth Century Literature* 17, no. 4 (October 1971):247-56.

The author feels that *Why Are We in Vietnam?* was the end of Norman Mailer as a novelist. His next group of nonfiction novels show that he is repeating himself.

1439 Kazin, Alfred. "The Decline of War: Mailer to Vonnegut." In *Bright Book of Life: American Novelists and Storytellers from Hemingway to Mailer*. Boston: Little, Brown, 1971, 71-93.

William Eastlake's *The Bamboo Bed* is compared to World War II novels in this discussion. The changes in attitude toward the war and how wars are and will be fought is explained.

1440 _____. "Vietnam: It Was Us vs. Us: Michael Herr's *Dispatches*: More Than Just the Best Vietnam Book." *Esquire* 89, no. 3 (1 March 1978):120-23.

Kazin feels that Herr's *Dispatches* is not only the best book to come out of the Vietnam War but "it is the only book I know on Vietnam that brings to us intact the specific environment that sooner or later hallucinated Americans at war."

1441 _____. "The War Novel: From Mailer to Vonnegut." *Saturday Review* 54 (6 February 1971):13-15, 36.

Notable American war novels are compared including *The Naked and the Dead*, *Catch-22*, *Slaughterhouse Five*, and *The Bamboo Bed*.

1442 Kermode, Frank. "Tell Me Lies about Vietnam . . .; Peter Brook and *US*." *Encounter* 28, no. 1 (January 1967):62-64.

A discussion of the play *US*, staged in London. The author finds the play useless as a way for audiences to find out what they feel about the war. He calls it a "breakthrough into sheer non-drama."

1443 Klein, Jeffrey. "The Vietnam Connection." *American Scholar* 44 (Autumn 1975):686-88.

A review and discussion of Stone's *Dog Soldiers*.

1444 Klinkowitz, Jerome. "Fiction: The 1960s to the Present." In *American Literary Scholarship: An Annual, 1986*. Edited by David J. Nordloh. Durham, N.C.: Duke University Press, 1988, 283-302.

   American Literary Scholarship contains a brief discussion of the literature of the Vietnam War as viewed thrrough literary criticism in Part X, "Literature of the Vietnam War," 299-300, a small part of the larger "Fiction: the 1960s to the Present." The 1980 volume in the series contains an article on the new journalism as a subgenre by J. Albert Robbins, 344-45.

1445 ____. *Literary Disruptions: The Making of a Post-Contemporary American Fiction*. Urbana: University of Illinois Press, 1975, 18-20, 27-30, 112-15.

   A study of contemporary American fiction which sees Vonnegut, Barthelme and Kosinski as real leaders in the advancement of the "disruptive school" of American literature. Included are discussions of James S. Kunen's *Standard Operating Procedure* and James Park Sloan's *War Games*. Bibliography.

1446 ____. "Vietnam" in *The American 1960's: Imaginative Acts in a Decade of Change*. Ames: Iowa State University Press, 1980, 75-88.

   Klinkowitz discusses Herr's *Dispatches*, Greene's *The Quiet American*, Halberstam's *One Very Hot Day*, movies about Vietnam, and the war protests at home.

1447 ____. "Writing under Fire: Postmodern Fiction and the Vietnam War." In *Postmodern Fiction: A Bio-Bibliographical Guide*. Edited by Larry McCaffery. New York: Greenwood Press, 1986, 79-92.

   The article focuses on the fiction published during our actual involvement in Vietnam. Klinkowitz notes that "Vietnam affected our literary imagination in ways that no other war has, and the result has been a body of fiction that relies on various innovative formal devices, similar to the experimental features that characterize other postmodern fiction, to capture a sense of that war's assault on language and on our sense of reality."

1448 Kneeshaw, Stephen. "Voices from Vietnam: The New Literature from America's Longest War." *Teaching History: A Journal of Methods* 13, no. 1 (Spring 1988):22-29. EJ 369 545.

A review essay of seven books written since 1983: *Bloods, Home Before Morning, A Piece of My Heart, In the Combat Zone, Dear America, Vietnam Voices,* and *The Bad War.*

1449 Koning, Hans. "Films and Plays About Vietnam Treat Everything But the War." *New York Times,* 27 May 1979, sec. 2, p. 7.
      Noting that the subject of Vietnam is now acceptable to film makers and readers, the author discusses the films and plays that deal with Vietnam and points out that the large moral issues of the war have not been addressed in these forms of expression. There has been no view of "the other side" and the idea of American guilt has been ignored.

1450 Kroll, Jack. "Passion Plays of Vietnam." *Newsweek* 93 (30 April 1979):97-98.
      A review and discussion of the plays and productions of *G. R. Point* and *Dispatches.*

1451 Lahr, John. "Indians: A Dialogue Between Arthur Kopit and John Lahr, edited by Anthea Lahr." In an unpaginated insert of *Indians.* New York: Bantam, 1971.
      Kopit discusses his play *Indians* noting that he wrote it because he wanted "to expose the madness of our involvement in Vietnam." He discusses the extended metaphor used in the play.

1452 Larsen, Eric. "Reconsideration: *The Quiet American.*" *The New Republic* 175 (7, 14 August 1976):40-42.
      Larsen discusses the prophetic quality of *The Quiet American.* He assures us that books don't make events happen. Although the book was written even before the French left Vietnam, the book is about Americans there.

1453 Leepson, Marc. "Vietnam War Legacy." *Editorial Research Reports* 11, no. 1 (6 July 1979):483-500.
      Leepson addresses three areas: "Reexamination of the War" (novels and movies), "Problems of the War's Veterans," and "Reassessment of the War's Impact."

1454 Leland, John C., and Tobey Herzog. "Comment and Response: Writing About Vietnam." *College English* 43, no. 7 (November 1981):739-74.

    The author, writing in response to Tobey Herzog's article in *College English*, feels that "Herzog does not treat the literature of Vietnam as examples of literary tradition" and proceeds to point out what is traditional in the Vietnam novels. Herzog responds and concludes by saying that "too many soldiers, civilians, politicians, tutored by World War II literature and John Wayne movies, simply exchanged Vietnam and World War II. The result was disaster."

1455 Lewis, Lloyd. *The Tainted War: Culture and Identity in Vietnam War Narratives*. Westport, Conn.: Greenwood Press, 1985.

    Nineteen personal narratives form the basis of this study of the soldier's view of the Vietnam war. "Their responses illuminate both the nature of that unprecedented military disaster and the larger cultural forces that made it possible." Conclusions drawn. A very useful bibliography of primary and secondary sources included.

1456 Linenthal, Edward Tabor. "From Hero to Anti-Hero: The Transformation of the Warrior in Modern America." *Soundings* 63, no. 1 (1980):79-83.

    Linenthal discusses "the shift in perception of the nature of war and of the symbol of the warrior in America" since the Vietnam War. The changing concept of the "hero" and the "warrior" are explored in this important article which focuses on *Friendly Fire* and *Dispatches*. Bibliography.

1457 Little, Stuart W. *Enter Joseph Papp: In Search of a New American Theater*. New York: Coward, McCann & Geoghegan, 1974.

    A study of the influential New York theater director Joseph Papp. Discussed are his work techniques, how he manages his theater on artistic, managerial, and financial levels, and his importance in the theater world. Papp describes his work with David Rabe and the production of *Sticks and Bones*.

1458 Lockwood, Lee. "Book Marks: Trips to Hanoi." *Nation* 208 (24 March 1969):374-77.

Lockwood reviews several books that concern themselves with trips to Hanoi including Berrigan's *Night Flight to Hanoi*, Mary McCarthy's *Hanoi*, and Susan Sontag's *Trip to Hanoi*.

1459 Lomperis, Timothy J. *Reading the Wind: The Literature of the Vietnam War–An Interpretive Critique.* Durham, N.C.: Duke University Press, 1987.

An important and useful work, *Reading the Wind*, is the result of a conference held by the Asia Society on May 7-9, 1985. Most of the major Vietnam writers spoke. A discussion of the Vietnam novel and its role in American literature was explored. John Clark Pratt's bibliographic commentary (117-54) places the novels within the framework of the history of the war.

1460 Lubow, Arthur. "Natty Bumppo Goes to War." *Atlantic Monthly* 243, no. 4 (April 1979):97-98.

A discussion of the film *The Deer Hunter* and its relationship to Cooper's *The Deerslayer*, *Going After Cacciato*, *A Rumor of War*, and other major Vietnam novels.

1461 Ludington, Townsend. "Comprehending the American Experience in Vietnam." *Southern Humanities Review* 18, no. 4 (Fall 1984):339-49.

Ludington discusses and reviews Philip Beidler's *American Literature and the Experience of Vietnam* commenting on Vietnam literature's attempt to make people understand what those who were there experienced. Attention also is given to *The Short-Timers*, *Fields of Fire*, and *Going After Cacciato*.

1462 Lyon, Jeff. "Author 1st Class." *Chicago Tribune Magazine*, 7 February 1988, 10-15, 18-19, 22-25, 29.

A profile of Chicago author Larry Heinemann following his winning of the National Book Award for *Paco's Story*. Heinemann discusses his war experiences, his experiences since returning home, and his views on writing.

1463 Lyons, Gene. "Pieces of a Vietnam War Story." *Nation* 224, no. 4 (29 January 1977):120-22.

Lyons discusses Tim O'Brien's work, particularly *Going After Cacciato* (prior to its publication).

1464 McCabe, Stephen. "The Literature Born of Vietnam." *Humanist* 46, no. 2 (March/April 1986):30-31.

McCabe comments on the uniqueness of Vietnam literature in comparison with the literature of other wars and notes that "Vietnam War literature is such overwhelmingly good art while its source and inspiration was such a resoundingly bad war." *In Country, Friendly Fire, Close Quarters, Going After Cacciato, Fields of Fire, One Very Hot Day,* and *Dispatches* are discussed.

1465 McCaffery, Larry. "Interview with Tim O'Brien." *Chicago Review* 33, no. 2 (1982):129-49.

McCaffery recalls the memorable 1968. He was drafted and wondered how he would react. Could he really shoot someone? Could he run? Luckily his asthma made him ineligible. After years of thinking about the war and of those who went, of reading the books, viewing the films, and interviewing vets, the author met and interviewed Tim O'Brien, asking him particularly about *Going After Cacciato* and his Vietnam experiences. O'Brien suggests that the basic question of *Going After Cacciato* is "What if I *had* deserted?" Comparisons are made to other war novels and the body of O'Brien's work is discussed along with his response to other Viet novels and the films, which O'Brien calls "cartoons." A very useful, interesting interview. This same article may also be found in LeClair, Thomas and McCaffery, eds. *Anything Can Happen: Interviews with Contemporary American Novelists* (Urbana: University of Ilinois Press, 1983), 262-78.

1466 _____, ed. *Postmodern Fiction: A Bio-Bibliographical Guide*. New York: Greenwood Press, 1986.

The purpose of this collection of essays is to allow easy access to information about specific postmodern authors and critics as well as to discuss the theoretical issues that have shaped the fiction of this period. Included are Jerome Klinkowitz's "Writing Under Fire: Postmodern Fiction and The Vietnam War" (1447) and several other references to the Vietnam War. A discussion and bibliography of three Vietnam authors also appears: William Eastlake, 345-48 (1343), Tim O'Brien, 477-79 (1512), and Robert Stone, 508-11 (1537).

1467 McCaffery, Larry, and Sinda Gregory. "An Interview with William Eastlake." *South Shore: An International Review of the Arts* 1, no. 2 (1978):41-65.

McCaffery interviewed William Eastlake on January 11, 1977 in Rio Rico, Arizona. Biographical information is provided. Eastlake discusses his views on writing, his style, the western settings, specific books, and his experiences in Vietnam.

1468 McCarthy, Eugene J. "Poetry and War." *Confrontation*, no. 8 (Spring 1974):131-36.

McCarthy, the presidential candidate, discusses the difficulty in writing war poetry. Notable war poems, those of Sigfried Sassoon in particular, are explored. "If most wars are beyond poetic treatment, certainly one would think this of the Vietnamese War. It was beyond poetry, but it was also beyond prose and somehow came back to the poets. They did not refuse." The poetic anthology *Winning Hearts and Minds* is briefly considered.

1469 McCarthy, Gerald. "Static Essentials: Voices of Vietnam War Literature." *Mid-American Review* 4 (Fall 1984):96-100.

McCarthy notes that the "voice" coming out of Vietnam War literature is "a voice out of the dust of the American dream, instinct with the tone of lost youth and innocence." These men can never feel the same again about war, their country, or themselves. McCarthy used Kovic's *Born on the Fourth of July*, O'Brien's *Going After Cacciato*, and Wright's *Meditations in Green* to illustrate this literary voice.

1470 McCarthy, Mary. "Sons of the Morning." In *The Seventeenth Degree*. New York: Harcourt Brace Jovanovich, 1974, 413-40.

A much-discussed, negative critique of David Halberstam's *The Best and the Brightest*.

1471 McInerney, Peter. "Straight and Secret History in Vietnam War Literature." *Contemporary Literature* 22 (Spring 1981):187-204.

The concept and definition of "straight" history as opposed to "secret" history–the manipulation of history as seen in Lyndon Johnson's "A Pattern for Peace in Southeast Asia" speech–are explained and the place of literature as history. The history of Vietnam

War literature is discussed from Greene's visionary *The Quiet American* to novels by Mailer, and personal narratives by Kovic and Caputo.

1472 Magistrale, Anthony S. "Stephen King's Vietnam Allegory: An Interpretation of *Children of the Corn.*" *Cuyahoga Review* 2 (Spring/Summer 1984):61-66.

The symbolic and thematic content of Stephen King's work is discussed noting that the horrors he describes often symbolize contemporary situations. The short story "Children of the Corn" is seen as an extended metaphor for the U.S. situation in Vietnam.

1473 Maloff, Saul. "Vietnam Mon Amour." *Commonweal* 55, no. 3 (3 February 1978):84-87.

Maloff reminds us of how we were overwhelmed with information about the Vietnam War at its height, especially by television, but that Americans never really allowed it to register in their conscious minds. He says that we knew too much and too little, and really didn't want to know anything at all. However, Herr's *Dispatches* not only reports what happened but makes readers *feel* it. Maloff says "no one who has written of Vietnam has caught it as powerfully as he in *that* book."

1474 Maness, Mary. "War Is Glorious: War Is Hell: War Is Absurd." *Language Arts* 53 (May 1976):560-63.

The author researched the treatment of war in children's literature, limiting her study to the fiction of WWII, Korea, and Vietnam. Her title sums up her findings. She discusses Dunn's *The Man in the Box: A Story From Vietnam* and Graham's *Cross-fire*. List of references included.

1475 Marin, Peter. "Coming to Terms with Vietnam." *Harper's* 261, no. 1567 (December 1980):41-56.

An excellent article on the moral quandary that was Vietnam and our inability or unwillingness to face what happened and why. The author fears that this inability will set us on the path to another war. A discussion of attempts to deal with the war through literature and film is presented as well as other wars' literary responses. American guilt is explored.

1476 Marnanca, Bonnie. "David Rabe's Viet Nam Trilogy." *Canadian Theatre Review* 14 (1977):86-92.
 David Rabe's Vietnam trilogy, which follows the soldier's cycle from basic training to war to the return home, is discussed. Marnanca calls Rabe "the voice of the American conscience."

1477 Marowitz, Charles. "The Royal Shakespeare's *US*." *Tulane Drama Review* 11, no. 2 (Winter 1966):173-75.
 A review of The Royal Shakespeare Theater's presentation of Brook's *US*. The author calls it an "artistic failure" in his discussion of the play and its production.

1478 Martin, Charles E. "A Good One Is a Dead One: The Combat Soldier's View of Vietnam and the Indian Wars." *Kentucky Folklore Record* 26 (July-December 1980):114-32.
 Martin begins his article with a comparison of an account of a 1868 General Custer battle against a Cheyenne village with a 1968 battle in My Lai with Charlie Company and discusses other similarities between the two wars. Some of the material utilized in the article is taken from Glasser's *365 Days*.

1479 Mazzaro, Jerome. "David Ignatow's Post-Vietnam War Poetry." *Centennial Review* 30, no. 2 (Spring 1986):219-27.
 Ignatow's poetry and its anti-Vietnam war imagery and theme are discussed. The author notes that Ignatow's body of work reflects an ongoing concern for the human being, especially underdogs. Particular attention is paid to his post-Vietnam poems.

1480 Melamed, Lisa. "Between the Lines of Fire: The Vietnam War in Literature for Young Readers." *Lion and the Unicorn* 3, no. 2 (1980):76-85.
 Vietnam War fiction for young people is discussed. Melamed divides fiction into two categories: war as a social phenomena (Hentoff's *I'm Really Dragged But Nothing Gets Me Down*) and books where Vietnam is the actual setting (Garfield's *The Last Bridge*, Graham's *Cross-fire*, and Haldeman's *War Year*).

1481 Merideth, Robert. "The 45-Second Piss: A Left Critique of Norman Mailer and *The Armies of the Night.*" *Modern Fiction Studies* 17, no. 3 (Autumn 1971):433-49.

A memorable scene from *The Armies of the Night* is used to illustrate what the author feels is Mailer's "present political inadequacy" for a New Left moving into a new decade.

1482 Merrill, Robert. "*Armies of the Night*: The Education of Norman Mailer." *Illinois Quarterly* 37, no. 1 (1974):30-44.

A discussion of the unusual structure of *The Armies of the Night*. Merrill comments on the importance of studying Mailer's artistic achievements rather than Mailer as a personality. The relationship between the two parts of the book—"history" and "novel"—are discussed. This article was reprinted in *Norman Mailer*, Robert Merrill, ed. Twayne (Boston, 1978), 108-28.

1483 Mersmann, James F. *Out of the Vietnam Vortex: A Study of Poets and Poetry against the War*. Lawrence: University Press of Kansas, 1974.

An important thematic analysis of the poetry written during the 1960s protesting the Vietnam War, focusing on the work of Allen Ginsberg, Denise Levertov, Robert Bly, and Robert Duncan with a survey of other poets who wrote against the war. An attempt is made to determine:

1. Whether war protest is a legitimate and natural outgrowth of a writer's world-view.
2. Whether the experience of war alters a poet's beliefs and practices.
3. Whether common themes and attitudes toward war and culture are tied to similar backgrounds and philosophic tempers or arise equally from different backgrounds.
4. Whether a poet's protest is based in opportunism (protest being the fashion) or whether he is deeply committed.
5. Whether protest poetry is generally inferior to the more detached and objective work of the same poet.
   Bibliography. See also 1646.

1484 Merton, Thomas. "War and the Crisis of Language." In *The Critique of War*. Edited by Robert Ginsberg. Chicago: Henry Regnery Company, 1969, 99-119.

Merton comments that war causes a "sickness of language" – words become twisted. Examples are given from various wars with Vietnam receiving special emphasis. The notorious example of a town being destroyed "to save it" is used. The corruption of language always peaks in periods of war, Merton notes.

1485 Messerly, Carol. "Literature of the Vietnam War." *Louisiana Library Association Bulletin* 35 (Summer 1972):56-57.
    The literary importance of the war novel and the particular themes of the Vietnam War novel from Greene's *The Quiet American* to the novels of the 1970s are discussed. A bibliography of novels and poetry is included.

1486 Middlebrook, Jonathan. "Can a Middle-Aged Man with Four Wives and Six Children Be a Revolutionary?" *Journal of Popular Culture* 3, no. 3 (Winter 1969):565-74.
    A study of Norman Mailer and his *The Armies of the Night*. Middlebrook explains how the man of the title can be, as Mailer asserts, a "central man, the locus of real American values."

1487 Mierau, Maurice A. "Carnival and Jeremiad: Mailer's *Armies of the Night*." *Canadian Review of American Studies* 17, no. 3 (Fall 1986):317-26.
    Mierau critiques *The Armies of the Night*, noting a failure to wed the political with the literary in the work.

1488 Miller, Wayne Charles. *An Armed America: Its Face in Fiction: A History of the American Military Novel*. New York: New York University Press, 1978.
    The development of the American military novel is traced from James Fenimore Cooper to Joseph Heller. A chapter concludes the book titled "The Military Novel in the Nuclear Age." The book was published in 1970 and contains no information on Vietnam specifically, but the book is useful for its study of the genre. Bibliography.

1489 Misra, Kalidas. "The American War Novel from World War II to Vietnam." *Indian Journal of American Studies* 14 (July 1984):73-80.

1490 Morgan, Thomas B. "Reporters of the Lost War." *Esquire* 102, no. 1 (July 1984):49-60.

The Vietnam War demanded a new kind of reporting. Morgan discusses the major Vietnam journalists including Just, Halberstam, Herr, Page, Sheehan, Emerson, Greenway, Laurence, Arnett, and Mohr. A list of those journalists who died in the war is included.

1491 Morrow, Lance. "The Forgotten Warriors." *Time* 118 (13 July 1981):18-25.

The story of the Vietnam veterans and the difficulty of their reentry into American life and the problems the rest of society imposed on them is recounted. A brief discussion of the literature of this war and its place in war literature is included.

1492 Murphy, John. "Like Outlaws: Australian Narratives from the Vietnam War." *Meanjin* 46, no. 2 (June 1987):153-62.

Murphy notes that "the Australian intervention in Vietnam presents some dilemmas for a culture which has relied all too heavily on a military past for images of a national character." He discusses the Australian literary response to Vietnam in novels and personal narratives.

1493 Myers, Thomas. "Diving into the Wreck: Sense Making in *The 13th Valley*." *Modern Fiction Studies* 30, no. 1 (Spring 1984):119-34.

Myers comments on the early lack of interest in literary works on the Vietnam War and the resurgent interest in the 1980s, briefly discussing the key works of the late 1970s. The purpose of all of these novels appear to be an attempt to make some sense of the war. A full discussion of Del Vecchio's *The 13th Valley* is included in which the author comments on the reviews and compares the novel to others of its type.

1494 _____. *Walking Point: American Narratives of Vietnam*. New York: Oxford University Press, 1988.

An excellent critical study of American writing on the Vietnam War. Myers discusses the nature of war writing and Vietnam War writing in particular, the language of the war, its history, the cultural climate, the narrative styles used, and the major novels and personal narratives. Extensive bibliography.

1495 Naparsteck, Martin J. "The Vietnam War Novel." *Humanist* 39 (July 1979):37-39.

Naparsteck argues that even though the Vietnam War is an unpopular topic with publishers at the time of this article, it has produced a large and "admirable" body of literature. He proceeds to discuss the important novels of this genre.

1496 Nelson, Cary. *Our Last First Poets: Visions and History in Contemporary American Poetry*. Urbana: University of Illinois Press, 1981.

A collection of essays about poets who were involved in protesting the Vietnam War. The war's impact on them and on their poetry is discussed. The basic theme in contemporary American poetry appears to be the conflict between vision and history. Essays that are included are "Whitman in Vietnam: the Poetry of History in Contemporary America" (see 1497), "Ecclesiastical Whitman: Galway Kinnell's *The Book of Nightmares*," "Between Openness and Loss: Form and Dissolution in Robert Duncan's Aesthetic," "Meditative Aggressions: Adrienne Rich's Recent Transactions with History," and "The Resources of Failure: W. S. Merwin's Deconstructive Career."

1497 ____. "Whitman in Vietnam: The Poetry and History in Contemporary America" in his *Our Last First Poets: Visions and History in Contemporary American Poetry*. Urbana: University of Illinois Press, 1981, 1-30.

A discussion of the poetry of professional poets who viewed the war as a betrayal of the democratic vision of America. He comments that this poetry is "not likely to survive." Denise Levertov, W. S. Merwin, and George Hitchcock, among others, are critiqued. This article also appeared in *Massachusetts Review* 16 (Winter 1975):55-71.

1498 Nelson, Marie. "Two Consciences: A Reading of Tim O'Brien's Vietnam Trilogy: *If I Die in a Combat Zone, Going After Cacciato*, and *Northern Lights*." In *Third Force Psychology and the Study of Literature*. Edited by Bernard J. Paris. Rutherford, N.J.: Fairleigh Dickinson University Press, 1986, 262-79.

Nelson compares the three major works of Tim O'Brien, noting that each is written in a different narrative style, but all grow out of his war experiences and ask the question "What law must a man who wants to be good obey?"

1499 "Now Read in . . . Vietnam Is Now the Business of Poets." *Times Literary Supplement* 3350 (12 May 1966):407.

A discussion of American poets response to the Vietnam War, particularly the American Writers Against the War Read-In and those poets involved.

1500 O'Neill, Michael C. "History as Dramatic Present: Arthur L. Kopit's *Indians*." *Theatre Journal* 34, no. 4 (December 1982):493-504.

O'Neill traces the evolution of the experimental, "collage" form, symbolism, and thematic content of *Indians* and discusses its various productions.

1501 Palm, Edward F. "James Webb's *Fields of Fire*: The Melting Pot Platoon Revisited." *Critique* 24, no. 2 (Winter 1983):105-18.

In World War II novels, men of vastly different backgrounds come together and work as a unit – the "melting pot" platoon. The author notes that in Vietnam, the men in the platoons were more homogeneous than ever before, drawn mostly from the working and lower middle classes. The nature of the platoon, as used in *Fields of Fire*, is stressed in this critique of the book.

1502 _____. "Search for a Usable Past: Vietnam Literature and the Separate Peace Syndrome." *South Atlantic Review* 82 (Spring 1983):115-28.

Palm, a Vietnam veteran, discusses war novels of the past, including *The Red Badge of Courage*, *A Farewell to Arms*, *Slaughterhouse Five*, and *Catch 22*, and compares them to the unique presentations of war in Tim O'Brien's *Going After Cacciato*. Palm states that "O'Brien's *Going After Cacciato* has presented the first serious challenge to Heller's particular form of tyranny over the literature of war."

1503 Pasquali, Marco. "The Americans in Vietnam: War and Literature." *Revista Militare* (Rome), January/February 1985, 62-77.

1504 Pearce, Richard. "Norman Mailer's *Why Are We in Vietnam?*: A Radical Critique of Frontier Values." *Modern Fiction Studies* 17, no. 3 (Autumn 1971):409-14.

Pearce discusses *Why Are We in Vietnam?*, the American "tall tale" and western frontier mythology. The values of the western hero,

278

the author says, can be seen in Huck Finn, Natty Bumppo and D.J., the hero of Mailer's story.

1505 Pierce, Peter. "The Australian Literature of the Viet Nam War." *Meanjin Quarterly* 39, no. 3 (October 1980):290-303.

Although much of Australian Vietnam poetry was written by noncombatants, most of the novels were written by veterans and seem intent on admonishing Americans as well as blaming Australians. The author seeks the repercussions of the war in modern Australian writing. Australian and American works in various genre are discussed and compared.

1506 Pochoda, Elizabeth. "Vietnam, We've All Been There." *Nation* 226 (26 March 1978):344-46.

Going After Cacciato and *Dispatches* are discussed and compared.

1507 Powers, Thomas. "Vietnam in Fiction." *Commonweal* 101 (15 March 1974):39-41.

A review and comparison of three Vietnam novels: Robert Roth's *Sand in the Wind*, William Huggett's *Body Count*, and James Trowbridge's *Easy Victories*. Powers analysizes the Vietnam novel.

1508 Puhr, Kathleen M. "Four Fictional Faces of the Vietnam War." *Modern Fiction Studies* 30, no. 1 (Spring 1984):99-117.

Puhr notes that the majority of Vietnam novels are written in a realistic mode. She discusses this and four other modes of writing, using a representative example of each to compare and contrast: John Briley's *The Traitors* – political propaganda; James Webb's *Fields of Fire* – realism; Charles Durden's *No Bugles, No Drums* – realism/absurdism; Gustav Hasford's *The Short-Timers*-absurdism; John Clark Pratt's *The Laotian Fragments* – documentary fiction.

1509 Rabinovitz, Rubin. "Myth and Animism in *Why Are We in Vietnam?*" *Twentieth Century Literature* 20, no. 4 (October 1974):298-305.

A discussion of *Why Are We in Vietnam?* and Mailer's use of mythic themes to discover how the novel resembles primitive literature. The use of animism as a metaphor in the novel is explored.

1510 Ramsey, Roger. "Current and Recurrent: The Vietnam Novel." *Modern Fiction Studies* 17, no. 3 (Autumn 1971):415-31.

Ramsey critiques *Why Are We in Vietnam?* and studies the characters, particularly D.J. and his (and America's) schizophrenic nature.

1511 Raymond, Michael W. "Imagined Responses to Vietnam: Tim O'Brien's *Going After Cacciato*." *Critique* 24, no. 2 (Winter 1983):97-104.

Raymond discusses the narrative structure of *Going After Cacciato* and compares the book and O'Brien's style and purpose to Caputo's *A Rumor of War*.

1512 ____. "Tim O'Brien." In *Postmodern Fiction: A Bio-Bibliographical Guide*, edited by Larry McCaffery. New York: Greenwood Press, 1986, 477-79.

A short biography and critique of Tim O'Brien and his work with a brief bibliography of primary and secondary sources.

1513 Reynolds, R. C. "Exploring the Myths: One Author's Response to War." *Journal of the American Studies Association of Texas* 16 (1985):42-48.

Every writer who tries to write of the Vietnam War brings his own uniquely personal viewpoint to the work. The author notes that in Anthony Grey's *Saigon*, however, Grey attempts to capture all the different points of view through his characters. Both sides are shown and the myths exploded to "discover Vietnam's place in 20th century American affairs." The author discusses character, theme and plot.

1514 Ringnalda, Donald. "Chlorophyll Overdose: Stephen Wright's *Meditations in Green*." *Western Humanities Review* 40, no. 2 (Summer 1986):125-40.

The use of green imagery in the treatment of the Vietnam War is explored in the major novels.

1515 ____. "Fighting and Writing: America's Vietnam War Literature."
Journal of American Studies 22 (April 1988):25-42.
    The author maintains that Americans feel that the symbol of
something can replace the object itself – an attitude he feels led to the
Vietnam War – that American could "tame the untamable." He notes
that the Vietnam War literature tries to do the same thing – tame it by
naming it – putting it in the traditional mold of literary realism. Those
novels that succeed "emulate the ways the Viet Cong fought." Specific
novels are discussed.

1516 Robertson, R. T. "Nightmare of Kiwi Joe: C. K. Stead's Double Novel."
Ariel 6 (April 1975):97-100.
    A critique of C. K. Stead's Vietnam novel *Smith's Dream*.
Stead envisions a New Zealand dictatorship and urges New Zealanders
to wake up from their dream of security. He fears for the
"Vietnamization" of New Zealand.

1517 Rollins, Peter C. "The Vietnam War: Perceptions through Literature,
Film and Television." *American Quarterly* 36, no. 3 (1984):419-43.
    Rollins gives a statistical history of America's involvement in
Vietnam, a discussion of the climate of the times and the antiwar
movement. The major works of the war are discussed (Ehrhart,
Caputo, Del Vecchio, Mason, O'Brien, Kovic) as well as the films about
Vietnam, including television presentations.

1518 Rosenheim, Andrew. "After Vietnam: Two Writers Revisit the Scene of
the Crime." *Politicks* 1 (25 April 1978):23-24.
    A discussion of Vietnam novels that attempts to "penetrate the
American psyche" with particular attention to *Dispatches*, *Going After
Cacciato*, and *A Rumor of War*.

1519 Rowe, John Carlos. "Eye Witness: Documentary Styles in the American
Representations of Vietnam." *Cultural Critique* 3 (Spring 1986):126-50.
    Rowe notes that the majority of personal narrativea about the
Vietnam War will never be read by the masses. These accounts are
often privately printed from a desire to explain and understand the
experience, yet he feels that they make an important statement. He
notes that "Vietnam is unique among other American wars for the
volume and variety of subjective accounts it has generated." Rowe

discusses the new journalism, the documentary films and histories, and some of the lesser known personal narratives such as Flavio Bisignano's *Vietnam – Why?* and Munson's *Letters from Vietnam*.

1520 Rowlands, Graham. "Preserving the New Past: Australian Vietnam War Poetry." *Island Magazine* 6 (March 1981):35-36.

Rowlands responds to Peter Pierce's article "The Australian Literature of the Vietnam War." Pierce criticized Australian Vietnam poetry because the authors were not fighters. Rowland objects, saying that people do not need to directly experience something to be able to write effectively about it. He illustrates this with examples of Australian war poetry which he compares and contrasts in this interesting article.

1521 Ruas, Charles. "An Interview with Robert Stone." In *Conversations with American Writers*. New York: Knopf, 1985, 265-94.

Biographical information and an interview with Robert Stone in which his major themes, characters, and their relationship to Stone's personal life are discussed. Stone discusses the process of making the book *Dog Soldiers* into the film *Who'll Stop the Rain*.

1522 Rutherford, Andrew. "Realism and the Heroic: Some Reflections on War Novels." *Yearbook of English Studies* 12 (1982):194-207.

The author feels that literature has dealt too naively with themes of war and heroism, under the influence of the traditions of epic and romance and discusses the corrective realism of modern literature *The Red Badge of Courage*, WWII novels, and James Webb's *Fields of Fire* are examined.

1523 Sale, Roger. "Robert Stone." In *On Not Being Good Enough*. New York: Oxford University Press, 1979, 66-73.

A critique of Robert Stone's *Dog Soldiers*.

1524 Salzman, Arthur M. "Betrayal of the Imagination: Paul Brodeur's *The Stunt Man* and Tim O'Brien's *Going After Cacciato*." *Critique* 22, no. 1 (1980):32-38.

The author comments that "Vietnam remains for us an incontestable metaphor for nightmare and waste" and discusses how reality has become surreal in this war. *The Stunt Man* and *Going After*

Cacciato are examined and the novels' depicting of the effects of a war, where reality is a nightmare, on the individual consciousness.

1525 Sanders, Clinton R. "The Portrayal of War and the Fighting Man in Novels of the Vietnam War." *Journal of Popular Culture* 3, no. 3 (Winter 1969):553-64.

A discussion of war novels written while the war was in progress. The author sees the prowar works as "patterns of affirmation" and the antiwar works as "patterns of despair" and describes the world of the Vietnam soldier based on six novels: *M, One Very Hot Day, The Killing at Ngo Tho, Incident At Muc Wa, The Green Berets,* and *The LBJ Brigade.*

1526 Saul, E. Wendy. "Witness for the Innocent: Children's Literature and the Vietnam War." *Issues in Education* 3, no. 3 (Winter 1985):185-97. ED 335 769.

Saul studied the treatment of the Vietnam war in children's literature. Her findings treat war events as isolated incidents and show the horrors of war. No overviews exist.

1527 Sayres, Sohnya, Stanley Aronwitz, Anders Stephanson, and Fredric Jameson. *The 60s Without Apology.* Minneapolis: University of Minnesota Press, 1984.

A collection of essays that attempt to show the positive as well as the negative affect of the 1960s on the culture and politics of the United States from the viewpoint of the 1980s. Vietnam and 1960s literature is mentioned throughout, but discussed particularly in "Vietnam: The Thousand Plateaus" by Herman Rapaport, 137-47, and "Why You Will Never Read the Novel You Might Like To" by Jay Boyer, 309-10. The book discusses the major issues of the 1960s – Vietnam, the sexual revolution, women's liberation, rock music, civil rights, etc.

1528 Scheurer, Timothy E. "Myth to Madness: America, Vietnam and Popular Culture." *Journal of American Culture* 4, no. 2 (Summer 1981):149-65.

Scheurer discusses the affect the Vietnam War has had on American culture since its end in 1975. Grappling with our role in the war in an attempt to make sense of it all, novels and films are discussed and compared to those of other wars. The John Wayne myth is explored.

1529 Schroeder, Eric James. "Two Interviews: Talks with Tim O'Brien and Robert Stone." *Modern Fiction Studies* 30, no. 1 (Spring 1984):135-64.

   A transcript of interviews with two Vietnam War novelists. The interview with O'Brien is separate from the one with Stone. Questions on the distinction between fiction and nonfiction in their novels, their style, opinions, and the background to their characterizations are explored.

1530 Scott, Nathan A., Jr. "Catholic Novelist's Dilemma." *Christian Century* 73, no. 31 (1 August 1956):901-2.

   Scott presents a review article of *The Quiet American* – its political and moral implications. The author sees a "romantic diabolism" espoused by Greene.

1531 Searle, William J., ed. *Search and Clear: Critical Responses to Literature and Films of the Vietnam War."* Bowling Green, Ohio: Bowling Green State University Popular Press, 1988.

   An excellent collection of sixteen essays on Vietnam and its portrayal in literature and film, each with a bibliography. Included are:

   a. Anisfield, Nancy. "Words and Fragments: Narrative Style in Vietnam War Novels." 56-61.

       The author shows how the use of language in Vietnam novels conveys the confusion of the Vietnam War as much as do the novel's stories.

   b. Christie, N. Bradley. "David Rabe's Theater of War and Remembering." 105-15.

       A discussion of Rabe's Vietnam trilogy, its place in the theater, and its relationship to other Vietnam dramas.

   c. Cronin, Cornelius A. "From the DMZ to No Man's Land: Philip Caputo's *A Rumor of War* and Its Antecedents." 74-86.

       An excellent discussion of *A Rumor of War* and its relationship to earlier war writing, particularly soldier's accounts of World War I.

d. Gilman, Owen. "Vietnam Writing and the Paradoxical Paradigm of Nomenclature." 62-73.

    A discussion of the unique features of Vietnam War literature.

e. Gotera, Vicente F. "Bringing Vietnam Home: Bruce Weigl's *The Monkey Wars*." 160-69.

    A discussion of *The Monkey Wars* which emphasizes the work's successful use of words and color images.

f. Herzog, Tobey C. "John Wayne in a Modern Heart of Darkness: The American Soldier in Vietnam." 16-25.

    A discussion of the Vietnam War, war movies in general, American myths about war, and the John Wayne image.

g. Jeffords, Susan. "Born of Two Fathers: Gender and Misunderstanding in *Platoon*." 184-94.

    Jeffords shows the ways in which the movie *Platoon* is very much like the Vietnam movies that came before it even though it was claimed to be more realistic and effective than the others.

h. Kern, Louis J. "MIA's, Myth, and Macho Magic: Post-Apocalyptic Cinematic Visions of Vietnam." 37-54.

    A discussion of how the movies have dealt with the war since its end.

i. Lawson, Jacqueline E. "'Old Kids': The Adolescent Experience in the Nonfiction Narratives of the Vietnam War." 26-36.

    Lawson discusses Vietnam War personal narratives, emphasizing particularly the affect of this war on the adolescent soldier raised on the myth of John Wayne.

j. Prasch, Thomas. "*Platoon* and the Mythology of Realism." 195-215.

    A discussion of *Platoon* and it's relationship to literature. The author calls it a "fictional film."

k. Puhr, Katherine M. "Women in Vietnam War Novels." 172-83.

    One of the few discussions of the women involved in the Vietnam war and their depiction in novels and personal narratives.

l. Quivey, James. "When Buffalos Fight It Is the Grass that Suffers: Narrative Distance in Asa Baber's *Land of a Million Elephants*." 95-104.

A discussion of *Land of a Million Elephants* that notes that this novel is stylistically more like the novels written aften the war's end than those of its own time period.

m. Robinson, James A. "Soldier's Home: Images of Alienation in *Sticks and Bones*." 136-46.

A discussion of Rabe's Vietnam trilogy emphasizing the image of the alienated veteran and his affect on the American family as seen particularly in *Sticks and Bones*.

n. Schroeder, Eric James. "The Past and the Possible: Tim O'Brien's Dialectic of Memory and Imagination." 116-34.

A discussion and comparison of the work of Tim O'Brien and other major Vietnam War novels, with special emphasis on *Going After Cacciato*.

o. Searle, William J. "Walking Wounded: Vietnam War Novels of Return." 147-59.

Searle discusses the image of the returned veteran in novels written after the war, most of whom are portrayed as mentally and physically broken.

p. Slabey, Robert M. "Fact, Fiction, and Metafiction in James Park Sloan's *War Games*." 88-94.

The author discusses *War Games*, pointing out its successes and failures of style.

1532 Searle, William J. "The Vietnam War Novel and the Reviewers." *Journal of American Culture* 4, no. 2 (Summer 1981):83-94.

Searle notes that because reviewers are so familiar with the Vietnam War through TV news, there is a tendency to review the Vietnam War books without considering their own complexities and subleties. A discussion of how these books have been treated by publicists and the media is discussed as well as the novels themselves.

1533 Sedlackova, Jaroslava. "Some Remarks on Formal Innovations in Norman Mailer's *The Armies of the Night*." *Brno Studies in English* 14 (1981):139-48.

A discussion of *The Armies of the Night* in which the author considers the form and structure of the novel in detail in order to determine it's exact nature (nonfiction or novel) and whether or not Mailer's purpose was achieved.

1534 Seib, Kenneth A. "Mailer's March: The Epic Structure of *The Armies of the Night*." *Essays in Literature* 1, no. 1 (Spring 1974):89-95.

An analysis of *The Armies of the Night* which notes Mailer's use of "traditional and clear-cut forms."

1535 Shafer, George. "The Dramaturgy of Fact: The Testament of History in Two Anti-War Plays." *Central States Speech Journal* 29, no. 1 (Spring 1986):25-35.

Shafer discusses Peter Weiss' *Discourse on Vietnam* and the ProVisional Theatre's *Xa: A Vietnam Primer*.

1536 Shaw, Robert B. "The Poetry of Protest." In *American Poetry Since 1960: Some Critical Perspectives*. Cheadle, Cheshire, England: Carcanet Press, 1973, 45-54.

An explanation, in thirteen essays, of the history of poets response to the war, social conditions, and the United States government during the sixties (including Robert Lowell's refusal to read his poems at the White House) and the resulting collections of antiwar poetry. The poems are classified as being of three types: diatribe and documentary, autobiographical, or apocalyptic and satiric. A discussion of individual poets and poems are included.

1537 Shelton, Frank W. "Robert Stone." In *Postmodern Fiction: A Bio-Bibliographical Guide*. Edited by Larry McCaffery. New York: Greenwood Press, 1986, 508-11.

A short biography and critique of Robert Stone and his works with a brief bibliography of primary and secondary sources.

1538 _____. "Robert Stone's *Dog Soldiers*: Vietnam Comes Home to America." *Critique* 24, no. 2 (Winter 1983):74-81.

Shelton presents a complete discussion of Robert Stone's *Dog Soldier* with an emphasis on the characters, especially the noncombatants. A bibliography of primary and secondary sources is included.

1539 Slocock, Carolyn. "Winning Hearts and Minds: The 1st Casualty Press." *Journal of American Studies* 16 (April 1982):107-17.

Slocock provides a history of the 1st Casualty Press ("In war, truth is the first casualty") – a Vietnam veteran, independent publishing group established in the early 1970s. Its publishing philosophy, authors, publications, and the problems involved in publishing Vietnam War literature in the last decade are explained.

1540 Smith, Leroy D. "No Simple Truths: A Selective Survey of the Literature of the Vietnam War." *Book Report* 7, no. 3 (November/December 1988):22-26, 29.

Designed for school librarians as a selection tool, this article discusses the major anthologies, novels, and personal narratives of the war. The author comments on the major theme of the Vietnam soldier's readjustment to civilian life as it is seen in the novels. Bibliography.

1541 Smith, Lorrie. "A Sense-Making Perspective in Recent Poetry by Vietnam Veterans." *American Poetry Review* 15, no. 6 (November/December 1986):13-18.

Ehrhart's *To Those Who Have Gone Home Tires* is compared to Weigl's *A Romance* and *The Monkey Wars*. Smith suggests that Vietnam War poetry may be a more valuable source of truth about the war than works of fiction.

1542 Solotaroff, Ted A. "A Witness of Vietnam." In *A Few Good Voices in My Head*. New York: Harper & Row, 1987, 128-34.

Solotaroff discusses Philip Caputo's *A Rumor of War*, noting that the book is "a true story of the transformation of one of the knights of Camelot, whose crusade was Vietnam and whose cause could only be noble and good, into a vindictive, desperate, and chronically schizoid killer in a war that he had to realize was futile and evil."

1543 Soper, Steven P. "Perspectives and Prejudices: Writing on the Vietnam War." *Teaching Political Science* 11, no. 3 (Spring 1984):130-41.

This essay does not concern itself with the creative literature of Vietnam, nor the personal narratives, but deals instead with the histories and political science treatises which have attempted to explain the "whys" of the Vietnam Conflict. It is useful as it relates to the same quest in the novels and personal narratives.

1544 Sossaman, Stephen. "American Poetry from the Indochina Experience." *Long Island Review* 2 (Winter 1973):30-33.

This article focuses on Casey's *Obscenities* and *Winning Hearts and Minds*. The author notes that veterans have been slow to express themselves in poetry and also that due to the nature of the war, traditional poetry is impossible. A discussion of the two anthologies ensues with reference to individual poems.

1545 Spark, Alasdair. "The Soldier at the Heart of the War: The Myth of the Green Beret in the Popular Culture of the Vietnam Era." *Journal of American Studies* 18, no. 1 (April 1984):29-48.

The Green Berets assume almost mythic proportions in the popular imagination of the Vietnam War. This fact has "served as a vehicle to express the purpose and experience of Vietnam." Moore's *The Green Berets* is discussed as well as the movie treatment of this work.

1546 Special Issue on William Eastlake. *Review of Contemporary Fiction* 3 (Spring 1983).

1547 Stegenga, James A. "Books on Vietnam." *America* 155 (29 November 1986):348-51.

The author discusses the sudden interest in the Vietnam War and it attendant flood of books, articles, and memoirs. Historical works are viewed as well as Hellman's *American Myth and the Legacy of Vietnam*, Santoli's *To Bear Any Burden*, Donovan's *Once A Warrior King*, and Ketwig's . . . *And a Hard Rain Fell.*

1548 Stein, Jeff. "The Morning After." *Washington Monthly* 18 (December 1986):49-52.

Stein reviews several histories of the war including David Chanoff and Doan Van Toai's oral history *Portrait of the Enemy*.

1549 Stephens, Michael Gregory. "Vietnam: The American Ronin." In *The Dramaturgy of Style: Voices in Short Fiction.* Carbondale: Southern Illinois University Press, 1986, 129-83.

Stephens examines the quiet warrior type and the John Wayne myth as they relate to the soldier that came out of the experience of Vietnam. The old images, John Wayne and the samurai, disappeared and the ronin, the masterless samurai, emerged. The circumstances particular to the Vietnam War that caused this new type of soldier to emerge and the literary forms that were subsequently adopted are illustrated in the major novels. An excellent, important article.

1550 ____, moderator. *Back in the World: Writing after Vietnam*. New York: American Poets Project, 1984.

A two cassette sound recording of a 1984 Vietnam writer's conference in New York City in which writers gathered to discuss fiction from the war and to read from their works. The panelists included Smith Hempstone, Chuch Wachtel, Joseph Ferrandino, Stephen Wright, William C. Woods, John Del Vecchio, W. D. Ehrhart, Larry Heinemann, John Clark Pratt, and Robert Olen Butler.

1551 Stephenson, Gregory. "Struggle and Flight: Tim O'Brien's *Going After Cacciato*." *Notes on Contemporary Literature* 14, no. 4 (September 1984):5-6.

The motif of flight from the battlefield and the moral struggle between private conscience and public duty are discussed as they relate to *Going After Cacciato* and other major American war novels.

1552 Stewart, Margaret E. *Ambiguous Violence: Myths of Regeneration and Proficiency in U.S. Novels of the Vietnam War*. Center for Southeast Asian Studies. Madison: University of Wisconsin, 1986.

One of the Wisconsin Papers on Southeast Asia (no. 10), this analysis of Vietnam novels attempts to understand the conflicting attitudes in the United States today. The desire for no more Vietnams exists side by side with the Rambo figure and the attitude which made the invasion of Grenada popular. The author discusses two myths: Regeneration, in the defense of civilization from its enemies, and Proficiency, job performance for its own sake. These myths can be seen illustrated in Moore's *The Killing at Ngo Tho*, Ford's *Incident at Muc Wa*, and Halberstam's *One Very Hot Day*. Bibliography.

1553 Stone, Robert. "Me and the Universe." *TriQuarterly* 65 (Winter 1986):229-34.

Stone was part of a symposium sponsored by *TriQuarterly* in which he spoke along with Ward Just and Gloria Emerson on the Vietnam War and its literature following which the three authors interacted with the audience and each other. Just and Emerson's essays are included in this bibliography. In Stone's presentation, he discusses the limitations of language when describing war.

1554 Styron, William. "A Farewell to Arms." In *This Quiet Dust and Other Writings*. New York: Random House, 1982, 208-17.

In an essay first printed in the *New York Review of Books* on June 23, 1977, Styron discusses Caputo's *A Rumor of War* noting the similarities and differences between his own war experiences and those of Caputo.

1555 ____. "The Red Badge of Literature." In *This Quiet Dust and Other Writings*. New York: Random House, 1982, 203-7.

Styron notes the dearth of literature emerging from the Vietnam war by 1972 and that "the further we remove ourselves from wars in which a vestige of idealism exists . . . the more we engage in waging wars that approach being totally depraved, the less likely we are to produce imaginative writing that contains many plausible outlines of humanity." Styron discusses Glasser's *365 Days*. This article first appeared in the *Washington Monthly* in March 1972. *This Quiet Dust* also includes two other essays of interest: "Chicago, 1968" and "Calley."

1556 Suther, Judith D. "French Novelists and the American Phase of the War in Indochina." *Selecta: Journal of the Pacific Northwest Council on Foreign Languages* 4 (1983):1-9.

Suther reviews the French novels which deal with America's involvement in Vietnam with an awareness of France's own involvement. Similarities in the two situations are noted. Only one of the novels discussed, *Ears of the Jungle*, has been translated into English. Some comparisons to American Vietnam War novels are made as well as American reaction (reviews) to *Ears* noted.

1557 ____. "French Novelistic Views of America and the Vietnam War." In *Explorations: Essays in Comparative Literature*. Edited by Matoto Ueda. Lanham, Md.: University Press of America, 1986, 312-25.

See 1556.

1558 Taylor, Gordon O. "American Personal Narrative of the War in Vietnam." *American Literature* 52 (May 1980):294-308.

Taylor discusses the importance of Graham Greene's prophetic *The Quiet American* and relates it to the personal narratives coming out of the war, particularly Herr's *Dispatches*.

1559 ____. "Cast a Cold I: Mary McCarthy on Vietnam." *Journal of American Studies* 9 (April 1975):103-14.

A critique of the three Vietnam works of Mary McCarthy, *Vietnam, Hanoi,* and *Medina*.

1560 ____. "Debriefed by Dreams: Michael Herr." In *Chapters of Experience: Studies in 20th Century American Autobiography*. New York: St. Martin's, 1983, 120-35.

Graham Greene's *The Quiet American* is the first and still powerful Vietnam novel. But many novels have been written since, each searching for an effective form for the narrative. Taylor feels that Herr's *Dispatches* has found this form. It is considered in the light of the "definitive presence" of Greene's novel.

1561 Taylor, Sandra C. "Vietnam through a Different Lens: Fiction, Memoirs, and History." Paper presented at the Annual Meeting of the Organization of American Historians. Los Angeles. 8 April 1984. ED 247 176.

Taylor comments that literary accounts of the war fill the gaps of information missing from more conventional histories. She discusses the basic themes and issues of the Vietnam War novels and the importance of the memoirs in providing the human aspect of the war.

1562 Tetlow, Joseph A. "The Vietnam War Novel." *America* 143 (July 1980):32-36.

Tetlow observes that the number of well-written Vietnam War books is increasing and discusses the genre, dividing the books into four types:

1. Novels of personal experience, "guerilla picaresque" – *Close Quarters*
2. Realistic novels about one part of the war – *The Lionheads*

3. Big war novels which try to encompass the whole war – *Better Times Than These*
4. Fables and fabulous tales – *Going After Cacciato*
    Omitted are novels of intrigue and assassination like *Dog Soldiers* and *The Killing at Ngo Tho*.

1563 Trilling, Diana, and Philip Rahv. "America and *The Quiet American*." *Commentary* 22 (July 1956):66-71.
    The two authors discuss American liberalism in connection with a review Rahv had written previously in which he had dismissed *The Quiet American* as a thriller. Trilling notes the importance of the political content, particularly in view of what was to come. Rhav responds.

1564 True, Michael. "War and Poetry." *Confrontation*, no. 8 (Spring 1974):137-44.
    True says "the only good war poems are antiwar poems." The heroic soldier, like Rupert Brook, won't do for modern wars. He discusses the modern relationship of war "one of man's most destructive and witless activities" and his poetry, "one of his most purely and intelligently creative activities." Vietnam War poems from the *Winning Hearts and Minds* and *Obscentities* collections are discussed.

1565 Valentino, Claudia. "The Vietnam Veterans Advisor." *Penthouse* 16 (June 1985):94.
    A discussion of the creation and production of the play *Tracers*.

1566 Van Deusen, Marshall. "Unspeakable Language of Life and Death in Michael Herr's *Dispatches*." *Critique* 24, no. 2 (Winter 1983):82-87.
    Van Duesen discusses the "literary echoes" in Herr's nonfiction novel style *Dispatches*.

1567 Vannatta, Dennis. "Themes and Structure in Tim O'Brien's *Going After Cacciato*." *Modern Fiction Studies* 28, no. 2 (Summer 1982):242-46.
    The problem of bringing literary structure to the chaos of Vietnam are discussed with reference to the pattern utilized by O'Brien in *Going After Cacciato*.

1568 Vargo, Lisa. "*The Quiet American* and 'A Mr. Lieberman.'" *English Language Notes* 21, no. 4 (June 1984):63-70.

An interesting essay in which the author discusses Graham Greene's efforts to get his hero in *The Quiet American* to speak *American* English. Many corrections and rewrites were necessary. Vargo also recounts Green's reactions to critic A. J. Liebling who criticized his use of the American idiom.

1569 Vogelgesang, Sandy. *The Long Dark Night of the Soul: The American Intellectual Left and the Vietnam War*. New York: Harper & Row, 1974.

A discussion of the history of the intellectual left's reaction to the Vietnam War, which they saw as a threat to the American Dream. The author maintains that most Americans did not hold this view. A sizeable bibliography of antiwar literature, mostly nonfiction, is included.

1570 Walsh, Jeffrey. "Towards Vietnam: Portraying Modern War: Satiric Fabrication or Epic Biography?" In *American War Literature, 1914 to Vietnam*. New York: St. Martin's, 1982, 185-207.

This important book provides an introduction to modern American war literature and discusses the work of American authors such as Hemingway, e. e. cummings, Dos Passos, Pound, Fitzgerald, and Faulkner, among others, and their reactions to the two world wars and Korea. The last chapter, "Towards Vietnam: Portraying Modern War: Satiric Fabrication or Epic Biography?" notes the differences between poetry, drama, and fiction of the Vietnam War with special attention focused on Herr's *Dispatches* and Caputo's *A Rumor of War*.

1571 Weales, Gerald. "Ronald Ribman: The Artist of the Failure Clowns." In *Essays on Contemporary American Drama*. Edited by Hedwig Bock and Albert Wertheim. Munich: Max Hueber Verlag, 1981, 75-90.

This overview of the work of Ronald Ribman contains a brief discussion on *The Final War of Ollie Winter*.

1572 Weber, Ronald. *The Literature of Fact: Literary Nonfiction in American Writing*. Athens: Ohio University Press, 1980.

The Literature of Fact explains and discusses the new journalism with attention to Mailer's *The Armies of the Night* (80-87) among other works. Brief mention is made of Halberstam's *The Best and the Brightest*.

1573 ____, ed. *The Reporter as Artist: A Look at the New Journalism Controversy*. New York: Hastings House, 1974.

Twenty-eight essays on the new journalism provide a good explanatory background work for the literary style that has emerged from the Vietnam War. This work was written too early, 1974, to discuss many of the Vietnam books, but Mailer's work is discussed. Also useful is Wilfred Sheed's essay "A Fun House Mirror," which includes a discussion of David Halberstam's *The Best and the Brightest* and Vietnam (296-98).

1574 Werner, Craig. "Primal Screams and Nonsense Rhymes: David Rabe's Revolt." *Educational Theater Review* 30 (1978):517-29.

Werner explains Rabe's use of language in his Vietnam trilogy.

1575 West, Richard. "Graham Greene's Vietnam." *Far Eastern Economic Review* 105, no. 35 (31 August 1979):75.

A reappraisal of Greene's *The Quiet American* twenty-five years after it was written. In light of current events it appears prophetic.

1576 ____. "Vietnam and the Imagination." *Books and Bookman* 24 (February 1979):57-58.

West traces the history of literature about the Vietnam War from Graham Greene to Tim O'Brien with special emphasis on a discussion of *Going After Caciato*.

1577 Wilson, James C. *Vietnam in Prose and Film*. Jefferson, N.C.: McFarland, N.C., 1982.

A primary source, Wilson's book traces the history of the best of the Vietnam literature from *The Quiet American* to *Dog Soldiers*. He also discusses how the war has been presented on film. A chronology of the war and a bibliography and filmography including secondary sources is included.

1578 Wolfe, Geoffrey A. "Vietnam Allegory." *New Leader* 50, no. 22 (6 November 1967):22-23.

An interesting discussion of Victor Kolpakoff's *The Prisoners of Quai Dong*, written while the book's author was a student at San Francisco State University. Kolpacoff had never been to Vietnam, but Wolff notes that he has "turned Vietnam into a metaphor of our own unrestrained willfulness and luxurious cruelty." He is sure that this book will survive the war.

1579 Wolter, Jurgen. "Arthur Kopit: Dreams and Nightmares." In *Essays on Contemporary American Drama*. Edited by Hedwig Bock and Albert Wertheim. Munich: Max Hueber Verlag, 1981, 55-74.

A discussion of the work of Arthur Kopit including *Indians*. A full explanation of its form and theme are provided.

1580 Woolf, Cecil, and John Bagguley. *Authors Take Sides on Vietnam: Two Questions on the War in Vietnam Answered by the Authors of Several Nations*. London: Peter Owen, 1967.

The authors submitted two questions by mail to a large group of writers: "Are you for, or against, the intervention of the United States in Vietnam?" and "How, in your opinion, should the conflict in Vietnam be resolved?" Some of the writers who responded are: James Baldwin, Simone de Beauvior, Babbette Deutsch, Robert Creely, Graham Greene, Joseph Heller, Doris Lessing, Arthur Miller, Jessica Mitford, Iris Murdoch, Harold Pinter, Edna O'Brien, Philip Roth, C. P. Snow, Susan Sontag, Kingsley Amis, John Updike, Auberon Waugh, and many more. A fascinating book. In 1937, a similar book was done on the Spanish Civil War.

1581 Wright, Robert A. "History's Heavy Attrition: Literature, Historical Consciousness and the Impact of Vietnam." *Canadian Review of American Studies* 17, no. 3 (Fall 1986):301-16.

Wright discusses Vietnam War literature, pointing out that history and literature in this area are not necessarily compatible and describes the impact of the war on the re-telling of history. The major novels and personal narratives, and their treatment of historical events, are described. Bibliography

1582 Yoshida, Sanroku. "Takeshi Kaiko's Paradox of Light and Darkness." *World Literature Today* 62, no. 3 (Summer 1988):391-96.

Kaiko was a cameraman for Tokyo newspaper *Ashi Simbun* in Vietnam in 1964, after which he wrote *Vietnam War Journal* (1965) and a series of essays describing his experiences. Yoskida discusses Kaiko's works relating to the war with particular emphasis on his novel *Into A Black Sun* and its sequel *Darkness in Summer* in this informative essay.

1583 Young, Perry Deane. "Nightmares in Print." *Saturday Review* 55, no. 41 (7 October 1972):54-58.

A discussion of the 1st Casualty Press' *Winning Hearts and Minds* and how it came to be published, plus a history of the press.

1584 Zins, Daniel L. "Imagining the Real: The Fiction of Tim O'Brien." *Hollins Critic* 23, no. 3 (June 1986):1-12.

Zins provides biographical information and comments on the work of Tim O'Brien and his approach to the novel, noting that his Vietnam War experience impacts heavily on both *Northern Lights* and *The Nuclear Age* although neither are directly about Vietnam.

1585 Zukerman, Stephen. "ProVisional Theatre's *XA: A Vietnam Primer*." *Drama Review* 19, no. 3 (September 1975):73-74.

A review of the ProVisional Theater, an eleven member, highly political group, and the performance of *XA: A Vietnam Primer* at the University of Michigan. The play, which changed its content and theme as the war progressed, is described in detail.

Bibliographies

1586 Andrew, Malcolm. "American Novels of the Vietnam War: A Bibliography." *American Notes and Queries* 10 (January/February 1982):80-82.
A list of forty-three Vietnam war novels.

1587 "Background Books: Vietnam." *Wilson Quarterly* 7 (Summer 1983):136-39.
A short discussion, in chronological order, of books on the Vietnam Conflict. The list is primarily historical but concludes with a short list of fiction and personal narratives.

1588 Brown, F. C., and B. Laurie. *Annotated Bibliography of Viet Nam Fiction: 500 Titles Dealing with the Conflict in Viet Nam, Cambodia and Laos*. Mesa, Ariz.: Rice-Paddy Press, 1987.
In this limited edition bibliography (300 copies), 500 fiction works are listed with very brief annotations. Included are some dramas and short stories and books that are peripherally about Vietnam.

1589 Buss, C. A. "Books in the Field: Our Current Crisis in the Far East." *Wilson Library Bulletin* 43, no. 3 (November 1968):228-38.
A bibliographic essay of books on the Vietnam Conflict which includes some fiction and personal narratives.

1590 Calloway, Catherine. "Vietnam War Literature and Film: A Bibliography of Secondary Sources." *Bulletin of Bibliography* 43, no. 3 (September 1986):149-58.

A comprehensive bibliography of secondary sources on the films, dramas, novels, and poetry of the war. Not annotated.

1591 Clifton, Merritt, ed. *Those Who Were There: Eyewitness Accounts of the War in Southeast Asia, 1956-1975 and Aftermath – Annotated Bibliography of Books, Articles and Topic-Related Magazines, Covering Writings both Factual and Imaginative.* Paradise, Calif.: DustBooks, 1984.

A large bibliography of works on the war written by those present during the conflict who are able to describe what happened first-hand. The ending date for inclusion of material is 1975. Included are novels, dramas, poetry, short stories, personal narratives, some critical essays, and magazines devoted to the war. Not all entries are annotated, the section divisions complicate easy use, and some of the titles listed as short stories are actually poems.

1592 Colonnese, Tom Graydon. "Robert Stone: A Working Checklist." *Bulletin of Bibliography* 39, no. 3 (September 1982):136-38.

A specialized bibliography on Robert Stone.

1593 Colonnese, Tom Graydon, and Jerry Hogan. "Vietnam War Literature, 1958-1979: A First Checklist." *Bulletin of Bibilography* 38, no. 1 (January-March 1981):26-31, 51.

The bibliography is divided into two sections: books and short fiction. The section on books includes novels, personal narratives, and drama. Not annotated.

1594 Dougall, Lucy, comp. *War and Peace in Literature: Prose, Drama and Poetry which Illuminate the Problem of War.* Chicago: World Without War Publications, 1982. ED 245 960.

Designed for high school and college humanities teachers, this bibliography discusses the literary works that may be used to foster a better understanding of war and peace. An annotated bibliography of materials from the Bible to Vietnam, this work includes prose, drama, poetry, anthologies, reference works, a chart of literature on specific wars, and a title index. The poetry section is very well developed. Key themes are traced. Poetry and five Vietnam war novels are included.

1595 Eckert, Edward K., and William J. Searle. "Creative Literature of the Vietnam War: A Selective Bibliography." *Choice* 24, no. 5 (January 1987):725-35.

A useful bibliographic essay which includes poetry, short story collections, drama, and novels.

1596 "Ethnic Groups in Children's Books: Southeast Asians." *Booklist* 83, no. 3 (1 October 1986):278-83.

A listing of books about Vietnamese legends and folklore, life, culture, history, and the Vietnamese War for children. Includes fiction and nonfiction by Americans and Vietnamese.

1597 Grefrath, Richard W. "Everyday Was Summertime in Vietnam: An Annotated Bibliography of the Best Personal Narratives." *Reference Service Review* 8, no. 4 (October-December 1980).

Ten full annotations and twenty-eight brief annotations of personal narratives.

1598 Grochowski, Barbara. "The Vietnamese Conflict: A Selected List of References." *Library of Congress Information Bulletin* 44, no. 30 (July 29, 1986):207-12.

An annotated bibliography that includes basic reference books, bibliographies, resource guides, periodical indexes, collected documents, general histories, campaigns and battles, policy analyses, official histories (air force, army, marine corps, navy), and literature and film about the war.

1599 Groh, Pat, and Steve Oserman, comp. "Vietnam: Ten Years After." Skokie, Ill.: Skokie Public Library, 1985.

An annotated bibliography of nonfiction, fiction, drama, and poetry.

1600 Jackson, Dennis, Edward A. Nickerson, and James R. Bennett. "The Language of Literature about War: A Selective Annotated Bibliography." *Style* 13, no. 1 (Winter 1979):60-88.

A general war study tool which includes material about war in general and specifically about the American Civil War, World Wars I and II, the Spanish Civil War, and Vietnam. The bibliography stresses the relationship between war and language.

1601 Lockwood, Lee. "Book Marks: Trips to Hanoi." *Nation* 208, no. 12 (24 March 1969):374-77.

A bibliographic essay of five books which relate journalists experiences in Vietnam and the effect the war had on them.

1602 Newman, John. *Vietnam War Literature: An Annotated Bibliography of Imaginative Works about Americans Fighting in Vietnam.* 2d ed. Metuchen, N.J.: Scarecrow, 1988. Original edition 1982.

An important bibliography. Newman bases his bibliography on the Vietnam War Literature collection at Colorado State University. Listed are 429 novels, 192 short stories, seventy-six poetry collections, and nineteen dramas, all annotated. The citations in the work are arranged by genre and then chronologically. Author and title indexes are included. Newman's evaluation of the military aspects of the novels is particularly effective.

1603 Ott, Bill. "Quick Bibs: New and Recent Books on a Timely Topic: Vietnam in Fiction." *American Libraries* 18, no. 5 (May 1987):324.

Seven novels annotated.

1604 Peake, Louis A. *The United States in the Vietnam War, 1954-1975: A Selected, Annotated Bibliography.* New York: Garland, 1986.

A large bibliography of 1549 items that includes general reference works, military accounts, film, music, literature, art, oral histories; information from both sides of the conflict. The emphasis is on non-literary materials. Includes an index, chronology of the war, list of principal characters on both sides, and a glossary of terms. The organization of the material into many small sections makes usage difficult.

1605 Pickett, Calder M. "Recent Books in Journalism History: A Bibliographical Essay." A paper presented at the 61st Annual Meeting of the Association for Education in Journalism, Seattle, 13-16 August 1978. ED 159 695.

A bibliographic review of journalistic books published between 1969 and 1978. Includes oral history, memoirs, magazine journalism, cartoons, photography, and the "new journalism." Brief annotations.

1606 Pierce, Peter. "A Checklist of Australian Literature of the Vietnam War." *Australian Literary Studies* 12, no. 2 (1985):287-88.

A listing of poetry, fiction, memoirs, and articles on the Australian view of Vietnam.

1607 Saul, Wendy E. An annotated list of children's books about the Vietnam War. Untitled. Unpublished. University of Maryland (Baltimore, n.d.).

A list of twenty-nine books for children in grades 1 through 6+. Includes novels, histories, and personal narratives.

1608 Smith, Myron J. *War Story Guide: An Annotated Bibliography of Military Fiction*. Metuchen, N.J.: Scarecrow, 1980.

The section entitled "The Years of Cold War and Hot Police Actions, 1945-1978" includes seventy annotated entries on Vietnam. The bibliography includes an index of authors, titles, pseudonyms, and battles, and a war and warrior index.

1609 Sugnet, Christopher L., and John T. Hickey. *Vietnam War Bibliography*. Lexington, Mass.: Lexington Books, 1983.

Items included were selected from Cornell University's Echols Collection. This is a computer generated bibliography of 4,000 items reflecting the period 1940-75 and designed for research on the war. The items are arranged by title and author only and are annotated. The index can be subject searched with some difficulty. The printing method makes reading difficult.

1610 Totten, Sam. "The Lessons of Vietnam." *Curriculum Review* 25, no. 1 (September/October 1985):87-89. EJ 324 155.

An annotated bibliography which includes factual overviews, personal accounts, fiction, and news analysis, designed for high school educators.

1611 Van Klaveren, Tricia. "An Annotated Bibliography of Recent Books on Vietnam Particularly Germane to Political Science Courses." *Teaching Political Science* 12, no. 4 (Summer 1985):195-98.

An annotated list of twenty-two basic works on the war including histories and political analyses, particularly useful for teachers.

1612 *Vietnam in Children's Books*. New York: United Nations Children's Fund, United States Committee, June 1975. ED 117 269.

A list of twenty-five nonfiction and eighteen fiction and folklore works, annotated. Films are also included. The items were selected to give a view of the culture and history of Vietnam as well as providing information about the war through 1965.

1613 Welch, Elizabeth H. "What Did You Write About the War, Daddy?" *Wilson Library Bulletin* 46, no. 10 (June 1972):912-17.

An annotated bibliography of twenty books about the war for young people. Fiction is excluded. The bibliography takes a decided antiwar slant and is introduced by a disclaimer from the editor commenting on the author's bias.

Dissertations/Theses

1614 Aaron, Chester. "Hello to Bodega." Thesis, San Francisco State University, San Francisco, 1975.
 See 1.

1615 Appy, Christian Gerard. "A War for Nothing: A Social History of American Soldiers in the Vietnam War." Dissertation, Harvard University, Cambridge, Mass., 1987.
 A study of oral histories, personal narratives, fiction and history to analyze the impact of the war on the soldiers who fought it. The author notes the social inequality of those who fought, the importance of the experience of basic training on later fighting, and the contradictions between official government accounts of the war and what was actually experienced.

1616 Arlett, Robert Michael. "Narrative Voices in the Contemporary Epic Novel." Dissertation, Tulane University, New Orleans, La., 1984.
 Discusses modern novelists' desire to examine contemporary affairs in their work. Norman Mailer's *Why Are We in Vietnam?* is one example of this trend that is discussed.

1617 Baker, Weldon Paige. "A Study of Literary Methods Employed by Three Writers on the Vietnam War: Norman Mailer, Michael Herr,

Frances Fitzgerald." Thesis, East Tennessee State University, Johnson City, 1981.

A survey of the literary styles of Mailer, Herr, and Fitzgerald writing on the Vietnam War. The author notes that all of the writers studied concluded that the war was a "disaster for all concerned."

1618 Bartz, Michael Omar. "United States Cultural Movements as Reflected in the Fiction, Journals, and Oral Histories of the Vietnam War." Dissertation, St. Louis University, St. Louis, Mo., 1987.

A study of the major cultural movements at the time of the war – civil rights, ecology, women's liberation, and the antiwar movement – and how they are reflected in the works about the Vietnam War.

1619 Brown, Harvey Ray, Jr. "Modern American War Drama." Thesis, Lamar University, Beaumont, Tex., 1981.

The thesis traces the American war play as a separate literary form from civil war dramas through Vietnam and the experimental theater of the 1960s to the starkly realistic dramas of the 1970s.

1620 Callincos, Helen. "A New Voice: Vietnam Veteran Prose and Poetry, 1967-1977." Dissertation, Bradley University, Peoria, Ill., 1977.

1621 Calloway, Catherine E. "The Vietnam War Novel: A Descent into Hell." Dissertation, University of South Florida, Tampa, 1987.

An examination of the "decent into hell" motif used in Vietnam war novels.

1622 Cavallero, Joseph, Jr. "Reflections on a Little War: The Vietnam Conflict as Portrayed in Selected Examples of Art, Literature, Film, and Popular Music." Thesis, Northeast Missouri State University, Kirksville, 1980.

The author discusses how creative artists rebelled against the war and, in some cases, influenced public opinion, and how this is reflected in music, art, film, and literature.

1623 Cawelti, Gerald Scott. "Norman Mailer and the Hipster: An Approach to 'The Armies of the Night' and 'Maidstone.'" Dissertation, University of Iowa, Iowa City, 1978.

    Mailer's "hipster" character is discussed as well as the author's emergence as a character in his work, particularly in *The Armies of the Night*.

1624 Chase, Geoffrey William. "Connection and Complicity: Five Playwrights of the Sixties." Dissertation, University of Wisconsin, Madison, 1981.

    A study of five playwrights of the 1960s including David Rabe. Rabe's use of violence and the era's antiwar sentiment are noted.

1625 Chung, Youn-son. "War and Morality: The Search for Meaning in American Novels of World War I, World War II, and the Vietnam War." Dissertation, Emory University, Atlanta, Ga., 1985.

    A comparison of the war novels of the last three wars which, notes basic patterns in theme. World War I novels see war as a cultural phenomenon, a search for beauty, World War II novels see war as a social phenomenon, a struggle between individual ethics and a collective ethic, and Vietnam War novels see war as a natural phenomenon, the transformation of the individual as a result of the horror of war. Webb's *Fields of Fire*, Durden's *No Bugles, No Drums*, and Del Vecchio's *The 13th Valley* are discussed.

1626 Colonese, Tom Graydon. "The Vietnam War in American Literature." Dissertation, Arizona State University, Tempe, 1981.

    Vietnam War novels are divided into three categories for discussion: conventional combat novels, unconventional, innovative war novels, and unconventional nonfiction war novels.

1627 Creek, Mardena Bridges. "Myth, Wound, Accommodation: American Literary Response to the War in Vietnam." Dissertation, Ball State University, Muncie, Ind., 1982.

    A discussion and analysis of fiction and nonfiction written by soldiers and correspondents between 1969 and 1981.

1628 Ely, Scott. "Starlight." Thesis, University of Arkansas, Fayetteville, 1986.
    See 148.

1629 Follows, Peter Campbell. "The Evasion of Atrocity: An Essay on the Moral Subjectivity Inherent in Three American Works of Literature Written about the Vietnam War." Thesis, Harvard University, Cambridge, Mass., 1986.

    A discussion of Caputo's *Rumor of War*, Groom's *Better Times Than These*, and Webb's *Fields of Fire*.

1630 Furrow, Larry D. "Vietnam Voices: Four Personal Accounts of America's Most Misunderstood War." Project (M.S.), University of Kansas, Lawrence, 1983.

    A one-hour radio program containing the thoughts and reflections of four Vietnam veterans. The text is free form with author narration rather than interview-style. Included is a very powerful description of one soldier's memory of the first Viet Cong he killed.

1631 Gaspar, Charles Jamieson, Jr. "Reconnecting: Time and History in Narratives of the Vietnam War." Dissertation, University of Connecticut, Storrs, 1983.

    A comparison of the various styles of writing employed in six major Vietnam war novels: *The Armies of the Night*, *The 13th Valley*, *Fields of Fire*, *A Rumor of War*, *Dispatches*, and *Going After Cacciato*.

1632 Greene, Barbara K. "Poems of the Vietnam War." Thesis, Cleveland State University, Cleveland, Ohio, 1975.

    The author studied twenty volumes of Vietnam poetry collections and discusses theme, tone, imagery, and poetic devices. Thirty-four poets are discussed.

1633 Hall, Henry Palmer, Jr. "The Enlisted Man's War: A Study of the Vietnam War Novels." Dissertation, University of Texas, Austin, 1984.

    Hall discusses the common soldier in the Vietnam war and his lack of commitment to the politics of the war or to the Vietnamese people. This soldier's main concern was to survive. The dehumanization of the Vietnamese, the contempt with which officers were held, and the racism within the troops are noted and major themes in Vietnam War novels are discussed with particular attention to the morality expressed.

1634 Heiss, Andrea Brandenburg. "On Foreign Grounds: Portraits of Americans in Vietnam." Dissertation, University of Iowa, Iowa City, 1983.

    The Vietnam War novel is studied through five major stages in the war:

1. Advise and Resent, 1961-65: Halberstam's *One Very Hot Day*.
2. The Build-Up: The Personal Narrative Record of War, 1965-67: Caputo's *A Rumor of War*.
3. Violent Realism: The Infantryman's Novel: Heineman's *Close Quarters*, Hasford's *The Short-Timers*, Durden's *No Bugles, No Drums*, Bunting's *The Lionhead*, Webb's *Fields of Fire*.
4. Corresponding Visions, 1968-69: Herr's *Dispatches*.
5. Winding Down and Out: Fables and Fantasy, 1969-73: Eastlake's *The Bamboo Bed*, O'Brien's *Going After Cacciato*. Bibliography.

1635 Hellman, John. "Fables of Fact: Studies in the New Journalism and the Non-Fiction Novel." Dissertation, Kent State University, Kent, Ohio, 1977.

    Hellman notes that in the 1960s and 1970s conventional novel forms for realistic fiction were not adequate for the events described, such as the Vietnam War. He discusses the subsequent rise of the new journalism, the nonfiction novel, using Capote, Mailer (*The Armies of the Night*), Thompson, and Wolfe as examples. This work was later published as a book, with some changes. See also 1407.

1636 Hough, Robert Winslow. "The Ethical and Religious Dimensions of the Poetry Produced by the American Soldiers in Vietnam." Dissertation, Harvard University, Cambridge, Mass., 1980.

    The author utilizes the poetry of American soldiers in Vietnam to show that the conflict between the acts of brutality the war demanded and the moral, ethical, and religious values of the soldiers had a profound affect on them and provides an effective antiwar statement.

1637 Kearns, Katherine Sue. "Some Versions of Violence in Three Comtemporary American Novels: John Irving's *The World According to Garp*, Tim O'Brien's *Going After Cacciato*, and Alice Walker's *The*

Color Purple." Dissertation, University of North Carolina, Chapel Hill, 1982.

A study of the use of violence in the three novels of the title. It is noted that after the horror and chaos of the Vietnam War, honorable action is impossible.

1638 Keating, Cletus. "The Rhetoric of Extreme Experience: Michael Herr's Nonfiction Vietnam Novel *Dispatches."* Dissertation, University of Denver, Denver, Colo., 1987.

Herr's *Dispatches* is discussed, noting how it differs from the literature of other wars. His writing style is an example of the new journalism – the nonfiction novel.

1639 Ladin, Sharon Lee. "Spirit Warriors: The Samurai Figure in Current American Fiction." Dissertation, University of California, Santa Cruz, 1979.

Ladin discusses the myth of the spirit warrior in the work of four American novelists, including Robert Stone's *Dog Soldiers*.

1640 Lander, Faye A. "War and Peace in Adolescent Literature." Thesis, University of Akron, Akron, Ohio, 1981. ED 248 169.

An examination of war and peace and how it they are presented in adolescent literature with emphasis on the role of historical fiction. Designed for teachers of high school students, this thesis also includes a critical, annotated bibliography of books dealing with the themes of war and peace from the Revolutionary War to Vietnam.

1641 Lennox, William J., Jr. "American War Poetry." Dissertation, Princeton University, Princeton, N.J., 1982.

Poets' moral search for any justification for war is studied through the poetic work of five American wars: the Revolutionary War, Civil War, World War I, World War II, and Vietnam.

1642 Lewis, Lloyd Bart. "The Thousand-Yard Stare: A Socio-Cultural Interpretation of Vietnam War Narratives." Dissertation, University of Maryland, Baltimore, 1982.

Using soldier's personal narratives, an attempt is made to construct a view of the war, noting the extraordinary nature of the war and the cultural atmosphere that allowed it to happen.

1643 Lister, Paul Anthony. "War in Norman Mailer's Fiction." Dissertation, Kansas State University, Manhattan, 1974.
A comparison of Mailer's treatment of war in *The Naked and the Dead* and *Why Are We in Vietnam?*, noting the differences in life philosophy and writing technique.

1644 Malone, Anne. "Once Having Marched: American Narratives of the Vietnam War." Dissertation, Indiana University, Bloomington, 1983.
A study of the personal narratives of the Vietnam War and the differences between personal history and public history. The author argues that these narratives enable the meaning of the war to be discovered.

1645 Marquis, Harriett Hill. "Cries of Communion: The Poetry of Denise Levertov." Dissertation, Drew University, Madison, N.J., 1984.
The Vietnam War changed the direction of Denise Levertov's poetry and had an impact on her recurrent theme of communion.

1646 Mersman, James F. "Out of the Vietnam Vortex: A Study of Poets and Poetry against the Vietnam War." Dissertation, University of Kansas, Lawrence, 1972.
See 1483.

1647 Misceo, Giovanni F. "War and Identity: An Analysis of the Personal Documents of Vietnam Veterans." Dissertation, Kansas State University, Manhattan, 1987.
A psychological study of soldiers' wartime experiences and how they affected the men themselves as seen through their personal accounts. The author comments that most of the soldiers studied experienced a tremendous change in their sense of personal identity as a result of their experiences.

1648 Myers, Thomas Robert. "Envisaging a War: Vietnam and the American Historical Novel." Dissertation, Purdue University, West Lafayette, Ind., 1985.

A new figure to emerge from the literature of the Vietnam War is the soldier who rejects the activity in which he is engaged. Thus, basic American beliefs, perceptions, and values are called into question in this literature. The author explores the tone and style of these war narratives.

1649 Palm, Edward Frederick. "American Heart of Darkness: The Moral Vision of Five Novels of the Vietnam War." Dissertation, University of Pennsylvania, Philadelphia, 1983.

Five novels of the war are viewed within the framework of American literary history and compared to other novels of their kind according to theme, symbol, and style. Vietnam emerges as a very different kind of war. The novels considered are *Fields of Fire*, *Close Quarters*, *Better Times Than These*, *The Short-Timers*, and *Going After Cacciato*. Bibliography.

1650 Ponpoak, Piengjai. "Americans in the Vietnamese War Novels." Thesis, Colorado State University, Ft. Collins, 1977.

1651 Puhr, Kathleen Marie. "Novelistic Responses to the Vietnam War." Dissertation, St. Louis University, St. Louis, Mo., 1982.

A comprehensive discussion of thirty-eight major Vietnam War novels noting similarities and differences between these works and those of other wars. Four literary approaches utilized in these works are described: propaganda, realism, absurdism, and documentary-fiction. Bibliography.

1652 Ramsey, Rebecca J. "The Literature of the Vietnam War: A Picture of Individual and Cultural Conflict." Thesis, East Tennessee State University, Johnson City, 1980.

Four novels, *Going After Cacciato*, *A Rumor of War*, *Dispatches*, and *Dog Soldiers*, are examined. In each, soldiers' enter an untypical war with typical American values and ideas about patriotism. The personal turmoil created by the disparity between ideals and reality is mirrored by the chaos of the war around them.

1653 Roundy, Peter Edward. "Images of Vietnam: *Catch 22*, New Journalism, and the Postmodern Imagination." Dissertation, Florida State University, Tallahassee, 1980.

Joseph Heller's *Catch 22* has had an impact on the writing style to emerge from the Vietnam War. This can be particularly noted in Mailer's *Why Are We in Vietnam?* The author discusses the "postmodern imagination" and its characteristics. *A Rumor of War*, *Dispatches*, and *Going After Cacciato* are also discussed. Bibliography.

1654 Sanders, Joseph Elwood. "Modern American War Plays." Dissertation, University of California, Los Angeles, 1975.

American dramas about war from 1914 to Vietnam are studied. *Viet Rock*, *Summertree*, *Hair*, *Sticks and Bones*, and *The Basic Training of Pavlo Hummel* represents Vietnam in the discussion.

1655 Schroeder, Eric James. "Truth-Telling and Narrative Form: The Literature of the Vietnam War." Dissertation, University of California, Los Angeles, 1984.

Established literary genres are often unable to tell the story of the Vietnam war, thus, writers eventually reject traditional literary forms. As a result a new style has emerged in which the novel merges with journalism. Fantasy is used as an alternative form. The works of Sack, Herr, Mailer, Stone, and O'Brien are discussed.

1656 Shea, John Robert. "The Imagination of Alternatives: (New) American Review and Contemporary American Writing." Dissertation, University of Pennsylvania, Philadelphia, 1984.

The literary paperback magazine *New American Review* was published from 1967 to 1977 and reflected the upheaval of the period in all areas of cultural life in America. The section of this dissertation called "The Matter of Vietnam" studies how Vietnam became a catalyst of the era.

1657 Smith, Douglas George. "The Best of Both Worlds: The Poetry of Robert Bly." Dissertation, University of Manitoba, Winnipeg, 1984.

In this discussion of the poetry of Robert Bly, a chapter is devoted to his *Sleepers Joining Hands*, a study of the reasons for the Vietnam War. The role of the political poem is discussed.

1658 Stewart, Margaret E. "Death and Growth: Vietnam War Novels, Cultural Attitudes and Literary Traditions." Dissertation, University of Wisconsin, Madison, 1981.

Eight Vietnam novels are examined and related to previous American war literature, with particular attention being given to those aspects of the American culture which gave rise to the attitudes that allowed us to become involved in the war. These attitudes are traced in the novels. Bibliography.

1659 Stringer, Kenneth Thompson, Jr. "A Substitute for Victory? Fictional Portraits of the American Soldier and Combat in Vietnam." Dissertation, American University, Washington, D.C., 1984.

Films and novels that examine the Vietnam War aid us in understanding and explaining the lessons of the war. Moral perceptions and responses are examined. The author notes that literature's attempt to change America's idea of combat may be one positive outcome of the war. Bibliography.

1660 Stromberg, Peter Leonard. "The Long War's Writing: American Novels about the Fighting in Vietnam Written While Americans Fought." Dissertation, Cornell University, Ithaca, N.Y., 1974.

A comprehensive, annotated discussion of each of the Vietnam novels up to 1974 with some information on the authors who responded to questions from Stromberg. Their letters are included. Major themes and ideas are traced. Bibliography.

1661 Swenson, Catherine Kitty Clayton. "Vietnam: Coming to Terms through the Mediums of Art." Thesis, University of Utah, Salt Lake City, 1987.

A discussion of the Vietnam War as viewed through literature and film. Bibliography.

1662 Tackach, James M. "The Huck Finn Hero in Modern Fiction." Dissertation, University of Rhode Island, Kingston, 1986.

Tackach identifies the characteristics of the archetypal Huck Finn character in American literature, and how he is employed in modern novels such as *Catch 22*, *Semi-Tough*, *The Bear*, *The Adventures of Augie March*, *The Invisible Man*, *The Southpaw*, and *Why Are We in Vietnam?*

1663 Weigl, Bruce. "A Romance." Dissertation, University of Utah, Salt Lake City, 1979.
　　　See 997.

1664 Wigley, Karla. "Vietnam: Putting the Conflicts on the Stage in the 70's and 80's." Thesis, Smith College, Northampton, Mass., 1984.
　　　In the last two decades of drama, the Vietnam War has come to be seen a both an American and Vietnamese tragedy. The plight of the veteran has been showcased.

1665 Winn, David. "Gangland." Thesis, University of Colorado, Boulder, 1978.
　　　See 473.

1666 Winner, Carole Ann. "A Study of American Dramatic Productions Dealing with the War in Vietnam." Dissertation, University of Denver, Denver, 1975.
　　　Ten plays dealing with the Vietnam War are compared. Included are Daniel Berrigan's *Trial of the Catonsville Nine*, Terrence McNally's *Tour*, and David Rabe's *Sticks and Bones* and *The Basic Training of Pavlo Hummel*.

Teaching Materials

1667 Alexander, William. "The Holocaust, Vietnam, and the Contemporary Student." *College English* 39, no. 5 (January 1978):548-52. ED 173 277.

Describes a course on the Holocaust and the Vietnam Conflict. Social responsibility is the main theme.

1668 Anderson, Terry H. "Focus on Civil Rights, Vietnam, Women's Liberation." *OAH Magazine of History* 1, no. 1 (April 1985):11-13. ED 319 088.

Information to aid high school teachers in selecting significant books for use in the classroom on the major topics of the 1960s including Vietnam.

1669 Barber, Sandra Powell. "A Role Simulation: Escalation of U.S. Troop Commitment in Vietnam, October 1961." *Teaching Political Science* 5, no. 4 (July 1978):405-20. EJ 184 077.

An activity designed to teach foreign policy decision making to undergraduate college students. The role playing technique is evaluated.

1670 Benedetti, Charles. "We Must Not Let Them Forget Vietnam." *Social Education* 52, no. 1 (January 1988):43. EJ 364 263.

The author was a draft deferred civilian who actively opposed the war. He discusses both his experiences as a peace activist and the course on the war he taught.

1671 Berman, David M. "'Every Vietnamese Was a Gook': My Lai, Vietnam, and American Education." *Theory and Research in Social Education* 16, no. 2 (Spring 1988):141-59. EJ 376 906.

Berman argues that the American educational system is reponsible for the way Americans see the world and contributed to our experience in Vietnam.

1672 ____. "Perspectives on the Teaching of Vietnam." *Social Studies* 77, no. 4 (July/August 1986):165-68. EJ 343 111.

Describes using Vietnamese literature and cultural history to teach the Vietnam War to high school students. Vietnamese fiction and poetry used.

1673 ____. "Teaching Vietnam Through Vietnamese Sources." *Social Studies Journal* 14 (Spring 1985):30-37. EJ 312 823.

Same as 1672.

1674 Bigelow, William. "Role-Playing the Origin of U.S. Involvement." *Social Education* 52, no. 1 (January 1988):55-57. EJ 364 269.

Describes a role playing activity which allows students to see how U. S. involvement in Vietnam began. Student handouts are included.

1675 Braestrup, Peter, and Leona Hiraoka. "Using and Misusing Media Resources in Teaching on Vietnam," *Teaching Political Science* 12, no. 4 (Summer 1965):161-68. EJ 325 823.

Discusses Vietnam War news film and the government's problem with the press during the war. The author emphasizes ways to promote classroom discussion on this issue.

1676 Brandy, Patricia, ed. *Perspectives*. Arlington, Va.: Close Up Foundation, 1984. ED 243 764.

Designed to foster critical thinking on political issues for high school social studies students. The media coverage of the Vietnam War is one of the topics covered.

1677 Brown, Frederick Z. "Myth and Misperception Abound in Our Courses on the War in Vietnam." *Chronicle of Higher Education* 34, no. 37 (25 May 1988):A48.

Discusses the problem of objectivity in teaching Vietnam War history and literature courses.

1678 Butterfield, Fox. "The New Vietnam Scholarship." *New York Times Magazine* 132 (13 February 1983):26-35, 45-46, 50, 52, 54-57, 60-61.

A discussion of historians' recent work in Vietnam War scholarship providing new information based on disclosures from Hanoi, documents in presidential libraries, and war memoirs. Included in the article is a section titled "Teaching the War" (34-35) which describes the revival of interest in the Vietnam War on college campuses with the development of courses on the war. The author discusses how these courses are being taught and by whom – in most cases not by Vietnam veterans or specialists on Vietnam.

1679 Casciato, Arthur D. "Teaching the Literature of the Vietnam War." *Review* 9 (1987):125-47.

1680 Chilcoat, George W. "The Images of Vietnam: A Popular Music Approach." *Social Education* 49, no. 7 (October 1985):601-3. EJ 322 862.

The author discusses the use of country-western and rock music to analyze the different points of view on the Vietnam War for high school students. A song list is included.

1681 Cohen, Steven. "Vietnam in the Classroom." *Social Education* 52, no. 1 (January 1988):47-48. EJ 364 265.

A description of a four week course on the Vietnam War with an emphasis on the development of critical thinking skills. Classroom techniques for higher education are outlined.

1682 Cussler, Elizabeth B. "Vietnam: An Oral History." *English Journal* 76, no. 7 (November 1987):66-67.

A discussion of how a unit on oral history in a high school communications class utilized the experiences of local veterans and others affected by the war to give background on writing, history, and oral history techniques. The class was taught in Edina High School, Edina, Minnesota.

1683 Dunn, Joe P. "Teaching Teachers to Teach the Vietnam War." *Social Education* 52, no. 1 (January 1988):37-38. EJ 364 260.

The author designed a course for high school teachers to teach then techniques for teaching the war.

1684 ____. "Teaching the Vietnam War in High School." *Social Studies* 74, no. 5 (September/October 1983):198-200. EJ 288 888.

A discussion of recommended readings for high school students.

1685 Ehrhart, W. D. "Why Teach Vietnam?" *Social Education* 52, no. 1 (January 1988):25-26. EJ 364 255.

The author, a Vietnam veteran and major name in Vietnam War literature, discusses the need to teach critical thinking skills and identifies curriculum materials that may be used to teach Vietnam as a framework within which to teach these skills.

1686 Elias, Stephen N. "American Newspaper Editorials on the Vietnam War: An Experimental Approach to Editorial Content Analysis." A paper presented at the 61st Annual Meeting of the Association for Education in Journalism, Seattle, 13-16 August 1978. ED 163 497.

The author discusses a course in which editorials about four news events (the Tonkin Gulf incident, 1968 Tet Offensive, President Nixon's 1969 Vietnamization announcement, and the fall of Saigon) that appeared in five newspapers (*New York Times*, *Los Angeles Times*, *Wall Street Journal*, *Chicago Tribune*, and *Washington Post*) were examined and compared considering content, tone, page placement, and length in an attempt to develop critical thinking.

1687 Elterman, Howard. "The Vietnam War and the Media." *Social Education* 52, no. 1 (January 1988):33-34. EJ 364 258.

The author contributed to the curriculum developed by the Center for Social Studies Education. He discusses this curriculum, particularly the section on the role and responsibility of the press.

1688 Endres, William Bliss. "Teaching Vietnam: Reflections Beyond the Immediate." *English Journal* 73, no. 8 (December 1984):28-30. EJ 308 219.

A discussion of the "complexity and moral ambiguity" of the war with particular attention to *A Rumor of War*, *Fields of Fire*, and *Dispatches*. Also included is his evaluation of his course "The Literary Response to the Vietnam War" and a discussion of the purpose of teaching Vietnam War literature.

1689 Englade, Kenneth F. "Some Schools Decide It's Time to Tackle America's Most Divisive War." *American School Board Journal* 175 (September 1988):21-23.

A discussion of the renewed interest in the Vietnam War in the schools since the erection of the Vietnam Memorial in 1982. The author notes the inadequacies of many high school texts but mentions other curriculum materials, books, and film programs being developed or already available. A twenty-seven item nonfiction bibliography is included, mostly personal narratives, for classroom use.

1690 Fernekes, William R. "Student Inquiries About the Vietnam War." *Social Education* 52, no. 1 (January 1988):53-54. EJ 364 268.

Presentation of a unit on the war that utilizes oral history interviewing techniques rather than texts with high school students.

1691 *Front Lines: Soldiers' Writings from Vietnam*. Cambridge, Mass.: Indochina Curriculum Group, 1975. ED 210 231.

Intended for high school students, this text presents a human side of the war through the personal accounts of veterans. Poems, interviews, and diary excerpts are included. In each account, a situation exists in which the individual is required to make a decision based on their personal beliefs. In some cases, the decision could mean life or death. Discussion questions, a bibliography of print and audio-visual materials, and a glossary are included. Photographs. The Indochina

Curriculum Group is a collective of Boston area high school teachers developing curriculum materials on Southeast Asia for high schools. See also 674.

1692 Garrahy, Dennis J. *Revolution*. Vista, Calif.: Vista Unified School District, 1982. ED 241 439.

A social studies unit designed to develop the reading and writing skills of low achieving high school students. The unit focuses on the theme of revolution and includes material on draft dodgers, hippies, and the Vietnam War.

1693 Glassman, Joel. "Teaching Students and Ourselves about the Vietnam War." *Social Education* 52, no. 1 (January 1988):35-36. EJ 364 259.

Describes a graduate course on the techniques of teaching the Vietnam War including a textbook analysis.

1694 Goldstein, Jonathan. "Teaching the American-Indochina War: An Interdisciplinary Experiment." *Teaching History: A Journal of Methods* 12, no. 1 (Spring 1987):3-9. EJ 353 077.

A description and evaluation of a college level course on Vietnam.

1695 Goodman, Allen E. "A Symposium on Vietnam." *Teaching Political Science* 12, no. 4 (Summer 1985):140-98.

The entire issue is devoted to Vietnam. The introduction (ED 325 820) notes that over 100 college departments of political science were studied to determine the extent of course offerings on Vietnam. An overview of the problems of teaching these courses plus a three page chart listing course names, university, name of professor, level, enrollment, and date offered in included. The issue includes articles by Douglas Pike, Harry Summers, Peter Braestrup, Seth Tillman, John Israel, David Trask, and Tricia Van Klaveren which are included as separate citations in this bibliography.

1696 Griffen, William L. "Telling It Like It Was: Vietnam History in the Schools." *Phi Delta Kappan* 55, no. 9 (May 1974):616-18.

The author notes that the schools have always been used to interpret wars and urges that every effort be made to accurately and honestly portray and discuss our involvement in Vietnam. He notes that some current inaccuracies are being taught and lists the steps that must be taken to ensure that the war be honestly presented to students.

1697 Griffen, William L., and John Marciano. *Teaching the Vietnam War.* Montclair, N.J.: Allenheld, Osman, 1979.

The authors express fears that the distortions in textbooks "foster a dangerous atmosphere akin to what existed prior to the Vietnam War." Part I of the book is a study of twenty-eight high school texts used in history and social studies classes while Part II is a concise history of the war. The authors conclude with their thoughts on the social function of secondary history texts.

1698 Halperin, Irving. "Taking the Radical Risk: Diary of a San Francisco State Professor." 1980. ED 207 447.

A professor describes his experiences during the Vietnam War and discusses the importance of teaching literature during such times of upheaval.

1699 Heath, Douglas E. "Map Exercise for Teaching About the War in Vietnam." *Journal of Geography* 80, no. 3 (March 1981):101-4. EJ 255 544.

A description of a two-part exercise to explore Vietnam's ethnic and political geography for college students. Students analyze maps, noting geographic factors affecting nationalism. The political changes in the country from 1946 to 1968 are emphasized.

1700 Israel, John. "Vietnam in the Curriculum." *Teaching Political Science* 12, no. 4 (Summer 1985):181-86. EJ 325 825.

Problems of teaching Vietnam War history are discussed.

1701 Kennedy, Joseph. "Today's Student Meets Yesterday's Vietnam." *Media and Methods* 20, no. 1 (September 1983):8-10, 40.

A discussion of the importance of teaching Vietnam War history and the new scholarship that is making effective teaching of the subject possible. Problems in teaching the subject are described.

1702 Kirschner, George, and Eric Weisberg. "Teaching and Learning About the Vietnam War." *Social Education* 52, no. 1 (January 1988):51-52. EJ 364 267.

The authors describe a one semester high school course which uses television, press coverage, and primary sources to teach the war.

1703 Kitfield, James. "The Vietnam Veterans Advisor." *Penthouse* 18, no. 6 (February 1987):92.

A discussion of the proliferation of courses on the Vietnam War in American colleges and the role vets are playing as guest speakers.

1704 Lander, Faye A. *War and Peace in Children's Literature: Pre-School through Grade Four.* 1981. ED 248 170.

Designed to provide elementary school teachers with information on children's attitudes toward war. The author reviews children's war literature, including materials on Vietnam. A critical, annotated bibliography of children's books of the 1960s and 1970s is included.

1705 Low, Robert, et al. "Mylai: Some American High School Students' Views." *Intercom* 13, no. 1 (January-February 1971):47-53.

A description of a twelfth-grade government class in which efforts to use law to regulate and control war was emphasized in a unit. The My Lai massacre was studied and it's "historical, moral, legal, and psychological implications" discussed. Information on the massacre was revealed when this unit was being taught in 1969. Students reactions were noted.

1706 Lukens, Rebecca. "War Is for Children." *PTA Magazine* 67, no. 2 (October 1972):20-22.

The author writes that parents and teachers can't prevent children from hearing about wars in the news. They need to know what is happening, and the best way to instruct them is through good children's books. Specific books about war for children are discussed including Harold Keith's *Rifles for Watie,* William Steele's *The Perilous Road,* and Meinert de Jong's *House of Sixty Fathers.*

1707 McNergney, Robert, and Martin Haberman. "Teaching Today's Kids About the Vietnam War." *NEA Today* 5, no. 9 (June 1987):12.

A discussion of books about the Vietnam War for children based primarily on the work of E. Wendy Saul.

1708 Mandel, Norma H. "The Use of the Novel to Discuss Vietnamese Refugee Experiences." *English Journal* 77, no. 5 (September 1988):40-44. EJ 376 067.

The author describes her techniques used in teaching Maureen Crane Wartski's *A Boat to Nowhere* in her high school remedial reading classes that include Vietnamese and other immigrant students. Her initial goal was "to foster interchange of ideas between the Asian and non-Asian students, using the novel as a catalyst." Bibliography.

1709 Matlaw, Martha. "Teaching the Vietnam War at a Full Circle High School." *Social Education* 52, no. 1 (January 1988):44-46. EJ 364 264.

A high school course on the Vietnam War is described with specific teaching techniques. A bibliography of print and audio-visual materials is included.

1710 Metcalf, Lawrence, et al., eds. *War Criminals, War Victims: Andersonville, Nuremburg, Hiroshima, My Lai – Crises in World Order.* New York: Institute for World Order, 1974. ED 170 182.

A pamphlet for high school students that studies international law as it applies to individual rights and responsibilities in wartime. A bibliography of books and films, to be used as a basis for discussion, are included.

1711 *NEA Today* 7, no. 3 (November 1988):19.

This untitled article briefly describes the course on the Vietnam War being taught in Pryor Junior High, Pryor, Oklahoma, by social studies teacher and Vietnam veteran Bill McCloud. McCloud wrote to 150 of the major people, from politicians to military leaders, involved in the Vietnam war asking each what we should tell our children about the war. Over 100 responded, out of which fifty-two were reprinted in his article "What Should We Tell Our Children About Vietnam?" *American Heritage* 39, no. 4 (May/June 1988):55-77. McCloud uses the letters in his class to teach the lessons of the war. No author is listed on the *NEA Today* article.

1712 Oldham, Perry. "On Teaching Vietnam War Literature." *English Journal* 75, no. 2 (February 1986):55-56. EJ 329 373.

Oldham, a Vietnam veteran teaching English at a high school in Oklahoma City, describes his class in Vietnam literature. The class focuses on *Rumor of War, Going After Cacciato, Fields of Fire, Dispatches, Tim Page's Nam,* and *Everything We Had.* Students' reactions to the literature are noted.

1713 Olson, Karen, and John Low. "Vietnam in the Classroom: Fact, Fiction and Truth." 1985. ED 265 912.

The authors describe a course called "Reading and Writing About Vietnam" that was taught at Dundalk Community College in Baltimore. The development of the course is described as well as the teaching methods utilized: journal writing, class discussion, essay assignments, guest speakers, and a research project. A course reading list with films is included.

1714 O'Reilly, Kevin. "Spanish-American War to Vietnam" (Booklet 4 of *Critical Thinking in American History*). South Hamilton, Mass.: Hamilton-Wenham School District, 1985. ED 257 757.

Part of the Project on History and Logic (HAL) series, this unit provides curriculum materials in high school U. S. history. A teacher's guide, source envelope, and student manual as well as ready-to-use lesson plans and test questions and answers is provided. The unit stresses critical thinking skills.

1715 Pike, Douglas. "Teaching the Vietnam Experience as a Whole Course." *Teaching Political Science* 12, no. 4 (Summer 1985):144-51. EJ 325 821.

A discussion of the new information available on the Vietnam War. The author charges teachers with the task of presenting all sides when teaching the war.

1716 Rice, Joseph A. "Let's Frag Old Sarge: The Viet Nam Experience Becomes Relevant." *Journal of English Teaching Techniques* 5, no. 3 (February 1972):15-21. EJ 069 338.

Description of a communications course assignment centered on the veteran's experience in Vietnam.

1717 Sanoff, Alvin P. "Vietnam Comes of Age." *U. S. News and World Report* 102, no. 4 (2 February 1987):58-59.

Discusses the renewed interest in Vietnam and the courses being taught.

1718 Silverman, Sherman E. "Using Primary Source Material as a Supplement to the U. S. History Survey Course." A paper presented at the Annual Meeting of the Eastern Community College Social Science Association, Harrisburg, Pa., 19 April 1985. ED 259 781.

Primary source documents are used to provide understanding of how individuals and groups reacted to events as a technique to approach history teaching. A letter from Ho Chi Minh, asking for U.S. support in establishing the Vietnam Democratic Republic in 1933, is one of the documents used in this discussion.

1719 Spector, Ronald H. "What Did You Do In the War, Professor?" *American Heritage* 38, no. 1 (December 1986):98-102.

A discussion of the current "trendiness" of Vietnam and the courses being taught on the subject. The author maintains that historians have not helped Americans learn from the war. Bibliography.

1720 Starr, Jerold M. "A Curriculum for Teaching About the Vietnam War." *Education Digest* 53, no. 8 (April 1988):28-31. .

A condensed version of an article originally appearing in *Social Education* 52, no. 1 (January 1988):29-32. Starr describes his efforts to create a program to teach the history of the Vietnam War and to promote critical thinking in drawing conclusions on the decision and events of the period. The objectives of the curriculum and twelve teaching units are described.

1721 ____. "The Making of *The Lessons of the Vietnam War*." *Social Education* 52, no. 1 (January 1988):29-32. EJ 364 257.

Starr describes the development of a Vietnam curriculum. See 1721.

1722 ____, ed. *The Lessons of the Vietnam War: A Modular Textbook*. Pittsburgh: The Center for Social Studies, 1988.

A one-volume loose leaf binder which includes a teachers manual, "Strategies and Resources for Teaching the Vietnam War," and twelve units for high school students. Terms are defined and activities listed in each unit. Information on speakers and films also included. Of particular interest is Unit 9, "The Vietnam War in American Literature."

1723 _____, ed. "Teaching the Vietnam War." *Social Education* 52, no. 1 (January 1988):23-24. EJ 364 254.
    Describes the difficulties in teaching the war which include the lack of materials. Starr describes some approaches currently being used.

1724 Stewart, Margaret E. "Vietnam War Novels in the Classroom." *Teaching History: A Journal of Methods* 6, no. 2 (1981):60-66.

1725 Summers, Harry G., Jr. "Teaching Vietnam: A Critical Military Analysis." *Teaching Political Science* 12, no. 4 (Summer 1985):152-60. EJ 325 822.
    A discussion of the Army War College's analysis of the U. S. Strategic failure in Vietnam.

1726 Taylor, Sandra. "Teaching the Vietnam War." *History Teacher* 15, no. 1 (November 1981):57-66.
    Taylor discusses the reasons for teaching the war and how to prepare a course. Key background works are discussed – both histories and novels.

1727 Taylor, Sandra, and Rex Casillas. "Dealing with Defeat: Teaching the Vietnam War." *SHAFR Newsletter* (Newsletter of the Society for Historians of American Foreign Relations) 11 (December 1980):10-18; concluded in 12 (March 1981):1-10.
    The authors surveyed college and university instructors to learn how they were teaching the war and the nature of their background experience in the subject. This essay presents the techniques involved in carrying out the study and how the data was tabulated. The results are discussed and include examples of the teaching techniques employed by the instructors and significant books

utilized in the classroom. Also included is a sample of the questionnaire, an appendix of data, and a bibliography.

1728 Tilford, Earl H. "Teaching the Vietnam War at Air University." *Social Education* 52, no. 1 (January 1988):41-42.
    A course on the Vietnam War taught to air force officers and the special problems inherent in such a setting are discussed. The author urges readers and educators to utilize techniques to enable the country to face the moral question raised by the Vietnam War.

1729 Tillman, Seth. "Vietnam and the Teaching of Congress and Foreign Policy." *Teaching Political Science* 12, no. 4 (Summer 1985):169-80. EJ 325 824.
    A discussion of the "imperial presidency" and the inevitability of the war.

1730 Toplin, Robert Brent. "Teaching the Sixties with Film." *OAH Magazine of History* 1, no. 1 (April 1985):24-25.
    Films that can be used in high school classrooms to teach the major events of the 1960s are described.

1731 Totten, Sam. "The Lessons of Vietnam." *Curriculum Review* 25, no. 1 (September/October 1985):87-89. EJ 324 155.
    Totten noted the renewed interest in Vietnam and the need for high school educators to teach the subject. Factual overviews, personal accounts, news analysis, and fiction are discussed.

1732 Trask, David F. "Official Histories of the War in Vietnam: Why They Are Produced and What Is Available for Classroom Use." *Teaching Political Science* 12, no. 4 (Summer 1985):187-94. EJ 325 826.
    The United States government is making an effort to produce a comprehensive historical account of the Vietnam War. The author discusses the potential use of such histories. Bibliography.

1733 *The Vietnam Era: A Guide to Teaching Resources*. Cambridge, Mass.: Indochina Curriculum Group, 1978. ED 201 565.

An annotated resource guide for high school teachers which includes general information and learning activities. Materials include primary source material, general interest books, films and slide shows. Several points of view represented. The eight chapters are "History of the War," "Land and People of Indochina," "U.S. Foreign Policy," "Vietnamese Liberation Movements," "GI Experiences," "Anti-War Movement," "Impact of the War," and "Vietnam Since the War."

1734 Wade, DallaGrana. "Vietnam in the High School Curriculum." *Social Education* 52, no. 1 (January 1988):49-50. EJ 364 266.
       Description of a seven-week high school course utilizing simulation exercises, songs of the period, and guest speakers.

1735 *War and Peace*. (Resource Unit VI, Project Social Studies). Minneapolis: Project Social Studies Curriculum Center, 1968. ED 083 106.
       A twelfth grade unit, number six of seven units, of a course on value conflicts and policy decisions. Vietnam is suggested as a case study.

1736 Wilcox, Fred A. "Pedagogical Implications of Teaching Literature of Vietnam." *Social Education* 52, no. 1 (January 1988):39-40. EJ 364 261.
       Wilcox discusses how primary materials may be used in teaching the war.

Periodicals

1737 *Deros*.

     Deros was a quarterly poetry journal devoted to men who served in Vietnam, published in December, March, June, and September. The first issue was published in December, 1981, by editors Lee-lee Schlegel and Ken Rose of Miriam Press, Alexandria, Virginia. Publication ceased in 1987. *Deros* means "date of expected return from overseas."

1738 *National Vietnam Veterans Review*.

     A monthly journal for veterans published in Fayetteville, N.C.

1739 *Perimeter: National Vietnam Veterans Monthly Newsletter*.

     Founded in December 1980 and edited by John B. Dwyer of Dayton, Ohio. *Perimeter* reviews books on the Vietnam War.

1740 *Vietnam Magazine*.

     A quarterly publication by Empire Press of Leesburg, Virginia, founded in 1988, this is a glossy publication that includes articles on battles, book reviews, and subjects of interest to Vietnam War veterans. Photographs, color and black and white, and advertisements throughout.

1741 *Vietnam Veteran.*
A monthly publication for veterans begun in 1986 in Gastonia, North Carolina.

1742 *Vietnam War Newsletter.*
A monthly newsletter that is an information clearinghouse for Vietnam veterans. It has a heavy emphasis on books. There are also articles, interviews, letters, and news items. Founded in 1979 and edited by Thomas W. Herbert of Collinsville, Connecticut.

1743 *Win.*
A biweekly publication devoted to nonviolent political action, *Win* includes poems and reviews. It was founded in Brooklyn in 1966 and is now published in New York.

SPECIAL ISSUES OF PERIODICALS

1744 *Confrontation* 8 (Spring 1974).
The issue is called "War Literature: Checkpoints."

1745 *Critique: Studies in Modern Fiction* 24, no. 2 (Winter 1983).
The entire issue, called "The Fiction of Vietnam," is devoted to Vietnam War literature.

1746 *Journal of American Culture* 4, no. 2 (Summer 1981).
The issue, called "Focus: The Vietnam War," includes five articles on various cultural implications of the war, three of which are on Vietnam War literature, and the other three on Vietnam's impact on music and on TV news. The issue also includes an article on Nixon.

1747 *Modern Fiction Studies* 30, no. 1 (Spring 1984).
Four articles are on Vietnam War fiction. The issue is called "Modern War Fiction."

1748 *Poetry* 70, no. 6 (September 1972).

       The entire issue, "Poetry: Against the War," is devoted to Vietnam War poetry.

1749 *Social Education* 52, no. 1 (January 1988).

       The entire issue is devoted to the topic of teaching the Vietnam Conflict.

Author Index

Title Index